Forbi   Rites

Your Complete Guide to Traditional Witchcraft

First published by O Books, 2009
O Books is an imprint of John Hunt Publishing Ltd., The Bothy, Deershot Lodge, Park Lane, Ropley,
Hants, SO24 0BE, UK
office1@o-books.net
www.o-books.net

Distribution in:

UK and Europe
Orca Book Services
orders@orcabookservices.co.uk
Tel: 01202 665432 Fax: 01202 666219   Int.
code (44)

USA and Canada
NBN
custserv@nbnbooks.com
Tel: 1 800 462 6420 Fax: 1 800 338 4550

Australia and New Zealand
Brumby Books
sales@brumbybooks.com.au
Tel: 61 3 9761 5535 Fax: 61 3 9761 7095

Far East (offices in Singapore, Thailand,   Hong
Kong, Taiwan)
Pansing Distribution Pte Ltd
kemal@pansing.com
Tel: 65 6319 9939 Fax: 65 6462 5761

South Africa
Alternative Books
altbook@peterhyde.co.za
Tel: 021 555 4027 Fax: 021 447 1430

Text copyright Jeanette Ellis 2008

Design: Stuart Davies

ISBN: 978 1 84694 138 2

Printed by Chris Fowler International
www.chrisfowler.com

O Books operates a distinctive and ethical publishing philosophy in
all areas of its business, from its global network of authors to
production and worldwide distribution.
This book is produced on FSC certified stock, within ISO14001
standards. The printer plants sufficient trees each year through
the Woodland Trust to absorb the level of emitted carbon in
its production.

Forbidden Rites

Your Complete Guide to Traditional Witchcraft

Jeanette Ellis

BOOKS

Winchester, UK
Washington, USA

Contents

Introduction   1

Chapter 1- An Introduction to Witchcraft   7

Chapter 2- Goddesses and Gods   25

Chapter 3- Elemental Quarters   68

Chapter 4- Magical Equipment   98

Chapter 5- Wheel of the Year- Sabbats   130

Chapter 6- How a Witchcraft Circle Works   159

Chapter 7- Gem and Metal Magic   199

Chapter 8- Herbs and their Magical Uses   283

Chapter 9- Essential Oils and their Uses   380

Chapter 10- Charms and their Meanings   416

Chapter 11- Esbats and Spells   535

Chapter 12- Familiars or Spirit Animals   584

Chapter 13 - Self Dedication   620

Dedicated to my two wonderful daughters, Debbie and Gayle and to Fred & Uzo, Pam & John, Steve, Sarah, Dee, Suzanna, Jacqui & Colin, Thorskegga & Dragon, Shaun, Zia, and Mary who have been so supportive.

Introduction

This is a book on traditional Witchcraft; written to discuss the journey we travel to gain a deeper knowledge of the Goddess and God. I don't want to upset my many friends in Wicca, just explain the differences in our tradition and answer the many questions that have been asked when we perform public rituals. No form of witchcraft is more valid than another, all bring light to a dark world. There are many aspects that overlap in both traditions and often it's just a question of emphasis. The exercises described in this book can be used whichever system of witchcraft you practice.

There are so many books written on the subject of "The Craft" as it is known by those within (unlike when I started on the long journey towards understanding). So why one more? In part, it's because though there are many books on Wicca there is little on other forms of Witchcraft and also due to the nagging of all my students asking me to record our belief system for others. I have based the book on the teaching course that I have run since 1998. It is designed so that it can be worked through at a rate of one chapter per month, so with thirteen chapters it will take you just over a year and a day to complete, the minimum before initiation. I'm sure if you are anything like me, you'll read the book through like wildfire, but do go back and re- read it at a more leisurely pace. Do the exercises at the end of the chapters. If you follow them, you will learn from your own inner guides and from the Goddess and God, the secrets of Witchcraft.

This book covers all the questions I have been asked on Witchcraft over the years resulting in a very wide range of subjects, for novice to the advanced. Forgive me if in places it seems too simple. I have provided lots of subheadings so you can use this later for reference. Take from it what feels right for you, learn to be intuitive when reading; if a tingle runs down your spine, this will work for you.

If it feels wrong, don't do it.

The form of Witchcraft I follow is (or perhaps I should say was) a verbal tradition. Our ancestors followed the seasons, noting the changing fields and the sky. How life progressed and changed, birth, love, food and death are the guiding forces. How can we change our fate? It is the same cry that has echoed down the years, from the dawn of man. How do I take control of my life, my universe?

Witchcraft was a religion not of the rich but of the farmers in the fields, not of the educated but of the illiterate. Just because they could neither read nor write please do not confuse this with unintelligent. They had the same dreams as you and I just without the opportunity to learn to write, reading was a different skill and many more could read than is generally given credit. If a letter was needed, it was to a church scribe they must turn. Even more reason to continue with a verbal tradition when you whisper of "Witchcraft". I find it unsurprising that so little is written down about any form of Witchcraft. There is very little written about other religions of the past that are re-blossoming again today, the Incas in Peru, the worshipers of Mae Toranee and the Nagas in Thailand, under the guise of Buddhism the Bon religion still flourishes in Tibet, the list is endless.

I have been a witch since 1986 officially, unofficially all my life. It took me many years of searching to find what I was looking for. When I did, it felt like coming home.

My first taste of the unusual came when I was ten; my father was helping me with my maths homework. He was sitting at the table and I was standing looking over his shoulder, when his distinctive green pen dropped onto the table from about my head level. There was no where for it to fall from. My father had lost his pen several days ago and wanted to know why had I dropped it on the table? He never accepted that it had just materialized and fell and I can't say I blame him. It did teach me that there are more things out there than can be easily explained.

I was very lucky to meet a now elderly couple who passed on to me, their local style of Witchcraft. My father's family (my maiden name) name came from Southern Ireland and this form of Witchcraft also comes from that area. There are very few covens, if any, still using this dying system. Making it extremely important to record these beliefs before they are forgotten. My family name is deeply associated with this area, owning the land and building many castles at one point in history, but time passes and fortunes change. According to legend the name descends from the Ancient Kings of Ireland and so I was astounded to realize that it was my ancestors that the stories of my Goddess were intertwined with. This form of witchcraft has no name, I tried to think of one; but to invent a name seemed deceptive and so after much thought, I left it as it is now known- Witchcraft.

I have always loved making things, whether it be costumes, painting or mask making. So in 1986 when I opened a jewelers shop, I wanted to feature more and more Witchie items, but none were available way back then. So I started to learn the art of Silver and Goldsmith by beginning to design and craft my own esoteric jewelry.

Eventually my partner and I started our coven, The Raven and The Rose. One day I had an idea- and so The Halloween Bash was born, so that Pagans of all denominations could gather together and enjoy each other's company.

The Halloween Bash and later the Beltane Bash Festival with its The Pagan Pride Parade (see the chapter on Sabbats), great fun, everyone loves it. Run so that Pagans can meet, enjoy time together, attend workshops, lectures, dance, have fun and; finally meeting together in ritual.

I shut the shop when the lease came to an end; Pagans of all paths are far more interesting to talk to than the more normal general public. So now I sell my jewelry mail order, through the Internet and of course at the Festivals.

At the festivals, we have different groups from one of the many Pagan paths to open the proceedings; my own coven always leads the closing ritual at both The Halloween Bash and Beltane Bash. These events brought us so many requests to join the coven that I started a teaching group, with new entrants each year. In turn this led to the start of a group called the Ravens, old members of my teaching course who meet together on a regular basis to celebrate the Goddess, God and participate in folk festivals around the country. In truth I could not run the festivals without their help.

As the Ravens and all our students wanted more gatherings, we began to organise regular Moots, which is an Anglo-Saxon word for meetings, which we have speakers from all Pagan paths.

My own journey into Witchcraft is by no means completed, I hope that I have many years of study ahead.

I could not ask for a more rewarding and full life.

To start on the path of the craft is a wonderful experience; I envy you, the joy of discovery.

Blessed Be,

Jeanette Ellis

THE MORRIGAN

By Jeanette Ellis

I am Maiden.
The primal scream, was wrenched from My lips,
From My fingers, roses fall to the Earth,
The Raven is held aloft by My will,
I am the fire of all beginnings,
I was born from the ninth wave of the sea,
I am the muse of the artist and the music within the flute,
I give joy and laughter to the Universe,
For I am Birth.

I am Mother.
It was I, that brought order to Chaos,
I gave birth to the Universe,
I struck the egg with My mighty axe,
One moment after creation atoms crashed against atoms,
Dark and light was formed,
I am the song of the stars,
Within My womb, lies all,
For I am Creatrix.

I am Crone.
You call to Me for dark mysteries and spoken spells,
I weave the magic, that enchants and binds,
I sweep the old and weary into My comforting arms,
I am the Dark Mother that stands in the shadows,
I see all from the darkness, for no light blinds Me,
I am the spinner of the web of your fate,
You will look upon My face only once,
For I am Death.

I am The Morrigan!
The Lady of Nine, Alpha to Omega,
Maiden, Mother, Crone, the archetypal woman am I,
The Grey Lady that stands between Dark and Light,
I protect those that walk in My shadow,
I am knowledge hidden beneath the wing of the Raven,
I am She that stands at the end of all time,
I gather all unto Me,

I AM.

CHAPTER 1

An Introduction to Witchcraft

Shall we write about the things not to be spoken of?
Shall we divulge the things not to be divulged?
Shall we pronounce the things not to be pronounced?
"Hymn to the Mother of the Gods" 1888 by Julian

If you have never felt the call of the old Pagan Gods, close the book now for it is not for you.

What is Witchcraft?

Witchcraft opens the door to strange vistas and dimensions. The rituals broaden your perspective by letting you look beyond the horizon, not just lift your face toward it. It is more than just a collection of spells. I don't want to remove the mystery from the Craft, far from it but to help you to find the enchantment and beauty within the rituals.

Witch means wise one, helping the community by being there. It means holding hands, at the times in life when help is needed. It means casting spells, which will aid the local community to get through their individual problems. Witchcraft is not only about helping others, it is a complete change of journey.

When you first take your tentative steps on the path of Paganism there seems so much to learn. The path lies in front of you strewn with knowledge and it seems so daunting. To begin, there are many paths to choose from, The Northern Tradition of Heathenism (followers of the Norse and Viking Gods), The Egyptian Mysteries, Paganism, Shamanism, Druid or Witchcraft with all their very different facets, to name but a few. Unless you are drawn to a particular path, research all available avenues of Paganism until you find what you are drawn too.

Witchcraft teaches intuition. It strengthens decision-making and develops emotional and spiritual strength. It will teach you a maturity of spirit, through the many rituals and meditations you perform. It will deepen your appreciation of life, teaching you not only to watch but to feel the changing of the seasons, becoming one with the Earth. Witches have their eyes wide open, experiencing life to the full, seeing the beauty that surrounds us. Even in the city there is beauty, a spider's web dripping with crystals of dew, take time to watch the clouds that in itself is a meditation. The Craft is not shallow; there is a deep spirituality within, which will take you the rest of your life to unravel.

Above all, Witchcraft is also FUN! It is not the somber path of Christianity but joyous and filled with laughter. In all Witchcraft circles there are wine and sweet cakes symbolizing the sweetness of life. And absolutely no hair shirts! Or discussion of sin! All Witchcraft circles contain laughter; no matter what tradition you follow.

Closing Ritual at Beltane Bash – A Spiral Dance

Finding the right group for you

All of the Pagan community is very welcoming. Don't be worried about attending your first Festival or Open Ritual, even if you go alone. You will soon get to know people and start to make friends.

In many cities, there are meetings and open rituals where everyone is welcome to attend. For those wishing to investigate deeper, there are open groups, with only a little commitment. You may feel that only a coven (pronounced cuvven) will answer your needs, then this can be harder to track down. Go to all Pagan events that you can, make contacts, only then will you find the elusive covens you seek. Once found, you will need to fit in with the other members of the Coven, have the same sense of humor, and enjoy time spent in the company of the group. When you finally find a coven to accept you, it will need your deep commitment, for teaching nights, for full moons and Sabbats. Can you offer this much time and effort? You must be of stable mind, this is paramount. Dealing with the energies that you will invoke is not easy. Magic will tear at any mental weakness you may have. If you take any form of tranquilizers then your first job is to strengthen your mind, so that you don't need their support daily living. Only then are you ready to explore the path of the Goddess.

Your first year in coven before initiation is a hard one; this will drag up a lot of psychological issues from your past for re-examination and re-classification. You will walk the dark side of your soul, re-examining what is important to you. If you are walking there not from choice; but from depression, you may find yourself hopelessly lost. You will need to be psychically strong, not on drugs, alcohol or have any other form of addiction. You need maturity not of age but of mind, I have met fourteen year olds I would rather have in circle than some forty year olds! I'm sorry if this seems hard, but you disregard this advice at your peril. Stick to open rituals, which are designed for everyone, until you have strengthened both mind and body. It is worth the work, Witch first heal yourself before healing others.

What ceremonial dates do we celebrate?

As with all forms of Witchcraft, our tradition has eight Sabbats (celebrations) per year, and thirteen full moons. If you join a Coven then there are at least thirteen teaching nights and as well as Open Rituals. You must come along to Beltane Bash and The Halloween Bash and there are lots more conferences and festivals to go to. You may be asked to private rituals held by covens as a guest. There are also less formal groups, where you can participate as deeply as you choose. Be aware, it can take over your life. If you decide to take up this challenge after initiation by a coven, you will take similar responsibilities to a Christian Vicar ministering to his or her diocese, blessing babies, doing spells, even counseling the dying. Can you cope? When I first found Witchcraft and found all the yearnings I have had over the years were real, I had no idea what a change in lifestyle I would be taking on.

A Witch is a follower of the old religion in Britain and Europe before Christianity arrived, and not a Devil worshipper. **The Devil and Satanism are part of an anti-Christian religion and nothing to do with Witchcraft.** Satanism is the darkside of Christianity. This reputation started and grew during the Middle Ages when the Catholic Church was still not truly established in Europe and it became determined to spread the word of Christ across a very resistant pagan population. The act of changing our Horned God from a benevolent force to an evil imp was an act of pure politics and propaganda. To try and convert Pagans or stop newly converted Christians backsliding to the old religion.

This propaganda continued throughout the centuries with comments such as "Never suffer a witch to live" According to the King James version of the Bible (Exodus 22:18). These words were thrown at many a supposed witches in 17th century. James 1 was 'witchophobic' with many people losing their lives during his reign through Witch trials up and down Britain. This statement however is a poor translation from the original Greek and Hebrew, the translation of the passage should read "Never suffer a poisoner to live", somewhat different.

Unfortunately this negative and false impression is still common. After our second Beltane Bash festival we went to the local woods next day, for a picnic. There were eleven of us, most as usual dressed in black, including a couple of bikers in black leathers and with all the items for a picnic packed in one box. Both handfastees, from the Witches Wedding (Handfasting) the day before, had been given a gift of black capes and one had chosen to wear his. We found our place, an old ritual site that we no longer used. We set the picnic and proceeded to eat our sandwiches, sausage rolls and drink our wine. As this was a Handfasting celebration, there was rather a lot of wine, mead and champagne. After an hour, two policemen and three rangers came up to us demanding to know where we had buried the body. I assumed they were joking!

"Under the blanket" quoth I, as no ground around was disturbed, it seemed the only answer.

"Who's in charge?" said the policeman, ten fingers point at the only High Priestess with "She is!" "Where's the one in the strange clothing?" well, the hanfastee still wearing his cape was up a tree at that moment, so eleven fingers pointing and saying,

"Up there", was not helping the situation.

"No really, where did you bury the body?" We began to realize they were serious. "Where's the coffin?" now this had us truly flummoxed! Then a female ranger with them said,

" I think we can put this down to a picnic, don't you?" with this they shot off across the woodland as fast as their big black boots would carry them!

The nice young lady ranger stayed to explain that the local police station had received a call, saying that thirteen Witches dressed in black capes, had gone into the forest carrying a coffin. This of course was the box with the picnic food in!

So be aware Big Brother is still watching you!

If Witchcraft is a mystery religion, what does that mean?

When Witchcraft was a dangerous calling (remember it was illegal until the 1951). It used to mean that mysteries were kept from you until after initiation, for your safety and your coven. Now after a relaxation in laws and to the general population most secrets are available in books these days. So is it still a Mystery Religion? In Witchcraft all rituals are done within a cast circle, and in our tradition. the High Priestess (HPs) allows the Goddess to speak through her. This we call the "Calling down of the Moon", in which the Goddess or God in the "Calling Down of the Sun" gives advice and prophesies events to come.

The Goddess and God in each ceremony and in your visualizations, hold all answers to the secrets, but they are different for all. You must find your own answers to the eternal questions and they are happy to teach you.

The Mystery is in the knowing how to look.

Whilst in circle, many years back, allowing the Goddess to speak through me, I started to tell a story. I was just repeating Her words. This is worrying when you have no idea where the story will lead!

"Many years ago," said the Goddess, "There was a young girl who wished to learn all knowledge, and she went to the wisest man in the village and asked him.

"I do not know the answers to your questions" he said. So she packed her bags and set out for the big city. On reaching the city she went to the wisest person in the city and asked again. Still no answers came; she traveled on from country to country always searching. Finally old and tired, without her answers, she returned to her village. Stories of her leaving had survived in the village and so on her return the villagers poured out of their houses to meet her.

"What have you learnt?" they all said, as they pushed and shoved to get near.

Suddenly all was clear to her "I have learnt that the answers to my questions are with in and not with out. All answers to the great questions are within your own heart."

In the Craft, you stand before your Gods without any mediator, unlike in Christianity where the congregation stands behind the priest, allowing him to intercede with his god on their behalf. When you speak to the Goddess not only does She answer you but taps you on the shoulder to make sure you get the point! In Witchcraft, you touch the divine. This can be very daunting, not something to be undertaken lightly.

Tapping you on the shoulder is not as far fetched as you may think. One of our coveners (a member of the coven) was told by the Goddess to be careful what he asked for. In our early years in the craft, before one particular circle he said that he wished he could feel things. Circle started and not long into it, as we were circling singing "Lady Spin Your Circle Bright", when he felt a tap on the shoulder, and turned expecting to see me with my hand raised to tell him something. He was astonished to see me a good half way round the circle and not within reach of his shoulder. I remember his face went ghostly white. After circle he found a knot tied in his robe. To remind him, we think, not to question who feels what!

Although that robe has long been consigned to the recycling bin, the knot was cut off and he still carries it in every circle.

The Goddess listens and gives Her comments, freely. Remember that what you ask for may well come true.

Why Thirteen Witches in a Coven?

In Witchcraft there are a maximum of thirteen in a coven, the same number as fullmoons in most years, inclusive of a High Priestess and High Priest. The reason for thirteen in a coven, over and above this being a magical number? The larger a Coven becomes the less opportunity each person has to truly know other member within the circle and of the High Priestess knowing the problems that individual members have.

The High Priestess is the thirteenth member, even if there is not thirteen in the coven and so has the deciding vote.

The grand name of High Priest and High Priestess only means

you just have to work harder organizing dates, transport and equipment. You work for your Coven, they do not work for you. Remember, to lead is to serve. The more people there are in the coven, the more necessary the structure of the ritual, with everyone knowing and understanding his or her part. This also applies to Wiccan covens. If you practice on your own, you can be as fluid as you please with your ritual.

In our tradition of Witchcraft there are no all-male covens but the High Priestess can take the role of warrior and High Priest by taking up the ceremonial sword if necessary in times of war, when no man is available. Today covens of all traditions of Witchcraft are experimenting with many ideas; there are gay covens, single sex covens as well as mixed covens.

The period of initiation is a year and a day.

This may seem a strange measurement of time but in medieval England a year and a day was often used in contract law. This time frame was used to bind people to many types of agreement, from employment to tenancy on the land. So with this link to the past we choose to use a long initiation period to prepare for changes in our lives and, actively seek to change our spirit. People misunderstand the dark side of witchcraft; the dark side you will face is within your own soul.

Take a long look at your life, what about you, would you most like to change?

Have you a job? If not, why not? If it is for health reasons, this is understandable.

If you are of sound mind and body, you can no longer blame others. Within the year and a day, find employment. If your are embarking on a spiritual path, you should not be reliant on others to feed and house you. That can hardly be considered standing on your own two feet.

Are your relationships as good as they could be, if not, why not? Fix it.

Then turn to your darkside, face your fears.

You must now take responsibility for yourself, before looking to heal and protect others.

Now is the time to assess who you are.

Take a long look at your life, what do you fear?

Fear will stunt your mental growth, hold you back from achieving all you are capable of. Allow the fear, from whatever root it stems, to pass through you. Hold it, look at it closely see fear for what it really is and then allow it to pass on. You are left; fear and anger have passed. You are stronger for having fought fear and won.

Mine was a fear of fire; I set myself the task of running my finger though a candle flame. This will seem simple to many; but it was not for me. I am glad to report by the time initiation came round I had conquered my fears and could do this small task with ease and confidence. For others it may be a deeper problem, learning to forgive a mother or father, or learning to take responsibility. No longer can you blame anyone for your life and how it has turned out. No one is perfect, but now is the time to move a little closer to the goal of growth and development.

Information common to all forms of Witchcraft

* The origin of the word Witch is lost in the mists of time it might derive the Middle English *wicche*, from Old English *wicca*, a masculine magic user and *wicce* feminine magic user. Witchcraft or *Wiccecræft* may derive from the Middle High German *wicken* to bewitch, Old English *wigle* divination, or the Old High German *wih* meaning holy + *cræft* meaning power, skill, strength and might, no one is to sure.

* A Witch can be male or female; either is called a Witch. Some books refer to a male Witch as a Warlock, but a Warlock is a swear word meaning oath breaker in Scotland, not a male Witch, hopefully. Neither is the term Wizard this comes from fairy tales

and should not be used to address a male Witch either.

* No Witchcraft Coven of any tradition will ask you to join them; you must always seek to join a coven. One of the coven members involved will let you know if you choose to ask, whether you will be given a positive answer. Don't feel that a rejection is personal and that you won't make a good Witch. It may be that you don't fit with that group, either too serious or too bubbly. Keep trying, you will find a group that is right for you. One good thing comes from this; you won't see me on street corners singing "Come and join us". You don't know what a blessing this is until you have heard me sing!

* It can be a problem if only one half of a couple wishes to take up Witchcraft. Imagine a wife or husband coming in at 3 am smelling of consecrated wine! Please think very carefully about how your partner will take to your interest in Witchcraft. I have seen many a partnership break over this.

* Witches mainly believe in re-incarnation, after many re-incarnations joining and eventually re-uniting with the Goddess and God. What you do in this life reflects on your next re-incarnation. We do not consider that you will be reincarnated, as the Buddhists believe, as a lower life form, for doing wrong. But you will have to repeat and repeat your lives in a cycle until you understand your lesson for that life correctly.

* As with all forms of Witchcraft, it is a nature and fertility religion centering on the Goddess and God union and their interaction with the wheel of the year. We work with the God and Goddess in balance. Working fullmoon rituals to the Goddess at night, and Sun rituals to the God in the day, when ever possible. In our tradition of Witchcraft, the High Priestess is the holder of the magic, the "chalice", if you will. It is her responsibility to see that

the spells are done. The High Priest is represented by the sword, on him rests the defense of the Coven, with help from the male members of the group. This kind of defense is largely symbolic rather than actual. In truth, of course, both do either job; men are as good as women at spell casting.

* In Witchcraft of all denominations, honor is nearly as important as breathing. Without honor you are not a Witch. For a Witch your word is your bond, whether this be a Handfasting (Witch Wedding), an initiation or at any time that you give your oath to the Gods. In Pagan cultures of the past, no matter what your social standing, an oath was never taken lightly. Their sense of honor was especially strong and they knew they would be held accountable.

The Romans thought that The Furies (the Greeks called them Erinyes, the Roman borrowed all of their myths from the Greeks) who were three black bird (or in some descriptions bat) winged female angels, their heads wreathed with serpents like the Gorgans, their eyes dripping with blood, and their whole appearance was frightful and repulsive, would swoop down and drive their victims insane, for daring to break an oath. The Egyptians thought that when you died your heart was weighed against Maat's (the Goddess of Justice) feather by Anubis (the Jackal headed guardian of the Underworld), all your lies and bad deeds would make your heart heavier. If you failed this test your heart would be eaten by a monster and you would truly die, rather than living forever. Honor applies particularly if working with Celtic or Viking Gods and Goddesses, an oath was central to their society if an oath was broken the person earned themselves the name of Nithing, so close to our own word 'nothing'.

A Rune stone found on the Isle of Man, was erected so that future generations would know this man to be a Nithing.

Rosketil betrayed under trust
A man bound to him by oaths.

To take an oath to the Gods, in the past was to risk death if you broke your word; today we tend to make light of this important undertaking. But when you work with such old energies you must expect to hold to the same principles.

* It is very important that during pregnancy, that women do not attend circle; the magic is too strong for an unborn baby. You are of course also dragging in to circle a human that has no choice, something that must never happen.

* A Handfasting, a Witch Wedding can take one of three forms.
A Handfasting for a year and a day, which is the most common.
A Handfasting for this life.
A Handfasting for this life and all others.

Be very careful here, only undertake this if you are very sure of each other. For neither party can change their mind. An oath once sworn is sworn, there is no way of undoing this, you pledged yourself in both life and death. Neither party can re-Handfast with anyone else, it is invalid. Remember we spoke of honor, of standing by your word. If you have Handfasted for this life and all others, you must now keep to your commitment or face your God and Goddesses displeasure.

What are the differences between our form of Witchcraft and Wicca?

I am not setting out to prove that our branch of witchcraft is better than Wicca, just different. All branches are equal. Due for the need for secrecy in the past, covens across the country lost contact with each other and developed in their own ways, and like Chinese whispers small differences arose. In modern times I find more and more that the sharing of information is beginning to standardize all branches.

Wicca There are two traditions within Wicca, Gardnerian and

Alexandrian.

Gardnerian- Taught to Gerald Brosseau Gardner by Dorothy Clutterbuck, High Priestess of the New Forest Coven. He wrote the first book on Witchcraft disguised as a story, "High Magic's Aid" under the name of Scire. In 1951 the Witchcraft Act was repealed and this allowed him to write the first book on Witchcraft legally. At this time Witchcraft was a dying religion with only a few practitioners and would have quickly sunk into oblivion. To Gerald we owe the revival and the start of the acceptance of Witchcraft in England and the world.

Alexandrian- Alex Saunders was initiated by Pat Kiminiski a High Priestess in Manchester before coming to London. He worked with, amongst others Janie Robertson (Janie became Artingstall on marriage) who was originally initiated into a Scottish coven, of neither the Alexandrian nor Gardnerian lines in 1946, well before it became legal in England to be a Witch.

The Alexandrian form of Witchcraft is more formal than Gardnerian tradition and with more Cabala (a Judaic-Christian form of magic) taught in Alexandrian Witchcraft. Alex was a Ceremonial Magician before being initiated as a Witch and this flowed into his teachings.

Wicca means Witch and so all Witches can call themselves wiccan, but in England Gerald Gardner was the first to write about Witchcraft, the name of Wicca has attached itself to people initiated into Gardnerian and Alexandrian lines. Now Wicca forms a title of their combined form of Witchcraft. To claim to be Wiccan and not be initiated into a Wiccan coven by a person ordained to do this, is claiming something you are not entitled to. This would equally be true in our own Coven.

Wicca was the main form of Witchcraft to cross the Ocean from England to America, and so became the norm there. Gardener himself visited America in 1936, for a short time. But Wicca did not catch the imagination of America until 1963 when Raymond Buckland, the granddaddy of American Witchcraft, initiated several

Priestesses who went on to start Covens of their own. In America, most think of Wicca as Witchcraft. Although Wicca even in America, has splintered into many sects and many would not be recognized as such in England.

Hedgewitch- A Hedgewitch is a lone witch, who chooses to practice without a coven. Hedgewitch or solo witches have the freedom to choose how to worship and when, making their own rules for how they work and what they believe. This can give you a great deal of freedom; but if you lack the discipline to celebrate full moons and other important festivals by yourself after a hard days work, you may need the structure of a coven to provide the incentive.

Cyber Coven- More and more Witches doing rituals on the Internet, a modern way of working Witchcraft. This does not need involvement, dedication; or a commitment to change your way of life. It might be fun but it is not Witchcraft, in my opinion.

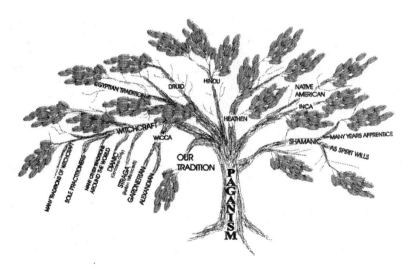

The Tree of Paganism with all its Branches

Traditional Witchcraft
There many forms of traditional Witchcraft from Britain and Europe. This is only one. It is said that Wicca is a religion and Witchcraft is

more centered on spellcrafting. But I can not agree with this, as all the traditions come from the same source, including Wicca. Possibly some traditions have developed with less emphasis on religion than others.

Both Witchcraft and Wicca are an amalgam of different practices; you can trace the influences from Ancient Egypt, Rome and Norse quite easily. Each civilization has added to the potion of enchantment, within the cauldron that was to become Witchcraft.

* If you choose to follow our path; and work with just one God and Goddess as their priest or priestess, it does not mean that you deny the other Gods existence. Be respectful to all traditions and pantheons even non Pagan and in that way hopefully, we can build a respect for who we believe in. As Pagans we must hold our heads high and walk proudly, all spiritual callings are to be respected.

* We have no degrees in our Witchcraft, only initiated and uninitiated. There are three degrees in Wicca, on acceptance by a coven, on knowledge, on leadership and a deeper spiritual understanding of the Goddess and God. Our initiation is equivalent to a Wiccan second degree. We have a welcoming ceremony, an initiation, and only if an initiate wishes to start a new coven of their own, would we then have a leaving ceremony to wish them well and pass on the magical words enabling them to open their own coven. In Witchcraft we all strive at our own pace with out the prizes of degrees, aiming at communion with the Goddess and God.

* One of the major differences between the Wicca and Witchcraft traditions is the formulisation of sacred writing. In Witchcraft we have no set words for our rituals each Coven writing their own. The Wiccan tradition has 'Book of Shadows' which standardizes celebrations and gives guidance to initiates, across England origi-

nally and now the world. The Book of Shadows is copied down after initiation by hand, and it is then added to by each covener. This means that there is no standard work and every Book of Shadows varies. Our method is based on the Celtic oral tradition, with no words handed down from Coven to Coven, only ways of more deeply understanding the seasons, of spellcraft and how to contact the energies within.

* Wiccans use the scourge (whip) for purification and to improve psychic ability. This draws blood away from the brain to the skin by the rhythmic beating of the scourge, giving a natural high and opening the physic centers. We do not use the scourge; it is thought that there are other ways to achieve enlightenment.

* The Covener, awaiting initiation wears a white cord. This will have been worn by every initiated person into the coven, each placing a knot to mark their passing until thirteen knots are placed within the cord. Then it will be retired and a new cord started. On initiation the white cord is exchanged for a plaited cord.

* For us the High Priest and High Priestess are always Handfasted, a Witch Wedding. So that, as in sympathetic magic, the love they share is passed on. This also makes for a more stable coven. Unfortunately, now days with marriages not lasting for life, this is not always possible.

* Our Coven carries out spellwork at every full moon.

* During all rituals we call down the Goddess or God into the High Priestess or High Priest, this is an oracle or channeling of the deities. Both the men and women within the Coven strive to open themselves to the God and Goddess, allowing them to hopefully meet the Goddess and enable Her to express an interest and join in with the circle directly.

We do not have the Wiccan set words called 'Charge of the Goddess' so naturally, we do not have Doreen Valiente's beautiful words (Doreen was Gerald Gardner's High Priestess and completed much of the Book of Shadows) for this.

* Our elemental candle colors are different from the Wiccan. This is more fully explained in chapter on Elemental Quarters.

* We introduce a new covener slowly, firstly only to Sabbats, which is a celebration of the cycle of the year. On their first Sabbat they come as a guest and only join after the circle is constructed, waiting in another room until everything is set, circle cast and elementals called. Only then are they invited into the circle and re-introduced to everyone with their magical names and titles.

At the next Sabbat, they enter at the start to experience the full ritual.

On the third Sabbat, hopefully all nerves are past, and it is time to start to work by calling an Elemental Quarter to the circles edge.

As members become more proficient, they attend the full moons rituals. They take many parts in the circle throughout their year and a day, before initiation, with the exemption of blessing the wine, cakes and anointing, as this is only done by the HP, HPs and initiated Priest or Priestess.

* When ever possible we do not wear shoes in circle. Sometimes in the forest, you may think it advisable if acorns or such have been falling from the trees. But better to concentrate on the magic than prickly feet!

* Very soon after picking up your first book on Witchcraft, you are thrown from student to teacher. This seems silly? Believe me it isn't. I see it every year in our course. When people from your work place know that you are studying to be a Witch, they will

ask questions, ask for spells or ask you to read their Tarot. Can you cope with this so quickly! If not, don't show your pentagrams at work or school, if you don't want strange looks and whispers. Keep it hidden; find your feet before starting to teach, because it will happen. You are one step ahead; you have read that first book and are therefore the expert, but remember what Sir Edmund Hillary once said; "X is an unknown quantity and spurt is a drip under pressure!" Wait until you are more confident of your chosen avenue before donning the trappings of a witch.

Exercise-

Magical or Dream Dairy call it what you will, start to put down your thoughts, visualizations and dreams into a diary. If you only keep it for your year and a day it will help you track your progress. Put into it all magical events that happen to you no matter how trivial you may think them.

CHAPTER 2

Goddesses and Gods

The style of Witchcraft that we practice, first and foremost is a religion. Not the religion of the Christian, solemn and heavy but joyous and with paths that lead as deep as you choose to follow. The Goddess will not lead you further than you can handle at this time in your life, nor this particular life in your many lives.

In the Craft we work with (not you notice worship) the Goddess and God equally, well almost. The Sabbats, that are celebrations of the changing wheel of the year, are equally divided between them both. We work magic with the Goddess at the full moon, so the year does have a Goddess bias, although we try to fit in as many God rituals during the day at noon (the height of the Sun's power) as work and other constraints allow.

So who is this Goddess and God?

The oldest depictions of deities we have in Western Europe are possibly the Great Mother, from the Upper Paleolithic era. They are grand figures of the Goddess with great child bearing hips and enormous breasts to feed the world. The face is obscured, not because the artists of the time were unable to depict such a complicated shape but possibly because only in a personal encounter with your Goddess, does She reveal Her face to you. As man's part in procreation became evident, She was joined by the Deer Horned God, both becoming worshipped by the hunter-gathers of Indo-Europe, the mother culture of Western Civilization. It would be wonderful to be able to trace a direct line of descent from the oldest religion in Europe to today's Witchcraft but this sadly is impossible. But the energies that we work with are the same as used by peoples thousands of years ago. Witchcraft is a returning to mankind's origins, for modern people new to the craft it becomes a reconnection to the oldest of our ancestors.

Although, I was taught to contact the Celtic Gods and Goddesses of legend, the same principle applies to all the Gods and Goddesses from pre-Christian folklore, which abound from all countries. All are connectable and will visit you in your circle.

When in school I was told there was only one god, I wondered if this was true, could the people of history be so wrong? Might they be right and my Religious Education teacher wrong? Why couldn't the Gods of the Celts, Romans or Egyptians be as real as the Christian god? If they are, why must one pantheon be true and not the rest? In any case I decided at the age of ten, that I didn't like the Christian god. Damning everyone to hell just because they didn't believe in him. Not a nice god, there were so many more with a sense of humor in history.

As I grew, I found Witchcraft that answered all of my questions. In the Craft, the Goddess and God will communicate through the High Priestess and High Priest, telling stories, prophecies and giving information to the coven. I have spoken the words the Goddess has told me, many times. Life will not necessarily be a bed of roses, you learn nothing in this life by walking in bliss. Life must challenge you, it was summed up well by Nietzsche "What does not kill you, strengthens you". Walk boldly into both the light and dark within your own spirit, for you do not walk alone.

I have read books that strip away all religious aspects of Witchcraft and yes, the spells will still work, though not as well without the guiding hand of your God and Goddess. When working magic you are using the energy of the Universe however spells are not all there is to Witchcraft.

In many other traditions of Witchcraft, the Goddess and God are thought to be within you, a projection of your own inner consciousness; you access the light and dark within your own spirit. This I feel is a very modern concept, in this modern age we can't conceive of anything greater than ourselves.

Many feel that the Gods and Goddesses are Archetypes, that is, standard personalities, one good and loving, one war like etc. From these you can choose the best for your spell or working, giving you something to aim your thoughts at. This keeps ideas sharp and to the point, Venus for a love spell, Jupiter for joy and happiness.

Others believe that you can create gods by worship, does this mean Elvis is a god? Many people worship him all over the world; there are even Churches to Elvis in America. I see no reason to choose (except perhaps Elvis); to me all are true, I believe the Gods exist. As real as you or I, they are higher beings on other dimensions, which kiss our planet occasionally. If they choose, they may show themselves as archetypes or be within us. Is this just a simplistic answer? Perhaps, but I'm a simple person and it works.

I even know a Christian vicar and congregation that worships their god in Witchcraft circle, even calling the elemental quarters. I'm sure they would say its not the how but the whom they call that's important. Who they call and who I call may be different but we all strive toward divinity, the improving and strengthening of the innerself to make it possible at the end of many lives to become one with your deity. This is at the core of what all religions have always been about once you strip away the trappings of ritual.

Both the Goddess and God have light and dark within them, this is not evil and good but life and death, something that we all must face. Nothing is ever black or white, everything is shaped by opposing forces as in the Yin-Yang the Chinese symbol of male-female, a little of the Yin in the Yang and a little of the Yang in the Yin. A witch stands between the light and the dark, if you stand in the darkness you see both the light and into the dark, if you stand in the light you are blinded by the light and see nothing else, we must see both light and shade to understand.

Is the God or Goddess the Stronger?

From our standpoint on the Earth, the Sun and Moon are equal in size. When the Sun is eclipsed by the Moon, the Earth is darkened, temperature drops, birds stop singing and all nature holds its breath, the Moon appears to have the power to nullify the Sun, this in the past would have proved that the Goddess to be the stronger. As the swollower of the sun it appears she is the holder of the magic in some ways She is stronger, She endures throughout time. The God must die and be reborn every year and so She is the pivot, the rock on which the Universe is built.

In times past Priests and Priestesses were initiated into the service of one God or Goddess, this follows in our tradition of Witchcraft. If joining an established coven you must accept the Gods and Goddesses that the coven work with but if approaching this book fresh then you have a wonderful chance to find a rapport with your chosen Goddess. By all means investigate many Gods and Goddesses, find who calls you to this path. When you are ready, if you choose to follow our tradition, initiate to your specific Goddess and God of whichever pantheon you find them in. With only one Goddess you form a closer understanding, a unity that is missing from working with many. You begin to understand her ways; She gets to know the way you think and how She can best teach you.

Creation Myth

In Witchcraft, for some reason, I can find no trace of a creation myth.

In this scientific age we live in, we tend to over analyze everything, so can a modern person accept the existence of Gods and Goddesses? Here is a creation myth read it and judge for yourself.

"When the Goddess was old and time but young, She was alone in the darkness, floating a spark of consciousness in an infinity of nothing, time passed, and She grew lonely. Time as we cannot conceive passed and She grew even lonelier. She created from herself an egg barely three yards wide, full of something and nothing under intense pressure. The something and the nothing were opposing forces and so each strived to separate itself, as She knew they would. An almighty explosion occurred, that threw the opposing forces into the darkness in all directions, matter collided with antimatter and stars were born. In infinite time stars gave birth to planets and planets gave birth to us and so the Goddess is no longer alone. All the matter and antimatter that forms the Universe was contained in that three yard wide egg. Across the sky hangs the shock wave of the explosion She left, that we may remember Her loneliness and that She created us from Herself and to Her we will eventually return."

I'm sure you will recognize this, as the latest scientific theory called the BIG BANG as told in myth form, obviously the Goddess does not feature in the scientific explanation. They have tried their best to construct a creation theory without a creator but without success. To try to compensate they then expanded on this with the Multi-Universe theory but I can't see how this helped at all, you still need a creator, you have just made the plot bigger. Cosmologists can't accept a creator only because a science needs proof before accepting an idea, but the theory does not stand up without Her. Without Her (or a Him, if you are Christian) did a ball of anti matter and matter start as a sphere of energy without a divine creator? How did the egg appear; however with a Creator in the equation we have balance. No matter how cosmologists seem to wiggle they can find no other route but to bring in a Creator or give it any name you care to, 'The Great Computer Programmer in the Sky', if that pleases you.

It is interesting to realize that if there had been equal quantities of antimatter as matter, the stars and therefore eventually us would not have formed, but the darkness would have been washed away in a sea of light. As it was, the matter outweighed the antimatter by JUST enough for the Universe, as we know it, to form and for us to come into being.

The Big Bang Theory does resemble many creation myths of culture thoughout the world. The Ancient Egyptians tell us of a sea of chaos (meaning nothingness) from which the Gods formed the Land. Bible tells a similar story of Jehovah creating the world (or

Universe) from nothing, which borrowed from many creation stories before it. The Akashic Egg that held all within, is another symbol depicted in the scientific explanation of how the Universe was formed.

In deep space there is untold beauty, that our eyes will never see. I have seen some pictures from the Hubbell space telescope, so we have some idea of our very small corner of the Universe. There has to be more to the Universe than science can ever put a label on or we can ever comprehend.

In days past, before artificial light polluted the sky, the heavens were awash with stars, have you ever been deep in the country, at night, near no other light but the stars? This is how it would have been all over the world, in the past, nothing to spoil the beauty of the stars and the Goddess and God.

It is easy to see the Gods then.

In the world all around us from an atom to the sunset, from a drop of water poised on the tip of a leaf about to fall to the great Oceans, there must be more to the Universe than we mere mortals can conceive.

What proof is there for these other dimensions?

I refuse to go into the "String Theory" even if I understood it! Which is the latest scientific theory that sets out to prove that other dimensions exist. All I can say is, find a magical place in the country make friends with it. Allow it to open up for you and be astounded. There is more out there than you can imagine. I can't prove it to you, if you're lucky it will be shown. I was in a wood where many rituals have taken place, many campfires have been lit, and much singing and jollity has poured onto the land. One night about three a.m. the fire had been dowsed for the evening, revelers had drifted off to bed, a friend and I were just checking to be sure no candles where left burning. Quiet seemed to fall over the wood, my friend and I stood in silence, over my friends shoulder I saw a deep purple light begin to form. I placed my hands on my friend's shoulders and silently turned him round to face the light, whispering "Can you see it?" By then it had grown to a fan shape about fifteen feet tall by thirty feet wide. Two flesh pink glowing figures formed, like two giant five pointed stars, just off center of the fan. They moved around each other caressing, sinking to the floor, then rising. I at first, wondered if it was not friends from the party making love in the woods but quickly realized that the two star shapes were very tall indeed and they glowed. I was racking my brain for a logical explanation, grabbing at silly straws. We watched and whispered, as my friend described how they were sinking to the floor and I described them now rising. We were quite obviously watching the same thing. How long did this go on? I have no idea. I think about five minutes but my concentration was distracted for a moment as I saw torchlight coming through the trees toward the entities. I then looked to see how far away they were, but they had gone.

It was impossible for a purple light to be there, there is no electricity, no way of forming purple ultra- violet light but we both saw it. What was it, the God and Goddess or spirit of wood? Who knows, I had my camera by my side and was too shocked to remember it, whether it would have taken a picture or not I have no idea. Many other visitors to the wood have seen purple lights but only smaller lights and occasionally golden globes have also been seen. Others have seen a fire that was not there and found no burn mark the following morning. I hope that at some other time I will be honored with another chance to look through the dimensions, into the realms of the Gods.

The traditional view of magic being the left hand path and the Christian god right – why?

Throughout history the left-hand side has been thought of as female and the right male. Where the Sun is a male God and travels across the sky from its dawn in the East and setting in the West, it travels clockwise. The Sun with all its golden life-giving glow must be good. The Moon has the same twenty eight-day cycle as women and in many religions this made the moon female. The Moon gives light in the darkness, which is the time of mystery, magic and witchcraft. It travels across the sky anti-clockwise and must therefore be bad. When Christian evangelical priests from a male centered religion tried to covert pagans across Europe from 300 CE (Pagans and many other religions don't use BC or AD but Before Common Era BCE or Common Era CE) onwards they changed or degraded any symbol or sign that was not connected with the Christian / Jewish tradition. Making the moon, left handedness or indeed any female symbol, evil. These symbols were buried deep in the pagan's spiritual subconscious and proved difficult to remove, making the Catholic Church more and more determined to eradicate these signs. As the drive to remove previous religions became more extreme women in the Middle Ages began to be considered a bad influence on good men. As women were the guardians of Magic, so Magic was consigned to the left-hand female path, which they feared held dark forces. Men in the Christian Middle Ages were considered good, standing for the virtues and represented the right. They are the Sun, guardians of the sword and the right hand path. The Moon Goddess walks in magic and mystery and to the medieval mind this was to be feared. The Sun God, strong golden warrior, fertilizing the fields, was easier to understand and except. With no Gods but the Christian god now allowed, the only option was to demean even the Sun God to the role of hero knight or His fertility aspect to that of the Greenman in churches. Of course, in Witchcraft we do not consider either path evil or good; merely that it is another misunderstanding of our religion.

Europe was not the only center of Sun and Moon worship, it can be found all over the world. In Peru in South America indigenous people originally crossed the Bering Straits, ten thousand years ago. Travelling down through North America to finally settle on the coast, reaching there some 4000 years ago. They had no contact with cultures outside the Americas until the 16th Century but amongst the magnificent pre Inca treasure of the Lord of Sipan burial site can be found many familiar symbols of witchcraft. On each hip he wears a large ceremonial axe, one in silver on his left for their Moon Goddess and gold on his right for their Sun God. Also a superb necklace of enormous peanuts, a symbol of fertility and duality (two nuts within each shell), gold on the right for their Sun God and silver on the left in honor of their Moon Goddess.

The Egyptian Pharaohs, who were buried with either both arms, crossed holding a shepherds crook and a flail. If however just one arm was placed on the chest, it would be the right holding a scepter. Egyptian Queens however, would be buried with their left arm across her breasts holding a scepter.

Ancient Rome developed this theme by inventing the handshake with the right-hand, for their army they invented to the salute, by raising the right hand to show that it is empty and that no weapons were held. Rome of course became the Holy Roman Empire and the prejudice against the left grew. In the Middle Ages if a man were born out of wedlock but entitled to a coat of arms this would show a black line across going backwards to the left and known as a bar sinister. In Latin the word for left is sinister. Men being assigned the right and women the left seems to be a universal constant in magic, although only Christianity deems this bad. Because of the Christian prejudice against woman in the middle ages, we still have a prejudice against the left hand, children up until recently were admonished in school for using their left hand to write with.

The symbols of Sun and Moon, left and right can be found across the world. These signs exist deep in all of our spirit and are universal, why? Does this prove that we instinctively know these signs and feel in tune with what they represent?

So whom do witches work with?

There are two points to be taken into consideration before starting to work with a God or Goddess, the Land and your Heritage.

The Land and Your Heritage

Witchcraft is a fertility religion; the land and the Goddess are one, as the Goddess blesses the land so the land flourishes, in this She is the Goddess of Sovereignty. Bestowing kingship on the worthy. You will recognize the story from many a folktale, of the prince who meets an ugly, twisted, old woman, who is the Goddess of Sovereignty in disguise, offering him Her favors (or in modern versions asking for water or help in some way). Some of the princes in our tale will not lay with the hag (or kiss or help, as the case may be). For the prince that satisfies the crone, She turns in the morning to a beautiful maiden who would confer royalty onto him, blessing the land and his reign. Like all good folktales they live happily ever after, until that is, he gets too old to forfil his marital duties and is sacrificed for the next young prince, but that is another story.

But every Goddess must have a God; fertility is a male and female business.

The God has been traditionally seen as procreative and fierce, as befits a warrior God. In the mating, the crops are fertilized the land refreshed becomes strong, this we see as symbolic of the process that repeats every Spring.

In the Middle Ages the Witch's God was depicted as a goat, this possibly originated with the Goat headed Sun God of the Egyptians, Amon. He was deliberately misconstrued by the church, to become their Devil; the Gods of the Old World have always formed the devils of the new.

There is a wonderful extract of a letter by Red Jacket at Missionary Meeting at Buffalo, New York.

You say that you are sent to instruct us how to worship the Great Spirit agreeably to his mind, and if we do not take hold of the religion which you White people teach, we shall be unhappy hereafter; you say that you are right, and we are lost; how do we know this to be true? We understand that your religion is written in a book; if it was intended for us as well as you, why has not the Great Spirit given it to us, but why did He not give to our forefathers the knowledge of that book, with the means of understanding it rightly? We only know what you tell us about it; how

34

shall we know when to believe, being too often deceived by the White people?......We also have a religion, which was given to our forefathers, and has been handed down to us, their children. We worship that way. It teaches us to be thankful for all the favours we receive: to love each other, and to be united; we never quarrel over religion'.

Nothing changes.

Red Jacket's reply is so poignant echoing down the years. I'm sure the same words were spoken by the Celts about their Gods and Goddesses becoming the Devils of the Christian Church, in the same way as the Native Americans in 1805.

Gods and Goddesses are great wanderers, wherever a tribe or army marched they took their Gods with them. Invasions have swept across the world from the dawn of time and new Gods have strode boldly into the lives of the invaded.

From the **Celts** we have legends of Tuatha Dé Danann (People of the Goddess Danu) flying there boats through the skies (or flying on black clouds) to invade Ireland, with them came their Gods, The Morrigan, Lugh, Brigit are but a few

Rome goose stepped its way across Europe, taking with them not only Jupiter and Venus but also Isis and Hathor, Egyptian Goddesses, which they had already incorporated into their pantheon. Rome chose to take these and similar deities from other cultures to help subdue the native population. The closest to the Triple Goddess that is so popular today are the Tres Matres meaning Triple Mothers of life and death (more later in this chapter).

The **Vikings** sailed all over Europe and even as far as America (which they named Vineland) smashing monasteries marauding until finally settling down, building communities and bringing their own religion to the lands they conquered to add to the mix Odin, Thor and Freya.

Many influences have come to make Europe and on to America and Australia, the people we are today. Even now, new influences of Hoodoo (African/American magic) and Hinduism with more to follow add to the rich stew that Paganism is at this time.

Although the magic of the land is the strongest, the Goddesses and Gods that have been worshipped for centuries are part of our blood; our ancestors literally spilled it in their defense. Christianity is a relative new comer with only the antecedence of two thousand years!

Your bloodline is important in contacting the old Gods and Goddesses but that does not mean that if you have only just moved to a country this religion isn't for you. Feel your bloodline, research your heritage, and honor your ancestors. Blood and land have caused untold wars but now is the time to look upon this with a new educated sight, honor the difference and honor the magic that various cultures hold within.

Perhaps we should take one thing from the Roman conquest of Britain. When bringing their Gods and other cultures deities, they sort similarities with Celtic Gods already worshipped here. By amalgamating similar Gods together and hyphenating the names they respected both the land and heritage, this perhaps is an idea that we can adopt today.

The Gods and Goddesses

The Gods and Goddesses of Witchcraft, are approachable, tell them your problems, and feel free to ask for proof of their reality. When I first started along the path of Witchcraft I was told to ask if I wanted something. Being brought up in a Christian household, I was taught not to ask for things for myself but eventually I fought off conditioning and found the courage. I had opened a small shop, selling conventional jewelry, it was not doing too well, and the previous owner had let it run down. A change of ownership new and fashionable jewelry had done nothing to improve the business. So, after taking the great amount of £12.50 all day I decided to ask the Goddess for her help.

" If there is a Goddess out there, can you give me help with the shop, as I don't want to go bankrupt just after I've opened!" five minutes later brought in a customer who spent £100, I was delighted! This was not enough to pay the lease that was soon due. So the next day, I asked again, five minutes later a customer came in and spent another £100! That evening on closing, my friend who was helping in the shop commented on how well we had done, I explained to her what had happened. Come next day again I asked the Goddess's help, and again a customer but this time she spent £200! Sarah asked me if I had asked, I said I had,

" Yes, so had I."

This is not a religion based on faith but on fact. Ask for proof and it will be given, but ask for something practical, not for the sky to turn green, or to win the lottery but something that is a little unlikely and your wish will be granted. Although it is impolite to keep asking for proof, so once only please!

The Goddess

To Her belongs all the uneven or magical numbers - 3, 5, 7, 9 and 13

The Goddess is the chalice and the holder of the magic and is represented by the High Priestess and all other Priestesses within the circle (women in Anglo-Saxon times were also considered to be holders of the magic, as magic users became devalued in the normal community they became the 'old wives' of tales). This explains why magic was not traditionally done without at least one woman present in circle. This is not to say that men do not participate in the making of the magic, merely that they are not the traditional guardians of the magic.

The Goddess is worshipped in many guises, She can be Venus the Goddess of Love, Heath and Wealth, She can be The Morrigan of Celtic legend or simply call Her- The Goddess. Honor which ever Goddess chooses to appear to you. You can choose any Goddess from the beginning of time, if you choose or should I say; if She chooses you.

Here are some to think about, the most common Goddess, if you can use that word about a Goddess, in witchcraft is The Triple

Goddess. Many say that She is a product of the twentieth century, others point to the Celtic Triple Goddess votive offering found in a well in Kent England very like the Tres Matras (Three Mothers) of Ancient Rome worshiped in Britain. Perhaps we just don't know at this point in time. Has She chosen to remerge from the past now or is She like Elvis the god, a product of Her time. One thing that can not be denied, is Her popularity.

Many Goddesses that have been worshipped in history can fall into one of the Triple Goddess categories. Use the visualization that we will start to do at the end of this chapter, then research the Goddess that appears to you. Like a great puzzle, start to assemble the pieces left to us from history to flesh out the bones of your chosen Goddess and God and make them real.

Triple Goddess
Her symbol is the Moon, in all its stages.

In Witchcraft, The Goddess is very often thought of as her symbol the Moon. This then splits into the three phases of the moon - waxing, full moon and waning moon. These are said to typify the three ages of women Maiden, Mother and Crone.

Her magical metal is Silver (see metal magic).

English folklore says that the Moon should be bowed to, perhaps this is a memory of a time when the moon was more important than it is now to most people.

"New Moon, New Moon, fust time I've seed thee,
Hope before the week's out I'll ha'summat gi'ed me".

On seeing a new moon, the folktale goes that you should turn over your silver in your pocket or purse three times to make it grow, particularly the first moon of the New Year and bow to Her.

Maiden

Young, innocent ~ look to her to do growing magic, plants, animals and health.

The maiden is pre-menstruating, young and innocent and is the waxing or growing moon.

Color is White

Waxing Moon ~ First quarter of the Moon, in it's growing cycle.

Blood- None- She is young life, pure uncomplicated, She has no wisdom to give away and so does not bleed.

Mother

Strong in mind, sexually rampant, mothering, battle Goddess, ~ ask from Her all magic. The mother is of course also sexually active, an enchantress, as well as mother to the world.

Color **Red**

Full Moon ~ she affects the tides, of magic as well as the seas, causing high and low tides.

Blood- Red of blood is the color of seductress and mother, there are many pulls on Her time, others dependant on Her, but still giving away Her blood and wisdom, leaking it to the world. It is thought that in tribal societies, without electric light to disturb the Pineal gland on the third eye area, all woman of a village will menstruate together at the fullmoon. This would make it a very strong time for magic.

I remember seeing a documentary many years ago, where an anthropologist was learning of the ways of a tribe in the jungle. He stated that at the full moon the women would leave the village and go into the jungle. Of course he sat with the men expecting some great ritual, but they just sat around drinking beer. I feel that like Cecil Sharp, who only documented the men's Morris dances in England not considering the women to be of any importance, this chap had missed the point.

A mother must first become pregnant to give birth and so She is very much a sexual creature not just a mother but as sexual as the God. To Pagans sex within a loving relationship is pure, with no taint of Christian evil. The Goddess is a strong and full woman in all Her attributes, though I do not deny Her motherhood, a state to be honored. She is the beautiful primal Mother, mother of creation, our mother, in this She can be warm and cozy like an old blanket, a time to love and nurture. Her color is also the red blood of the Battle Goddess, to understand Her in this form think of Her as a Lioness defending Her cubs. Any mother defending her children will be a fearless fighter, could a Goddess be less?

Crone

Often known as The Dark Goddess of Wisdom, death, the old one that sweeps all into her arms at the end ~ Divination, decreasing magic (as in decreasing pain), binding magic.

Color is Black

Waning Moon ~ decreasing Moon

Blood- None.

Finally Crone, post menstruation, alone once more, pure wisdom, protection, death. Deep within a lifetime of wisdom, looking both to the past and deep into the future, knowing all that has ever been and ever will be. Said by tradition to reabsorb her own blood, not giving any away and by this becoming more and more wise. There at the end of your time, waiting to cut the threads of your life and end this cycle and life time. She is Death. The Dark Goddess is not to be feared, She takes the old, the crippled to her breast, remaking them and replacing them for a new life free from the pain and disease of the last. She is not the scary man in a cowl with an hourglass and scythe ticking away the seconds but an old warm kindly grandma waiting to take you in Her arms and remake you young and strong once more.

If you believe in reincarnation, death is not the end but a moving forward. We all have something to learn or do in this life, once learnt; it is time to move on. Witches do not fear death; we have visited the Dark Goddess many times, only the unknown is fearful. At death, the Goddess sweeps all to her dark wings once again, a time to rest and in time to be reborn. In many areas of England in the Middle Ages, it was considered unlucky to light three candles, on the third you brought death. This same belief traveled to the trenches in the First World War, and was transferred to lighting cigarettes with one match. It was thought on the first cigarettes the enemy saw the light, the second he aimed the gun and the third he shot. As a witch however we understand the Crone and the third candle that is Hers, to us she is a comfort to others She can be frightening. Death is not evil, our modern perception denies death it's place in life, banishes the Crone from our society prevents the old having the dignity their wisdom deserves. That is wrong. Honor all ages, all have something to teach us, from the innocence laughter and purity of youth, through to the combined wisdom of all that has gone before. It is time to accept the Crone with Her dark mysteries, without fear.

Dark Moon In all diaries this is marked as the New Moon but the symbol that they use of the dark circle is more accurate, for us it is called the Dark Moon. No moon can be seen in the sky, at this time. By this we know that the Goddess does not wish to be disturbed, the time of change, for the Goddess back to Virgin, not a time to call Her. I always visualize Her in a chrysalis form during this phase or sleeping and regenerating.

The myth of the Descent of the Goddess Inanna in its original appearance helps to explain this. How she descends to the underworld through the gates leaving her jewelry and then robes (waning, decreasing moon), is dead in the underworld for three days, (dark moon) resurrected and brought back to life. Returning through the gates (waxing, increasing moon) as She grows in size to the full moon, once more.

Triple Goddess Pendant

You can see from the pendant I made, left, that the Moon travels widdershins (anticlockwise, starting on the left hand side, the female side) through its cycle, as perceived from Earth. Starting on the left-hand side with the Maiden, increasing moon, center the Mother- full moon, right hand side with the Crone-decreasing moon.

Gaia

Dr James Lovelock studied chemistry at the University of Manchester within the United States he has conducted research at Yale, Harvard and Baylor College.

In his book called *'Ages of Gaia.'*, written in 1988 in which he says that the Earth is alive, guides human evolution and She has a thinking but primitive mind. Since the evolution of humanity She has preserved us, never making the Earth too cold or too hot for the plants that we need to preserve life. Always keeping a constant balance, that allows us to survive. One of the old names for the Earth Goddess was Gaia, so Lovelock borrowed that name; it fits very well. Although modern Pagans interpretation of the Lovelock theory is a little more intense than he visualized it. For us She has a thinking mind and strong personality, able to change and direct evolution to Her will. Will She when She feels the time is right change Global Warming? Perhaps, but not until after we have learnt our lessons.

Aradia

Charles Godfrey Leland was born in 1824 Philadelphia, Pennsylvania, into a Puritan family. But surprisingly Leland seemed to have been surrounded by people either practicing The Craft or folklore rituals or learning Voodoo from servant women in the kitchen.

His niece Elizabeth Robins Pennell in a biography wrote

In both the "Memoirs" and "Memoranda," he tells how he was carried up to the garret by his old Dutch nurse, who was said to be a sorceress, and left there with a Bible, a key, and a knife on his breast, lighted candles, money, and a plate of salt at his head: rite that were to make luck doubly certain by helping him rise in life, and become a scholar and wizard.

It is said that he could not pass a bit of red string without picking it up or a stone with a hole within without popping it into his pocket, which clanked from the amulets that he carried from his travels.

Leland was a traveler, journalist, an expert on folklore and on the Gypsy traditions, no doubt stemming from his early influence.

Leland eventually moved to Tuscany Italy in 1886, where he met a young woman Maddalena Taleni who read the future using playing the cards. She told him that she practiced the Italian form of witchcraft, Stregheria, which she said, had been in her family since the ancient Etruscan times. Maddalena and her friend Marietta slowly began to reveal to Leland the secrets held by the local Stregheria families. But it was eleven years before Maddalena would part with a copy of The Vangelo (Gospel) which Leland later published as *Aradia: Gospel of the Witches*. She posted this to him on New Years day 1897 in her own handwriting, telling him that she was to be married to Lorenzo Bruciatelli and was emigrating to America- he never saw her again.

Leland's description of Meddalena

"a young woman who would have been taken for a Gypsy in England, but in whose face, in Italy, I soon learned to know the antique Etruscan, with its strange mysteries, to which was added the indefinable glance of the Witch. She was from the Romagna Toscana, born in the heart of its unsurpassingly wild and romantic scenery, amid cliffs, headlong torrents, forests, and old legendary castles. I did not gather all the facts for a long time, but gradually found that she was of a Witch family, or one whose members had, from time to immemorial, told fortunes, repeated ancient legends, gathered incantations, and learned how to intone them, prepared

43

enchanted medicines, philtres, or spells. As a girl, her Witch grandmother, aunt, and especially her stepmother brought her up to believe in her destiny as a sorceress, and taught her in the forests, afar from human ear, to chant in strange prescribed tones, incantations or evocations to the ancient gods of Italy, under names but little changed, who are now known as folletti, spiriti, fate, or lari - the Lares or household goblins of the ancient Etruscans."

Charles Godfrey Leland   **Maddalena**

In his book *Etruscan Roman Remains* Leland says
> *It was their rivals and enemies who were maladette streghe, etcetera, but the latter I never met. **We were all good***

and in another passage he says
> *came to practice **our** noble profession.*

Could Leland have been initiated as a Witch?

The book centers around Diana and Her daughter Aradia, detailing the rituals and spells taught to the Straga, the Italian word for Witch, by Aradia. Diana was a one of the many Goddesses beloved of the

Romans before Christianity, could this be a continuation of that tradition going underground? As with the Incas in Peru and those still worshipping the Nagas the Water Dragons and Mae Toranee an Earth Goddess in Thailand, that is traditional thought of as a Buddhist country to this day.

Diana can easily be interpreted as a Triple Goddess. Traditionally thought of as a Virgin Goddess, She is also the Mother of All Creatures in her aspect as Diana of Ephesus and but is also the Huntress, note the arrows on Her back, the death giver. Her worship was not confined to Rome but traveled with them to all parts of the Roman Empire. The Canon Episcopi (an edict of the church) published in 906 CE (Common Era), states that Witches were deluded heretics who worshiped Diana, Goddess of the Pagans but it is the Devil that seduces them to do this (they had to get that bit in). Here again we have mention of Diana.

Beneath St Paul's Cathedral in London is a Roman Temple to the Goddess Diana, this temple survived until the 7th century Common Era. In John Stone's Survey of London in 1598, he tells of a strange rite that still took place at that time in St Paul's, even though it was a Christian Cathedral. On May Day hunters from the closest woods would bring a doe and a stag, Diana's sacred animals, to the high altar of St Paul's and there on the altar their throats would be cut, the heads would then be carried around the cathedral. At that moment horns would be blown to announce their sacrifice and answered  from every quarter of London. People at the time that witnessed the ritual were said to comment that the Goddess Diana had returned to them again.

There are also suggestions the Leland invented the book, but his background in folklore and the high esteem that he was held by the Gypsies for his work in documenting there beliefs, tends in my opinion preclude this.

Hecate

I was surprised and delighted on re-reading Shakespeare's Macbeth, after finding Witchcraft that the three Witches worshipped Hecate a Roman Goddess and not the devil as you may have thought Shakespeare would conclude. Perhaps he knew more than we give him credit for.

Similar examples of the Goddess can be found all over the world and in many cultures. Equally her consult can be found nearer to home than you think.

The God

The God is both the child of and husband of the Goddess. As husband, He fertilizes The Goddess and with Her, the land. Spring returns and Winter recedes to become a memory. The Earth blooms, crops grow tall, all is well with the land. The Goddess is the pivot of the year, never changing, but the God dies and is reborn fresh and young each year. As the year changes the Goddess appears to mate with Her own child. This may seem strange to modern people, although in both the Egyptian and Celtic royalty it was quite common. In our tradition however this legend is a metaphor for re-incarnation. The God, as all Gods are, is perfect. He is born again and again, unchanging but for us mere mortals, we must strive for perfection and this will not be found for many lives. We work from one life to another, ever striving toward our goal. Not as with the Buddhists fearing to be born as a lower life form but only treading water until the lessons of this life are achieved. I feel this brings an understanding to the problems of disability, everyone experiences this problem in one of our many lives. Those who help and under-stand have worked through that life, those who are uncaring have yet to experience this problem. Learning how to cope with disability, learning how to cope with being poor and even learning to cope with being rich, all are lessons to be learnt. You must have met many naive people that you felt were experiencing their first life and many a child that had an understanding far in excess of their years.

The God is the sword, warrior and guardian of the circle and is represented by the High Priest and the Priests of the Circle. They are the guardians of the circle and traditional holders of the sword within our tradition, representing the God as warrior, protector.

To Him belongs the even numbers- 2, 4, 6 and 8

The God's symbol commonly used is the Sun, His magical metal is Gold (see metal magic).

There are many Gods that you can choose to work with in Witchcraft, Gods of the Sun, the Greenwood, Smithing, War and many more. Although the God most commonly worked with is the Horned God of the Forest.

The Stag Horned God

Most modern Witches, perhaps because of the confusion with the Medieval Devil in the minds of the public do not work with a Goat God, although the Egyptian Sun God Amon would be a perfectly exceptable God to work with. Most Witches prefer to work with Cernunnos or Herne.

Although Cernunnos is depicted with horns this has nothing to do with the Christian concepts of the devil but is far older than Christianity. The worship of the Horned God goes back to the hunter-gather peoples of Indo-Europe. The Christians don't add the horns and tail to their devil until the 6th century Common Era. In our earlier extract of the thoughts of Red Jacket it is common practice for the conqueror to make the Gods of the conquered people into the devils for the new regime. Changing the Sun God Amun's horns into the horned dark one.

There are approximately sixty depictions of Cernunnos the Celtic Horned God, across the Celtic lands, the earliest from Northern Italy in the BCE 400.

Cernunnos, was depicted with the antlers of a stag, He is a God of fertility and plenty. He is strength, warrior, protector a nature God and the fertilizer of the land. Images of Red Deer stags are used to symbolize Cernunnos in His non-human form. Horns and Antlers in particular are representative of forest deities, the stag antlers of Cernunnos and Herne are like the trees of the forest. Stags drop their horns like leaves yearly, their tines (points) representing the branches of the tree as in the Song of Amergin when he says he is a stag of seven tines.

Amergin, Bard of the Milesians, lays claim to the Land of Ireland
I am a stag: of seven tines,
I am a flood: across a plain,
I am a wind: on a deep lake,
I am a tear: the Sun lets fall,
I am a hawk: above the cliff,
I am a thorn: beneath the nail,
I am a wonder: among flowers,
I am a wizard: who but I
Sets the cool head aflame with smoke?

On the Gundestrup cauldron found in a peat bog at Gundestrup, Denmark in 1891, made about 2nd or 1st century BCE (in the La Tene 111 period) and is possibly Celtic. It stands a magnificent fourteen inches high, twenty-eight inches in diameter, weighs twenty pounds and is made of solid silver. On the cauldron Cernunnos is also depicted with seven tines on each beam of His antlers. In folk tradition a deer with this quantity of tines is called an Imperial Stag and would be the lead or master of the herd. So we are told both in the song and on the cauldron that The Horned God is a leader of both men and animals. Cernunnos is depicted on the cauldron holding in his left hand a rigid horned snake and in his right a torc, is this a phallic representation? Telling us that he is a God of

fertility.

Remembering that the Celts had no written language, only one carving of Cernunnos bears a name in Latin, carved by sailors from the Gallic Parisii tribe (Paris) in the first century CE that by then was a Roman province. It is carved on the Pillar of the Boatman which stands 5.5 m high and nearly 1 m wide at the base and would have stood outside a Roman temple on an island in the middle of the river Seine, where Notre-Dame de Paris now stands. Cernunnos does not appear alone on the pillar but is in grand company, with many other Gods, both Gaelic and Roman. He is carved with a neck torc (a form of necklace) hanging from each beam of His antler, this is similar to the torc He is depicted with on the Gundestrup Cauldron. But this time the horn is placed within the torc, leaving us in no doubt that He is a God of fertility. This time the act is forfilled not just hinted at, in fact twice over, one for each horn.

The name Cernunnos is similar to the Latin for Horned One and it has been suggested that it may not have even been His original name. It may have been just a description of the God, but as the other Gods on The Pillar of the Boatman are mentioned by their name I see no reason to think that it was not.

The legends of Herne the Hunter from England, have also been attached to Cernunnos, some today preferring to call Him by this

Anglo-Saxon name. Herne the name may have come from stags at mating time, in late spring use the call of "H-H-HERNE", trumpeting it across the countryside, as a challenge to other mature males to fight for lead male position.

Many great historical leaders used the symbol of both horns and antler, as the horn was seen as a sign of wisdom and kingship. When Rome annexed Egypt, the Father of the Roman Gods was Jupiter, He was hyphenated with the Amon, who sported a fine set of horns, and was considered the oldest and mightiest of the Egyptian deities becoming Amon-Jupiter.

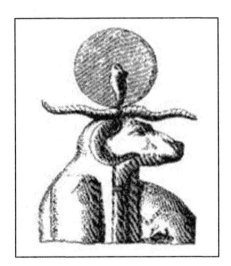

Alexander the Great claimed that his father was the Egyptian Sun God Amon, Alexander borrowed His "fathers" ram's horns and was depicted wearing them on some of his coins, giving himself kingship and the wisdom of a Sun God. From this the Sun came to represent all horns and so Cernunnos' antlers also represent the rays of the Sun.

In Hebrew 'radiated' and 'horned' are the same word and a mistranslation appeared in some versions of the bible. Moses was thought to have solid physical horns in the Middle Ages. There is a statue in the Vatican by Michaelangelo at the tomb of Julius 11, 1513 Common Era of Moses with horns. You'll find it tucked behind a column out of sight. Not that Moses was the only Christian to acquire horns, Bishop Reginald of Bath, 1174-1191 thought himself sufficiently praise worthy to wear them on his seal too.

There are even legends of people being born with horns. I can remember an article in the newspaper when I was very young, which stated that a woman in Italy had been admitted to hospital for an operation and would not remove her scarf. After much coercing they eventually managed to persuade her to remove it, only to find that she had horns, the doctors promptly offered to remove them. But she would have none of this. Which as a teenager at the time, was beyond my understanding. But it seemed that she was greatly revered in her home village and considered a holy woman, dare I say Witch (was she one of Leland's Straga?). Although at the time, to report Witch in the newspapers would have given her a different persona than holy. She had her operation and all went well but one of her horns was "accidentally" broken during the operation. She quite rightly demanded its return and returned to her hill village. Unfortunately I can find no photos which I assume would have been taken and so no proof for the reality of this story. Which is a great shame, I can only say it strikes me as true. If only that the horned woman was reported to be holy, not a concept a reporter back then would have imagined.

In 669 Common Era Paganism was still the religion of many people in Europe and was a threat to the still establishing Holy Roman Empire. The Pope Vitalian became active in the destruction of many pagan sites and sent missionaries all over Europe to convert the heathen. In Southern England, Pope Vitalian had little success and had eventually been forced to send a high profile mission led by Theodore the Greek, who was later to become Archbishop of Canterbury. Theodore carries out the Pope's orders and began to ban Pagan traditions. One of many was...

'Whoever at the kalends (first) of January goes about in the form of a stag, that is changing himself into the form of an animal, dressing in the skin of a horned beast and putting on the head of a beast, for those who in such wise transform themselves into the appearance of a wild animal, penance for three years, because it is devilish'

Not you notice any other wild animals, only the stag. The 1st January is the last day of the old Yule celebrations; Yule the day of the rebirth of the Sun God. A relation of mine still takes her Yule decorations down (yes, she's Pagan too) on New Years Eve and cleans the house. It is the tradition in my family not to wait for the Christian Twelfth Night, is this remembrance of an old Pagan custom I wonder? The more I look, the more information I seem to find.

Pashupati means ' Lord of Animals' (Pashu - animal, Pati -Lord).

He may be the predecessor of all the Horned Gods, stretching across Asia into Europe, being the oldest yet found. He strode the area of Northern India and Pakistan, approximately 6000 years ago. Did Pashupati along with the Mother Goddess His consort, travel with migrating people across Asia into Europe? Is Pashupati the true name of our own Horned God?

From many seals that have been found in the area of the Indus Valley, there is a striking resemblance to Cernunnos on the Gundestrup Cauldron. Pashupati on the seals sits cross-legged surrounded by animals, as does Cernunnos, but very understandably the animals are different. Pashupati's animals are a rhinoceros, elephant, tiger, bull and a musk deer, animals of the area and time that he lives. Cernunnos sits surrounded by a stag, wolf, bull, a human figure riding a dolphin and a strange feline, never satisfactorily identified, is this a corruption of Pashupati's tiger? In modern times, Cernunnos has acquired Pashupati's title of ' Lord of Animals'.

If we except the assumption that the torc and the horned snake carried by Cernunnos on the Gundestrup Cauldron are phallic, although Pashupati has His hands on His knees, on some of these seals we find that the God' s penis is visibly erect and the testicles prominent. Leading to the conclusion that both have a connection to fertility, with Cernunnos being a little subtler with the information. Unfortunately, the scripts that bare a resemblance to Runes, has never been satisfactory deciphered. But there are references to Pashupati in other Indian and Nepalese religious texts. The Indian God Shiva is a development from Pashupati

Shiva says in the Skanda Purana -

As I reside here in the forest of Sleshmanta in the form of a beast,
My name will hence be known as the Pashupati the world over.

And

'the wilderness of this forest in merry-making assuming Himself (Shiva)
the form of a deer' .

Silvanus a Roman God or spirit "of the woods" far older than Rome itself, not part of the "official" pantheon of Roman Gods but well loved by the people. He is a version of the still older Etruscan deity Selvans. The stag was His sacred animal and He would be sometimes depicted with a fine set of deer's antlers. If clearing woodland, it was though best to make an offering to Silvanus before doing so. The first fruits of the Harvest were always offered to him by the farming communities, to Him as Mars (Mars is a very old God of Vegetation and protector of the fields) Silvanus, farmers would turn for heath for there animals. He was worshiped in the heart of Rome as well as the countryside, with 21 shrines dedicated to Him. This may have been because the land that Rome was built on was thought to be His and if Rome and Her people were to prosper a sacrifice must be offered.

Borevit (also spelled *Prove, Porewit* or *Borewit*) a Slavic God. He either roomed the woods as a bearded man or in the form of a human-stag (like a Pan character), with deer horns and big genitalia, the symbols of fertility and nature. Borevit helped travelers lost in His woods, punishing those destroying trees or harming the animals in his care. He was a shape changer or at least size changer, being able to stand as tall as a tree or have lunch with a squirrel within its hole.

Green Man

A Pagan symbol of nature and fertility, often depicted with leaves sprouting from His Mouth, sometimes from His eyes. Perhaps more a spirit of the Greenwood than a God but worked with in circle by many in the Craft. The Green Man first made his appearance 2300 years ago in India or possibly His first incarnation was as Osiris who is always depicted with a green face, not the color of petrifaction but the color of new life and growing things. Then travelling to Ancient Rome then moving to Turkey he can be seen in carvings on 2nd Century Roman Columns. The Greenman is carved in Jain temples of Rajasthan and in many Medieval churches in Europe.

The Green man is very often carved near the Sheela- Na- Gig (see charms) the female spirit of fertility. Fertility needs both the Greenman and the Sheela- Na- Gig, so obviously showing us her womb, pointing to Her fertility and allowing it to flow free over all that acknowledge Her. So why I wonder did the church retain these two figures, which seem to fly in the face of the chastity that they hold so dear?

Farming communities all round the world are reliant on fertility, of crops, animals and of children. Without Father nature and Mother Earth fertility will not take place. I have seen them on my travels again and again. Although the new religion has been adopted the old religion lives on tucked into a corner but still loved and revered by the ordinary folk.

Thailand is a Buddhist country, isn't it? Well possibly, but Mae Toranee, Mother Earth, helps the Buddha to overcome evil. She is always depicted washing Her hair, this is the rain that pours on the crops to make them grow and bring happiness. For this life giving rain there are many gifts of flowers and incense left by Her statues. She is never forgotten.

In Peru the Roman Catholics killed many in an attempt to convert the Incas to Christianity. Inca Temples were torn down and Roman Catholic Churches were built on sacred Inca sites. Mary mother of Jesus in Churches in Peru to this day, is depicted with a big cape to look like a mountain, which is the symbol of the much loved Pachamama the Peruvian Mother Earth Goddess before Spain insisted on the native's conversion. Mary is even depicted in many statues and paintings with a snake slithering up Her "mountain" for the Incas this is a creature of the underworld, the heart of the Earth Mother. A halo looking very much like the Sun, rises behind every statue of Mary, just as the Sun God rises behind Patchamama, she is never forgotten in the Inca peoples heart. The Incas were encouraged into the grand and awe inspiring Catholic churches to worship the new god. Mary dressed in the Incas own melted down gold and silver. But the Inca people, I believe continued to worship their Pachamama in the guise of Mary.

There is a modern legend that tells of a Catholic procession parading through the streets of Cusco, the old Inca Capitol City. There the Virgin Mary is carried shoulder high, but the statue slips and Mary crashes to the ground! Out from under the statue rolls the embalmed body of an Inca princess thought to be a reincarnation of Pachamama. It was Her that they were venerating in the guise of Mary. I would think every Roman Catholic priest was looking under Mary's skirts, that night.

During the last days of the Inca Empire, Manco Capac the last ruling Inca, made a speech to his people before one of the final battles with the Spaniards. These words vibrate down the centuries to me today. He is recorded as saying

'Outwardly you can give the impression of complying with their demands. Give them small tribute........I know that some day, by force they will make you worship what they worship. When that day comes and you can no longer resist, do it in front of them but on the other hand do not forget our ceremonies.......keep the rest hidden, close to your heart'

I feel that the Inca people really have kept their religion close to their hearts. I am pleased to say the old Inca religion for so long hidden, is now blossoming again, now the Peruvians can be seen to show their allegiance freely. The Inca rainbow flag flies side by side with the counties national flag, the past and the present standing balanced.

In Peru I came across a procession, at night in a small village at Easter. The Inca Rainbow flag was being paraded down the only street and was followed by the Christian Cross. Outside the church, it was strange to see the cross, bowed to the four Elemental Quarters three times, only then was it allowed into the church. Their brass band played one more rendition of the tune to cover the noise of the cross being hefted into its usual spot. The Christian priest started his mass and most of the people walked out! Like all Pagans they enjoy a good parade but weren't interested in staying for the Mass. I'm sure Manco Capac would have approved.

The Incas had no written language, we know nothing of their beliefs apart from that written by a few Spanish and that handed down by word of mouth from their Inca forebears, from priest to Shaman. Yet the similarity in the Shamanic rituals I participated in, all round the country are remarkable. Can this be considered a continuation of an old tradition, although nothing is recorded? I'm sure it can and if so, can that apply to Witchcraft too?

If we study of the techniques used by the Roman Catholics in Peru, might this throw light on the tactics that were used in England, so many years ago. If the Inca people dealt with the Roman Catholic Church supplanting Pachamama in 1632 was the same strategy used in Celtic Britain far earlier?

In England early Churches were always built on our sacred Pagan sites, as they were in Peru, if the Pagan religions were so evil why are images of the Green Man and Sheela- Na- Gig such a very pagan image, retained in a church that seems on the face of it to have no use, are they the Celtic Pachamama and Pachpoppa?

The Wild Man

The Wild Man, like the Greenman, is another very ancient concept, from the Arctic Circle to the Mediterranean. These are hirsute men with leafy loincloths, crowns of green leaves and most carry a big club. The wild man, with not too much stretch of the imagination, could be a development of the Green man. It was said that if you moved into the woods, eating berries and wild plants, you too would turn into a Wild Man, this process was considered irreversible. Was this some sort of veiled reference, threatening Christians returning to Paganism? Could this have been the last vestiges of the Deer Horned Gods that roamed the countryside in the popular conciseness?

The Wild Man also plays a part in what we now call Mumming plays; He is Nature, killed and resurrected. In some plays He mates before He dies. Is this the Goddess of the Land that He mates with? In English hereditary in the Middle Ages there are many instances of Wild Men supporters on many Coat of Arms. There are also stag horned men amongst these coats of arms these are said to again represent Moses. But I wonder if this is whom they really represented or was it safer for the mason to tell the church this horny man was a representation of Moses rather than Herne? In Medieval times it was no a time to shout "Pagan" or "Witch", best to cover your tracks with a nice respectable name of "Moses".

Pan

In my early days before finding the path that I was to be initiated into, I worked with many Gods, one time the Coven called Pan to our circle. Don't take Pan as your God unless you are fond of practical jokes or you may have a circle like this one evening. Pouring the beer at the Lammas Sabbat, our coverner found himself getting wetter and wetter. He thought at first that the jug that held the beer was leaking. Try how he might, the beer flowed more over him than into the chalice that all held, until his robe was a dripping mess. The jug was refilled after circle; not one drop spilled and at the many uses in circle since it has never dripped again.

Pan is not evil and most defiantly not the Christian Devil, as I have heard people say. He is God of the forest and it's woodland inhabitants. Sometimes in the wood you can hear his tunes played on the wind. Panic is said to be named after Pan but to me that is his warning sound that He blows on his pipes to warn the animals in His charge of any danger or of fire within the forest. Read the chapter 'Piper at the Gates of Dawn' from 'The Wind in the Willows' for a wonderful insight into The Great God Pan. The chapter is unfortunately cut from most children's illustrated books. Another interesting book is Rudyard Kipling "Puck of Pooks Hill".

Unknown Gods and Goddesses

You may find that in visualization you come across a deity that you have never heard of. You may choose to work with them and you may find an explanation later. It might be that a God or Goddess, (as with our own Coven's God's name) no longer exists. This does not make them any less valid than a God whose name is remembered.

My own God, is something like Cernunnos but not identical. In a visualization to my Astral Temple (more later), I suddenly found myself somewhere completely different. Standing in front of me was a type of stag horned centaur. He stood in front of an old half-timbered pub with the pub sign of purple grapes, swinging in the wind. I asked his name. He tried to tell me, but His name just seemed to hang on the air like a silver pattern of sound. He tried again but then just laughed and throwing back his head and said 'You may call me Hesphestios'. On researching the name Hesphestios, I found he was a Smithing God, which fits perfectly as I am a jeweler but strangely He is also responsible for wine making and brewing. Which explained the connection of the pub symbol with the sign of grapes, this made the visualization even more powerful. I carried on working with him, for many years but with no further information. After ten years a friend found a representation of a stag horned centaur on a Celtic cross in Ireland. On further investigation it appears that the designs on the cross is thought to be of Celtic Myth that predated

Christianity but no more is known. I had no idea that the design was on the cross in Ireland and so this memory could not have come from the recesses of my subconscious memory. I still do not understand the name He gave me. I tried another time when meeting Him again on the Astral Plane. This time he gave me a word, when I got back I looked it up in all the books I could think of, to no avail. I suddenly thought to look it up in the dictionary, to find the word meant that the explanation was more difficult than the fact! I looked again to check the spelling for this book and the word is not there. Interesting. Like the stories that tell of a shop or house that when you return is no longer there. Visualizations can communicate through space and time. Perhaps one day I will be given His true Celtic name or there again, perhaps not. Just before sending this manuscript to the printers I was given new information, both through visualization and then backed up by little known historical fact. At long last after many, many years, his true name was revealed, again under unusual circumstances but this is between my God, the coven and I.

How to do a Visualization

I've given below a visualization to start to find your Goddess and then God. Visualization is one of the tools of Witchcraft of all paths and one you will find invaluable.

It is not easy, you may not achieve this at the first attempt or you may not do it at all! This does not make you a bad Witch, it just means your power lies elsewhere. But practice will always improve your visualization skills. Men do find visualization more difficult than women. Visualization opens a path to the Astral plane, most will be trips within your own mind, finding out more about yourself. But just occasionally, you walk through the gate that leads to the Astral plane; we don't open it from our side, it is opened from the side of the Gods. We can however, refuse to see it open or block the door, not allowing entrance. This can take many years of hard work to rectify once the offer has been made, perhaps visualizing removing a brick wall stone by stone? Only you can find the answer for yourself, if you are too afraid to let go and allow the Gods to guide you.

How do you know that you are there, not just wondering in your mind? Things happen that you don't expect and would not dream of. Normally in a visualization, you think about what you are about to do, "I'll put a pot of flowers over there" flowers appear. This may be a fleeting deliberation but there is a small time lapse between thought and deed. When you have truly wandered into the Astral plane however, events make you jump, they happen before you think about them. Suddenly, you are transported to another location and faced with a new person that you may have never dreamed existed. He or She may teach you of magic or things that will come to pass. It will always be important information, write it down as soon as you return to your circle. It may not at first make sense or you may be unable to check the facts but proof will turn up eventually, as with our stag horned centaur. I have been lucky enough to be allowed through the gate many times and always given information I did not know, which has always been proven to be true, with time.

Exercises: Visualization to find your Goddess and God.
This visualization will guide you in and at a certain point will leave you to see what is conveyed to you, and then the visualization will guide you home. Remember, this is only a guide, you must do the work and you can come out of it at any time you choose there is nothing to fear.

Try making a tape of the visualization so that you can concentrate more easily.

When you have finished the visualization, write down everything that you remember. Examine everything you saw and everything you are told. Look for clues as to who your Goddess is. Has she any Raven qualities? Then look to The Morrigan or other Goddesses that have raven symbols. Has She a dress with flowers growing, which Goddess typifies this for you? Has She Egyptian clothing, what symbols does She carry?

After working to find your Goddess, then start to work finding your God. I leave you to raise the veil of your Goddess.

Finding Your Goddess

Relax; allow the cares of the day to fade away.

Slowly tighten the muscles of your feet, and then your legs. Tighten the muscles of your chest, shoulders and then your face.

Allow your body to relax, float on a sea of nothing.

Breathe out the dark air of the day; breathe in the white light of the universe. Do this for a little while.

Visualize yourself at the top of a flight of stairs, descend slowly and as you descend allow your breathing to slow.

Descend again, breathing in and out more slowly.

Descend again, feel the banister under your hand.

Descend again, feel the tread of the stair under your feet.

Descend again.

At the bottom there is a door, knock on the door and you will find that it opens, allowing you to enter.

Beyond the door.....

It is night, the sky is cloudless, it is early spring the air, is crisp and cold but dry. You are wearing a black robe; with a white cord tied around your waist; from the cord hangs a pouch. You have carefully packed this, with every thing you may need for the coming ritual.

For you are on a Vision Quest.

Before you is a steep hill, your eye drifts to the top, for it is there, that your Goddess awaits.

You start your walk; there is a path to follow, for many have walked this path before you.

It is a long and hard walk and you becoming out of breath from climbing.

You reach the brow of the hill and rest for a moment to get your breath back.

You chant repeatedly, as you start to gather wood for a fire.

I come to your call
The call, from deep in my spirit
Guide my hand least I fall.

Lighting the leaves, the thin twigs then catch and then the branches finally begin to burn.

Sprinkling more dried leaves onto the fire the flames leap high.

The smell of wood-smoke drifts to you, making your eyes sting, for the moment, you move and it passes.

You take a moment to think of what you are about to do, looking up at the sky, there is a full clear moon and she is smiling down at you.

The sky is a velvety blackness but scattered from horizon to horizon with stars, so many; you feel that they could never be counted.

The Milky Way splashes across the sky like a river, as if thrown by the hand of the Goddess.

From your pouch, at your waist, you take incense and toss it into the fire; the perfumed smoke slowly rises.

Perhaps from your mind, or by unseen hands, a drum begins to lightly beat.

You sway to the rhythm.

You begin to circle clockwise around the fire.

The steps get faster; you leap, even if normally you have pain, now you have none.

If normally you are shy, you are alone with your Goddess; your awkwardness has gone.

No one can see you; allow your imagination to soar as faster and faster you dance twirling and leaping...........

You stop. Dropping to one knee, with your hands on the floor to steady yourself, you allow the world to stop reeling and you to catch your breath..........

Stand and throw incense onto the fire the perfumed smoke sends your senses reeling.

Raise your arms, and call

"Great Goddess, hear my call, I invoke you,
From the glittering ice and cold mountains of the North I invoke
you,
From the perfumed and mystical plains of the East I invoke you,
From the burning heat of the deserts of the South I invoke you,
From the Lands across the distant Ocean in the West I invoke
you.
As of long ago I called you,
It is now the time for me to remember
And awake from my long sleep.
Come, grant me your presence here."

A mist begins to flow around you.

Across the fire, the mist forms thickest, there a heavily draped figure emerges.

She puts her hands to the edge of her veil, and speaks.........

(Here take 5mins. to see listen to Her words)

"Thank you Great Goddess, for coming to me" you say.

The Goddess raises her hand in blessing.

A shower of stars sprinkles from her hands, and is absorbed into your body.

She turns and leaves the same way she appeared.

You douse the flames with water.

And return down the hill, and back toward the candles and the room.

Return now to full wakefulness.

"We may enter the circle tired and weary,
But with Spell chant and rhyme, give our help to all that ask,
And with merriment go forth to face the world once more".

Finding Your God

Relax; allow the cares of the day to fade away.

Slowly tighten the muscles of your feet, and then your legs. Tighten the muscles of your chest, shoulders and then your face.

Allow your body to relax, flout on a sea of nothing.

Breathe out the dark air of the day; breathe in the white light of the universe. Do this for a little while.

Visualize yourself at the top of a flight of stairs, descend slowly and as you descend allow your breathing to slow.

Descend again, breathing in and out more slowly.

Descend again, feel the banister under your hand.

Descend again, feel the tread of the stair under your feet.

Descend again, at the bottom there is a door, knock on the door and you will find that it opens, allowing you to enter.

Beyond the door.....

It is night, the sky is cloudless, it is the eve of the Summer Solstice, the air is chill, the time nears dawn. You see before you a wood with tall beech trees.

You are wearing the same black robe and with a white cord around your waist; from the cord hangs your pouch. You have carefully packed this, as before, with every thing you may need for the coming ritual.

For once more you are on a Vision Quest.

Tall beech trees with their high canopy are above your head; no undergrowth impedes your walking. Follow the path through the beech trees, this is Ancient woodland, near sacred sites and has an intense magical feeling, that wraps around you like a warm cape. The Beech trees clear, you come to a more open clearing in the forest, you walk from the dark of the beech into the Moonlight with high ferns, with oak, ash and rowan trees scattered around. May abounds on the Hawthorn trees and normally the Bluebells too, would have gone by now, but for you they stay and the perfume dances on the wind.

Across your path just ahead wanders a Munt Jac deer, it stops to look at you, judging the distance between you both, you make no move. It seems to incline its head, as if acknowledging your presence, and then wonders on. Squirrels start to chatter in the treetops, an owl hoots, bats fly between the trees.

You stroll towards the pond that lies at the border between the Beech and the Oak. Many years ago a great tree has fallen, tearing its roots from the earth, leaving a large indentation in the ground. A pond has formed here, that the animals may drink, bats flit in and out of the branches feasting on the insects that hover around the water. The wood was cut and used many years ago. But the old tree refused to die and from the great old tree roots, two new trees have grown, on these hang offerings and ribbons of many colors, put your hand into your pocket and draw from it a ribbon. What color is it? Pink for love- Blue for healing- Green for money- Red for passion- all colors have a meaning, you will draw from your pocket what you need. Tie the ribbon to the tree as you tie it, tie in the magic of the color and the tree will see that it comes to pass.

Now return your steps to the beech trees and the ritual area, to find a fire burning in the firepit. You sit upon the ground, you now have a feeling of being watched, but you are not frightened, the ancient Wood is not a collection of trees but one living being, it welcomes you and enjoys your company.

From the oak wood, glowing balls of purple light move toward you, there is no feeling of panic, they are very friendly, they come and dance around you never touching, always moving. They drift quietly way but still the feeling remains that you are being watched.

You sit watching the fire Elementals play in the flames, purple balls of light drifting up, sideways and down.

You look up as you sit in the clearing and see The Milky Way splashed across the sky like a river, as if thrown by the hand of the Goddess into the lap of the God.

From your pouch, at your waist, you take incense and toss it into the fire; the perfumed smoke slowly rises.

Throw another handful of incense on to the fire, the perfumed smoke sends your senses reeling.

Raise your arms, and call

"Great God, hear my call, I invoke you,
From the glittering ice and cold mountains of the North I invoke
you,
From the perfumed and mystical plains of the East I invoke you,
From the burning heat of the deserts of the South I invoke you,
From the Lands across the distant Ocean in the West I invoke
you.
As of long ago I called to you.
It is now the time for me to remember,
And awake from my long sleep.
Come, grant me your presence here."

A mist begins to flow around you.

Across the fire, where the mist forms thickest, a figure emerges from the ferns.

He stands strong and proud ...(fill in His description)......behind him the Sun begins to rise, an aura of golden light shines behind Him. The air warms, he speaks.........

(Here take 5 mins. to listen to His words)

"Thank you Great God, for coming to me
May we meet again soon." you say.

The God raises his hand in blessing.

A shower of sunbeams pours from his hands, and is absorbed into your body.

He turns and leaves the same way he appeared.

You douse the flames with water.

And return to your door, in what is now full daylight.

Back toward the candles and the room you are in.

Return to full wakefulness.

"We may enter the circle tired and weary,

But with Spell chant and rhyme, give our help to all that ask,
And with merriment go forth to face the world once more".

Make notes of all you have seen, and repeat the exercise frequently to get to know your God.

CHAPTER 3

Elemental Quarters

When Witches start to make magic, they erect a temple to the God and Goddess to do this first cast a circle and then call the Elemental Quarters. This is called setting circle and cuts the mundane world away from the world of magic. It "takes us out side time and place", the circle is the temple of the Witch.

The circle is divided into the four quarters; these are guarded by the four elements. They are Earth, Air, Fire, and Water. These are assigned to the four Cardinal points of the compass. All things on the Earth are made of these four elements. These are guardians of the circle and friends to be invited into your home.

Each Cardinal of the point of the compass is ascribed an element, this is standard with all branches of witchcraft and magic.

Different Traditions visualize the Elemental Quarters in many varying ways.

Lords of the Watch Towers

Angels- Earth- Auriel, Air- Raphael, Fire- Michael, Water- Gabriel.

Kings of the Elementals-

Paralda King of the Sylphs,

Djin the King of the Salamanders,

Niksa King of the Undines,

Ghob the King of the Gnomes.

Our tradition works with the basic elemental energies,

Gnomes and Elves in the North,

Fairies in East,

Fire Dragons in the South and

Undines in the West

In fact all "The Little People" or fairy folk of legend, guard our

Elemental Quarters. Don't be worried or feel silly about calling fairies, elves and undines to your circle. To Witches they are especially friendly. I feel it is because we come to them with open hearts, wishing to see them and understand their world. They reach out through the veil to help us create a magical circle that both can share.

In your magic working you will slowly acquire your Elemental Quarters, do not expect this to happen in one sitting but slowly over time and as you become stronger and able to handle the energies that each element brings to the circle. Follow the visualizations below and when you are ready an elemental will be called to your circle, representing each quarter Earth, Air, Fire and Water, guarding and helping with the magic that is shaped within. These Elemental Quarters are friends to humans but at all times must be respected. Get to know your quarters, they are unseen members of your circle.

Elemental Candle colors-

	Our Tradition	Wicca
Earth	**Brown**	**Green**
Air	**Blue**	**Yellow**
Fire	**Red**	**Red**
Water	**Green**	**Blue**

Alexandrian Wiccan colors were at one time very close to ours; now due, I think, to inter-handfasting and the mixing of covens, they have standardized with Gardanarian. All over the world colors are an important part of ritual in the Manchu period of China, the Emperors wore girdles of stone according to the different ceremonies that they presided over. These were very similar to our colors, at the Temple of Heaven he wore a girdle of Lapis Lazuli, as blue as the night sky. For the Temple of Earth he wore a girdle of yellow Jade (the earth in China is not as dark as ours). For the Altar of the Sun he wore red coral and white Jade for the Temple of the Moon.

In Tibet the prayer flags string across the roads, as you walk or drive under them you are blessed. These also are in the same basic colors of Earth yellow, air blue, fire red, water green and clouds white.

Although we may give them different names and colors, I'm sure that they are the same energies and common to all circles. At the various festivals I have run, we have had guests from all over the world. They always say how much they feel at home and how like their own ceremonies they are. They may call the elementals the four winds and they may have different names for each, but the essence is always the same.

Elemental quarters are kept separate on our altar, why?

We keep all four representations of the Elemental quarters separate on the altar, to be used in spells.

In the North we keep Salt
East, Incense
South a red Candle
West a small bowl of Water.

By keeping them pure and unmixed we can use the energies of each individually. You can charge an amulet by all the quarters or by only one, you are more in control of the spell to be cast.

If we choose to add energies from all quarters, this we do by taking an amulet or spell around the circle diesiel (clockwise, this is the oldest spelling of this word I can find, predating any books on Witchcraft), passing it through the elements to add the energy of each to the spell.

To cast this spell
Starting with North.

1. Of Earth we sprinkle with salt and ask protection.
2. Of Air we pass through the incense smoke and ask knowledge.
3. Of Fire we pass through the candle flame and ask passion and energy.

4. Of Water we dip into the water asking for emotion, usually of course, this is happiness.

For example if you wish to use only one quarter, for protection perhaps.

Choose elements from the Earth Quarter(see the list below) possibly-

Patchouli oil,

Tigereye tumble stone.

Oak Bark and a piece of Deer horn (deer's drop their horns every year and there is no problem even for a vegetarian to use deer horn and it is reasonably easy to get), representing the God.

Put this into a brown or black bag ask the element of North to help by putting in its energy or write a little poem and you have created a strong Bag of Protection.

Each quarter in our coven, is assigned a covener to act as Guardian, to call each of the Elemental Quarters to the circle and to thank them for their attendance. The uninitiates try their hand at calling all quarters and are moved around the circle, month by month to experience the energies of all the elements. Start by experiencing you favorite element, to help you relax, this is very important. You cannot work well until you relax in circle. When you are comfortable with your favorite element, work towards your least favorite as this holds the key. What you instinctively turn from, you need to understand the most, what comes easy, you know already.

Each quarter is thought to hold an essence of either male or female. In Medieval times men were though to be made of humors that are hot and dry; women cold and wet and so the elements were assigned them accordingly.

Women- Earth (stability and ethereal protection) and Water (emotions).

Men- Fire (passion and will) and Air (intellect).

Don't feel that you need to stick to this particular man- woman orientation when calling quarters. All must experience and learn from the energy and magic of each quarter, accessing to male and female energies within us all.

Elemental Correspondences
North

Unlike most traditions of Witchcraft our ritual starts from the North, moving clockwise around the circle, this is known as Diesel or Sunwise. North to us is the most important of the elements, we call North "The Gates of Death" but death, in a tradition that believes in re-incarnation is also rebirth. The end is also the beginning, as with the Ourobourous Snake eating it's own tail. The tomb becomes to womb, in ever repeating cycles.

The Craft over the years has acquired many traditions from the many peoples that have visited our shores. The stories of the Byfrost (Rainbow) Bridge, from the Heathen traditions of Norse and Viking, which I'm sure is the Aurora Borealis or Northern Lights, which can be seen from as far south as Scotland, arching like a rippling multi-colored bridge, from the world of mortals to the worlds of the Gods.

This they called Valhalla and lies to our North and is possibly the reason that we start our circle from this quarter. Perhaps due to the Byfrost Bridge, when calling their Gods and Goddesses into the circle the Wiccans also face the Northerly direction, Although they start to call their circle from the East and the rising Sun.

In Pagan times how did priests find north one of the most important quarters of our circle? With a mineral called Lodestone, its magnetic properties had been known since at least the Classical Greeks period. Later the magnetic compass was developed at least a 1000 years ago, its unchanging magic always pointing to the North. It seems strange the magic of the lodestone hadn't been turned into a compass earlier; there are of course theories but no concrete evidence that this happened. One way of magnetizing the blade of your Athame, is to sit facing North (find this through your compass) pointing your Athame at the North and tap the blade with your finger, this will align the molecules of the metal in one direction along the length of the blade. In doing this you are connecting with the magnetic fields of the Earth. The science behind magnetism and magnetic fields is not full understood, even today. Strange that one of the most potentent quarters is the least understood. Before the knowledge of the compass was discovered, priests and Shaman may have been able to tune into the magnetic energies emanating from the North. I have pointed to a single stone in a stone circle and known it to be the Northern and most important stone, just by the energies emanating from it. With powerful magic like that originating from one direction, the North is the obvious place to start to call your quarters from, in any magical working. Of course, there is also Polaris the Northern Star, to guide travelers on the seas, and to aid magic users in their work. Polaris never sets, all the constellations revolve stately around this most important star called "the Immovable One". Due to the Procession of the Equinox of course, Polaris was not always the Immovable One, but one lone star in the north always guides those with the knowledge to safety.

However, the idea of North being the most important quarter of the circle may go back to pre history. Archaeologists determine the religion of a burial from it's orientation, if it's east-west it's Christian, if it's north–south it's Pagan. This seems to apply across the world strangely. Whilst in Tunisia I had an opportunity to test this, I were looking at the Roman site at Utica. This had a number of yet older Punic graves; and as it is a site difficult to get to, my friend and I were alone there. The Curator in charge very kindly gave us a tour of the site and we were able to determine the orientation of these very oldest graves were still North – South. In far Peru, The Lord of Sipan along with his fabulous treasure was also buried with his feet in the North and head in South so that if he stood he would also face the Gods in the North. North must have had important associations for many different Pagan cultures from many different eras and in many different countries.

Earth- North

Elemental- Gnome or Elf

This element is Female

Season- Winter

Tarot Suit- **Pentacles or coins**

Funa- **Wolf, Snake, Deer**

Gem- Smokey Quartz, Tigereye, Imperial Topaz

Color- Brown, like the dark rich earth itself (Wiccans use Green).

Be silent- Earth teaches that once a spell is cast, no more must be said.

The Sun only reaches the North Pole for six months of each year, so it is the land of darkness and silence, and secret knowledge. Even in the North of Scotland in Winter, it is only light for a short time each day.

Powers- All things grounding, Protection, Prosperity, Stability, Work, Food and all growing things, Secret Teachings.

Material Content- Salt

Symbol on the Altar- Pentacle

Incense used when working with this quarter- All woods, Mugwort, Oakmoss, Patchouli- dark and woodsy smells.

East

Air is also carrier of the sacred sounds and bringer of knowledge.

In Ancient Greece they had names for all the winds, the names are mentioned in Homer's works and have their own myths and legends. The most important winds being the four Cardinal Directions and then the cross quarter winds. These are engraved into the Tower of Winds that stands to this day in Athens and was built BCE 100. The names of the winds were still in use in medieval times.

North- *tramontana*, North East- *greco*, East-*levante*, South East -*siroco*, South -*ostro*, South West- *libeccio*, West- *ponente* and North West- *maestro*.

East- Air

Elemental - Sylph or Fairies (Fairies always appreciate a gift of ginger, milk and honey.)

> *This element is Male*
> *Season* - Spring
> *Tarot Suit* - Wands or Rods
> *To know*- knowledge.
> *Powers*- Knowledge, Intellectual
> Thought, Messenger.
> *Material Content*- Incense
> *Color*- Blue as the sky

(Wiccan use yellow-Mercury bringer of knowledge)

Symbol on the Altar- Wand (Wiccan- sword) and all musical instruments if used.

Funa- Bat, Bird in particular a Raven, Crow (as messenger to many Gods and

Goddesses) and Owl.

Gem- Blue Topaz, Lapis Lazuli- night sky, Turquoise- day sky, Blue Sapphire (Wiccan- Citrine or Yellow Sapphire).

Incense used when working with this quarter- Acacia, Benzoin, Lavender, Gum Mastic, Honeysuckle.

To the East lie the lands of the Orient with its fabulous perfumes.

South

To the South of England lie the hot countries of Egypt, Morocco, and Tunisia with all of Africa below and so for us Fire is in the South of the circle. Fire of all the elements is perhaps the one that is easier to understand as being a living entity. It dances upon the wood as it burns, even singing as the gases from the wood escape. Pyromancy, the art of scrying in the flames is possibly one of the oldest forms of divination. Most Smithing Gods and Goddesses would have practiced this form of divination; most notably the priests of Hephaestus the Greek God of fire and the forge, as did the priestess of Athena Goddess of War and Wisdom. Fire was considered a direct link with the Gods and Goddesses that used this mystical, moving, never resting element.

South- Fire
Elemental- Salamander or Dragon
This element is Male
Season- Summer
Tarot Suit- Swords
Funa- Lion.
Gem- Ruby, Garnet, Carnelian.

Color- Red (Wiccan- Red- Mars)
Will- To have the power to carry out the spell.
Powers- Energy, Purification, Warrior, Confidence, Sex.
Material Content- Flame (on a red candle)
Symbol on the Altar- Sword or Athame (Wiccan- Wand)
Incense used when working with this quarter- Cinnamon, Dragon's Blood, Chilli, Ginger, Red Sanderswood,
To the South lie the hot countries of Egypt, Morocco, and Tunisia with all of Africa below.

West

To the West is the great sea that separates us from Vineland (America) and so the element of water is to the west of England.

Water is the prime source of life, without this simple substance, no life on Earth would survive, rivers wells and springs were considered to be the home of the Gods. Water to many countries, was THE most valuable commodity. With water, happiness abounds, without water death walks the land.

Visualize a stream at full flood, a waterfall, the hidden depths of a dark well, feel the energy that they produce, this is all part of water's mystery. Phenomena like the River Severn Bore, (part of the Bristol Channel in England) in which a massive wave 2 meters high, runs up a river against it flow for 25 miles at the Spring Equinox, only serves to connect us to the awe in which our ancestors held water. The Moon and Water are of course inexorably linked, the Moon affecting the tides twice a day. Stories of water (this extends to mirrors) and magic abound, since Celtic times, they have been linked and were thought of as a doorway into the realms of the Fay (fairy) or the underworld. Many rivers in the British Isles are still named after Celtic Goddesses who were symbols of fertility, The Clyde was named after the Goddess Clota the Divine Washer, the River Dee is named after Deva meaning Goddess. The River Braint in Anglesey and the Brent in Middlesex is derived from the Goddess Brigantia. In Ireland Anu Mother of the Celtic Gods is commemorated in the name of St Anne who has many sacred wells named after her. Skulls have been found in sacred Celtic wells, this is thought to have bestowed life on the waters, as well as fertility, healing and luck to those who drink the waters.

It is an ancient tradition to throw money or bent pins (is this a remembrance of throwing broken swords into water or bogs?) into water, Mid Summer is a good day to do this, but first you must walk round the well three times, jump across and then speak respectfully to the Goddess or water spirit or not only will your wish not be for filled but something nasty will happen to you instead! At Silver Well near Otterburn in Northumberland if you threw pine cones into the well, they would be changed to silver for you. Many other wells needed an offering of white stones, to quell stormy weather.

In Scotland broken pottery was placed beside water as an offering, is this because a broken pot could not carry away water?

West- Water

Elemental- Undine (a water spirit)

This element is Female

Season- Autumn

Tarot Suit- Cups

Funa- Dolphin, Fish, Frog, Toad

Gem- Emerald, Peridot, Green Aquamarine, Pearl, Shell, Mother of Pearl.

(Wiccan- Blue Topaz, Blue Aquamarine)

Color- Green (Wiccan- Blue- Neptune)

Care- Signifies the compassion to work the spell.

Powers- Emotions (to cry with sorrow or happiness), Dreams, Inner Vision and Creativity.

Material Content- Water

Symbol on the Altar- Cauldron, Chalice.

Incense used when working with this quarter- Willow, Jasmine, Hyacinth, Ylang-Ylang.

If starting to call your Elementals from the North, as with us, this enables you to rise spiritually as you pass through the elements.

North

North being the strongest of the quarters is assigned the element of Earth. When we call the Elementals to our circle we start with the most stable of the elements. The element on which we all stand, the most grounded with money and protection as its characteristics. From this we move around the circle calling to the circles edge the remaining elements, as each is called so we pass through many emotions.

The negative essence of North is to be bogged down and unable to move forward.

Air

After Earth the next element that we encounter is Air- its higher qualities are intelligence and knowledge, Airs negative quality is cold uncaring intellect.

Fire

Next through Fire- passion and rage are its qualities, passion not only in a sexual sense but passion for work, art or any human quality. Rage on the other hand is mostly a destructive energy burning away intellect.

Water

Until finally we reach Water with its emotions of love and caring, the drawback of water is depression, to drown within its depths. Waters other attribute of love and caring, however, is perhaps the height of human emotions. So focusing on all the Elemental Quarter's higher attributes, we rise as we call each quarter within our circle.

By starting calling your quarters from the North and progressing through East and South, you inevitably find yourself in the West and the setting Sun, a place of finishing and closure.

But do what ever feels right for you to do, if you are more used to the Wiccan system of starting to call your Quarters from the East and the rising Sun, then follow that. Call your quarters as your heart dictates.

I met my first Elemental Quarter unsurprisingly, for North, while on a walk in the woods. I was out walking along a path by the side of a small stream and stepped onto a tree that had fallen, to cross to the other side. Suddenly a whole story started to unfold in my third eye. Although I know that it was not taking place in this plane of reality, it seemed so clear. An Elf started to jump up and down on one of the branches of the tree, accusing me of walking into his sitting room, although even if you could not see the Elf, you would have seen the tree moving. The Elf had a strange way of moving his legs, coming up vertically, so that his knees were out at his sides in a flat line with his body, a movement quite impossible for a normal human being. I apologized for disturbing him; he seemed to quieten down immediately. Seeming surprised that I could see and hear him, we became best friends after that. He then became my Northern Elemental and has often helped out with finding both lost items and knowledge. One time, some friends and I were walking in nearby woods and one had decided to take his divining rods. Hoping to find a good place for his circle, he happily walked round and round many interesting sites but to no avail. The reason was quite simple; my little Elf was jumping up and down knocking his rods all over the place! "I can't get a thing!" my friend announced "the rods are going all over the place!" This may not be the normal way to meet your Elemental but it is perfectly valid, but if an opportunity like this does not come your way give it a little push, with the visualizations below.

Exercise

Building your temple on the Astral Plain

This is a visualization to find your temple on the Astral plane, this is a place to go when you are searching for knowledge or are stressed. When ill, a place to send your consciousness too. There you can lay on the cool grass when your body has a temperature, helping to improve your recovery. Sometimes travelers will pass; some times they will impart esoteric knowledge to you. They may be Goddesses or Gods, elementals or any person or creature from any mythology whether you have read about them or not. Strangely I have met people within a visualization that I had no idea existed in myth, until in some cases many years had passed and I found a reference to them. This is where your magical diary comes in, always record in it as much detail as possible, every magical thing you see and feel.

As with all visualizations it is a form of self-hypnotism, you can go to your temple and bury your fear or throw it into the running water, if that is what holds you back. For example someone I knew with a deep problem, as I guided the visualization down the stairs, (which is a way of deepening the trance). I had the idea of two doors, one leading to the temple, the other to a toilet where they could dump any unwanted psychic rubbish. If ever they felt depressed or angry, she could go to her psychic toilet and throw it down and flush it away. Although it is not very spiritual, it works and saves cluttering the Astral plain with psychic junk.

It is said that when you become very proficient at visiting your Astral temple, at the time of your death you merely move into your temple on a more permanent basis and your loved ones can come visit, if they know the way.

Light some incense of visualization or divination, both allows the mind to relax and ideas to surface. You can record them on tape or read and remember them, in some ways that is better, as it allows your mind to interpret the symbols within this visualization how you please and gives you as much time as you wish at any location. If you choose to record them, visualizations work best if recorded in a singsong voice.

But it depends on how confident you feel. Another approach might be to do the visualization as it is written and then revisit with a freer approach, at a later time.

Close your eyes; settle back and relax; allow the cares of the day to fade away.

Slowly tighten the muscles of your feet, and then your legs. Tighten the muscles of your chest, shoulders and then your face.

Allow it all to relax, float on a sea of nothing.

Breath out the dark air of the day, breath in the white light of the universe. Do this for a little while.

Visualize yourself at the top of a flight of stairs, descend slowly and as you descend allow your breathing to slow.

Descend again, breathing in and out more slowly.

Descend again, feel the banister under your hand.

Descend again, feel the tread of the stair under your feet.

Descend again, at the bottom there is a door, knock on the door and you will find that it opens, allowing you to enter.

Beyond the door you see in front of you, a stretch of grass with flowers sloping down to a thick wood, on your left is a river with woodland beyond and on your right the ground slopes up and gets rockier. If it is day here, it is day there, if it is night here, it is night there. Whatever the stage of the moon at this moment, it will be the same there. (Some times I have found the weather to be different.)

Walk out onto the cool grass, feel it between your toes. This is your land. On the stretch of grass in front of the forest is where you will build your Astral Temple. It can be any size you like, defy the laws of science if you choose. It can look like Stonehenge, a castle or a cloud, what ever takes your fancy. This is your perfect place; you can with a sweep of your hand erect it or you can build it stone by stone what ever suits your personality. Take some time to do this, there is no hurry...... The same with the decorating any color or none, place an altar within, candles or a perpetual flame or what ever your mind can dream up.

When your temple is completed to your specifications, return to the door, which shines out like a warm and inviting opening on a dark night. Up the stairs, with each stairs you climb, your breathing will return slowly back to normal until by the time you reach the top step you will feel happy and fully awake.

Go to your temple as many times as you can for the first few months to establish it fully. Go there at least a few times before continuing with the next visualization.

Visualization to the Elemental Quarters

Don't be put off by the simplicity and childishness of these visualizations, they are designed to appeal to the child with in, the child that understands the meaning of myth and legend. Brave deeds and quests teach us important lessons. Within the stories that will unfold, are symbols that your brain will understand and that help you to connect with each of the Elemental Quarters. Hopefully they will also point you in the direction of improving your inner spirit, as this too is part of your mystical journey.

Visualization to the realm of Earth

Light a brown candle.

Place incense on the charcoal block and have a bowl of salt and a crystal on your altar. Put your fingers in the salt and feel its texture, scatter some around the edge of your circle, take the crystal in your hand and sit facing North.

Close your eyes; settle back and relax; allow the cares of the day to fade away.

Slowly tighten the muscles of your feet, and then your legs. Tighten the muscles of your chest, shoulders and then your face.

Allow it all to relax, float on a sea of nothing.

Breath out the dark air of the day, breath in the white light of the universe. Do this for a little while.

Visualize yourself at the top of a flight of stairs, descend slowly and as you descend allow your breathing to slow.

Descend again, breathing in and out more slowly.

Descend again, feel the banister under your hand.

Descend again, feel the tread of the stair under your feet.

Descend again, at the bottom there is a door, knock on the door and you will find that it opens, allowing you to enter.

Beyond the door is your land and you can see your temple, just as you left it. Walk out onto the cool grass towards your temple, the sky is clear the Moon (or Sun) is shining, bend over and pick a flower for your altar, if you have them growing in the grass. You know this will cause no harm to pick wild flowers, for if you wish to you can fill the whole field with plants. Walk into your temple let your hands feel what it is made from. Place the flower on the altar, perhaps you may wish to lift your arms to the Goddess and thank Her.

Leave your temple when you are ready and walk on to the forest just beyond. As you enter the atmosphere changes, it is darker, there is no Sun/Moon, little light trickles down onto the forest floor. The trees stretch high above you.

You walk farther into the forest; you begin to hear a strange singing, a bit off key and high. "Hello" says the high voice; he is a small man slim and young looking dressed in green and red. "Not seen you here before, not many of your sort wander this way". You explain that you have just moved into the neighborhood

"Let me be the first to welcome you to Darkling Wood" he says, "I will be your guide", he clears his throat importantly.

" Where do you wish to go". You answer that, as you have never been here before, than you have no idea what there is to see.

"I'll take you somewhere interesting." That seems to settle it.

You both walk on together exchanging questions and answers of name and histories, until you get to a small, rounded, almost polished, stump in the ground not more than a few inches high. The Elf bows deeply and kicks you to do the same, this you do.

" This" the Elf says "is the brainiest tree in all the wood, all the decisions about what grows where are made by Breen. He doesn't say much but he thinks a lot. Follow, follow, this way" and you are off again.

"That is the dog tree" another tree is pointed out to you. "Come, come" This is a tree that has what looks like a dog's head carved from wood protruding from the trunk but there are no joins to the tree, it has just grown naturally that way. A clearing is ahead and you follow the Elf into it. There is a very old stone circle hidden within the wood, some of the stones had fallen at some time in the past.

"This way, this way" pipes up a little voice. You follow, around one of the fallen stones and there, there seems to be a passageway going down into the Earth. Before you can say a word, your guide has disappeared within.

You reluctantly follow,

down the steps you go

and down

and down

down.

You begin to hear a noise from deep within the earth, tap, tap, come to your ears. You begin to see a light ahead. As you walk into the thin light, you see many gnomes mining crystals from the rocks. You wander oblivious of the gnomes, entranced by the wonderful gems but not daring to touch. Gems of every color lay piled high, energies from them are darting all around. Moving from one pile to another you find yourself at the end of the corridor and move into the next room. Within the room, there is a gigantic dark crystal that stretches from floor to ceiling but inside there is a shadow that appears to move, you look closer. You can barely make it out but there within, is an old, old woman.

"I am magic" she says " are you the one". You reply that you would not think so.

"Have you come to replace me, to allow me go free" she asks with hope.

"I do wish to help. But..." you hesitate.

"Then there is nothing that you can do" she says very disappointedly, her head droops.

A tear swells up from your eye and splashes onto the dark crystal. A deep rumble starts deep within the earth itself, the tremor spreads higher and higher, until with a shriek, which emanates from the crystal itself, it bursts apart. The old woman, trapped within changes to a young and beautiful woman and stands before you.

"Thank you for releasing me from the stone, I am forever in your debt, you have set magic free into the world again and into your own heart. Your tears set me free, I have waited a long time for someone who would take pity on my plight. Whenever you have need of me, call me", she gives you a pentagram with a long chain, from her neck.

"By placing your finger on the top point, moving to the bottom left point and then continue to following along the paths of this pentagram. Lay this on your altar in your temple, for it is invisible in the normal world. It will guide you through your new life" and with that she is gone. The Elf who was hiding in the corner while all this was going on, now bustles out jumping up and down in wild delight, asking to rub your new pentagram for luck. You retrace your steps through the tunnel, up the stairs and through the forest. As you both walk back you hear a dog barking,

"We must hurry" says the Elf "The Dog Tree has said so."

At last you see light coming from between the trees and know that you are not far from your temple. Arriving there you place the pentagram onto your altar, and it begins to glow. You notice the elf is still with you.

"Can I be your Earth Elemental when you cast circle? Just call me and I'll be there. Can I, can I, can I, thanks," as he disappears out the door. Whether you want it or not you have an Elemental of Earth.

With much reluctance you leave your new pentagram and your temple to return to your door.

Climb the stairs slowly and as you do, you return to normal breathing. By the time you reach the top step, you will feel happy and fully awake.

Write down, in your diary all that has happened during your visualization. Paying particular attention to any differences in the story between the one given and your own.

Visualization to the realm of Air

Do not be to quick to pass on to the next visualization. As with all aspects of magic, take your time.

Place incense on the charcoal block on your altar. Have a blue candle burning, wave your hand through the incense smell its aroma allow it to waft around you, sit facing East.

Close your eyes; settle back and relax; allow the cares of the day to fade away.

Slowly tighten the muscles of your feet, and then your legs. Tighten the muscles of your chest, shoulders and then your face.

Allow it all to relax, float on a sea of nothing.

Breath out the dark air of the day, breath in the white light of the universe. Do this for a little.

Visualize yourself at the top of a flight of stairs, descend slowly and as you descend allow your breathing to slow.

Descend again, breathing in and out more slowly.

Descend again, feel the banister under your hand.

Descend again, feel the tread of the stair under your feet.

Descend again, at the bottom there is a door, knock on the door and you will find that it opens, allowing you to enter.

Beyond the door, you see your land and your temple exactly as you left it.

Walk to your temple and place a little incense on a burner or throw it into the air and change it to smoke with your will power, as an offering to the Gods. Pick up the pentagram and place it over your head. Leave your temple when you are ready and walk towards the stony uneven ground that slowly rises to the East of your temple. It is a long walk, harder than the last. Finally you come to a cliff edge, the ground drops down dizzyingly from your vantage-point, the wind blows pitilessly. Only clouds are below you and the sky above. Your mind begins to drift, consciousness slips away and your legs begin to lose their control. You fall.......

Down through the air you tumble, the air rushes around you, as you fall faster and faster, unhurt you land! You find yourself on the back of a giant night black raven,

"Sit still, grab my feathers with both hands, he won't be pleased if I lose you". I won't be pleased if you lose me either, you think.

The Raven's feathers are deep, you are cushioned as you have never been before, the warmth of the raven comes up from its body, as the dry air of your flight flows around you. You fly farther and farther. The raven finally begins a slow descent. You slide on his smooth feathers further forward and hold on tighter for what you can only imagine will be a final quick descent, you hide your head in the feathers awaiting the stomach churning drop and stop but the raven glides smoothly to land. Wondrous perfumed smoke drifts all around as you alight from the bird. You are not sure what the smell is but it is light and refreshing to the very spirit.

"That way." Which way: 'that way', is not too clear. But no objection is called at your choice, the floor is strange, as you walk, your weight is supported but at different heights, it is very tiring to walk. Small flittering blue lights like butterflies drift in and out but they become more numerous, until many are flying around you, chattering? A blue light in the direction that you are walking becomes more evident and stronger and stronger. The breathtaking blue glow deepens until it becomes like nothing you have seen before. The light emanates from a throne made from blue Sapphire, on the throne sits a man of indeterminate age, dressed in finest of blue velvet, behind him are row on row of books on ethereal shelves. The fairies, for that is what the glowing balls of light are, rest on the bookshelves and throne, all around the man dressed in blue.

He then converses with you for a while, asking many questions of your home, family, he seems interested in all aspects of your life. He tells you of his own life and recounts for you his lineage.

"It is our tradition that a visitor must tell a story, will you continue this tradition?"

You smile and a chair is brought for you, everyone settles down comfortably in anticipation. After a small hesitation, you begin to tell the story of your favorite film. After a little you are so carried away with the enchanted looks of your audience, that you first hum, then whistle and then even sing the theme song or a song that fits the film. The notes of your song hang in the air and are perfect, as is the whistling even if you can't normally whistle, this is a magic place where all things are possible. The fairies bring out instruments to join in; tiny drums flutes and fiddles are played. A few more songs are demanded of their guest, they then reciprocate.

Finally everyone is sung out and you finish, to great applause!

"Thank you for your visit to our Kingdom, you have brightened this time, it is so nice to receive visitors," he says.

He thanks you and calls a fairy to his side and whispers in her ear. She flies off and returns within a moment, with a breathtaking wand, it has (fill this with your own description)....................... He hands it to you and thanks you for the wonderful gift of knowledge and sacred sounds, that you have given them and he bids you use the wand in your new life. But he warns you that it is not to leave this realm and is invisible in the outer world of mere mortals.

He tells you it is time to leave, claps his hands and the raven is there. You climb up on the raven and it flies into the sky, returning you in due course to the cliff side.

"Don't forget me," says a little voice and there is the fairy that was assigned to get the wand from its hiding place. "I am to do your bidding for the Air quarter, she stands proudly, I've been told". You hold out you finger which she grabs and shakes with glee.

You return to your temple and removing the pentagram, you place it next to the wand on your altar; the wand begins to glow with a blue light.

With much reluctance you leave your new wand and your temple to return to your door, that leads back to your normal world.

Up the stairs and as you do, you return to normal breathing, until by the time you reach the top step you will feel happy and fully awake.

Write down, in your diary all that has happened during your visualization. Paying particular attention to any differences in the story between the one given and your own.

Visualization to the realm of Fire

Place incense on the charcoal block. With a red candle burning or better still, by a bonfire in a wood and sit facing South.

Feel the heat that such a small flame puts out. If you are able, pass your finger through the flame of the candle (not the Bonfire!), as if announcing your intent to go visit the fire elemental, attune to the flame, while introducing yourself.

Close your eyes; settle back and relax; allow the cares of the day to fade away.

Slowly tighten the muscles of your feet, and then your legs. Tighten the muscles of your chest, shoulders and then your face.

Allow it all to relax, float on a sea of nothing.

Breath out the dark air of the day, breath in the white light of the universe. Do this for a little while.

Visualize yourself at the top of a flight of stairs, descend slowly and as you descend allow your breathing to slow.

Descend again, breathing in and out more slowly.

Descend again, feel the banister under your hand.

Descend again, feel the tread of the stair under your feet.

Descend again, at the bottom there is a door, knock on the door and you will find that it opens, allowing you to enter.

Beyond the door you see your temple, you walk towards it and enter. Remember you can add anything to your temple at anytime you choose. You light a red candle or an eternal flame on the altar within your temple. When you are ready, place on your pentagram and tuck your wand into your belt and leave on another of your great adventures.

This time you head towards the south, very quickly you find the air is getting hotter. As you walk further south the heat increases and the ground becomes more arid. No pretty flowers around now but stark rocks and boulders, ahead the skyline is mountainous and peaked. From one of these now erupts a colossal explosion, lava, shooting high into the sky and flowing down the mountainside. The glowing red lava contrasts starkly with the sky, it is a barren and austere landscape. You continue walking, as you round a rock you see small pools of lava, bubbling to one side. You now notice that farther ahead they become more frequent and larger, some with flames darting from them. You approach the largest lake of lava that bubbles and pops, fire dances around the lake, it has a beauty and fascination all its own.

You notice a disturbance in the center of the lake; something seems to be rising from the center. The head of a colossal red dragon appears from the lava; it swims to shore and begins to step out onto the land, is there no end to it! It shakes itself free of drops of the remaining lava; this flies in all directions. One seems to be flying straight at you; you move your arm up to defend your face. Your pentagram that you wear around your neck suddenly becomes a shield upon your arm and with a splat the lava lands on your shield and safely falls to Earth.

" So we have a knight come to kill the Great Fire Dragon, ha! I who am ignipotent!" the great booming voice, sends tremors through the nearby rocks.

" I have not come to kill you but to be your friend" you quickly state.

"A likely story, I have heard it all before, I picked my teeth with their charcoaled bones!" he lowers his head menacingly almost to the floor and moves it nearer to you.

You hold your shield a little higher, and draw your wand, as you have no other defense. As you do a blue light emanates from the tip of the wand. The dragon is entranced and almost hypnotized by the light. "I really wish to do you no harm," you say.

" No harm" the dragon repeats.

You tentatively move the wand down to your side. The dragon seems to regain control of himself.

" I see you are a friend, for you have been given 'the' wand; I too will be your friend but first you must prove that you are a true knight. Enter that cave if you dare, and rescue my son within, as you see I am too large to fit within the cave. Will you help?"

You tell him that you will but do your best.

You enter the cave; it is dark, hot and smells of sulfur. It slowly becomes lighter, as it opens into a big cavern, before you is a curtain of flames with no way around. You take a deep breath, raise your shield before your face and walk into the fire, you feel your temperature rise, feel your pulse quicken, feel the fire around you **not** burning as in life but tingling. Your pentagram shield is protecting you.

The color red suffuses the area; the fire surrounds you. Feel the flames run up your back swift, darting, dancing.

Play with the flames, hold them in the palm of your hand see yourself standing and dancing, allow your passions to spiral, dance with the passion of fire!

Suddenly, the fire is a ring around you protecting you but death to your enemies. You stand in the center unharmed, still, quiet, your arms by your side, the eye at the center of the fire.

The flames entrance you; you march out followed by your flames in lines like soldiers, the fire of aggression!

Your center becomes quieter now, a warming dance slow like the fire late at night with just a lazy flicker, the fire of comfort.

From the fire a creature emerges, a small red dragon comes toward you, it is young, and very fast. Each scale on its body flickers like a flame.

You say "Ye Elemental of the Palaces of Fire, I seek the pure energizing balance of your force, will you follow me?"

The flames are gone but the young dragon remains, you turn and leave and it follows.

You come out of the cave into the relatively fresh air, and return to the Great Red Dragon.

" You have passed my test, you are a true knight strong and brave. I give you this sword; it will cast a circle to enhance your magic. Return now but when you have need, my son this young dragon will answer your call." It is a sword of wondrous beauty it has.................................(use your own description).

You return by the same path that you followed to that spot. The arid landscape once more returns to green. You enter your temple and place the new sword, your wand and your pentagram onto the altar. The sword glows red, as it touches the altar.

With much reluctance you leave your new tools and your temple to return to your door.

Up the stairs and as you do you return to normal breathing, until by the time you reach the top step you will feel happy and fully awake.

Write down, in your diary all that has happened during your visualization. As usual, pay particular attention to any differences in the story between the one given and your own.

Visualization to the realm of Water-

As you may now guess, place incense on the charcoal block, place a bowl of water on your altar and sit facing West.

Relax; allow the cares of the day to fade away.

Slowly tighten the muscles of your feet, and then your legs. Tighten the muscles of your chest, shoulders and then your face.

Allow it all to relax, float on a sea of nothing.

Breath out the dark air of the day, breath in the white light of the universe. Do this for a little while.

Visualize yourself at the top of a flight of stairs, descend slowly and as you descend allow your breathing to slow.

Descend again, breathing in and out more slowly.

Descend again, feel the banister under your hand.

Descend again, feel the tread of the stair under your feet.

Descend again, at the bottom there is a door, knock on the door and you will find that it opens, allowing you to enter.

Beyond the door, your temple awaits. This time walk to wards the river that flows not far from your temple, you will find a green bowl on the river bank. Pick it up and fill with water from the river, carefully carry this back to your temple and place this on your altar. Place your hands into the water and feel it on your fingers. Put on your pentagram, pick up your wand and strap on your sword.

Walk back to the river and there you will see a fish shaped boat that strangely you never noticed before. Get in the boat, perhaps this time your journey will be easy. The boat pulls away from the shore into the middle of the river and sails swiftly onwards. Small fish jump out of the water all around you, as if trying to see what you look like; a sound that could be called fishy laughter seems to bubble from them. After a little, the river now starts to flow through a canyon, the walls getting higher on either side. The river becomes choppy and running between boulders, now you have to hold on to the sides of the boat, you can see ahead a complete stretch of white water!

Your boat is buffeted this way and that, as you are thrown from one side to the other. Eventually the river calms but the boat travels on. You leave the river behind as it opens up to become the sea and still you travel on. Abruptly the boat dips and begins to sink, prow first, you hold your breath as you sink under the waves. Around you, your wand has created a bubble of air for you to breathe. You see lights far below, as you draw closer you see that under the sea is a complete city, made from living green coral. People are swimming quite effortlessly around; they see you and wave. Some of them swim over and guide the boat safely to the sea bottom. Once there, a hand is offered to you that invites you to follow, this is no problem, as the air that you are breathing seems to follow you quite happily. You are taken to the Queen, she is incredibly beautiful with long streaming green hair or perhaps it is just the reflection of the water playing on it.

"Welcome my friend, I have been informed of your many exploits from the other Elemental Quarters that you have already visited. I sent my boat to fetch you and make your journey here as pleasant as possible." Her voice is like the rushing waves.

" I too have a quest for you but more perilous than the others. One of my undines has been captured; around her pool that she guards, a group of unsavory demons has camped. Can you rescue her?"

You answer that you will do your best.

" More than that I can not ask. When you find her, give her this; prepare yourself." With that she picks up from beside her throne a chalice that is..........................."

As your hand touches the chalice, you feel a whoosh and then you are somewhere completely different, it takes a moment for you to get your breath. Loud raucous music accosts your ears! So many people! All dressed in bright clothing. You have found yourself in a picnic area of a visitor's center in a wood. Litter lies every where, radios blare out music or football results, and children are chasing each other around screaming.

No one takes any notice of you; in fact you think that they can't see you. You look around, your element that you are here to help is water but you can't see any. You wander around and there behind the teashop you see it. A small pool three yards wide, rubbish stacked up on one side sliding into the pool. An undine, which looks to be made of water, standing in the center with her hands over her ears, crying.

" Hello, may I help?"

She looks up startled " Have you been sent?" she enquires.

You assure her that all will be well; some children run past screaming: you stand between the undine and the children. Without seeing you but in some way sensing your presence, they veer away. You draw your sword and you draw a circle around you and the undine, you then walk around twice more, saying words that you feel right.

As you finish and connect the third circle, it is like you have cut that area of the wood from reality. You then give the undine the chalice, as instructed a bright flash and you are in a silent dark wood, with the undine, pool and some of the rubbish from the visitor's center. You point your sword at the remaining rubbish, fire sparks from its tip and the rubbish is vaporized.

"Thank you for your help, I do not know how to ever repay you. You have turned sorrow into happiness for me" the undine says. "One last favor, could you pull that big branch over for me to sit on, you see I am unable to leave my pool."

This you do with pleasure but it is big and heavy and needs a good bit of pulling and pushing but you struggle and finish the task. She slips from the water onto the branch but you notice her feet are not to be seen, her dress is always connected and forms part of the water.

"Please take this chalice, I have no need of it now, thanks to your help. Remember this chalice cannot be seen in your world" she begins to comb her long hair. " Just walk in that direction and you will see your temple. When ever you need me just call and I will be with you, pool as well" see laughs.

You walk back to the river, for you are in the woods on the far shore; there is no boat so you swim across, your newly found tools weigh nothing in the water.

Still dripping with water you enter your temple but there is someone there! A woman has her back to you but turns as you enter. She is your Goddess and is old or young, fat or thin; however you feel She should be.

"I see you completed your tasks, I am pleased. Not only have you acquired these magical tools but have found your Elementals. They will mature and grow as you grow in magical knowledge" She says. " When you have need of them use your wand to summon them and then light a candle to hold their attention during your magical working. They will give you all the help that they are able. When you acquire your magical tools in your world you must blend them with the ones on this world, your Quarter Elementals will be able to cross the great divide with your help. You will have noticed in your travels how all elements complement each other. You have done well" She is then gone, only Her shadow remains and then that too is gone.

You place you pentagram, your wand, your sword and chalice that glows green as you place it upon your altar. It is time for you to leave. You follow the path that you are now creating, back to the door and your own world. Up the stairs and as you do you return to normal breathing, until by the time you reach the top step you will feel happy and fully awake.

As always write down, in your diary all that has happened during your visualization and of course paying particular attention to any differences in the story.

You have now acquired all four Elementals.

You might also like to try another exercise.

Find any bits of cloth or clothing, tea-shirts or such, the colors of the four Elemental Quarters, fold them into a neat square. Look around your home and see if you can find one or more items to make four altars from what ever you can find in the house, it will be a good exercise to cement in your mind the correspondences.

North you might find salt, a crystal preferably Smokey Quartz, a plant or branch, a pentagram and a picture of an animal that you feel relates to North.

East you might find incense, a feather, a book to represent wisdom, lapis lazuli or turquoise. Have you made a wand, then add that too?

South you might find a candle, a garnet or carnelian, a statue of a lion or dragon, your Athame and perhaps a phallic representation of the fires of passion or however you see passion expressed.

West you might find a bowl, chalice or cauldron of water, a drawing of a fish or frog, and a shell.

These are only ideas to start you off, add to them anything that comes to mind.

CHAPTER 4

Magical Equipment

What do I need?

You do not need all or even most of the equipment mentioned in this chapter, to work in the Craft as a Witch!

Start to work first, begin to understand what **you** need to work with and why, only then will you be ready to start to buy or better yet, make your equipment. Until then use your finger to cast circle, old glasses to hold salt and water, a flowerpot with some dry earth to burn incense.

Many years ago there were no shops for you to buy your magical equipment, you were expected to go to the wood, pick and make your own tools.

No one can be good at everything, but then do you need to be good at making ritual equipment, all you need to do is try your best. On the list below there must be something you can make?

Learn to use one item before making or purchasing another.

Don't go shopping to get Witchy, "one of those and one of those". Understand each piece of magical equipment first and only when you can cast your circle with your finger, buy an Athame (a magical knife) or change the wine glass for a chalice. In our own Coven, an apprentice will have to practice for the first six months without an Athame, while making her or his own.

If the magic will flow for you without equipment, so why have all these ritual tools?

An Athame or Wand will draw the power from you and enhance and refine the strength of that power, but you must first learn where the power lies within your body. Learn how to handle the power that you raise by yourself; only then are you ready to start to practice with your magical tools.

Each piece of ritual equipment changes the energy that you produce from within you. You supply the energy; the tool modifies it, in its own special way to produce the desired effect. With an Athame you are directing your energy with a straight piercing quality, with a wand it changes to a compelling light beam. Choose the right tool for the right job, like any good craftsperson.

All of the Witches ritual tools are dedicated to the Goddess, God or one or the Elemental Quarters, it tells us about the energy of the tool and how it works. The Goddesses tools symbolize the womb or are curvy like a woman's body and the Gods ritual tools symbolize the phallus. The Elemental Quarters, are easily categorized, a chalice or cauldron must symbolize Water but also the Goddess's womb.

When you first make or buy your tools consecrate them to your chosen Goddess and God.

How to use your tools.

Athames and Wands – project your energy down through them, I call it (possibly very irreverently) zapping. Imagine a lightening bolt passing down through your hand, into the Athame, which will enhance its energy and sharpening it as it travels through. When working with your Athame, visualize it as a white energy beam cutting your circle from this reality or zapping the water and purifying it in an instant.

If working with a wand visualize a white light beaming out, carrying your magic or call through the veil that separates the mundane from the ethereal worlds.

Traditionally all tools should be wrapped in black silk. Black silk scarves can be bought quite cheaply from New Age shops or more likely from Ethnic shops.

Tools

I haven't placed the Magical Equipment in alphabetical order, but in order of importance to the Witch, listing everything that you may possibly need and explaining ritual equipment not used in our circle.

This is not a shopping list; I can not stress this too strongly but a list of anything that you might come across in your travels and need a little fuller explanation.

If you are practicing with your finger instead of an Athame you will still need candles and a place for the candles to stand, this is your altar. So I have started with these items not because they are the most important tool but because you need them first. As the list progresses it was very difficult to decide the order of importance, items could equally be slightly higher or lower, the list is in no way definitive.

Candles, five- spirit- white, earth- brown, air- blue, fire- red, water-green.

Before ritual stars light the spirit candle, that represents your deities both Goddess and God. After casting a circle, then call the Elementals Spirits this powerful being needs a candle to entrance and hold them once invoked or they will drift away.

Traditional covens work with the colors of the world around us, as our forefathers were uneducated and worked with the colors in nature. Wiccan covens work with the colors of Ceremonial Magic (planetary colors). Ceremonial Magic has a Cabalistic and Jewish/ Christian origin used by the upper and educated classes in medieval times.

Witches have an old saying *'Beware of Witches that blow on candles',* always use a snuffer or your fingers. To blow on a candle is to use one male element against another, which draws bad luck. Perhaps in reality to use a snuffer preserves the wick better and made it easier to re-light when in the Middle Ages the wicks weren't as good quality as they are today.

Candleholders unless using thick candles, for safety you will need candleholders, buy as cheaply or as expensively as you choose. Perhaps buying cheap candleholders and painting them the elemental colors, decorating them with their elemental sigils or depicting the elements in some way that appeals to you?

Charcoal Blocks these are purchased from your occult suppler and are round with a dip in the center for holding and burning incense (see chapter on herbs). To light them hold them with tongs over a lighter or gas flame until the row of sparks have traveled over the block. Place down in a metal or ceramic container with dry sand or dry earth from the garden. Best to dry it first for a little time in the oven first or stand it on your radiator for a week, to be sure that it is in no way damp or your charcoal block will go out. Then place half a teaspoon of loose incense on the block, knocking of any burnt residue after five minutes and replacing with fresh incense.

Altar, placed in center of a traditional circle, and in the North in a Wiccan circle. The center of the circle is the most sacred place. A cupboard to hold your ritual tools, with an altar cloth embroidered by you (just because you're male don't think you can't do it;) over it, is a wonderful altar. Or if like us, you prefer a lump of tree sandpapered and beeswaxed, this also makes a great altar.

The Altar's element is Spirit (dedicated to both God and Goddess or perhaps Deity beyond gender).

White circle cord, used as a visual marker of the circle. This is not strictly necessary but very good for those new to the craft. In fact our Coven still use ours, it reminds apprentices where the boundary of the circle is set.

Athame (a-th-A-m-E) is a double edged straight bladed knife with a black handled, used to cast circle, cut a handfasting cake, bless wine, to cut away illusion (as with Tibetan magical knives), for psychic protection and can be used to open a door in the circle.

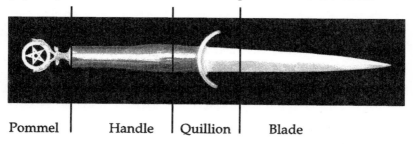

Pommel   Handle   Quillion   Blade

(The Tang is a continuation of the blade, inside the handle, screwing into the Pommel. Metal conducts magic as easily as electricity, this allows the magic to travel down the handle without hindrance)

In a Wiccan coven an Athame is used to call quarters, we feel as it is to aggressive to point at a friendly elemental and demand their presence in your circle. For us Elemental Quarters are friends, invited to join us within circle.

The first mention of an Athame, that I have found, is in a book written in 1572 on Ceremonial magic called "The worke of Salomon the Wise, called his Clavicle revealed by King Ptolomeus ye Grecian" in which an Arthany is mentioned. (before Dr Johnson wrote the first dictionary, people spelt as they thought fit). Although this Arthany was described as a blade with a white ivory handle, these and other knives were used to mark out, rather than cast the circle (never use an Athame to mark out a circle by thrusting it into the Earth this will ground it, use the white handled Boline). The book also mentions black handled knives but they have other names. It would seem at some point the name was reassigned, at least as far as Witches were concerned or perhaps Arthany was their original name that witches have preserved. As so much with Witchcraft, without written records it is impossible to prove it either way.

An Athame must never touch blood, if it does it must be retired, even when being made should the Swordsmith slip and it draw blood, the blade must never become an Athame, but used for some other purpose. The way to retire an Athame as you would expect would be to touch blood so either use it as a normal steak knife or cut your own your finger with it. This will ground it for any use in magic. But why you would want to retire an Athame is beyond me. The longer you use it, the more it becomes part of you and the better it works. I have had mine for since 1986 and it will be with me until I die.

What makes a knife into an Athame?

It is the dedication of the knife to the old Gods that enables it to channel the magic down the length of the knife that makes it into an magical tool. The words of power must also be whispered into the Athame as it is made and incense burnt. During the dedication of an Athame the molecules need to be aligned to direct the magic on its path. This is easier than you might think. Sit facing North, rub a piece of Lodestone (Magnetite see in the chapter on Gems and Metal magic) down the edges of the blade, from hilt to tip, and then along the face of the blade but not quite touching, at this point, as it will scratch the blade badly if you do. You will need to do this several times. This action magnetizes the Athame, drawing the energy in one direction along the blade, so it is very important to work from the handle to the tip, as this is the way your energy will flow down the blade. Alternatively if you do not have a piece of magnetite or a magnet and are worried about scratching the blade sit facing North. This is very important; aligning the molecules will not work unless you face Magnetic North. Gently tap the blade but it takes many hours of work to align the blade this way. This to my mind is another reason why the Athame is sacred to the Fire quarter rather than Air. You would naturaly sit in the South to face North, to prepare your blade to become an Athame.

With the dedication of the knife to the old Gods it finally enables the magic to channel down the length of the knife and turns a knife into an Athame.

The Athame a black handled knife, and is made from a protective wood such as Oak, Ash or Ebony, this I think is the true meaning of black, as black is the color of the Dark Goddess of Protection, part of the Triple Goddess. Today many ask for the handle to be left natural but I am a traditionalist and prefer to see a black handle on your Athame, but as ever, this is your choice.

Ebony has the advantage of being both a naturally black wood and also has a wonderful feel, like silk. Although this wood comes from Africa and Asia, it may have been traded in Europe since pre-

Celtic times, surprising Archaeologists as new evidence continues to be produced confirming how far early people traveled and traded. It is possible to get Ebony from renewable sources such as fallen trees or pruned branches. Obviously, these are preferable for magic than wood that comes from the result of deforestation. Another wood to consider would be Bog Oak but it is very difficult to get, this special wood is up to 7000 years old. Oak, Yew and Scots Pine trees are all called Bog Oak and are trees that have drowned in ancient times, due to spreading bog lands. The wood of the dead trees, over the years absorbs the water from the bog into the body of the fallen tree which due the chemical reaction between the iron in the bog and the tannin in the wood, darkens to a wonderful color. When dried, this special wood is very hard due to its age and special treatment by nature, which only enhances its magical properties. It is the same wood that is used on the handles of a real Skean Ddhu (there are many spellings of this word and all are right) Skean means knife and Dbhu means black, which is a knife that a can be seen in the full highland regalia of Scotland and peaking out of the sock when dressed in full kilt.

During the Iron Age, unsurprisingly, blades of knives and swords where made from Iron. Each blade represented both wealth and power. The legend of King Arthur may have some basis in reality, although if true, there is much conjecture about which period of history the story is set. Did Arthur with Merlin's help draw the Iron sword from the stone? If this stone was Iron Ore did it mean that they heated this in a furnace until the Iron ran hot from the stone and then forged the sword? In so doing, taking rock and turning it into a sword- from the stone. Or was King Arthur's story set in the Bronze Age? They cast Bronze swords in stone moulds, so Arthur would still have pulled Excalibor literally from the stone. Or perhaps this story represents King Arthur receiving his sword or Athame and magnetizing its blade. Changing an ordinary sword into the magical Excalibor, the Guardian Sword of England. The stone or loadstone drawing along the blade directing the magic, and enabling the sword to point truly. Many legends have some base in fact; perhaps we need to understand the importance of Smithing and the wealth that a chief would have to own a sword to understand this story and its magic.

Blades are today mainly made from either carbon steel or stainless steel, but Steel is merely Iron with carbon added which increases the strength of the metal. Steel is surprisingly old, the Saxons were masters at working with Steel; knowledge was lost until regained until the 18th century. Much of our knowledge, on many subjects, was lost during the Dark Ages of early Christian invasion of England.

The disadvantage of both Iron and Steel is that any liquid will stain the blade, even sweaty fingerprints will leave their rusty mark. Stainless steel was the next scientific advance, by adding a little Chromium to steel Smiths found that it stayed bright and clean. But if you really try, you can still mark even Stainless Steel. Traditionally, Horsetail herb was used to clean both knives and armor and is a good traditional way to maintain your athame, but I must admit, modern cleaners do give a better polish. Please, please keep especially a carbon steel blade well oiled, the best thing to use is a rust inhibiting oil, failing this, any oil, even cooking oil will do. Steel, if it marks, can be cleaned with wire wool or a little very fine wet and dry sandpaper, rub up and down the blade, not in circles. Although if you clean the blade with a dry cloth and oil it as part of your ritual after closing circle this should not be necessary.

It is traditional to carve sigils into the handle or to paint them on before consecration. If you have an antique Athame or you do not choose to carve sigils onto the handle for any reason, another option is to use water-based paint. It is then easy to wash the sigils off after consecration, so that no one would recognize it as a witch's Athame (dry and oil after). This is known as using "Phantom Script", as there is only a shadow of the charm that is known to only you and the Gods. Although hopefully, persecution is a thing of the past and we can feel secure in today's climate of religious freedom to have what sigils and trapping of our religion we choose. Another route between them both is to incise the sigils into the leather of the sheath; any good Swordsmith will leave the scabbard unfinished for you to do this. If you make the athame yourself you could add the sigils to the tang, which is a part of the blade that runs down through the handle, before assembling the knife.

What Sigils? There are five traditionally placed on the athame, one for the Goddess, one for the God, one for yourself, one for the eight festivals and one for your coven. Choose any that appeal to you, do some research, here are some to start you off.

For the Goddess

For the God

The eight Sabbats
Normally the sigils for yourself would be your birthsign, but if you have a bindrune this would personalize it nicely (see the Chapter on Charms).

One for the coven uniting you all, this may be any depiction of the name chosen for your coven or anything you see fit. If you are working as a Hedgewitch you may choose to leave this blank or mark it with a representation of a herb or have a completely different thought. There is nothing wrong with having ideas and adding them to established thought.

Wiccans use a different set of symbols, see books by Janet and Stewart Farrar and later with Gavin Bone. I highly recommend them. True Swordsmiths whisper words of power into the making of knives and swords, this is particularly true of magical weapons. Today, sadly most knives are mass-produced abroad, with no understanding of magical traditions and even the magical words are lost, with the exception of a few. If made by a witch then the words (hopefully) will be remembered and the powers energize your blade. No knife made by a Witch should be purified, as this will wipe from it work done by them to enhance your Athame or Boline. If however, it has been made in a factory as part of a production line by uncaring workers then it is advisable to purify it before dedication to your chosen deity. After all, the person making it might have been having an off day or a row with their partner, its best to clear it of all negative energy placed within. Some books I have read advise you to bury the tools in salt for a week or in the earth for six months. PLEASE DON'T DO THIS, it will total destroy an athame or any other ritual tool not made from stone, crystal or glass. It will cause the wood to rot; it will rust the blade and if made by Witches that have already started the magical process, drain its power. If it needs it, pass it widdershins (anticlockwise) through the elements, starting with Earth and salt; sprinkle a little **dry** salt from the pommel to the tip of the blade. Carefully shake all salt from the athame before moving on through the other elements and taking it next to Water and be as sparing with this as with salt. After consecrating it, carefully dry it and oil the blade. There is a fuller explanation at the end of this chapter. There is no traditional design for an athame, except that it should have a sharp double-edged blade. Needless to say you must be careful of waving around a sharp blade, but I have never seen any Witch slice into another during rituals. It has to be a sharp blade; if you are journeying on the Astral plane and encounter a problem; you can't pull out your plastic penknife as defense. You need to be able to rely on the knowledge of a good sharp knife to see the baddies off, although this does not happen very often it is best to be prepared, like a good boy scout. A Pentagram makes an apt pommel (the other end from the blade), and is seen on many a witches Athame today. Standing as it does for spirit and the four quarters, and being a barrier for evil to pass.

I personally prefer a moon Quillion (or cross-guard, set between the handle and blade) but the choice is yours. In our form of Witchcraft Athames are worn on a belt, as each covener will use their own Athame at some point during a circle.

I must just add that it is still illegal for you to carry your Athame in public in England, if you live in other parts of the world it is best to check the local laws. Be sensible, wrap it in a cloth and then in a plastic bag, wrap it with sticky tape, pack it at the bottom of your bag. Place with your robe and any other items you are carrying on top. If you are stopped tell the police about it immediately and why you are carrying it.

An Athame is sacred to the God although carried by both male and female Witches.

An Athame must never be given as a present; it must be paid for, even if with only the smallest coin or it will cut the friendship.

I once was privileged to be allowed to hold a modern blade made in the traditional Viking way. The knife and its brother sword were owned by Ragnor, a Viking I much respected, sadly now in Valhalla. This sword and knife was alive, it vibrated in your hand and you might even say sang in a note too high for human ears. I would dearly love to have owned such a knife and sword, my star sign is Taurus-gems and possessions are one of its attributes, it's not my fault.

In our tradition attributed to the element of Fire, Male. Although some attribute it to air.

Scabbard is protective as in the scabbard of Excalibur and is female, likened to the womb of the Goddess, containing the sword of the God.   **A Scabbard is female.**

Wand, a wand is gentler than an athame: an athame commands, a wand asks.

We use it to call the Elemental quarters, as they are your friends and not elementals to be commanded to appear. A wand is obviously phallic shaped, it opens the doors of life allowing the Elemental to pass through into this realm.

A wand acts like a torch, imagine a beam of light projecting from the tip of the wand, asking the Elementals to join the circle. It works much like a moth to a light, holding them at your circles edge until you light the Elemental candle that will keep them amused, until you put out the candle at the end of circle. But unlike a moth, the Elementals must choose to make a connection with you first, they come to be with friends for the evening.

A wand can be made from any of the sacred woods although my own opinion is that it is male and so needs to be made from a male wood. Wands can also be made from crystals, which are a fine amplifier of power or a combination of the two. If using a crystal, I have found the clearer the better. Quartz crystal is my own choice but Amethyst or if you are using the idea that the wand is male and needs a male crystal may I suggest Citrene, are also greatly prized for the work.

A wooden wand is easy to make, choose a piece that has energy for you.

Male wood
From Ash for healing and solar energy.
From Elder for exorcising negative spirits
From Hawthorn for great power.
From Oak for fertility and longevity.
From Pine with a Pine cone mounted (male cones are smaller from the lower branches and available only in spring), for fertility.

Female wood
From Rowan (Mountain Ash) for knowledge.
From White Willow for Moon work.

From Hazel for poetry, knowledge, love, fertility and childbirth.
From Apple wood for love and wisdom.

I went for a walk in the woods, and came across a poor broken Ash sapling, a vine had grown around it. It had grown tighter and tighter over the years making a wonderful twist into the wood but pulled too tight and snapped the baby tree. It was so long- dead that it had become air-dried. I unhooked it from the vine, shortened it for carrying and took it home. Once home it was the work of one evening to sand off the broken end cut to the right length (from the tip of your longest finger to your elbow or what seems in proportion for that piece of wood) sand, strip off the bark and bees wax it. You can add anything your heart desires to enhance the magic and personalize the wand; you can burn a design into the wood or add beads, crystals, feathers as your own artistic and creative imagination dictates. Of course you can leave it plain, there is nothing wrong with simple.

In our tradition attributed to the element of Air, Male. Although some attribute it to Fire.

Silver Pentagram worn by many witches today and as a protection against evil and as a recognition symbol to other Pagans. **Its element is Spirit.**

Silver Jewelry- being a Pagan jeweler I must comment on this. No, this is not an ancient tradition not even the pentagram, but a modern development of Witchcraft. All living religions develop and change, Witchcraft is no exception. People are richer and freer than they have ever been in history; we celebrate this by outward signs of our religion as any other religion so freely does.

Boline, a white (or horn) handled knife with traditionally a curved blade, although a straight blade is being used more and more. The Boline is your working knife in circle, whereas the Athame is a spiritual knife. Remember until recently every one would carry a knife with them at all times for every day business, cooking, work and even a clerk would need a knife to sharpen his quills. Although all tools used in circle are special and must only be used for your

magical purposes.

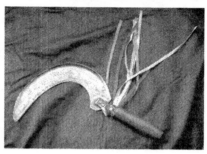

I use a Thatchers sickle, which is the smallest that is made, this I decorated with the elemental color ribbons (one of these days I will get round to rubbing down the handle back to the white wood). The Boline is used for cutting within the circle, Herbs, carving sigils into candles and corn at harvest time. It can also be used to mark out a magic circle, stick the Boline into the ground tie your nine foot cord to it and mark out a circle.

A Boline is female.

Altar Pentacle, a pentacle is protection, "a gate that no evil may pass". The five points stand for spirit and the four elements. This is set in the center of your altar, usually made of copper or brass, but can be made of pottery or even drawn onto paper or as cheaply as five twigs interlocked. When consecrated it should be offered to the North of your circle. **Its element is Earth, female.**

Thurable an incense burner (for incense see chapter on herbs). Obviously there is no need to buy expensive incense burners, an old flowerpot with some dry earth in will work very successfully. **Its element is Air, Male.**

Chalice, this holds the ritual wine and is sacred to the Goddess. The chalice can be found throughout history. Chalice and the Celtic Cauldron of Regeneration, were fused into one to form in Christian myth, into the Holy Grail of legend.

In Viking tradition the female head of the household would meet guests with a horn of Mead, we know that in the rites of Freyr and

Freya there was some form of fertility ritual performed. Could Freyr's famous sword have been plunged into Freya's Horn as in a witchcraft ritual? Was this the origin of our ritual?

A Chalice is an expensive item, and should if being correct, be made from solid silver; needless to say, no one I know owns a solid silver chalice. So don't worry about not being able to afford one, any nice wine glass or goblet will serve the Goddess. She will be happy with what ever you choose to offer Her. Consecrate facing West, the element of water

Its element is water, Female.

Anointing oil, this should be made from Essential oils-Frankincense, Myrrh, Amber, Sandalwood, Rose and Benzoin diluted with almond. No synthetic oils should be used.

Its element is Spirit.

Candle Snuffer or fingers never blow on candles, this uses one male element against another.

Salt is representative of Earth, as such should come from the bowels of the earth, not sea salt please. Rock Salt is the best to use, having few if any additives.

Incense –See herbs

Water and Dish if you wish to use tap water or to buy bottled water the choice is yours. When you zap (throw the energy down through your hand and down throw your Athame) it with your Athame, the water will be made pure in either case. Remember our religion was a secret for many years with a heavy penalty if discovered. Many ritual items needed to be very unremarkable and hidden amongst other kitchen implements

Besom (broomstick) In the past of course, a besom would have

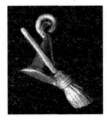

been the only form of sweeping utensil, the ancestor of the broom. A besom should have a phallic handle wrapped around with some birch or other twigs. If birch did not grow in your area, you used what was to hand. In the North of England at least, during the last century the plant

Broom was called besom. I was in an industrial museum in the North of England watching a old film on steel making, when I was surprised to hear them talk about throwing besom twigs onto the steal before it went under the great rollers. It is interesting to see how old Witchcraft rituals survive into a modern setting without people understand the true significance

The besom is also a fertility symbol this is easily understood on seeing one made, the twigs are tied into a tight bundle with willow and then the handle with its carved phallus is pushed into the center of the bundle of twigs. A Besom should never be made during May or over the twenty four days of Yule, this was thought very unlucky.

The Besom is used to purify the circle before use, this should be done widdershins (anticlockwise). A besom can also be used as a bridge between the worlds, a doorway into and from the circle.

In many countries around the world, to jump the broomstick was the only form of marriage, and is used nowadays in all Witch Handfastings but to do this properly the besom should be held over the threshold. As once more you jump between the worlds of dependency on your family to dependant on each other, a far bigger change in your status within the community formally. Even today in many parts of the England, if a girl has an illegitimate child, it is said she 'jumped over the Besom'. After childbirth, the house should be swept from the front door out the back door, to take all evil influences from both mother and child or earlier still, to protect from fairies stealing the child.

To ride the besom has another meaning entirely, remember the phallic symbol mentioned earlier. A besom was also ridden, like a child rides a hobbyhorse, around the farmer's fields and with sympathetic magic; a Witch would jump as high as possible to show the corn how high to grow. In the Craft there is a great deal of controversy as to whether the Besom should be ridden with bristles up, resembling a horses head or bristles down like the exhaust of a jet engine. There are many depictions in medieval illustrations showing both ways, but as the artist would no doubt have never seen a Witch riding through the air or around a farmer's field, I don't think that we can take either way as any proof. Watch a child play horsy with mothers broom and you will see it pick up the stick leaving the head on the floor, if it seems natural to the child, it will seem natural to the Witch and so I depict it that way in my jewelry.

To have a Besom leaning up against the wall near your door showed that you were at home, the house was tidy and ready to accept callers. With the satellites taking pictures of the house and seen instantly on the web, I wonder if this idea will re-establish itself? No other tool with the possible exception of the distaff has been more widely associated with women and female magic. The Besom is especially associated with the Roman Goddess Hecate, who is often linked with witchcraft. **Its element is air, Male.**

Cauldron is sacred to the Goddess, the cosmic womb of the Great Mother, used for divination, to hold special candles, as at Yule and to burn your regrets at Samhain, etc. The cauldron in the past, would have been used to brew potions. There were many cauldrons in Celtic myths. Ceridwen's cauldron of knowledge, the Dagda's cauldron of regeneration, The Morrigan's boiling cauldron of life, wisdom, inspiration and enlightenment. Branwen and Solomon the Great both had cauldrons of regeneration. In Egypt, the sign of the Goddess Mut was three cauldrons.

Its element is water and the Goddess, Female.

Stang is a staff with deer horns attached. You will see in the photo I carry one at the Pagan Pride Parade. The Stang is used in the West Country, instead of a sword to cast circle, developed from the pitchfork of the farmhands. The Stang varies in design from coven to coven, using decoration easily available in the country- horns, feathers, ribbons etc and with bells to ward off evil. Be careful if you choose to make one, to have the horns placed above most peoples heads as you do not want anyone to spear an eye on the points of the antlers. The wood used for the Stang is Blackthorn, a strong dark wood, with a will of its own (see Herbs). A long piece of Blackthorn, is difficult to find straight, a good substitute is Ash; Ash is straight and strong, used for fighting staves in medieval times but does not hold as much magic as Blackthorn. Some consider Blackthorn too "dark" a wood but personally, I just find its magic very intense.

A stang should be footed with iron; this has two purposes, the most practical being that it stops the end from rotting and damage, more importantly it grounds the stang to the earth. The problem today is that iron is almost impossible to get, on our stang we solved this problem easily and neatly by fitted a cast iron gas fitting. Giving us the only British Standard Kitemark stang fitting! If you are not lucky enough for your stang to fit neatly into a gas pipe fitting, steel is the next best option. Steel has the same consistency as Iron but with added carbon, so no big problem. The most basic answer is a nail driven into the foot of the stang, be careful here not to split the wood. If you are clever cut a disc, and nail this on or make a cup to fit on the bottom. You can use glue to attach the cup but only around the sides and not at its base, as this will form a barrier to the magic passing along its length.

A Stang is being used more and more as handfastings and as open rituals are performed more frequently. There is no problem about carrying a Stang to a ritual or a Handfasting, where there may be people unused to Witchcraft ceremonies and who may feel threatened by waving around a sword. Although it is not part of our tradition to use a stang, I find it convenient for open rituals, to start waving swords around does frighten some. If an accident should happen to a Stang and it is broken, the Coven will also break, so carefully look after your Stang.

Its element is Fire, Male.

Sword A sword is just a large athame, used for a coven. It is also used to swear an oath of allegiance or to direct coven energy. Like an Athame, the sword must never touch blood. To strap on a sword makes the High Priestess into a High Priest, as in times of war when no men where available to act as HP. In medieval times, all Yeomen (a type of middle class) owned a sword; it is a modern misconception that they did not (at the battle Agencourt all archers are known to have carried a sword).

There is controversy in The Craft as to the placement of the sword and Athame, whether they should be regarded as Air or Fire, like all things in Witchcraft be guided by your inner wisdom of what feels comfortable to you. For us the sword and Athame are fire elements. An Athame and a sword are made in fire, heated and then quenched and re-heated. At each part of the process of beating and tempering energy is added with every stroke of the hammer, annealing in the fire and then repeating the process, until the work is finished. A sword is usually being wielded in passion; oaths are taken on the blade of a sword with its inherent threat if broken, both an attribute of Fire. A wand may well never touch fire in its making, and has a slower but clear-thinking energy, for me I feel wand represents Air. Both Fire and Air are male elements and so this does not change which ever you choose, whether the aggression of fire or the cerebral quality of Air, is your final choice.

Its element is also Fire, male. Although some attribute it to Air.

Burin, an old name for jewelers engraving tool, used to carve the sigils onto the handle of your athame. I find it easier to use a burin to carve candles for candle magic, rather than a Boline to be honest.

Aspergent can have a handle carved with sigils but usually today it is a bunch of purifying herbs, such as rosemary, hyssop or lavender. An Aspergent can be used by dipping it into a bowl of Holy water (zapped by you) and sprinkling or splashing an area or people, to purify or rid a person or area of any psychic problem.

Necklace, A bead necklace should be worn by every woman with in a circle, a necklace of Amber and Jet is worn by the Highpriestess. Jet represents the Dark moon and Amber possibly the Sun.

Many Goddesses in the past are represented as wearing a bead necklace, to wear a necklace in circle honors all Goddesses, particularly the Egyptian Goddess Hathor, who wore a sacred necklace which was also carried in ritual and shaken as a musical instrument.

Robe We work robed rather than skyclad (naked). Robes cannot stop the flow of energy but do make you feel different when you dress for your circle, the smell of the incense clinging to them, changing everyday life into a magical time. After all, if you can't send your magic through a thin layer of cotton, how can you send it through walls when working within a building or over many miles to its destination?

When you slip your robe over your head the smells of the incenses used at the last Sabbat waft around you, this is a subconscious message to your mind that circle is about to start. It also unites a coven, everyone expressing themselves in different styles of robe but when the lights go out, circle starts, the robes disappear and only the important essence of a person, the face and hands are left. All different, all one, shapes and trappings of everyday life have gone. Most people start by working at home, so chose a thin fabric for your robe, it gets very hot in circle. Later you may decide to do out-door workings, then a thick wool or velvet robe may be a good idea. Although in our tradition of Witchcraft we wear robes, nothing is worn under your robe- no bra, no pants- naked under your clothes! But to tell the truth outdoor workings in Winter can be a bit chilly, so wear as many jumpers as you can in comfort, you need to be concentrating on the magic not the cold.

But Robed or skyclad (naked) the choice is yours.

A description of a quick and easy to make robe at the end of this chapter.

Cords, this is known variously as a Cingulem (a Roman military belt to hold sword of knife) or Singulum. We have no special name for the cord but then we do not use the cord to hold our Athame. I wear my Athame on a black leather belt around my waist (some wear it on a black cord that holds no significance).

Witches in the past were accused of caring cords, this was one of the accusations leveled at Joan of Arc and the Knights Templer, although they didn't stand alone in this accusation. Why carrying cords was considered such a crime is not detailed, it can only apply to there use in magic.

Traditional cords are red for both men and women (the blood red cord of Egyptian Goddess Isis?), or green for the women (the green cord of justice of The Egyptian Goddess Ma'at?) and red for men. In some Covens the High Priest wares a gold cord and the High Priestess a silver cord plaited into their other colored cords. In most Wiccan Covens white, red and blue cords may be worn to indicate degrees. With us, initiates wear the white initiation cord until initiation, when a knot is placed in the white cord to remember their passing, when thirteen knots are in the cord it is retired and another started. During Initiation three cords are presented to the newly initiated coverner and then braided by them, braiding into the cord the energy of their initiation.

Tying a knot in your waist cord should mark ideas, rituals or deeds that are important to you. Tying a knot in your cord for your initiation would of course be one very important example. Some Coveners have a complicated method of tying knots in the main cord for very important things and knots in the fringe for those of lesser import. It is best to be sure that the deed is worth noting as of course, this does shorten your cord quite considerably after a few years. So add only events that are very important to you, to your cord.

Cords are also used for magic but unlike Wiccans we use a new piece of cord each time, for if a knot is placed in the cord it must stay there until its work is done; and not untied until then. The exemption to this would be Tarot or crystal reading where you special cord can be placed in a circle and the cards dealt or crystals thrown within it, this enhances the magic of the reading. Handfastings are done with a red cord; this is given to the bride after the knot has been placed within and never unknotted, unless the two wish to part.

Wiccans also use their cord to bind and restrict the flow of blood causing the coverner to become light headed, all words spoken must be noted and the coverner encouraged to describe any visions they may be given, sometimes this is used with the scourge. Great care must be taken not to bind too tightly or for to long, or you can stop the flow of blood completely and cause great harm.

Your cord or come to that any form of flag, should never be

washed (please feel free to wash your robe).

Offering bowl to hold the cakes, and to hold those that you leave at the end of the circle for the elementals.

Pouch this is not strictly necessary but useful, a place to keep all the bits and bobs that you acquire over the years feathers, crystals, even lighters in case the Altar Candle goes out. This is very easily made even by those not able to sew, take a large circle of leather or non fraying fabric make small holes all round about an inch (2.5cm) from the edge and thread a piece of cord through, tie off, simple. Of course if you are clever it can be any shape and decorated in any fashion you choose.

Drum carrier of the sacred sounds but not a brilliant idea in a flat at midnight. Use the drum to raise power or to accompany chanting, wonderful in outdoor workings particularly if there are a few of you.

Cape worn for outdoor circles, even in Summer it can get cold at midnight.

Stag Horned Crowns more likely to be worn by traditional HP as well as Wiccans, as the horns are more easily available in the countryside and cheaper there.

Silver Moon Crown worn by the High Priestess this was and still is, an expensive item. Mainly used by Wiccans, but now being adopted by many other covens. In Victorian times, very possible further back still, only married ladies were allowed to ware a tiara, which is the same shape as the moon crown. This emphasizes the fact that the HP and HPs were traditionally thought of as a handfasted couple.

Scourge is not used by traditional witches, but by Wiccans only. The scourge varies between covens, some use it in token and some with more force. This can be either a silk whip or some prefer to wield something more sturdy, more of a cord. But all have nine strands and five knots on each strand, this is used to purify witches during rituals and to "get the sight" or prophesy.

Sacred Bottle Opener, well any bottle opener will do of course, just don't forget it!

Witches Hat no, I'm not suggesting you should wear this in circle. But...In Germany have been found no less than three, tall solid gold conical hats with brim, exactly like the traditional Witch's hat. This hat is three thousand years old! With 10739 stars and moons on. The moons cleverly work out to be our own moon's 18.6-year cycle!

In China they have unearthed mummies of blonde, European appearance not Chinese, one tall, beautiful lady was buried, again wearing a tall Witches hat. The only thing I can say is, interesting.....

Layout of your altar.

Below is a basic altar layout, every quarter has it's representation on the altar, the salt for Earth, incense for Air, red candle for Fire and a bowl of water naturally for Water. These are kept separate to honor each quarter and for spell workings on fullmoons, to add each elemental energy separately into any spell.

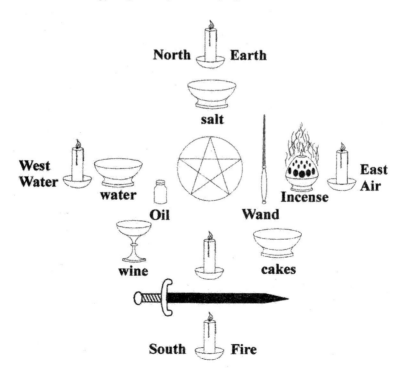

You may feel you would like to personalize your altar, fine, add any crystals or a fossil that adds power, of which you are particularly fond. Each Sabbat you can add an altar dressing, flowers in Spring and Summer, pinecones in Autumn let your imagination loose. A good excuse if one were needed, to go for a walk in the country and see what comes your way, needless to say don't pick wild flowers but some from your garden would be wonderful.

Although I have included the dedication of the Athame and Wand in this chapter, this should only be done after learning how to cast and prepare a circle.

Dedication of an Athame

At the Fullmoon
Cast circle with your finger
Draw up cone of power
Draw pentagram in the North, with your finger.
Call Elemental Quarters.

The first part of the dedication is for a commercially bought Athame, not one made by yourself or any Witch who you trust; and you should never be buy an Athame, your most important tool, from one you do not.

Turn to North
Sprinkle a little salt on your blade as you say:-

"Element of Earth, cleanse this blade, let nothing impure remain there in."

Turn to West
Sprinkle a little water on your blade as you say:-

"Element of Water, cleanse this blade, let nothing impure remain there in."

Turn to South

Wave the blade through the Red candle as you say:-

"Element of Fire, cleanse this blade, let nothing impure remain there in."

Turn to East

Wave the blade through the incense as you say:-

"Element of Air, cleanse this blade, let nothing impure remain there in."

Start here if this is a non-commercial blade.

Stand facing North and rub Lodestone along the blade as described above.

See in your mind's eye the merging of your Athame with the Sword that you were given during your visualization. Join the Athame in your hands to that on the Astral plane, see the energies of two, becoming one, knowing that now you have twice the power to draw upon.

"Lady of the silver rays of Moonlight
Mistress of Magic,
Spinner of Fate,
Goddess of the Dark cauldron of inspiration,
May You (if you have a Goddess name add it here) watch that
which takes place here, and give your blessings upon my path".

Oil the blade with anointing oil from hilt to tip.

" God of the fierce and golden Sun,
God of Warriors and all who hold courage with in their heart,
Lord of the Greenwood, mighty Stag,
Strengthen my Athame against all evil and embue it with your

power"

Wipe any excess oil from the blade.

Walk to South and hold the athame out on your two hands to the South

Athames and swords are sacred to Fire,

"I dedicate this Athame to your service, elemental of Fire and courage,
Help me to cut a circle that will take me outside of time and space,
And banish all malevolence from my circle."

Pass the blade of the Athame through the fire.

Turn to North
Sprinkle a very little salt on your Athame from Pommel to the tip of your blade as you say:-

"Element of Earth, imbue this blade with your protection."

Turn to East
Wave the blade through the incense as you say:-

"Element of Air, let me use this Athame with understanding."

Turn to South
Wave the blade through the Red candle as you say:-

"Element of Fire, imbue this blade with your energy."
Turn to West
Dip you finger in the water placing as little as possible from pommel to the tip of your blade as you say:-

"Element of Water, imbue this blade with the emotion of happiness."

Place the Athame on your breast and close your eyes, bonding with it.

"Thou art mine! I am thine! We are one!"

Hold high to the God and Goddess; adding anything you wish to say.

"SO MOTE IT BE!!! NINE TIMES ETERNAL!!!"

Kiss the blade to seal the bond,

Place on any dedicated magical tool you may already have, to absorb the energies.

Bless cakes and wine.

Use your new Athame to close circle.

Close circle in the normal way.

Place remaining cakes and wine on the Earth.

Dedication of a Wand

At the fullmoon

Cast circle

Draw up cone of power

Draw pentagram in the North

Call Elemental Quarters.

Purify Elements

Chant

Anoint

Call down the Moon

The first part of the dedication is for a commercially bought wand, not one made by yourself or any Witch who you trust. You should not of course be buying a Wand, from one you do not.

Turn to North

Sprinkle a little salt on your wand as you say

> *"Element of Earth, cleanse this wand, let nothing impure remain there in."*

Turn to West

Sprinkle a little water on your wand as you say

> *"Element of Water, cleanse this wand, let nothing impure remain there in."*

Turn to South

Wave the wand through the Red candle as you say

> *"Element of Fire, cleanse this wand, let nothing impure remain there in."*

Turn to East

Wave the wand through the incense as you say

> *"Element of Air, cleanse this wand, let nothing impure remain there in."*

Skip to here if this is a non-commercial wand.

Point the wand at the sky/ceiling holding it with both hands and with feet apart (forming a triangle).

> *"I ask the Goddess and God to imbue this Crystal/Twig (or what ever material has been made from), with energy*
> *That will allow me to use this as a wand to beam through the veil between the worlds,*

Calling to my circle's edge the powers of Earth, Air, Fire and Water."

Throw power down the wand, visualize a beam of light issuing from the tip.

"Lady of the silver rays of Moonlight
Strengthen my wand with your magical iridescent light.

God of the fierce and golden Sun,
Strengthen my wand with your radiant light and power."

Oil the wand with anointing oil from the bottom to the tip.
Walk to East and point the wand at the East
Wands are sacred to Air.

"I dedicate this wand to your service, elemental of Air and knowledge,
Aid me always to understand my path,
Assist me to call Spirits to my circle's edge,
And help with the magic I must do."

Pass the wand through the smoke of the incense

Turn to North

"I call to my Elemental of Earth,

Throw power down the wand, visualize a beam of light issuing from the tip, do this with all elements.

I present this wand to the elements
Help guard this place set outside of time.
Your power I invoke to aid me."

Turn to East

"I call to my Elemental of Air,
I present this wand to the elements,
Help guard this place set outside of time.
Your power I invoke to aid me."

Turn to South

"I call to my Elemental of Fire,
I present this wand to the elements,
Help guard this place set outside of time.
Your power I invoke to aid me."

Turn to West

"I call to my Elemental of Water,
I present this wand to the elements,
Help guard this place set outside of time.
Your power I invoke to aid me."

See in your mind's eye the merging of your wand with the wand that you were given during your visualization. See the energies of two, becoming one.

Place the wand on your breast and close your eyes, bonding with it.

"Thou art mine! I am thine! We are one!"

Hold high to the God and Goddess; adding anything you wish to say.

"SO MOTE IT BE!!! NINE TIMES ETERNAL!!!"

Place on your Athame or any magical tool already in use, if possible, to absorb the energies.

Bless cakes and wine.

Close circle in the normal way, using your new wand to say goodbye to your Quarters.

Place remaining cakes and wine on the Earth.

Exercises- Start to compile your magical equipment, think about what you can make; are you good at sewing? Painting? Leather work? Or just good at picking up a bargain at junk shops. You don't have to spend a fortune, make do and mend to start with. As you progress, then you can add one good piece to you collection of ritual equipment and only more as ability and money permit. Remember the Goddess knows you aren't rich, so don't spend vast quantities of money on equipment, build over many years; but I can understand how you can want your altar to look it's best. This can be helped with a little greenery at Beltane or fruit at Harvest.

How to Make a Simple Robe……
Take 3.5 – 4 meters of black fabric, cut off half a metro for the hood, for meditation.

Fold the fabric in half raw edges together; fold again lengthwise with all four salvage (neat) edges together.

At the point of all the folds cut a neck-hole, just sew up the sides, leaving room for your hands.

Fold the extra half-meter of fabric and sew along a raw side then stitch the neat sides to the neck of your robe.

Neaten hem and sleeves if you wish. This is a very basic robe. You can cut if you are a little more skilled, from the bottom inwards at an angle to underarms (chest measurement plus 6inches) turn and come back as far down as you would like your sleeves to hang.

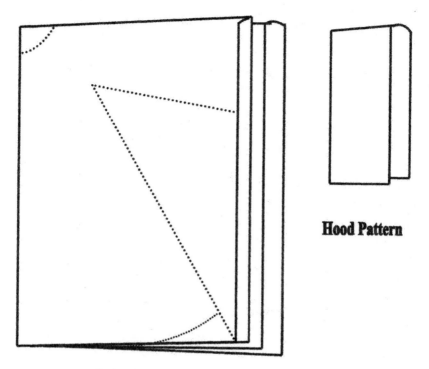

Hood Pattern

Robe Pattern

CHAPTER 5

Wheel of the Year - Sabbats

What is a Sabbat?

A Sabbat is a ritual and celebration of the changing seasons, the wheel of the year, in which we invite the Goddess and God to be with us.

Both God and Goddess are invited to all festivals.

The High Priestess represents the Goddess in ritual.

The High Priest represents the God in ritual.

If you are a Solo Witch then you represent your Goddess or God, according to sex.

The Sabbats reflect the changing tides of magic as they flow through the year. As the wheel of the year turns, at each turn, a different festival or Sabbat of the eight celebrations is prominent and a different energy flows through the land.

At Sabbats you celebrate with the God and Goddess a very special time. You give your energy to the Earth to strengthen the seasons to unite and become one with the very Earth itself. You bond with your God and Goddess, learn to connect on a deeper level the more Sabbats you do together. For us our deities are, like the quarters, extra Coven members, older, wiser and greatly respected. The knowledge they impart must be deeply valued. Many traditions of Witchcraft think that you must pay for a spell in some way, but by working Sabbats you also give energy to your deities when you work within circle. By giving your energy, in celebration at Sabbats you are in essence placing your energy into a pool of power, which can then be drawn at Esbats, (Fullmoon ceremonies), in which spells are cast. Without the Sabbats what energy would you have to draw on? You can't just take; you need to also give. If you like, it is a very an ethical principal or Eco Magic, taking only what you need without harm to you or the Universe.

You should begin your new life as a Witch by celebrating the seasons with the Goddess and God for at least six Sabbats before attempting Esbats and spell casting. Be sure you understand how to cast and dismiss a circle before attempting spells. If joining a Coven this would also begin to establish a group mind. So that when spells are attempted concentration on the goal is easy and there is less chance of worrying about knowing your words or feeling silly in your robe.

The God's special celebrations are the quarter days, the Solstice and Equinox. The time when the Sun takes eminence in the sky; and the God and High Priest takes prominence in the ritual. The calling down of the God or Sun takes place (where the God speaks through the High Priest), this is not to say that High Priestess does not get a look in, but she does not take the central role. The Solstices and Equinox's have been special days since pre Christian times, firstly for the agricultural communities and later for civilization as a whole. It is also the day that quarter rents are paid in businesses up and down the country. Many stone circles of Europe such as Stonehenge have markers that indicate the Summer Solstice or while other monuments such as Newgrange in Ireland, mark the Winter Solstice with the light traveling down a passage to mark the turning of the seasons. These are the easiest cycles for the priests in the past to have calculated. Although we know that they were able to perform far more complicated mathematical calculations to determine eclipses and the paths of the "Wandering Stars" or Planets as we now call them.

The Goddess's special celebrations are the cross quarter days, also known as Fire Festivals or Greater Sabbats. No nasty rents are collected, a time of celebration! At the Greater Sabbats the Goddess is called into the High Priestess and the High Priest a less prominent role. Samhain and Beltane are the two most important festivals of the year, representing life and death.

It has been speculated that the God festivals are a later addition the wheel of the year. But you can't have cross quarter days without something to cross. As you can see from Stonehenge and Newgrange these were the times of the earliest festivals celebrated over four thousand years ago, the Greater Sabbats must be a later addition, as they nicely equal out at about six week intervals.

For us, all Sabbats and Esbats (Fullmoons) are celebrated on the correct night. At all festivals, but most especially at Samhain (Halloween) the Veil between the Worlds is said to be thiniest on this special night. You therefore cannot celebrate Samhain three days or a week before or after when the veil has fallen again. Even at Samhain, I say celebrate because it is not a sad festival, calling back your loved ones through the Veil of Death to be with your once more, it is time for happiness. When the day is passed the energies change, the year flows inexorably onward and will not wait for the nearest Saturday to be convenient. Grab the day, most of us can change our timetable to cope with a few days a year, or perform the ritual when you return from your evening class or what ever, one late night will not kill you.

Bogie Drummer at Beltane Bash

But you will find it worth it, once it becomes a habit to always work on the right night, you will start to feel the subtle energies of the Sabbat and understand the deeper meanings of the year wheel.

But to enable all pagans to get together at The Halloween Festival we hold (a large public ritual) several days before Samhain but this is due to necessity, as all true Witches will be celebrating with their loved ones and covens, in a private ceremony on Samhain night.

You will notice that there are no words for each of the Sabbats, only the stories and suggested ways to express them. Write your own, as I did, and all HPs in our tradition do. Words in themselves are not important, borrow heavily from the wonderful poems of Doreen Valiente or write your own, or don't write them, let them surface from the heart, which ever suits you, only the symbol of the Sabbat is important.

Wheel of the Year

God's Year –Dates change every year, to find the dates for the God's year look in your diary. These are celebrated on the eve of the Solstice and Equinox, as the Celtic year ran from noon to noon the next day. The Solstice and Equinox are all about the progression of the Sun as it travels through the year and so are God festivals.

Yule- Winter Solstice, the time of the year when the Sun is at its weakest. It sits looking as if it hasn't the strength to grow stronger. In reality growing only by a few seconds a day far too short a time for the ancients, even with all their knowledge, to be aware of. The Sun appears to pause unable to climb the sky again, all would hold their breath and watch the sky for some movement to reassure them that Summer will come again. Then as if breaking free of its bonds the Sun starts to climb the sky steady and sure- reborn. The Winter Solstice is a time of death and birth; the God is old but wise and strong in His wisdom, if not in body.

Vernal (spring) Equinox or Oestara- Day and night stands in balance hence Equinox, meaning equal and Vernal meaning of cause virgin, the new and vergin year. The Young God in His wild and free aspect, like all teenagers more hormones than sense! The Earth goes wild, growing green, budding every tree, every bush, grass and crops spread across the country. The first of the fresh food, after Winters long sleep is available.

Summer Solstice or Litha- The longest day, the Sun God at the height of his strength. The Sun is at His strongest, the crops bathe in His heat. This is also a time to thank the Elementals for their help throughout the Year.

Autumn Equinox or Mabon- Once more day and night stand equal, the light is fading earlier from the sky every day, Winter draws swiftly on.

The Autumn Equinox is the Pagan Harvest Festival, as in every religion throughout the world, time to say thank you, that all the crops are safely gathered in or please help if they are not.

The God's Year

Yule- Winter Solstice
(The Sun's most Southerly rising point)

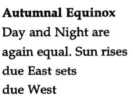

Autumnal Equinox
Day and Night are
again equal. Sun rises
due East sets
due West

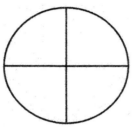

Vernal Equinox
Day and Night are
equal. Sun rises
due East and sets
due West

Summer Solstice
(The Sun's most Northerly rising point)

The ancients where able to see the Sun changing it's setting and rising position quite easily from early in history. The Sun then forms a pattern and that in many ancient cultures represents either the Sun or the Earth as a symbol, as above.

The Goddess Year

- this is always celebrated on the eve of the festival, as the Celtic year went from noon to noon next day.

These dates are the eve of the festivals and do not change.

Samhain- Halloween- the Celtic and Witch New Year, a time of death and re-birth.

The Goddess as Crone- 31st October.

The New Year, Samhain (pronounced Sawhain) is the old Celtic and witch name for the festival now called Halloween by some. Samhain is Summers end and an affirmation of life and recognition of death. It is also the Celtic New Year; a time for the old year to leave us and the New Year, with all it's fresh promise, to be born.

Imbolc- Candlemas- The Goddess as Maiden- 1st February.

A Smithing Festival and the career you earn your living by. A time to make and anoint the elemental candles and spirit candles.

Beltane- The Goddess as Mother- 30th April.

A celebration of life!! The Sacred Handfasting of Goddess and God.

Lughnasadh- Lammas- Loafmass - 31st July.

The first cut of the Harvest.

The Goddess Mature with the first hints at the Crone she will later become.

The Goddess's Year

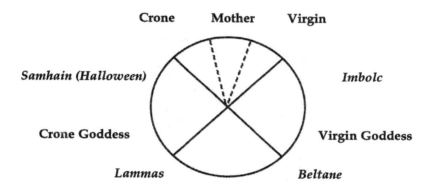

Crone   Mother   Virgin

Samhain (Halloween)   *Imbolc*

Crone Goddess   **Virgin Goddess**

Lammas   *Beltane*

The Mother Goddess

At Imbolc, as the Goddess year starts, She is Virgin Her color is white, She covers the fields in her blanket of snow.

As Summer dances in, Her color changes to red for the Mother and from Her fingertips She spreads the green of the fields.

But as Lammas approaches Her color begins to changes to the black of the Crone Goddess. The skulls and crone Witch faces you see at Samhain are the reflection of this, the bonfires that light the sky at the English tradition of Guy Fawkes Night, are part of the old

Samhain celebrations.

How the year of the God and Goddess coincide

Of course it is never as easy as all that. The Goddess attends every ceremony as does the God, but the emphasis changes, alternating between them both, with some festivals shared equally.

Samhain

The Witches New Year. Beltane in May is the witch festival of life; Samhain is the festival of death. At this Grand Sabbat, the most important of the eight festivals of the witches year, we remember those we have loved that have died. Passing a candle around the circle, for all to call back their loved ones. We also remember those killed in the persecutions in the name of witchcraft whether were a follower of our religion or not. On the 31st October, we say, "The veil between the worlds is thin," allowing our loved ones back with us for a short while. Witches leave a lighted candle to guide loved ones home, a glass of wine to remind them that they are loved and remembered and a cake to remind them of the sweetness of life that we shared together. But this is not a sad time, for we have our loved ones back for a little and so love, laughter, song, dance and drama, are the order of the season, a time to celebrate.

As this is the old Celtic New Year, it is a time to let go of the past and it's problems. Write down everything that you regret, from your life so far, light a candle and place it within the cauldron and burn your unwanted fears and regrets within in the flame. As your problems burn and turn to nothing but smoke, visualize them gone completely, your life new and clean of any regrets.

Many of our ceremonies are simple and reflect the earth that we celebrate, cut an apple in half to show the pentagram of the Goddess within.

For those that are not vegetarian and are meat eaters, bless all animals that have sustained us in the year past, thanking them for their energy and wishing them rebirth. In the legend of Thor, he would kill the goats that pulled his chariot for his nightly meal. Then wrapping their bones in the skin, finding them awake and munching grass in the morning.

In days gone past Samhain was the time to cull the herd, killing off all animals that would not survive the winter, keeping only the best of the animals to breed and restock in the Spring. If you had to kill animals, then it made sense to our ancestors to offer their animals to their Goddess first and so Samhain was a time of sacrifice. It was then followed by feasting, before the hard work of salting and drying the remains of the meat for the winter. We in the modern world would never dream of killing animals in circle now days. We are separated from reality in this day and age, all our meat comes in neat plastic trays from the supermarket but in many parts of the world, and people do not have refrigerators and deep freezes to keep meat fresh. Animals are still bought live in the markets, taken home and killed there for food for every day living. These people would have no problem with sacrificing within circle, as our ancestors did. I'm not saying I wish to do this, I don't, but it is not as far away as we seem to think. But respect for animals must be a priority to all Witches and Pagans. Although I am not a Vegetarian, I would never eat Battery Chickens or eggs, I buy my meat straight from the farm, so that I am assured of how it grew and roamed free. All fruit, grain and animals have life, I personally can't draw a line as to who has most, but respect for every living thing must be paramount to all witches.

Samhain is a time of remembrance for the dead, after death comes rebirth and so the Great Rite (more later) is performed by all coveners with partners, after circle, at home, in private.

Samhain is still is celebrated in Ireland and Scotland although it died out in England in the last century. The remains of the Celtic festival of Samhain has been adopted into the Christian as All Hallows where the poor would go from house to house asking for Soul Cakes in payment for praying for the soul of the family's dear departed. By the late 19th and early 20th century this was taken over by ruffians who would throw clumps of earth and broken pots at the doors of houses that would not give them cake, and an Anglified version of Trick or Treat was born. All Hallows of course sailed with the Irish immigrants to America in 1840 and became part of their heritage as well as our own and is more remembered there than in England with journalists asking why we practice an American tradition! Even the pumpkin so readily available growing wild in America, would have originally in England have been a Mangle Wersal. As this was cattle food, it was easily available and cheap, would be cut up and played with and then after Samhain fed to the cattle with no detriment to the farmers live stock. Mangle Wersal heads kept the demons and things that go Boo in the night way, on this most frightening of nights in the Christian Calendar. But for us of course, we just call them ancestors.

All harvests must be picked by Samhain as the Pooka (a nature sprite of Celtic folklore) now urinates on any harvest left in the fields and it is now unlucky to eat anything freshly picked.

Yule- The God knows that he is too old and unable to mate with the Goddess. She represents the land and He the fertility. It is time for the God to lay down His life for the good of the land which He offers freely so that he may be reborn young and fertile, to enable the land and trees may grow green once more.

The sacrifice of the God by the Goddess, and then the birth of the new God, is re-enacted by the Highpriest and Highpriestess. As there can be no birth with out a mother, the Goddess shares this festival equally with the God, although officially it is His festival.

The Goddess (enacted by the High Priestess) enters the festival as Crone with a black cape covering her, here the God (enacted by the High Priest) offers his life for the good of the land. The Goddess takes the sword from the altar and cuts his throat (please remember this is Ritual Theatre!) places over her dead lover her black cape, which reveals her red cape that she wears under her black. Now she has passed to Mother Goddess and as such, will give birth to the Sun God. He is then re-born as a new and inexperienced child (lift the

138

black cape) that needs to know the wonders of the land that he has inherited. After the birth she returns, like the legend of Venus rising from the foaming sea to Virgin, removing her red cape and revealing a white cape. (These capes can be made cheaply and easily from a few yards of fabric from your local market).

If you are alone in the circle enact the myth described above as visualization.

To prepare your alter for this celebration, have three candles on the altar as well as the spirit candle, one white, one red and one black for the crone. Gather mistletoe, holly and Ivy each represents a different aspect of the Goddess. The Mistletoe's white berries represent the Virgin Goddess, the Holly berries represent the Mother/Seductress, and the berries on the Ivy, which are black and poisonous, are of the Crone (it is remembered in the old carol "The Holly and The Ivy"). If at all possible decorate the base of your candles with these berries. Evergreen decorates your altar and room, to remind you that the Sun, Summer and the crops will return. (Bishop Martin of Braga 529-580CE forbade the "adorning of houses with green trees.")

Slowly the High Priest lights the candles that all hold, with either chanting or words by the HP to encourage the Sun to return with sympathetic magic, until the circle is aglow with light. If you are alone this can easily be done by lighting small candles or tealights around your circle (watch your robe on the ones behind you). Remember to leave the Yule spirit candle burning through the night but in a safe spot, your cauldron or sink. Be careful of any animals you may have, that they don't knock the candle over or burn their tail. It is said that if just one single witch does not leave a candle burning, the Sun will not find its way back home, to grow stronger each day until Summer returns. It is your duty to see to it, that the ceremony is duly carried out, don't leave it to someone else, it may never be done and the world will live in darkness from that day forth. It can be put out in the morning light, but never blown out or it will bring bad luck.

The Yule Log is a tradition that can be borrowed from our Pagan past, if your home is large enough. The ceremonial starts on Yule Eve, the log must be from either Oak, Ash or a fruit wood and ceremonially brought into the house at twilight (a time shared by both the God and Goddess). The Yule Log should enter the home through a corridor of candles and should be sprinkled with some life enhancing corn, wine or cider, as it crosses the threshold of the house. Odin was also the God of Alcohol and so we remember Him with this part of the ceremonies. The oldest member of the coven or household after placing the Yule log on the hearth before setting light to it, should bless all within the house and this little poem was used in some areas of England, as far back as 1648.

Kindle the Yule Brand, and then
Till sunne-set let it burne;
Which quencht, then lay it up agen
Till Yule come again.

Part must be kept wherewith to tend
The Yule Log next year;
And where 'tis safely kept, the Fiend
Can do no mischief there.

It should then be kindled with a fragment of last years log (but remember every ceremony starts somewhere). How long it should burn varied around the country, but a least twenty four hours to the whole of the Yule period. It must be extinguished at the end of the celebrations and never allowed to go out during it's burning time, as this was thought to be very unlucky. The Yule Log represents the Suns return, light in the darkness and continued life returning to the cold fields.

It was thought very unlucky to buy your Yule Log, does that apply to a Chocolate Yule Log so popular today? So you should even make your own chocolate Yule Log if that's the type you have. As with the sprig of plastic holly on the chocolate log, the traditional log was often decorated with evergreen before being brought into the house. The ashes were used as fertility and healing charms, so powerful were they thought to be.

As I am sure you know, many of the Christian trappings of Christmas are Pagan, feasting, Christmas Trees, evergreen decorations and Mistletoe. The three Wise men continued a good Pagan tradition by giving Jesus presents at the end of a year and the beginning of the new. At the Roman festival of Saturnalia and Brumalia that was the feast of Bacchus and the celebrations of the birth of Mithras, were all held at the Winter Solstice. The rich would give gifts to their poorer neighbors and receive a small gift in return. The gifts were chosen to bring good luck to the recipient, sweets and honey would give a year full of sweetness, candles light, gold and silver give prosperity.

And the wreaths that we hang on our door at this time of year? They symbolized from the time of the Roman Empire the victory of light over darkness and death. The returning sun at the winter solstice; like the victors crown they would have been made of laurel, they represent the Sun's triumph once more.

Later the Anglo Saxons continued Yule celebrations with the tradition of 'Wassailing', meaning "be of good cheer". This an Anglo-Saxon tradition, was continued, over the twenty-four nights of the old Yule. The Wassail Cup was taken from the cupboard were it had stood unused since last Yule, made of wood or for the rich silver, with two handles for ease of use of such a heavy item. The Wassail Cup was then decorated with some evergreen and filled with hot ale, spices, apple and perhaps a big shot of spirit. Added to that was a piece of toasted bread; guests to each house were offered a drink, "Toasts" were given and the treat of eating the toast was given to the Householder. There are many Wassailing songs.

Here we come a-wassailing,
Among the leaves so green,

Here we come a-wandering
So fair to be seen.
Love and Joy come to you,
And to you, your wassail too,
The Gods bless you, and send you
A happy New Year.
And send you a happy New Year.

Meet your to your neighbors and offer them a drink from your Wassail bowl, if you're brave ask them to refill it again.

Apple trees or any fruit trees are also traditionally Wassailed. At night go to your local orchard (ask permission first), with the Wassail Bowl, which should contain mulled cider this time. Find the best fruit tree in the orchard, stand round this tree, bang drums and blow horns and (for country folk, it was traditional to fire off shot guns) to frighten away the bad luck from the orchard (or your one apple or fruit tree in your garden). Toast the tree, pour some mulled cider around the tree's roots and hang the toast on a forked branch, as the host of the orchard.

Other customs on this night could be seen on a high hill tops, where twelve small fires were lit in a circle with a larger fire in the center and toasting friends, family and any on you could think of. Thirteen fires, ha!

I don't know about you, but I don't empathize with Christmas cards, have you looked at the pictures of camels and the three Wise Men and thought, "What has this to do with me?" Or looked at the Yule cards of a midwinter fullmoon and finding yourself slipping into the scene and empathizing with the cold midwinter? For me the men on the camels surrounded by sand, sweating in the heat, always felt alien, unreal. But the Midwinter snow and ice I could see that from my window, it was real, it called to me. I understood it. This could be recollection of our past lives well before Christianity, as Jung would put it, a 'collective unconscious'. The celebration held at that time would be Yule, the Solstice and the shortest day. But I'm a witch and that is understandable but most of the populace seems to feel the same, is this some sort of tribal memory? It is a remembering of who we are, where our path has led us and in some ways a wishing to retrace our steps, to re-find the religion of our own lands. This is what all Pagans quest for.

At this time of year we share a great similarity to the Christian birth of their Son of God; but in the Pagan religions of Mithras, Apollo and Sol Invictus, the rebirth of the Sun had been celebrated on the Winter Solstice far longer. In 46 Before Common Era, when the Roman Empire adopted the Julian Calendar the 24th December was approximately the shortest day of the year, therefore 25th was the first day of the growing light of the Invincible Sun. So Christians attached their festival, that is so much like ours, to that date. Even with the further change to the Gregorian Calendar restoring it to the same time.

Roman Emperor Constantine, a converted Christian changed the day of worship from the Jewish Saturday to the first day of the week Sunday, the day the pagans worshiped the Sun.

In 601 CE Pope Gregory I wrote to Mellitus, his missionary in England, telling him *"not to stop such ancient pagan festivities, but to adapt them to the rites of the church, only changing the reason for them from a heathen to a Christian impulse."*

Many religions celebrate at about the time of the Winter Solstice (or Summer Solstice in the Southern Hemisphere), Jews celebrate Hanukkah, Buddhists- Bodhi Day, Muslims- Ramadan, Christians-Christmas and of course Pagans the Winter Solstice, it's a nice thought that all the world with its beautiful diversity can celebrate together.

Imbolc - Honor the God and Goddess of Smithing. Make and anoint candles to be used in the year ahead, the pre-Christian Feast of Lights, where torches were carried around the streets in the Roman festival of Februa to which February was named.

Imbolc is a Smithing festival but not all are Smiths and so in our coven we bring an example of how you earn your living into the circle. This can be anything that you wish to expand, if you wish to make your hobby into your job, take that in to circle.

Smiths in the Bronze Age were considered magicians, drawing from Iron Ore, after many processes, daggers and swords. We whisper words of power into the making of knives and swords, this is particularly true of magical weapons (see Smiths in Metal Magic in a latter chapter), which is why Smithing is so closely linked to this festival.

How to make candles.

We also make, and anoint, our own candles that we may need throughout the year. By making the candles ourselves, is for us, a very important part of the Imbolc Sabbat. This Sabbat concentrates on work after all and it seems only appropriate to do some work for it. Ideally candles for magic should be made on a Waxing moon, but to find time to make candles at all is hard, so don't worry too much about this. To make our candles we use lengths of two inch (5cm) wide and any length that feels right to you, plastic water pipe as candle moulds, very cheap and very tough, available from any plumbing or DIY stores. Buy wick from hobby shops, cut and tie this to the center of a pencil, dropping the wick down through the pipe and out through a piece of tough card with a hole in and seal with

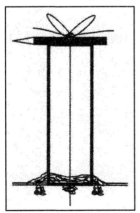

plastercine (you may need a little plastercine to get it to balance) and seal around the pipe. If you are feeling clever cut a wooden bung to fit. You will need to place this on a tray as some wax will leak out and make a mess.

This is easily cleared off the tray after finishing the candles by pouring boiling water over it. Heat the candle wax in a double boiler (not straight on the flame, as this will ignite!) as soon as it is melted pour the wax into the mould, carefully. As it cools it will contract and requires topping up for the next few hours. Of course, when you are making one color it is as easy to make a batch, so when making the white spirit candle, make all the Virgin white candles you need for the entire year. The Fire candles and Mother/Enchantress are made from a red wax and again are made as a batch. Crone black candles can be a problem, this can be over come by buying children's crayons and adding the black crayon to a batch of dark colored wax.

In ritual we anoint our elemental candles, brown, blue, red and green; this is done like a candle magic spell, if you look at the chapter on spells it will explain it in more detail. Mix the oil for each of the quarters, to bring attributes of Earth, Air, Fire and Water to the candles making them a beacon to hold the elemental spirit called to the circles edge. If you haven't got a coven this can be expensive, so use anointing oil instead. We then pass the light from the old candles, to the new. Light was thought to drive away the darkness of Winter. Imbolc with both the old candles and the new ones that we have passed the light to, the circle is awash with light, it is one of my favorite Sabbats, it looks so pretty. Last years candles are the basis of next years candles and so are renewed as a symbol of rebirth that we hope for in the next life. Some of the first candles I ever made are contained somewhere, in the newly made candles for this year, I like to think.

As the sun begins to grow in the sky and the earth warms, it starts the time of initiation.

Vernal Equinox or Ouster- God very lusty and single, before he meets and loves the Goddess, a physical manifestation of the life-force.

Light candles, circle and chant or dance. The High Priest then explains how this represents the balance of the forces that exist at this time of year, while he snuffs out half of the candles, so half of the circle is in darkness and half in light.

Time for chocolate eggs in circle! Yes, I know they never had them, but I ask you, would any have turned them down? Naturally, you can have real eggs and color the shells as is traditional by tying on onion-skins before boiling, cooking the eggs with beetroot or painting them after they are cooked. Vegans can purchase eggs carved from semi-precious stone as a representation for the altar, they are not very expensive and can of course, last for ever.

The Christian festival of Easter, which is at about this time, was named after the Goddess Oestara, Her sacred animal was the Hare. These have their nest in open land, rather than in a burrow like rabbits. Lapwing birds also lay their eggs in nests in open country, so country people confused both and thought that hares laid eggs that hatched into leverats and were therefore very magical. So Easter, the Christian festival, named after a Pagan Goddess has eggs and hares (or now nice bunnies instead) as their symbols. Fun isn't it.

Beltane - Beltane is a celebration of life!

It teaches us love, laughter and reminds us of the beauty of the world. The Sun once more begins to shine and we tentatively stick our nose out of the door to see if winter has passed. Down the road comes the sound of Morris bells jingling, the sound of drumming can be faintly heard, coming closer. When into view comes a bouncing bush, followed by Giants of all shapes and sizes. Beltane is here and the first day of Summer has arrived! The trees are blossoming, the flowers are growing, time to enjoy life. If you can't enjoy the Earth in Summer then you will never appreciate its beauty. The crops are growing in the fields all life is in flower.

Our ancestors would have been able to see a crop start to grow in the field. This they knew would have fed them through Winter and, if enough rain fell, if the wind didn't blow too strong, if the Sun shone and the Moon did its magical work, they just might live through the coming Winter.

Beltene is the old Irish name for this Celtic fire festival, meaning bright fire. In many Celtic areas the home fire was put out, that had burned day and night for a year. Need fires (started by rubbing two sticks together) were then lit by the Druids on hill tops, and a fire brand was taken from the new fire to re-light the hearth and bring with it new luck. From hilltop to hilltop a spreading chain of need-fires crossed the Celtic world, on the night before Beltane. The fires protected the people from the otherworld, where lived the fairy folk, as on all Sabbats the dividing line between the words grows tenuous. In some areas two fires were lit sometimes with Juniper wood for purification and the cattle driven through to bring both fertility and luck. Many people choosing to walk between the fires the same reason, in the hope that they too will be fertile in both children and luck.

The Romans first celebrated perfume around BCE 750 in religious ceremonies to celebrate the Goddess of Flora. Each year the ceremonies would be held to celebrate the first flowers of the season. Later, the ceremony was held on April 28, four days before May Calend, this celebration was adopted by the British and added to the Celtic celebration to become May Day.

In Medieval England, the principle place to enjoy the only half remembered Pagan festivities, was in the Town Square or in the Churchyard much to the annoyance of the local church. Here the Chain dance (carol), or in Pagan parlance Spiral dance was performed, throughout the Summer months. These carols (sung at all times of the year not only Christmas) disturbed the solemn services, with songs and laughter drifting through the walls from the Churchyard beyond. Religious laws were passed in many diocese to ban carols and other 'dissolute games' and 'carols and lascivious songs which are sung in churchyards and open spaces of the churches' in 1213.

'Old wrinkled women, rummaged in their boxes for dancing cloths to lend to the young girls who had none; maidens painted their faces and wreathed garlands of flowers for their heads, the very devils trophies'.

The girls and the young men linked hands moving in a circle to the left. Of course all this noise and pleasure must be accounted for at the next confession, not only the 'sin of voice' but that of 'the sin of movement' and 'the sin of touching'(holding hands to you and I)!

How old the Spiral Dance is none can say. We do know that

singing and dancing together was performed in Anglo-Saxon times but whether this was our Spiral Dance or whether it originated in the Christian Middle ages, we may never know. But the Spiral dance it always enjoyed at all large Pagan gatherings throughout the year. The leader whether it be the High Priestess or High Priest takes the hand of the nearest person of the opposite sex. All join hands preferably alternating sexes and to the sound of music or chanting, a large circle is made. The circle spirals widdershins and inwards until it becomes quite tight but moveable, then the leader turns and unwinds the spiral now moving Sunwards to bring festivity into the lives of all taking part. From there the dance gets wilder weaving in an out and round and round, the people at the end working up quite a speed. Until all is finished with a shout of energy, sent off into you universe to perform a healing spell.

The God and Goddess wish us to contact "the child within" at this time of year. But not with deep and emotional rituals, but with fun and laughter, greening our faces, putting flowers in our hair, running through the fountain at the Pagan Pride Parade in London, England and being blessed by the water quarter. Join Pagan Pride days wherever you find one or start one.

Make wild and passionate love to your partner. In short **Bonk for Beltane!**

Traditionally girls and boys would go into the woods to collect Hawthorn blossoms or 'May' for the parades the following day and to bring fertility of the fields into the villages and towns. The Puritans on stopping the practice insisted the young girls were no longer maids on their return from the woods! Too much fertility it seems.

On May Eve, May Birching was performed, where a branch was fixed to the house of your neighbors. Which twig you left gave a comment on the householder. A flowering branch of Hawthorn, was a compliment and very nice to receive but to receive Briar (liar), Holly (folly), Plum (glum), was not such a nice compliment. A nut branch outside the door meant that the lady within was of a dubious reputation, other branches that you didn't want to receive were nettles, sloes, elder and crab-apple. Better were Lime (Prime) and Pear which meant fair. I wonder how many got up early and attached their own branches to the front of the house? Or replaced ones already there.

The God is symbolized by the Maypole in all its full glory, with dancers circling around, half going whiddershines and half diesiel the intertwining of life and death. When you pass a Maypole for the first time at Beltane, you must always bow, for good luck to follow you through the year. In the last century, if a young man didn't pay due respect to the Maypole the old men would 'remind' them, with a clout!

In days passed the May Queen was a maid chosen to represent the Goddess, her crowning and then parading through the streets with her retinue of Maids in attendance. This would have been followed later by a re-enactment of the wedding feast and wedding night of the God and Goddess!!

The energies of Beltane were so strong, even as late as WW1. A soldier in the trenches hearing a Beltane folk tune being played from his home town of Helston, where the famous "Furry Dance" is held, had to be dragged back from dancing in no-mans-land, between the two armies.

Witches ideally practice their rites on the night before May Day under the moon and stay until the Sun comes up. We welcoming it by blowing cow horns and drumming up the Sun. Which is when ordinary people come out of their houses to dance in the streets, around the Maypole and crown the May Queen. 'Obby 'Orses, Greenmen, Bogies (Greened Drummers) and Giants dance to the sound of folk music.

Within circle the Handfasting of Goddess and God is re-enacted by HP and HPs. All Handfastings (Witch Weddings) are done at this time. Coveners are handfasted on Beltane Night, and all friends during the month of May, although nowadays it also tumbles on into June as well. Jump the Bel fire for luck. If you are in the great outdoors, this should be a small fire, if inside a candle in a cauldron will suffice.

Perform the Great Rite.

Go to watch the sun come up on a special place with other Pagans, if there is no tradition like that near you - start one! All were started by one person once, don't think that you haven't been doing it long enough, you have been doing it longer than the next person to join you.

Everyone is always welcome at the Beltane Bash's Pagan Pride Parade in London!

Pagan Pride Parade walking through the streets of London

Green is said to be an unlucky color, another tall tale told by Christians to stop us dressing in green, being handfasted and dancing in the streets.

'Married in May, kirked (married) in green,

Bride and Bridegroom won't long be seen'

Christians spread the story that it was unlucky to wear green, a death would soon follow. This was thought of as the color of the fairy folk and they would be angered by the disrespect shown to them. Perhaps the church felt that if no one would wear green, the customs of Beltane would soon die out. Sadly for them and happily for us May Day goes from strength to strength in England with thousands all round the country parading through the streets and happily wearing green. And what of the fairies? Well they seem to love the Pagans, and Witches. The drumming, the laughter, the magic and wearing their color, give us good luck throughout the year. And who knows perhaps they are there within the crowd, laughing and singing with us.

Summer Solstice, Midsummer or Litha- The Sun at his height of it's power. As a tribute to the elemental quarters, leave milk, ginger and honey outside the circle. At North for the Gnomes or Elves, for the Fairies of the East and for the Undines West, and not forgetting a charcoal block or lump of coal in the South for the Fire Dragon, that the elementals can share with you the gaiety of the evening. For as in Shakespeare's play A Midsummer Nights Dream it is the Elementals special night. The ordinary folk were frightened of the world of magic so to keep the fairy folk away on this magical night, many hung magical plants over doors to stop fairy folk from popping in to wreak havoc. In 1598 the historian John Stow wrote of the sight in London:

'Every man's door was shaded with green birch, fennel, St. John's Wort, orpin, white lilies, and the like, ornamented with garlands of beautiful flowers. They...had also lamps of glass with oil burning in them all night; and some of them hung out branches of iron, curiously wrought, containing hundreds of lamps lighted at once, which made a splendid appearance.'

Although it makes me wonder whether the people weren't also carrying on the yet older Pagan tradition where big bonfires were lit to encouraging the Sun and Summer to last a little longer before its inevitable sink into Winter. By lighting many candles or fires, you encourage the Sun to shine brighter for a little longer, which is a good example of sympathetic magic. Rather than solely trying to keep fairies away.

Beating the bounds was performed during Medieval times, land owner or villages marked out the ground they owned by parading around with rough music, banging drums, cooking pot and anything else they could get their hands on. A poor luckless apprentice was chosen to walk or be dragged around the bound it was his job, rather then the rich land owner to be dragged through ponds, over houses and through holly bushes without which of course the true bounds were not beaten.

The Summer Solstice ritual requires all coveners to carry candles within the circle, chant or dance while circling, on stopping the HP extinguishes all candles one at a time. Explaining as he does that from this point the land will become darker and weaker until the Winter Solstice, when the Sun will turn and start to grow stronger once more. Leave a red candle burning (in a cauldron or somewhere safe) to remind the Sun to shine a little longer.

Well dressings are carried on throughout the Summer; although this is now thought of as a Christian ceremony, they were originally Pagan, in which the Water Spirit was honored and placated. If you do have a well in your village, it would be lovely to see this charming old Pagan custom resurrected.

Lammas or Lughnasadh-

Lughnasadh is the Celtic name for this time, a celebration of the God of light, Lugh. This was celebrated with games, contests, fairs and feasts.

Lammas the Anglo- Saxon name for this Festival means Loaf Mass, commemorating the first cut of the corn harvest, the new corn was made into bread and offered to the Gods.

Now the crop in the fields is turning to gold, ready for the harvest. The long hard work of the harvest is still to come but just to know that if all goes well, the harvest will stand high in the barns, was a great relief to all. So a little merriment is in order, a festival that celebrates our beloved beer and bread. As with the wine and sweet cakes, always a little sweetness with the practical to enhance our lives. "John Barley Corn" is a good song for this time.

The Corn Spirit dwelt in the fields as the corn was cut so the spirit retreated and continued to retreat into the last sheaf of corn. No one wanted to be the one to cut down this down. So the laborers would throw their sickles at the last sheaf; this would then grace the Harvest table, be hang in the home through Winter and reburied in the fields the in the coming year.

Beer was a staple drink in Medieval times, water was rarely good enough quality to drink. So water was sterilized by turning it to alcohol! Choose and then draw your chosen rune in the beer, in drinking, draw that power into your life. You could use the same idea with the bread if you prefer, mark it with a rune or pentagram in some way before eating. A wonderful easy bread to make at this time of year is-

Lammas Bread mix equal quantities of flour, dried milk, with a pinch of salt and a little good quality beer. Just enough to mix it without going sloppy, it will get hot under your hand (you are using your hands to mix aren't you). Roll small quantities into round rolls with floury hands and pat them flat. Bake the dough at 180 degrees for an hour or so according to size.

But with the first swish of the scythe comes the first touch of the Crone Goddess into the year.

Autumn Equinox or Mabon – The God in His prime, wise and at full maturity.

Harvest home, light candles circle and chant or dance, HP puts out half, so half of the circle is in darkness and half is in light, balance reigns once more at the equinox. Time for the Summer to rest, and so The Cornman or Berryman (Russell to His friends) is made, he is the golden Autumn version of the Greenman of Summer. Russell is made on the Fullmoon before the Autumn Equinox, tie twigs together in a rough human shape, cover in berries and corn, sometimes with us, it is only a token amount, living in the city this is not always easy. He attends the full moon ceremony and the Autumn Equinox ceremony, by then his leaves have turned golden and brown. At the end of the ritual he is burnt, while we chant goodbye to the Greenman. Summer must now rest to come again.

All would now know in days passed, if all their hard work had come to fruition and if there is enough food that they may live through the coming winter. Even today there could be a world wide famine. In the past a meteor has hit our planet, throwing up great clouds of black dust blotting out the sky or some other devastating disaster. We take

"Russell" The Cornman

food too much for granted in today's easy come society, expecting it always to be there, moaning if we can't find mushrooms due to late delivery. So a thank you isn't perhaps, too much to ask.

It is the time of death of the crops, the cutting down of the harvest, the gathering. Now is the time to say good bye to Summer, to allow it to rest, before returning in its full vigor!

A Chant at this time of year might be

Greenman come, Cornman go,
The Sun shone bright upon your face
Greenman, Greenman,
Now it is time for you to leave,
Cornman, Cornman.
(Repeat as many times as necessary.)

As the Sun shrinks in the sky, it finishes the time of initiation.

The Wheel of the Year

Sacrifice &birth of the God
Three aspects of the Goddess

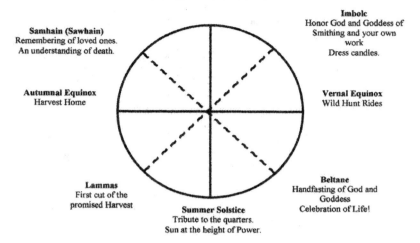

Imbolc
Honor God and Goddess of
Smithing and your own
work
Dress candles.

Samhain (Sawhain)
Remembering of loved ones.
An understanding of death.

Autumnal Equinox
Harvest Home

Vernal Equinox
Wild Hunt Rides

Lammas
First cut of the
promised Harvest

Summer Solstice
Tribute to the quarters.
Sun at the height of Power.

Beltane
Handfasting of God and
Goddess
Celebration of Life!

Greater Sabbats ~ ~ ~ ~ ~ ~ ~

Lesser Sabbats _____

Southern Hemisphere

Of course if you are working in the Southern Hemisphere the dates of the Sabbats must be changed around, as the wheel of the year circles differently. Halloween and the New Year will fall on our Beltane as the Southern Hemisphere closes down for winter. The dates change but the name of the Sabbat remains. In the Southern Hemisphere, Halloween is celebrated on 30th April. The same with the elemental Quarters; Fire is changed to the north, as the equator is above you, Earth is to the south as the land of ice and snow now lies in this direction. Cast your circle, the direction in which the bath water circles when the bath plug is pulled. I do understand this causes a problem for those on the equator.

What Are Giants?

Traditionally made of woven wicker, the giants and giantesses were

155

seen in medieval times at all festivals particularly in the Summer months and in all towns through out the country. It is a tradition that is I am happy to say, like Witchcraft, is returning. In Europe, with which we shared the hobby of gianting, its popularity never diminished, and is as admired today as in medieval times. I have always been interested in folk customs and in visiting stone circles. So when I got a chance to help in a folk parade, it seemed like a good idea at the time.

A giant is a large person, our own is 15 feet tall and carried by only one porter. When we decided to build one, there was no choice really; it had to be The Morrigan. Traditionally The Morrigan is thought of as a Celtic Warrior Goddess but for us She is so much more. Our Giant always wears black, except when she walks in the Pagan Pride Parade that precedes Beltane Bash festival, when she wears green to welcome Summer. After all, a girl can't have only one dress, Goddess or not. She has now been joined by two ravens, which stand 8 feet high.

Gianting is a very old pastime in this country and in fact in all the Celtic countries. In Europe giants are paid for by the towns themselves and are budgeted for with in the towns tax bill. Everyone within the town then feels a pride of ownership, as if they are their own personal giants. They are cheered through the streets, as the giants parade noblely past, as they would have been in England so many years ago.

No one has any idea at what date gianting started; Caesar speaks of the Celts burning Wickermen with people inside. It is commonly believed that Caesar was demonizing the Druids by writing of human sacrifice and it is always the victor's stories that are remembered. But could it have been the ancestors of our giants that processed to the spot where torches were then thrown, making it look as if the person inside had gone up in flames? When in fact, twelve people approached the giant and thirteen came away, an old stage magic trick?

Gianting remained popular in England down through the

centuries. Gogmagog the Giant of London, needed to bow to the King outside the walls of London, before the King was allowed to enter the city. During the Civil War, the female fish gutters of East London carried their Warrior Goddess Belona, who was wife to Mars (not unlike The Morrigan), to repair the walls of London.

Our Giantess The Morrigan, out for a walk in at The Pagan Pride Parade

Both Henry V111, thinking Gianting Catholic and the Puritans banned gianting as too much fun. There are only a few descriptions of giants in England in the whole of medieval history. In Salisbury Museum is a repair bill dating to the 1600's for their giant St Christopher, and passing references in Medieval manuscripts to "and there were giants", add a little more to our knowledge. So popular were Giants and so well known, dancing on every High Street in England and every festival, that it was thought too common place to write of, for so large and public a performance.

Many point to the fact that witchcraft has so little references other than the trials of witches, but gianting through the streets has so few references, for such a public display. If it had been a secret practice, like witchcraft, we would have never known it existed.

Exercise-

Look at the fields and watch the changing year, see how the Goddess and God relate to the seasons and how they relate to you. Begin in the simplest ways at first to mark the Sabbats.

What Sabbat is it?

How is it celebrated?

What signifies this time of year for you?

Turn off the Telly (you would be surprised at the amount of people that tell me they can do an entire ritual in the commercial break!)

Place a simple cloth over a coffee table or sideboard and place something that symbolizes this time of year on it.

Call the God and Goddess to be with you.

Do a meditation.

Thank the God and Goddess for being with you.

You have done your fist simple Sabbat.

CHAPTER 6

How a Witchcraft Circle Works

Sabbats- the Wheel of the Year and Esbats- spell work, are rituals carried out within a witchcraft circle. In fact, most Witchcraft work is done within ritual; nothing can harm you within circle. Within circle, you delve deep into the unknown and energies of the Universe. But it is no more alien than watching an apple fall to Earth. Both use the laws of nature. The gentle arms of the Goddess and God will guide you through.

There are many levels to a witchcraft circle; it will take you a long time to find your way through. Some of the earliest will be a light hypnotic trance but as your mind gets used to the freedom within the circle it will allow you to travel deeper. Don't think that by having been in a circle that you have felt the magic of witchcraft. It can take many years to develop.

A witchcraft circle takes you outside of time and place, but how?

By changing your consciousness, by a form of self-hypnosis.

The repeating of phrases, the circling, the candle flames flickering and the chanting, will change your perception of reality.

Or does it actually change reality?

Does it "Take us outside of time and place"?

For me it does.

First, we need to look at power, how to find it, how to manipulate it and how to cut our circle out of this realm of existence.

By each of the steps taken to create a circle, it helps you to reach down into the core of your being, to find the power that will take you outside of time and place. The energy that you use to build circle, lays deep within us all. It is an old energy, in some ways a primitive and primal energy, for many long forgotten. You need to reach deep into your very spirit to find its home. Practice this first, before you are ready to start your circle. Once you begin to use this power you will find it will flow more easily and steadily.

Take a bowl of water and with your finger or Athame if you have one, practice channeling power down your finger or blade into the water. You will feel silly at first, but hopefully after a few attempts you will begin to feel the power flow. When you are finished pour the water on your plants to give your energy back to the living universe rather than just throwing it down the sink, it is now Holy water. Water blessed by a Witch is as holy as any water blessed by a Christian priest, just dedicated to a different deity.

Don't expect the power to manifest on your first circle, it will take time. Even if you have found the power within yourself, when you are working with others it will take a while for you all to blend together, to build a group mind.

To call the Quarters to your circle or to perform any part of a ritual be confident. If you forget your words make them up or say them from the heart. Never apologize to your friends or to the Gods, this will break the concentration of yourself or anyone that you may be working with. Your part within circle must be second nature, thinking destroys magic, and it keeps you anchored to this reality. The more you think about other things, "I wish I was as slim as her", the more you lose concentration, stay focused. It is the energy that you raise that is important not the words themselves. I can not emphasis this enough, hold the magic. Do not be embarrassed about chanting or saying words to your sitting room wall. See through this reality into the realms of Fay, to the lands where the Elemental Quarters live. Thinking and analyzing is for before and after the circle activity, allow your mind full range during circle, we are not used to doing this and it can be quite hard at first. From childhood we are taught to put limits on our imagination, to eradicate our ability to see through reality to other planes of existence to awaken this skill can be hard at first. Now I am asking you to take the blinkers off, to look into the many worlds in all their full glory, to be found within the circle.

Magic DOES happen in circle. Time warps, a short time in circle can be two hours in reality, it touches the land of Fay and so as in old stories of the fairy folk, time has no meaning.

Visualization that we have been practicing over the weeks now comes to the fore; to visualize is not to "make things up" but to see with your third eye the truth that can be hidden by the mundane world.

Never kneel in circle but stand straight and tall with your hands held up high to your Goddess, who took you from the animals and raised you to a thinking being, standing on two feet. It gives Her no pleasure to see us groveling on the ground once more. The Goddesses and Gods are honored friends that you invite into your circle; neither demand Their presence nor fall on your knees to Them. Although They are a higher intelligence than us, They are still equals and should be treated like a revered Grandmother and Grandfather. Hold your hands high to your Great Mother, as any child would. Some times the treatment that you receive from Them is like Granny waving Her finger to a small child, other times it is just the whispering of a friend in the dark.

Hair should always be unbound, to symbolize freedom, if possible left to grow long, although this can be difficult with some jobs, some employers taking the symbol of freedom and interpreting it as a symbol of aggression and anarchy.

The words that you see at the end of this chapter are not the words that we use, but an idea to inspire you, please feel free to alter them in anyway that feels right to you. Hopefully in a year or two you will have written your own wording with real meaning just for you. For it's not the words that cast a circle and do magic, but the energy you produce and use, that causes the changes to take place. If you know a circle casting use it, feel free to use any ritual it is as valid as any other, make sure that the energy is right. Throw the force down the blade, zap the water when purifying the elements. It doesn't matter one iota if you don't kneel when blessing the wine, what does matter, however is the force concentrated down the blade of your Athame. Sit and write the words yourself, make them up as you go along, which ever seems right to you. You will not be blasted where you stand by the Gods.

What do I mean by zap down your athame? First you start by visualization, imagine energy coursing down the blade of the sword to cast circle; here visualize a pale blue or white light leaving a trail behind you. Next, feel your energy flow down your body through the blade and out of the tip, see it leaving a trail behind you as you walk around the circle. Practice holding your Athame in front of you not pointing at anyone of course, now project your energy through it and out like a light saber, swish it around you, if it helps visualize the color and noise of a saber made of light. Can anyone do this? Some people have more ability than others do, but most children learn to speak, some may learn quickly and others take their time, but at the end of the day most communicate and so with magic, you can do it if you have patience. Producing energy is probably the most important lesson in magic; in fact I would go so far as to say it is the essence of magic. Once you have learnt how to produce this energy, you can do everything you need to with it, cast circle, bless wine, and cast spells. When you produce the energy from your body, like electricity it is a raw energy. You can cast circle with out an Athame or sword; but these tools modify the energy emanating from your body changing it to suit the job you wish it to do, before that the energy is basic, uncontrolled, unrefined. Remember to let the pommel have contact with your hand, when holding the Athame. This allows the magic to flow the length of the Athame along the tang, which is part of the blade that runs through the handle and screws into the Pommel. If making an Athame yourself make sure that you place no insolating substance to block the flow of magic.

Whether you use Wiccan colors for your candles, or the colors from this book, whether you use music in your ritual or not, is unimportant: learn to use the energy from within.

A circle is never left lightly; there are some instances, during a Handfasting or initiation when it is done (but otherwise pee in the cauldron!). To cut a door in the circle for only such instances, take your Athame and by cutting around three times widdershins, make a person size door. In the same way as a stage magician places a patch of sticky-tape onto a balloon and then sticks a pin into the balloon without it going POP. This is the principle behind cutting a door in a circle. Have a Guardian of the door standing in the space with athame drawn or two priests with staffs crossed, or if alone in the circle close the door behind. To do this, redraw the door three times diesiel; never leave an unguarded porthole between the worlds.

If at anytime " Blessed be" is said by anyone within circle, the reply should always be 'Blessed be' twice in our traditional circle, as many things are done a total of three times within circle, three being a magical number. In all branches of Witchcraft 'Blessed be' is used both as a greeting and a farewell. In our tradition of Witchcraft it refers to the Medieval use as a greeting, with the reply "and with you sister (or brother)", although as with Wicca in modern times witches normally just repeat "Blessed be".

'Blessed be' is said only once in a Wiccan circle, this is a short hand for a Wiccan blessing

"Blessed be thy feet, that have brought thee in these ways".
At farewells, just BB is said for a type of short hand.

A ritual consist of three parts, Setting circle- Content- Closing circle.

A circle takes two-hours approximately to complete, don't rush it, take your time, slow and formal or fast and happy, but never rushed.

Below is a description of how to raise the energy of a circle. I have also added an explanation of the moves we make. If you do not feel comfortable with any, then change them.

Prepare
*Sweep the area to be used to cast circle with the besom (you could if you choose run the vacuum cleaner over the area too first). This not

only cleans the area physically but also by projecting your energies down the besom sweeps all psychic clutter too.

*Turn off all mobile phones; remove watches and any unconsecrated jewelry except handfasting rings that are of course consecrated or wedding rings, which you can consecrate at an Esbat if you choose.

*Change into robes; these you will need at all private events in your new Pagan life. Many Covens ask that robes be black as is traditional, for in the past, to quickly hide at the base of a tree when danger threatens, was to 'vanish' completely from sight. I say traditional but many a modern witch working on land that they don't own have 'vanished' with this trick.

*White cord around your waist, this you will use to link together in the chant.

Stand man, woman around the circle with High Priestess and High Priest in the South facing North.

*We set our altar in the center of the circle; the center is most sacred part of the circle. This then favors no one within the circle; all stand equal before the Goddess.

*Light the white Spirit candle, this represents your God and Goddess. The Spirit candle stands in the center of your altar, which is in the center of your circle, the sacred heart of the circle.

*Light the charcoal block and place a ½ a teaspoon of incense on to the charcoal block, refill as necessary through out, especially at the blessing of Air.

*For some, the start of the circle it is pulling on his robe with the smells of previous Sabbats, for me it is the smell of lighting the charcoal blocks that signals the start of ritual. We use many different incenses at fullmoons and Sabbats but only the charcoal blocks remain a constant smell.

*While setting the circle it becomes good practice to walk diesiel, at all times, I know it can be a pain if you have forgotten something and need to go all round the circle again. But ritual needs to be done ritually with no short cuts.

Meditation This takes place before any circle; it enables you to focus getting you in the right mood for what is to follow. How long is up to you, long enough to rid yourself of the cares of the day, short enough so that you don't fall asleep after a long hard day, 5 or 10 min should be ample.

Welcoming of the circle A short speech that triggers the subconscious that circle is starting now!

Casting Circle Ask a group of people to hold hands and you have a circle, not a square or a triangle. It is possibly the most basic shape that can be visualized.

If this was Ceremonial Magic, the circle would protect you from what was to be called, either Angels or Devils but they are called into a triangle set outside the circle. There is nothing evil called outside a witchcraft circle and so protection isn't a problem, although as with a Ceremonial Magic Circle, it does protect all within. The witchcraft circle is designed to concentrate the magic that is raised by the Witch. To step over the line where the circle is cast is to break the circle, if you do this dissipates the magic. So mark this line with a white cord, as big as you have room. In some forms of Witchcraft the Boline is pushed into the earth and a nine-foot white cord with a loop on the end is dropped over and the Witch walks round marking out an eighteen-foot circle. Nice if you have room, but not to worry, the magic will still work whatever size the circle needs to be. If you were walk through the boundary of the circle, like a burst bubble it disappears.

With the candles standing on the altar, your concentration is centered down towards the altar, rather than out toward the walls of your Living room, as it would be if placed on the edge of the circle. As circle is cast, even if like ours the white rope tends to be more of an oval than a circle, it will automatically form a circle on the magical plane, even if it be through the walls and into your kitchen. The room beyond the circle fades, you are out side of time and space. It does not matter, in some ways, whether you are out in the forest or inside in your living room, it is the space within the circle that is important. Walls and pictures diminish into insignificance, they become items that you look through not at. We always spoke about having banners to put up at the quarters to hide our pictures during ritual but over the many years this has become less and less important.

Having said that, when in the forest, we place the candles (being practical now you will need lanterns to hold the candles or tall glasses to be sure that they aren't blown our by the wind) out at the circle's edge, with a bonfire replacing the spirit candle. This being so much brighter, it illuminates the underside of the trees vaulting over our heads like the flying buttresses of a Medieval Cathedral. The forest does participate in your ritual more than your Sitting room does, it draws the animals and fairy folk to it, that abound in the wood. You can always hear animals moving about just outside the circle of light, we have had Owls fly over our circle as if they were taking a look at the proceedings. Eyes watch you from the shadows, but this is nothing to worry about, the animals are just curious and the fairy folk have come to share the magic. One hot summers night we had cast circle in our sitting room, when the door burst open and in came a hedgehog from the garden. On seeing so many faces he suddenly got scared and bolted for the corner, after circle we put him outside.

How to Cast a Circle-
The Sword in the Scabbard is offered to the High Priestess by the Guardian of East on one knee, this is not done subserviently but knightly, hence better done by a man. We have over the years tried this role with a priestess but for me it never felt right. The High Priestess takes the sword and proffers the sword hilt to the High Priest, and he draws it from the scabbard and proceeds to cast circle with it. This again is representative of fertility and the union of God and Goddess. If there are at least two of you the Priestess holds the Scabbard in front of her, this represents the womb of the Goddess. The High Priestess is the holder of the magic, while the High Priest is the Circle Guardian. So she gives him the magic and permission to cast circle, by passing him the sword. The High Priest then walks around diesiel (clockwise) three times casting circle. From now until

the close of circle the sword belongs to the High Priest in a purely symbolic representation of being the circle guardian. There are certain times when a High Priestess takes the sword during male initiations for instance, when the new priest is asked to place his hand on the blade and swear allegiance to the Goddess and God pledging his commitment to the coven.

With each cast the High Priest says one line of the words, one cast for each phase of the Goddess, Maiden, Mother and lastly Crone, many things in a witchcraft circle are done in threes. With each cast he strengthens further the circle bounds. If there is only one person, then there is no choice and of course you will have to cast circle alone.

Walking round three times to cast a circle with a sword used only for magic, is a very old practice and was documented by Theophrastus in BCE 230 in Ancient Greece and may of course go farther back still.

An Athame replaces a sword in a non-coven situation; but don't think that you must have an Athame to cast circle. An Athame enhances the magic that is produced from your body, it does not produce it in itself, use your first finger right hand or your left hand if this is your leading hand. If you are not sure which is your leading hand get someone to throw you a ball; the hand that you catch it with is your leading hand. Visualize a white light emanating from your index finger or athame but not only see, feel it running through you. Point your athame or sword, at the ground and walk around the circle. See the light left behind as a white fiery trail of power, cutting you off from the mundane world of everyday living. This will not happen on your first attempt but it will happen with practice.

How to Raise the Cone of Power (these words have a slightly different meaning in Wicca)- This lifts the cast circle to form the bubble or cone of magic, it also serves to bind all present into a cohesive whole.

Feel the Earth beneath your feet, and either lift the Earth energy by placing your hands on the floor and slowly standing, drawing the energy of the Earth up, as you stand. Or the Coven can all take hands, still standing reach down into the Earth through your feet, as before allow it to run up through your body, feeling the energy of the Earth Goddess pass through you.

In both cases ask Her for Earth energy, it will be freely given, allow it to heal you, energize you, and balance you as it passes through your body.

At first you may be just raising your hands as you visualize the Cone of Power lifting the circle higher and higher. But as time goes on you will begin to feel a circle of power rise up your body. It feels like climbing down the steps of a swimming pool, as the cold water rises up your body, taking away your breath as it gets higher. At first you may feel just a slight tingle but slowly it will become more intense, until it is breath taking in its power.

Pentagram of Protection This announces to the Astral plane that a circle is being cast, a pentagram also adds to the protection. Once more focus power down the blade; see the pentagram form before your eyes. Visualize this in light much like a sparkler on Bonfire

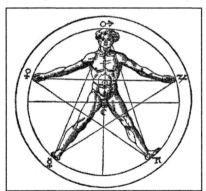

night, but a white light rather than red, allow it to hang in the air much as the sparkler's light does. When drawing your pentagram in the air or above the elements; think of Agrippa of Nettesheim's famous pentagram with a man standing inside.

Start at the top (or head) of the pentagram, draw a line to the bottom left corner (right foot), then follow up to the side right (left hand), from there across to the side left (right hand), down to the bottom right (left foot) and up to the top (head) again, sealing the pentagram closed.

The words I have underlined below are the attributes of the quarters and are there to emphasize the power each quarter brings to the circle as well as forming the Pentagram of protection.

When magic is performed it leaves a mark on the Astral plane, by drawing the pentagram it forms a gate that no trouble-making entity can pass through, although this does not form a barrier for your Gods and Goddesses. We never remove this pentagram in our home or in the circle that we use in our wood, it forms a patch over the hole made by magic. When, however, we wish to move, it is a time to clean house. It is polite to remove all traces of magic from houses and areas that you have worked magic in, before leaving. You don't want the people moving in to your old house having problems of a magical kind, due to your incompetence and disrespect by not tidying up after yourself.

Calling Elemental Quarters In calling the Elemental Quarters, you bring four extra coven members to the circle. So even a Hedgewitch has a coven of seven, you, Earth, Air, Fire, Water Elementals, God and not forgetting the most important the Goddess.

In our tradition, within circle we use the wand to call our guardians much as you would wave to a friend. It sends a beam of light through to the Astral plane and alerts the elemental that you have been working with, that a circle has been cast and their presence is needed. I carefully do not say requested, as once a mutual bond has been established they will find it impossible to deny your call. The act of then lighting the candle holds them transfixed, much as a candle transfixes a moth "Aha, pretty". Until you finish the circle, put out the candle and release them.

When working in your own circles you will have befriended your own quarter guardians by doing the visualizations in an earlier chapter. Now is the time to see you're new found friends, visualize them standing or sitting at your quarter positions, just out side the circles edge. If at any time you are given a name of an Elemental, then of course add that to your quarter calling.

You will note a dynamic increase in the heat within the circle once the candles are lit, far exceeding that of five small candles, because you now have a sealed space it holds onto the heat put out by the candles, until the moment the circle is cut.

Purification of the Elements As we may use the representation of the elements on our Altar to cast spells or for other uses in the ritual, all undesired vibrations must be driven out.

For this you use your Athame, draw a pentagram over each element in turn- the Salt, Incense, Candle Flame and Water, as you say your words and then with a sharp burst of energy down the blade and into the element, project all your will power to blast it clean.

Chant Waist cords are removed and linked in the center to physically and mentally link us. The chant is built slowly from almost a whisper to crescendo, whilst circling the timing of the steps matching the volume of the voice, the louder the chant the faster around you move. Remember that you are trying to blend as one, so therefore no one should be trying to out sing anyone else! It does not matter if you can't sing. I can't. It does however matter if you don't join in! I will never criticize anyone for their voice but I will if they don't sing. If you were in our coven, you would be on brass cleaning duty at the next teaching night, for not singing! The chant is both unifying and a hypnotic aid, deep breathing needed to sing, hyperventilates you. Coupled with repetitive words and the pace speeding faster and faster spiraling you down into another level of consciousness.

With this the circle is cast

Anoint The anointing, with a combination of sacred oils is a very special time; Kings and Queens are anointed at their coronation, it is as important as placing the crown upon a monarch's head.

To be anointed is an acceptance of your right to be within that witchcraft circle and as a blessing of the Goddess. This is done as a pentagram on the forehead, one dot on each wrist and one on each foot in temple (or Covenstead which is where the coven meets) as shoes and socks are banned. If working outside you may choose to keep shoes or sandals on, in which case if you can't see the feet you can't dab them with anointing oil. Don't worry.

Call down the Moon and/or Sun In our tradition we refer to the whole of this part of the circle, as a Calling Down of the Moon/Sun, rather than in Wiccan- Calling Down of the Moon/Sun and then Charge of the Goddess/God.

The High Priest will say the words to invite the Goddess to speak through the High Priestess or Call Down the Moon Goddess (or High Priestess Call Down the Sun into High Priest) to enter her. If this is a coven working, the calling down will be tried by all, at different times in training. The reason for repeating the phases of the Goddess, Maiden, Mother and Crone is not only to remind us of them but to keep grounded all those who are not having a deity called into them. The more often it has been tried, the easier it is to touch the divine. Not that this stops communication with the God or Goddess by other members of the coven during this time, and all thoughts, feelings and apparitions seen are discussed during the wine and cakes. Sometimes the Calling Down is shared between more than one, the three Goddesses or a Dark and Light God.

In a Wiccan circle, the beautiful Charge of the Goddess by Doreen Valiente is read, in our tradition it takes the form of an Oracle or channeling of the Goddess. This is a communication between the High Priestess and the Goddess (or High Priest and God). The Goddess using with permission from the HPs, her body to speak to those in attendance at the circle. Possession sounds a very frightening word but in fact it is more difficult to hold on to the Goddess and to repeat the words heard in your head than it is to let her slip away. Open your spirit and allow the Goddess (or if you are a man the God) to enter you, you may not know how to do this but they do, don't worry! No harm will come to you, if you are of sound mind. Please do not attempt this if you are very young, depressed or on tablets for any form of mental illness. Just start by repeating everything that comes into your mind, do not censor it in any way, nor think about what you might say before hand. At first it will be your own thoughts, with practice you will find messages coming through. Do not attempt to manipulate the Goddess' words to get people to do what you want, I have seen this in circle and believe me it stands out a mile. If you get no words be brave enough to say so. Sometimes I have said what seems nonsense to me, only to find after circle that it was answers to questions being silently asked by a covener. If I had changed the words because I did not understand what was being said, I would have inadvertently changed or censored the Goddess's reply. If you start a story this can be very disconcerting but can come as a revaluation when the Goddess has a very interesting allegorical point to make and you had no idea where the story was leading. I have been known to speak long poems, under the influence of the Goddess, deep and meaningful, far better than my poor rhymes here. But they are never remembered after circle, what little is remembered is written down. The Goddess has been known to tell of things to come and warn of danger but like the Sybil's prophesies it is very difficult to know what She refers to; until after the event.

Call God or Goddess to circle *The deity that has not been called is invited to join us.*

If you have called down the Moon, then invite the God to also join you.

If you have called down the Sun, then invite the Goddess to also join you.

At Beltane and Yule both the God and Goddess are invited to attend and speak through the HPs and HP.

Now you are ready to perform the content of the ritual
SABBAT – Celebrate seasons changing.
or
ESBAT (Fullmoon) – Spells
If an Esbat and a Sabbat fall on the same night, do both, spells and a celebration of the season.

Blessing of the Wine (RED) or Mead- The red wine represents love and laughter and the Goddess's menstrual blood. Mead is one of the oldest alcoholic drinks known to mankind and the honey that it is made from a product of the bees sacred to many Goddesses. The blessing has been a feature of Pagan rituals from the invention of wine and in no way is it a copy or a perversion of the Christian mass. It is far older than Christianity and was used in rituals for Apollo the Sun God, Mithras and many others far back in time.

The High Priest kneels on one knee before the High Priestess and holds the chalice up for the blessing; the High Priestess stands and places the Athame into the chalice, channels energy down the blade, from the God and Goddess, while repeating the wording. This is a fertility religion and the Athame dipped into the Chalice represents the union of God and Goddess, so whenever possible this should be enacted by a handfasted couple.

The Chalice is then passed around the coven with a kiss and a "Blessed Be"; it is not always possible to sit man, woman, man, so ladies if they are sitting next to each other, peck on the cheek and men- I'll leave that for you to workout.

A little wine is always left, this can be refilled but the chalice can never be drunk dry.

A Smith (or if the wine is homemade) if present in circle, he or she must always drink from the chalice first.

In times past the Smith would have been responsible for brewing both beer and wine. Each festival would have had a separate brew, this is at last is returning, at our local pub you can buy Rudolph Bitter at Yule (yes, it is red) and Witches Bitter Brew at Halloween. By drinking first, this ensured that the magic the Smith placed into the beer, different for each festival, was for the benefit of the community and on a more prosaic note that the beer or wine was not poisoned and that the wine was to a high standard.

Blessing of the Cakes High Priest places hand over cakes and repeats his words, sending his energy down though his arm and into the cakes. This is done standing or with the High Priestess kneeling.

Blessing of the Wine

To close circle

Now you begin to close circle, disassemble what you have so carefully assembled. As you built your cake, layer by layer now carefully take it down. As each layer is removed visualize yourself slowly floating down to Earth.

Thank Goddess by HP

Thank God by HPs

Thank Quarters Said by Quarter Guardians, as in the calling, visualize them leaving, always be careful to dismiss quarters thoroughly, especially Fire!

Cut Circle Once more the Sword and scabbard is picked up by the priest and passed to the HPs, holding the scabbard she proffers the hilt to the HP, as before. He draws the sword from the Scabbard, lifts it high, bursting the energy bubble created by the casting of the circle, drawing the sword down and dragging it across the circle boundary, returning the sword to the scabbard, held by the HPs.

With the last sweep of the sword all remaining energy is grounded. You can be tired from working all day but circle lifts you, giving you energy. You feel replenished and exhilarated when circle closes, but not high. If you still feel heady or dizzy in any way, place your hands on the Earth and send any remaining energy into the Earth or you will not be able to sleep that night.

This rite is done.

Place wine and cakes on the earth.
If this is a Sabbat, then all feast together.

What is The Great Rite?

Witchcraft is a fertility religion and The Great Rite expresses this, it is the sexual union of the Goddess and God, a joining, a holy wedding. The Great Rite has been conducted in Pagan rituals for thousands of years and was originally called Hieros Gamos; it was first recorded in early Sumeria, about 5500 years ago. Pagans do not see making love as evil, this once more is due to Christian influence. We feel that the joy of making love is a direct gift from the Gods and so must be thought of as a holy act.

It is performed at Samhain to represent the birth of the New Year, at Beltane to represent the marriage of God and Goddess and for some spells.

The Great Rite can be enacted in two ways, in actuality with a priest representing the God and a priestess representing the Goddess and is ritual sexual intercourse or in representation. Blessing of the wine with its union of the chalice and athame and withdrawing and replacing the sword in the scabbard as circle is cast, at every Witch ritual can also represent The Great Rite.

With us, in a coven situation, a handfasted HP and HPs would perform The Great Rite, or possibly all handfasted couples, after the ritual had ended in their own beds or under the moon if they were feeling adventurous! If working as a couple alone, The Great Rite is best performed in a cast circle, as part of the ritual. At the climax of the Great Rite the energy raised is given to the Gods or as with a calling down of the Sun or Moon open yourself to allow the Goddess or God, according to gender, to enter you. You are therefore making love to a God or Goddess.

Whether you choose to do The Great Rite in its fullest meaning, is of course up to you but within every circle it is done in representation.

Group Workings

If you stand alone within a circle, you must produce all of the energy that is being used. If on the other hand you stand in a coven or group, not only must you produce the energy but blend it into a harmonious whole. This allows, when in circle or spell work is to be done, everyone to operate as a single unit. Blending as a coven happens in ritual, but also when the coven socializes becoming close and good friends. When coveners begin to understand each other without the use of words, every piece of energy is concentration on the spell. Try to feel the energy being produced by other members of the group.

Raising the Cone of Power described above is a very good exercise for this, try practicing this frequently.

In group workings try to give everyone a role to play, not only because it shares the load for one person to learn, but also ensures that everyone feel involved. This again helps to blend all into a whole unit. The sum of the whole is greater than the individuals within. When all have reached initiation, this is a very powerful entity, enabling concentration on deep magics.

Always remember that the job of the HP and HPs is to encourage the quieter members of the group and to blend the noisy ones, whilst keeping everyone's individuality and building strength in all. It is not your job to shine the brightest but to bring everyone within the coven up to your strength, and beyond.

These are some suggested words change them in any way you see fit.

The Exercise at the end of the chapter is a simplified ritual, if you feel that the one below is too complicated for a first attempt, you should work towards this ritual as and when you feel ready.

Esbat and Sabbat Ritual for one person

Learn a little at a time, or write down the order of the ritual creating the words as you go along. It does not matter; it is the energy that you generate that is important. The more layers your cake has, the stronger magic you create but feel free to start simply and build your cake as and when you feel confident.

Sweep the circle with the besom, visualizing sweeping all evil from the area.

Lay out white boundary cord

Buckle or tie on your belt, on which hangs your Athame, if you have one.

Ladies place on your beads, a symbol of eternity and your connection to the Goddess.

Light spirit candle

Place incense on the charcoal block.

Meditate to clear the mind and prepare for the ritual.
 Opening of the circle
Stand with hands raised
"Goddess of the Magical shimmering Silver Moon,
God of the Powerful burnished Golden Sun,
Cast your circle of protection about this seeker after wisdom,
Hold me in your gentle arms,
Guide me on my path."

Cast circle with the Athame (clockwise three times)
 1st circle

"I cast this circle around me in purification and in the name of
the Virgin Goddess.

2nd circle

I cast this circle around me in love and in the name of the Mother
Goddess.

3rd circle

I cast this circle around me in protection and in the name of the
Crone Goddess.
In the three names of the Goddess the circle is made!"

Replace Athame into your scabbard, on your belt.
Draw up the Cone of Power, raise hands as you draw the power
higher.

"Reach down into the earth, through the many layers,
Down, Down to the earth's core,
The ever spinning, ever beating heart of the Earth Goddess,
Draw upon her power, draw it higher,

Up, up through the very earth itself
As you draw it through you,
Allow it to heal you, allow it to balance you, allow it to empower
you.
Higher and higher, until..... completion."

Draw a pentagram in the air, in the North and with every stroke say forcefully

"I call upon that powers that bide,
Beyond the veil to be my guide.
Of Earth, <u>silent</u> with no word I speak,
By Air, <u>know</u>ledge forever I will seek.
By Fire, my <u>will</u> I hone that I may dare,
By Water, with tears of joy I <u>care.</u>
(After, still with your Athame pointed at North say)
By the pentagram that shineth bright,
I form this a shield in the darkest night.
Blessed Be!   Blessed Be! Blessed Be!"

Stand facing north and holding your wand out before you.
North

"I call to my Elemental of Earth,
Come from the glittering ice caves and enchanted forests of the
North,
Guard this place set outside of time.
Your primal power, I invoke to aid this ritual,
Come share this special time with me.
Guard this circle invoked in the names of the Old Gods
   (When you know the names of your Goddess and God insert them here).
 Blessed Be!   Blessed Be! Blessed Be!

Light the brown candle on the altar, and say

Hail and Welcome!"
Stand East and holding your wand out before you.

"I call to my Elemental of Air,
Come from the perfumed and mystical East,
Guard this place set outside of time.
Your primal power, I invoke to aid this ritual,
Come share this special time with me.
Guard this circle invoked in the names of the Old Gods
    (when you know the names of your Goddess and God insert
them here).
Blessed Be! Blessed Be! Blessed Be!
Light the blue candle on the altar, and say
Hail and Welcome!"

Stand facing South and holding your wand out before you.

"I call to my Elemental of Fire,
Come from the heat and deserts of the South,
Guard this place set outside of time.
Your primal power, I invoke to aid this ritual,
Come share this special time with me.
Guard this circle invoked in the names of the Old Gods
    (when you know the names of your Goddess and God insert
them here).
Blessed Be! Blessed Be! Blessed Be!
Light the red candle on the altar, turn and say
Hail and Welcome!"

Stand facing West and holding your wand out before you.

"I call to my Elemental of Water,

Come from the primal waters of the West,
Guard this place set outside of time.
Your primal power, I invoke to aid this ritual,
Come share this special time with me.
Guard this circle invoked in the names of the Old Gods
(when you know the names of your Goddess and God insert them here).
Blessed Be! Blessed Be! Blessed Be!

Light the green candle on the altar, turn and say

Hail and Welcome!"

Purification of the Elements
Earth
Draw the sign of the pentagram over the salt, with your Athame.

"Out of thee, goes all that is impure,
May only the might of the Great Mother remain."

Air
Place more incense on the charcoal,
Draw the sign of the pentagram over the incense, with your Athame.

"Out of thee, goes all that is impure,
May only the might of the Great Mother remain."

Fire
Draw the sign of the pentagram over the red candle, with your Athame.
"Out of thee, goes all that is impure,
May only the might of the Great Mother remain."

Water

Draw the sign of the pentagram over the water, with your Athame.

"Out of thee, goes all that is impure,
May only the might of the Great Mother remain."

Chant nine times whilst circling

"Lady Dark, Lady strong
Queen of Wisdom hear my song,
We (you, the four quarters, Goddess and God, see there is already seven of you with in the circle) *are gathered here to night,*
Within your circle in your sight."
Or chant your favorite Pagan chant or write one.

Anoint on the third eye (forehead) the two wrists and feet.
I consecrate on the third eye, (Drew pentagram on forehead)
"May the Goddess (or your Goddess' name)
Enhance my inner sight, (two wrists)
May She bless and keep me, (feet)
And may I walk in the way of the Goddess (or your Goddess' name) *forever."*

The Circle is Set.
Calling Down the Moon (All moon rituals, Grand Sabbats and Yule)

"High the moon that rides the tides,
Virgin Goddess, She of new beginnings,
Mother Goddess, She, the Queen of Creation,
Crone Goddess, She, of the night black Ravens Wings,
Enter thy Priestess and servant, that we may hear your words."

Reply of the Goddess speaking through you. (Channeling the Goddess)

Calling Down the Sun *(Equinox, Solstice and Beltane)*

"Stag, Ram, Bull and Goat, Oh Horned One.
Warrior God, mighty hero,
Bright God of the golden day,
God of the dappled shade of the Greenwood,
Enter thy Priest and servant, that we may hear your words."

Reply of the God speaking through you. (Channeling the God)

SABBAT – Celebrate seasons changing.
ESBAT – Spells

Visualization

Consecrate the Wine
Draw your Athame, standing place tip of Athame into the chalice on the altar
"As the Athame (Knife) *is to the God* (or your Gods name)
So is the Chalice to the Goddess (or your Goddess' name)
Together they form the mystic union
And I unite with my God/dess (answer with your opposite, priestess says God, priest says Goddess)"

Consecration of the Cakes
Places hand above cakes
"I bless this food,
As seed it did go into the Earth,
Then as corn, did dance upon the wind,
And then stretching up into the warmth of the Sun,
And tasting the saltiness of the rain,
Now let us partake of the Elements, as we partake of the food."

To closing the Circle

"I may enter the circle tired and weary,
But with Spell chant and rhyme,
Give my help to all that ask,
And with merriment go forth to face the world once more."

Facing North.

"My guardian Elemental of the North,
I thank you for attending my ritual,
Return to you forests and realms of Earth,
My loyalty is eternally with you.
Blessed Be! Blessed Be! Blessed Be!"

Using a candle-snuffer or your fingers do not blow on, put out the brown candle.

"Hail! And farewell!"

Facing East.

"My guardian Elemental of the East,
I thank you for attending my ritual,
Return to your perfumed and mystical plains of Air,
My loyalty is eternally with you.
Blessed Be! Blessed Be! Blessed Be!
Using a candle-snuffer or your fingers do not blow on, put out the blue candle.
Hail! And farewell!!"

Facing South.

"My guardian Elemental of the South,

I thank you for attending my ritual,
Return to your lava and deserts of Fire
My loyalty is eternally with you.
Blessed Be! Blessed Be! Blessed Be!

Using a candle-snuffer or your fingers do not blow on, put out the red candle.

Hail! And farewell!!"

Facing West.

"My guardian Elemental of the West,
I thank you for attending my ritual,
Return to the your distant and primal plain of Water.
My loyalty is eternally with you.
Blessed Be! Blessed Be! Blessed Be!

Using a candle-snuffer or your fingers do not blow on, put out the green candle.

Hail! And farewell!"

Draw the Athame, holding it high above the cast circle saying,

"The circle is open but unbroken,
May the peace of the Goddess be in our hearts,
Until we merry meet, merry part and merry meet again!!!
Bring the Athame down, cutting through the bounds of the circle.
Blessed Be!! Blessed Be!! Blessed Be!!"
Put out spirit candle with snuffer.
This Rite is done

Places some cakes and wine on the Earth.

"I bless the Earth
That in it's turn the Earth
May bless all."

If this is a Sabbat, then have a little to eat to be sure you are grounded.

Esbat and Sabbat Ritual for a Group

If there are a group of you this is how the same ritual would translate for more people.

Sweep the circle with the besom, visualizing sweeping all evil from the area

Lay out white boundary cord

All buckle or tie on their belt on, which hangs your Athame, if you have one.

Put on white cord

All stand in circle alternating man, woman, ladies with beads.

Light spirit candle

Place incense on the charcoal block.

Meditate to clear the mind and prepare for the ritual.

The Opening of the Circle

HPs With hands raised

> *"Goddess of the Magical Shimmering Silver Moon,*
> *God of the Powerful Burnished Golden Sun,*
> *Cast your circle of protection about these seekers after wisdom,*
> *Hold them in your gentle arms,*
> *Guide them on their path."*

A male covener if possible, bends down and picks up sword in its scabbard whilst still on one knee (this is knightly not subserviently), offers the sword to the HPs.

She takes the sword (still in the scabbard) and proffers the hilt to the HP, who draws the sword. The HPs step forward to the Altar and holds the scabbard, in two hands, upright with feet apart. All follow HP around the circle while circle is cast, keeping an equal distance.

HP   Draw the circle with the sword (clockwise three times)

1st circle
"I cast this circle around us in purification and in the name of the
Virgin Goddess.

2nd circle
I cast this circle around us in love and in the name of the Mother
Goddess.

3rd circle
I cast this circle around us in protection and in the name of the
Crone Goddess.
In the three names of the Goddess the circle is made!"

After circle is cast, the HP replaces the sword into the scabbard held
by the HPs. She returns it to the covener who drops to one knee to
take the sword and return it to the altar.

HPs All take hands, raise hands as you draw the power higher.

"Reach down into the Earth, through the many layers,
Down, Down to the Earth's core,
The ever spinning, ever beating heart of the Earth Goddess,
Draw upon her power, draw it higher,
Up, up through the very Earth itself
As you draw it through you,
Allow it to heal you, allow it to balance you, allow it to empower
you.
Higher and higher, until….. completion."
HPs Draw a pentagram in the air, in the North and with every stroke
say forcefully

"We call upon that powers that bide,
Beyond the veil to be our guide.
By Earth, <u>silent</u> with no word we speak,

By Air, <u>knowledge</u> forever we will seek.
By Fire, my <u>will</u> I hone that we may dare,
By Water, with tears of joy we <u>care.</u>
(After, still with your Athame pointed at North say)
By the pentagram that shineth bright,
I make this a shield in the darkest night.
Blessed Be!"

All   *"Blessed Be!*
       Blessed Be!"

HP   *"Attend your Quarters!"*

All circle once, guardians finish standing at your quarters.

HPs takes wand from the altar, HP takes taper.

The Guardian of the North circles round (all following) to take the wand from the HPs, turns, holding out wand, facing North (brown) candle saying.

North
"I call to our Elemental of Earth,
Come from the glittering ice caves and enchanted forests of the North,
Guard this place set outside of time.
Your primal power, I invoke to aid this ritual,
Come share this special time with us.
Guard this circle invoked in the names of the Old Gods
(When you know the names of your Goddess and God insert them here).
Blessed Be!"

All   *"Blessed Be!*
       Blessed Be!"
North passes the wand to East and takes the taper from HP walk

halfway round the circle to the North candle and lights it, turns.

North "**Hail and Welcome!**
All **Hail and Welcome!**"

The Guardian of the East takes wand and circles (all following) to stand facing East (Blue) candle, holds out wand, saying.

East

"I call to our Elemental of Air,
Come from the perfumed and mystical East,
Guard this place set outside of time.
Your primal power, I invoke to aid this ritual,
Come share this special time with us.
Guard this circle invoked in the names of the Old Gods
    (when you know the names of your Goddess and God insert them here).
Blessed Be!"
All *"Blessed Be!*
 Blessed Be!"

East passes the wand to South and takes the taper from North, walks halfway round the circle (all following) to the East candle and lights it, turns.

East "Hail and Welcome!
All   Hail and Welcome!"

The Guardian of the South takes wand and circles (all following) to stand facing South (Red) candle, holds out wand, saying.

South

"I call to our Elemental of Fire,
Come from the heat and deserts of the South,
Guard this place set outside of time.
Your primal power, I invoke to aid this ritual,

Come share this special time with us.

Guard this circle invoked in the names of the Old Gods (*when you now the names of your Goddess and God insert them here*).

Blessed Be!"

All *"Blessed Be!*

Blessed Be!"

South passes the wand to West and takes the taper from East, walks halfway round the circle (all following) to the South candle and lights it, turns.

South "Hail and Welcome!

*All **Hail and Welcome!**"*

The Guardian of the West takes wand and circles (all following) to stand facing West (Green) candle, holds out wand, saying.

West

"I call to our Elemental of Water,

Come from the primal waters of the West,

Guard this place set outside of time.

Your primal power, I invoke to aid this ritual,

Come share this special time with us.

Guard this circle invoked in the names of the Old Gods (when you know the names of your Goddess and God insert them here).

Blessed Be!"

All *"Blessed Be!*

Blessed Be!"

West passes the wand to North and takes the taper from South, walks halfway round the circle (all following) to the West candle and lights it, turns.

West "Hail and Welcome!

All   Hail and Welcome!"

North (all following) walks halfway round the circle (all following) to the HPs and returns the wand to the HPs. West returns the taper to the HP.

Purification of the Elements

Earth
Draw the sign of the pentagram over the salt, with your Athame.

"Out of thee, goes all that is impure,
May only the might of the Great Mother remain."

Air
Place more incense on the charcoal,
Draw the sign of the pentagram over the incense, with your Athame.

"Out of thee, goes all that is impure,
May only the might of the Great Mother remain."

Fire
Draw the sign of the pentagram over the red candle, with your Athame.

"Out of thee, goes all that is impure,
May only the might of the Great Mother remain."

Water
Draw the sign of the pentagram over the water, with your Athame.

"Out of thee, goes all that is impure,
May only the might of the Great Mother remain."

All chant nine times whilst circling, with cords linked across the circle, like a spiders web.

> *"Lady Dark, Lady Strong*
> *Queen of Wisdom hear our song,*
> *All are gathered here to night,*
> *Within your circle in your sight."*

Anoint on the third eye (forehead) the two wrists and feet.
HPs

> *"I consecrate thee on the third eye,* (forehead)
> *May the Goddess enhance your inner sight,* (two wrists)
> *May She bless and keep you,* (feet)
> *And may you walk in the way of the Goddess forever.* (stand facing)"

With this the Circle is Set.

Calling Down the Moon (All moon workings, Grand Sabbats and Yule)

HP *"High the moon that rides the tides,*
Virgin Goddess, She of new beginnings,"
All *"Virgin Goddess, She of new beginnings,"*
HP *"Mother Goddess, She, the Queen of Creation,"*
All *"Mother Goddess, She, the Queen of Creation,"*
HP *"Crone Goddess, She, of the night black Ravens Wing,"*
All *" Crone Goddess, She, of the night black Ravens Wing,"*
HP *"Enter thy Priestess and servant, that we may hear your words."*
HPs **Goddess replies** (channel the Goddess' words)

HP *"Thank you great Goddess for your (empowering, kind, gentle thoughtful) words."*
Calling Down the Sun (Equinox, Solstice and Beltane)

HPs *"Stag, Ram, Bull and Goat, oh Horned One."*

All *"Stag, Ram, Bull and Goat, oh Horned One."*

HPs *"Warrior God, mighty hero,"*

All *"Warrior God, mighty hero,"*

HPs *"Bright God of the golden day,"*

All *"Bright God of the golden day,"*

HPs *"God of the dappled shade of the Greenwood,"*

All *"God of the dappled shade of the Greenwood,"*

HPs *"Enter thy Priest and servant, that we may hear your words."*

HP **God replies** *(channel the God's words)*

HPs *"Thank you great God for your (empowering, kind, gentle or thoughtful) words."*

Here the content of the ritual is done whether it be...

SABBAT – Celebrate seasons changing.

or

ESBAT – Spells

Visualization

Consecrate the Wine

HP takes chalice from the altar and kneels on one knee,

HPs draws her Athame, standing she places tip of Athame into wine.

HPs

"As the Athame (Knife) is to the God (or your Gods name)

So is the Chalice to the Goddess (or your Goddess' name)

Together they form the mystic union, that consecrates this wine."

Wine is first drunk by HPs and then past round circle with a kiss.

Consecration of the Cakes
HPs takes cakes from the altar,
HP places hand above cakes
HP

"I bless this food,
As seed it did go into the Earth,
Then as corn, did dance upon the wind,
And then stretching up into the warmth of the Sun,
And tasting the saltiness of the rain,
Now let us partake of the Elements, as we partake of the food."

Cakes are passed round circle
A time of magical chat (magical only! the Calling Down of the Moon or what each saw in the Visualization).

Closing the Circle
HPs

"We may enter the circle tired and weary,
But with Spell chant and rhyme, give our help to all that ask,
And with merriment go forth to face the world once more."

HP   *"Attend your Quarters."*

All circle until Quarter Guardians are in their places.
HPs takes wand from the altar, HP takes candle-snuffer
North takes wand from HPs, turns. Faces North (brown) candle.
North

"Our guardian Elemental of the North,
We thank you for attending our ritual,
Return to you forests and realms of Earth,
Our loyalty is eternally with you.

Blessed Be!"

All "Blessed Be!
Blessed Be!"

North passes the wand to East, and takes the candle-snuffer from HP.

North moves half circle to the North (brown) candle and snuffs it, turns.

North **"Hail! And farewell!**
All   **Hail! And farewell!"**

East takes wand from North, turns Faces East (blue) candle.
East

"Our guardian Elemental of the East,
We thank you for attending our ritual,
Return to your perfumed and mystical plains of Air,
Our loyalty is eternally with you.
Blessed Be!"

All   "Blessed Be!
Blessed Be!"

East passes the wand to South, and takes the candle-snuffer from North.

East moves half circle to the East (blue) candle and snuffs it.

East *"Hail! And farewell !!*
All   Hail! And farewell!!"

South takes wand from East, turns.
South
"Our guardian Elemental of the South,
We thank you for attending our ritual,

Return to your lava and deserts of Fire
Our loyalty is eternally with you.
Blessed Be!"

All "Blessed Be!
Blessed Be!"

South passes the wand to West, and takes the candle-snuffer from East.

South moves half circle to the South (red) candle and snuffs it.

South "Hail! And farewell !!
All   Hail! And farewell!!"

West takes wand from South, turns.
West

"Our guardian Elemental of the West,
We thank you for attending our ritual,
Return to your distant primal plain of Water.
Our loyalty is eternally with you.
Blessed Be!"

All "Blessed Be!
Blessed Be!"

West passes the wand to North, and takes the candle-snuffer from South.

West moves half circle to the West (green) candle and snuffs it.

West "Hail! And farewell!
All   Hail! And farewell!"

Half turn of the circle West passes the wand to HPs, and West passes the candle-snuffer to HP

East bends down and picks up sword whilst still on one knee, offers the sword to the HPs,

She takes the sword (still in the scabbard) and proffers the hilt to the HP,

Who draws the sword, holding it high above the cast circle he says,

HP

"The circle is open but unbroken,
May the peace of the Goddess be in our hearts,
Merry meet, merry part and merry meet again!!!"

Bring sword down and cut across the circle bounds (remember like popping a bubble), cut the circle.

HP   *"Blessed Be!!"*
All   *"Blessed Be!!*
        Blessed Be!!"

Put out spirit candle with snuffer.

This Rite is done

HPs places cakes and wine on the Earth.
HPs

"We bless the Earth
That in it's turn the Earth
May bless us."

If this is a Sabbat, all fest together, either one person cooks (this changes every Sabbat) and brings it to the Covenstead or all bring something to share.

Exercise: If you feel ready, start to find the energy within your body.

When you are confident, perform this simplified version of the Sabbat ritual, adding from the more complicated ritual above, a little at a time.

Simple Sabbat Ritual

Have ready:

. A elemental candles and candleholders

. Anointing Oil.

. Sabbat incense.

. A charcoal block.

Light the charcoal block. When lit add ½ a teaspoonful of incense and replenish as necessary.

Light Spirit Candle

Meditate for a while on what you are about to do.

Cast a circle, allowing the power to flow from your body.

Turn to the North (This is the realm of Earth.) and say:

"Earth most fair, come share this special time with me."

Light candle

Turn to the East (This is the realm of Air) and say:

"Air most gentle, come share this special time with me."

Light candle

Turn to the South (This is the realm of Fire) and say:

"Fire most warming, come share this special time with me."

Light candle

Turn to the West (This is the realm of Water) and say:

"Water liquid of life, come share this time with me."

Light candle

Anoint with oil

Call to the Goddess and God to be with you in your own words.

Toast the God and Goddess with a glass of wine and a biscuit.

Thank God and Goddess for their presence here in your own words

Turn to the North and say:

"Earth, I thank you for being with me, go and may we ever be in peace."

Snuff candle

Turn to the East and say:

" Air, I thank you for being with me, go and may we ever be in peace."

Snuff candle

Turn to the South and say:

"Fire, I thank you for being with me, go and may we ever be in peace."

Snuff candle

Turn to the West and say:

"Water, I thank you for being with me, go and may we ever be in peace".

Snuff candle

Put your hand out and cut the circle of light that you have created.

With this your ceremony is done.

CHAPTER 7

Gem and Metal Magic

Great is the force of herbs, but greater by far
The virtues that in stones inherent are
For in the stone implanted by mother earth
Eternal force, unfading, at its birth.
Shortlived the herb, it quickly fades away;
When past its prime it drys and withered lies:
And what help find in a thing that dies?
Plants as the source of death and health we own,
But scarce canst thou find mischief in a stone.
The Lithica by G. N. Giannakes

I have had a love of gems and crystals from a very young age. In one of my first comics as a child, the publishers tried to educate us by including a page on different unusual topics, one week pictures of large gems were very crudely reproduced. The Amethyst was printed in red and blue spots due to the lack of purple ink, and was depicted as oval, the emerald in which I now know to be an emerald cut, was oblong with straight facets along its length. Also depicted was Ruby and Sapphire, although these did not hold my attention like the Amethyst and Emerald did. I can still visualize that page to this day.

As a child I loved holding any gems that I could get my hands on, they tingled as I held them and this fascinated me. All the more so when I found out as I got older, that no one else had seemed to noticed this.

One day, my family went to the Victoria & Albert Museum in London, there they have a wonderful collection of Victorian Rings, great wondrous, colossal gem rings. I loved them all!! How I wanted to own rings like that! Some months later on a market stall I saw loose glass gems for sale, not as big as the wonderful ones at the V&A, but big. I saved my money and bought then. Yes, I know they weren't the real thing but it taught me to visualize! I handled the glass stones and designed settings for them; and dreamt they were real. Now many years later design and make jewelry, dreams do come true if you visualize hard enough.

A witch believes that everything has a spirit. Every rock, tree, plant, crystals and gems are no exception. This is now being confirmed by scientific research. Scientists can now measure the electrical signals given off by plants, in tests they have torn apart one bush whilst measuring the signals from a second and recorded its distress.

Crystals have been adopted by the New Ager's and as such, given them a 'Fluffy Bunny' image, if I do nothing else but convince a few witches to reconsider their use, I will be happy.

These beautiful products of nature are part of our heritage; Pagans have used them all over the world from the beginning of time to heal, to divine, as talismans and amulets. Quartz crystals are still used by the Shaman of Peru and their use stretches back in time to at least the Mochica, a pre-Inca tribe, where crystals have been found in the graves of both priests and kings. The Shamans of Brazil and North American Indians use crystals. But the quartz family are not the only gems used, every precious and semi- precious gem has been used at some time as an aid to magic. Diamonds were discovered in a Shamans pouch in South Africa, rather than by a geologist working for a mining company. Always, in which ever country gems are found, the local witch by whatever name they are known, will use them in ritual. Gems have been traded over vast distances from the dawning of time and still used today. There is something in their magic, surely. Why therefore cut ourselves off from a source of such strong magic? And strong magic it is, even if the New Agers have borrowed them, hold one in the palm of your hand and try to feel the energy; you won't be disappointed but pleasantly surprised.

Crystals are a very precious harvest of the Earth, formed millions of years ago at the Earth's dawn. Some people are unhappy about crystals being torn from the earth, but all births are painful. The Goddess knows our love of bright shiny things and so I find it no wonder that she has chosen to place healing quality with such beautiful packages.

Each gems crystalline form varies, a Diamond forming an octahedron, or a Topaz as an orthormbic, with the perfect specimens always forming the same pattern over and over again. As with humans one head, two arms, two legs, the pattern for each crystal was set at the dawn of time, and each crystal tries it's level best to grow in that pattern. Because each crystal holds a different crystalline pattern, different color and different atomic structure, it projects a different energy. X-rays can photograph the aura around crystals as well as the crystal itself, showing wonderful lace like patterns projected out to three times the size of the crystal. With each type of crystal the pattern varies, and experts can tell a clear quartz crystal from amethyst just by the x-rays patterns. Each type of crystal pulses at a given rate, this pulse can be scientifically measured. Each quartz crystal pulses at the same rate, each ruby at the same rate, but both at different timings and frequencies. This pulse enables a crystal to be used to power quartz watch, a small piece of quartz crystal regulates the watch by its accurate pulse, never varying and the battery of the watch then amplifies this. Without this piece of quartz your new watch will not work. In Witchcraft we say that each tree, pond, stone and therefore each crystal has a spirit. If each crystal has a spirit. The pulse is I like to think, is the spirits heartbeat.

Classic mechanical watches however are said to be seventeen jeweled or more but this only means that Ruby or Sapphire replace the metal cogs within, as they are far harder than metal, reducing friction and will therefore last so much longer. Rubies, now synthetic, are used in lasers and older people may remember the term Crystal Radio in which they were used. On oilrigs in the North Sea, a theory was developed that each crewmember should wear a different crystal, (probably disguised in a manly leather or plastic band). This pulse then could be tracked around the oilrig by a computer and used in the case of fire and dense smoke would hinder the search for injured crew members. The central computer would know if anyone were still left on board, where and who, by the individual signature given off by each crystal.

White light can be split by a prism, into all the colors of the rainbow, for it holds all within, Black is the absence of all light. One object might reflect green light while absorbing all other frequencies of visible light, some of the retained light will be converted into heat. In garnet, red will be reflected and orange, yellow, green, blue, indigo and violet will be absorbed. The hotter the temperature the closer to red the color, the closer to purple the cooler the temperature. This applies to everything of course, not only to crystals but combined with their inner energy it forms a wonderful healing tool.

If different crystals give off energy at different rates and different colors, they must affect us in different ways, this is why some heal and others protect. Within the group, each specific crystal is an individual, as with humans each has it's own personality and the power of each varies, a crystal may work better for one, than for another. You can train yourself to pick up the energy emitted by the crystals very easily, choose a crystal that feels most comfortable and that draws you to it. Pass your hand over it and try to feel an energy from the crystal, this may feel like a tingle in the palm of your hand, as the vibrations hit the skin. But with practice it can be like a bolt of lightening running up your arm, only you know if this crystal feels right for you. Some people prefer to use a pendulum and dowse for a suitable stone, allowing the pendulum to be affected by the vibrations.

New gems- Although all gems and crystals are millions of years old, some have only just been discovered and have no provenance as healers and protectors. Which isn't to say they are useless but that only a very few people have given their opinion of the gem, and your opinions are as valid as theirs. Hold it, feel the energies and listen to what the stone is telling you about its self.

How do crystals and gems look?

Raw Crystal – Many of the precious gems, as well as the well known quartz, grow before cutting as Crystals. Rubies, sapphires and emerald, are far more affordable in their crystal form.

The crystals vary in shape according to the stone type. The quartz crystals for instance have a point at one end and have rough sides, although some sides may look almost perfect, the base, where it was attached to the rock will be broken and is sold just Mother Nature made it. There is always an exception isn't there, in this case it's double terminated crystals (crystals with a point at both ends) and raw fluorite octahedral which are like two pyramids stuck together. These grow not on rock but in sand or similar soft substance, that will allow the crystals to spread in many directions at once.

Polished Crystals As above but with all sides as smooth as glass, the point perfect and a polished base, this will be a crystal that was broken in mining or a stone perhaps like Moonstone that has no crystalline form. It is then polished, shaped like this it makes a good pendant.

Which to choose? Personally I normally prefer the raw crystals untouched as much as possible. Some crystals that have been damaged in mining feel healed when polished and are stronger than they where before. So it's a matter of choice, choose what feels best for you.

Phantom Crystals- A very interesting and unusual stone, mainly quartz. It formed millions of years ago as the crystal grew in a cave, dust sprinkled onto the point, slowly more crystal grew entrapping the dust. You are then left with a shadow of the crystal point as it was. I have a crystal that this has happened to many times over its life, you can see layer after layer; the crystals whole life is there for you to read. I have heard of crystals where the layer of dust is so thick that they can be taken apart, the crystal having many 'hats', one on top of the next, unfortunately I have never seen one, but you never know.

Phantom crystals are very good to hold for regression work.

Tumble stone The type of stone that grows in large mass, when broken into bits small enough for the average person, are then tumbled in extra large washing machines to polish them smooth.

Faceted (from the French, meaning little faces)– Cut into beautiful angles that reflect and refract the light making some stones like liquid fire, as the light plays within. These are then usually set in rings or pendants.

Cabochon Normally round or oval and polished smooth gems. This is often used for opaque or second quality stones the very finest being reserved for faceting. These are then usually set in rings or pendants.

Which to choose? This one comes down to cost and use. It would be silly to place a wonderful faceted Amethyst in a Spell Bag to be sealed; when a tumble stone will work as well. But as a magical ring, you may prefer to choose the faceted or cabochon amethyst rather than the tumble stone. As always the choice is yours.

Should gems be perfect? In antiquity it is said that all gems used in magic should be perfect. I am not rich but I love gem magic, I can't afford perfect rubies and emeralds, even if I can afford a perfect Tigereye. Instead of a perfect ruby, use a slice of ruby crystal that can by very inexpensive, of course these are full of imperfections. I personally have never felt that the ruby does not wish to be used just because it is not perfect. If you are very rich please let me know if a perfect gem works better than an imperfect one.

Organics, these are not true gem stones but are produced from living organisms, Amber, Pearls, Jet, shells, horn and bone, in times past Ivory would have been included in this list. Organics are not as robust as gem stones and must be treated far gentler.

Shape and color
Natural stones make great charms and certain shapes and even colors in stones are considered of great importance.

Black- protects from the evil eye and bestows wisdom.

Brown – warded off sickness

Green – is used for vegetation, rain, fertility and virility.

Red – stop blood flow and to protect from fire and lightning

Stones that sparkle- were thought to contain a deity

Violet- protects children and calms them

White - protects from the evil eye and emits spiritual emanations

Stones with bands of color, water-worn stones, Hag stones which are stones with holes in, triangle, circle or semicircular are all traditionally of great protection against evil. You can find wonderful stones in fields or on the beach. I once found a strange stone while out walking in the country, in fact two, not far from one another. The first I found had two long points like the horns of the God, with strange squiggles on them, I'm sure they are natural but it looks like writing and I was very pleased when I found it. But just a few steps on, I found a wonderful Hag stone, the stone of the Goddess. So they sit together happily on my shelves of interesting things I have collected over the years.

Clearing and Attunement

You need to contact the spirit with in the crystal or gem, to truly bond and for it to help you in your work. When you have selected your chosen crystal, you must first to cleanse it, before you can work with it. The crystal must be cleansed from all the people that have handled it since it was taken from its bed deep within the Earth.

There are several ways to do this:

Your crystal can be washed in salt water, although I find this a little strong.

I like to wash the crystal in just warm water with a little washing-up liquid, rinsing in clean water, either leave it to dry naturally or wipe with kitchen paper. This is a very simple cleansing but I find it quite adequate and it does not shock the crystal but makes it feel at home. It may sound strange to talk about the crystal as having at character but the more you work with them the more you will feel it.

And/or you can bury it under the earth again, back in the womb of the Goddess.

Once cleansed, you need to contact the spirit within it. There are more ways to do this, than to cleanse your crystal.

Make a strong tea with a couple of tablespoons of Mugwort and boiling water, leave to get cold. Wash your crystal with the cold Mugwort tea.

And/or you can place it on the earth during a storm for 24 hours. This will bring the crystal in touch with three elements.

The Native American Shaman say that only the Sun can empower the stone for a man and only the Moon for a woman.

My preferred way, after washing it, is to rinse it in cold Mugwort tea. Then hold the crystal in both hands and blow gently on the stone. In magic, all of your body fluids holds the pattern of who you are, by breathing on the stone you are imprinting it with your personality. Allow your mind to drift, and to receive images from the stone, anything that it wishes to communicate to you, this attunement will need to be repeated over the next few weeks to attune with it completely, it is very unlikely that you will complete this in one step. Place it under your pillow and keep it with you as much as is practicable.

Choose whichever method you feel at home with.

After attuning it, please never let anyone else touch your crystal, the exception being your partner or your child, as they are considered part of you. Unfortunately because of the aura given off by the gem, many people find it irresistible if they see it hanging round your neck, to reach over and take it while admiring its beauty. This is the reason that Amulets and Talisman, gems and crystals are part of this group, should be kept out of sight, as they will imprint the crystal with his or her aura as well as yours. Until it has been cleansed again, it will not be truly yours.

Families of Gems and Crystals

Quartz

Many crystals come in families, quartz is the most interesting. The family consists of clear Quartz Crystal, Amethyst, Ametrine, Citrine and Smokey Quartz the darkest stones of the Smokey Quartz being called Morian Quartz. With the proper equipment you can move a single stone through all of these colors by heat and x-rays and back to its starting point. So the difference lies within the stone itself not by added elements as with quartz's cousin Rose Quartz that contains other substances.

Beryl

Other families are Beryl containing, Emerald, Aquamarine, Morganite, Golden Beryl and Red Beryl.

Corundum

Corundum the common name for Ruby and Sapphire. Ruby is always red but sapphire comes in many colors, not only blue, but pink, violet, yellow, green, brown, black or colorless, its different colors affecting its properties

Topaz

Topaz is yet another family, although Topaz has not been given exciting names for each of its colors.

Quartz Crystal Meditation

As this is one of the most important groups of crystals, you may feel that this meditation will attune you to the Quartz Family. You will need to lie down for this. Firstly meditate with Smokey Quartz placed on you feet, the darker the better, Smokey Quartz is very grounding. On your next meditation place a Citrine on your sexual area, for the God (this still applies whether you are male or female) for his sexual energy. Then an Amethyst on your heart for the

Goddess, for her love and sensitivity. Then Clear Quartz on your third eye for knowledge above and beyond gender. Finally you will need to bring them together placing the appropriate crystal in its correct place and retry the meditation with the full family. Note the impressions you get from each and then together. What does it tell you about the character of each gem, try changing them around, how does this feel?

What is the Third Eye?

You will come across this expression many times in your magical life. The Third Eye is by some thought of as literal and by some as merely as a short hand for the idea of psychic ability. The third eye is situated in the center of the forehead and lays above the Pineal and Pituitary gland which is the master gland of the body which regulates sleep, light, growth, and stores mood-enhancing hormones and has been known about since ancient times. There is a type of lizard found only in some small islands of New Zealand called the Tuatara, it is the sole survivor of a group of reptiles that have existed for 200 million years. When young it actually has a physical third eye, this is connected directly to the Pineal gland. It closes as the lizard type creature gets older but still retains its ability to distinguish at least between light and dark. I find it fascinating that an idea born in the East, has a basis in fact in the far shores of New Zealand.

How do you use Gems and Crystals?

Now your crystal is ready for use by you, or the person for whom you chose the crystal, as a gift.

Many people give a pure quartz crystal to a child at birth or an Amethyst for a girl and a Citrine for a boy, only charge the crystal if you are directly related to the child, Mum, Dad or Grandparent. Otherwise wash the crystal to clear it and get the child to grab it and so imprinting its spirit on to the crystal. Of course never leave it with the child in case of any problems, it may be small enough to swallow and crystals are sharp and pointed.

You can use your crystal to heal, point it to the problem to be healed, send your energy down through the crystal, like with the Athame. Your energy is then magnified by the stone as it helps to heal the problem.

Tumble stones and small crystals can be placed in spell bags (See the Chapter on Charms), their energy adding to that of the herbs and other items within. Consult the list and see what energies you feel you need to add to the Spell bag for it to enhance your work.

You can also place a healing spell on a crystal to be given to someone in need, after charging the crystal, place a healing spell upon it.

Crystal and Gems can be worn on the body, around your neck in contact with your skin or in a ring, for long term protection or healing. This needs to be worn for a time before any benefit is felt.

Tumble stones and small crystals can be kept in your pocket to bring into your life the energies of that stone.

Place Crystals in a room for healing, whether this be a person or the place.

Surround the patent with five large crystals equally distanced facing inward, see these as the points of a pentagram, connect the points by tracing a pentagram in the air with your finger, connecting the crystals, so that your patient lies within the pentagram of healing.

Place Laser (long thin) crystals in a pentagram shape, ten large on the outside following the lines as you would draw a pentagram in the air, five smaller in a pentagon shape in the center. Draw the energy into yourself with your left hand, very good as a tonic, after an illness.

Until you are more experienced never wear more than three crystals at one time and always make sure they are compatible. A rock crystal will magnify any other stone when put with it. Your can use a large rock crystal and a small ruby crystal to get

Crystal Pentagram

the same effect as a large ruby crystal.

Crystal Elixirs

Crystal Elixirs are excellent for taking the energy of a crystal into your body. The concept goes back to at least the Anglo- Saxon period, where crystals were dipped into water and sprinkled on cattle and humans alike, to protect them from fairies and the Evil Eye. Crystal balls all ways have been expensive items, only the rich could afford them. In Scotland at least, it is recorded that the Lord of the Manor would allow the family crystal ball, which was carried on standards as the clans went to war, to be dipped into his farmers water three times. The farmer must draw the water himself, bringing it to the great house, after dipping it must never enter any house until the farmer returned home or the magic would vanish.

As today we have our own crystals, we can be a little more lavish with the time, not just three quick dips. Take your chosen clean crystal and place it in a clean glass, top up with water and place it on a windowsill. Either during the day if you wish to imbue it with Sun energy (strength, fortitude and energy) or during the night of a full moon if you with to imbue it with Moon energy (improving magical and psychic ability). Drink this.

There are, however, only some crystals that should be used, any of the quartz, corundum, agate or jasper families. Stick to these and you will be fine, some of the other gems like malachite or turquoise are too soft and will dissolve in the water leaving you with metal poisoning. I lectured on this once, telling the class which crystals to use. Well, one young lady thought she would experiment with crystals outside the ones I had recommended. She tried Malachite, coming back to me a month later with a swollen tongue and copper poisoning!

Light and Crystals

Another way to work with gems and crystals is with light. This works on the same principle as a gem ring, allowing light to pass through a gem, energizing it and then allowing it to be absorbed by the body. Lay in the special rays of the sun with a crystal on the problem to be healed, please remember that a crystal magnifies the light from the Sun and can burn. Some crystals now come with a nice cut flat bottom, I hold this to a small torch. Switch on the torch and hold it to the problem about an inch away. Hold it there for about ten minutes, or shorter if any discomfort is felt. Use Citrine for low energy, anemia or for lack of sunlight called S.A.D., and use Amethyst for healing.

Legendary Mystical Qualities of Gems

Agate (this comes in many colors)

Magic: All agates are said to be good for protection while travelling and protects from storms and lightening.

Blue Agates are worn to promote general health.

Green Agates improve your prosperity. Both the old one pound note and the American dollar bill are green.

Red to Brown Agates improve the ego and self-esteem; this is especially good for Virgo, that have a tendency to suffer with this problem. Also works wonderfully in the Earth, plant agates in your garden to help a favored plant to grow, or hang them from a tree to improve the fruit yield. In Ancient Rome brown agates were worn on the left as a ring or bound to your left arm as a tribute to farming Goddesses.

Blue Lace Agate gives peace, happiness, relieving stress and gives confidence when speaking in public.

Black Agate (some times called Onyx) Protective, worn for success in deeds, probably by deflecting the Evil Eye.

Moss Agate This strange agate has the most realistic looking trees growing within, as with brown agate plant it in the Earth to improve crop yield. Worn by gardeners it helps to improve their green fingers and relieve the aches and pains associated with this job. (See also eye Agates in Amulets and Talisman)

Alexandrite

Alexandrite was discovered in April 1834 in the emerald mines of the Ural Mountains on the day that the ill fated Prince Alexander of Russia came of age. This green stone under daylight changes to blood red under candlelight, the colors of Imperial Russia. Alexandrite is a gem of great beauty and is far too expensive to ever own. its ability to change and its rarity dictates its price, far in excess diamonds. New deposits of the gems have been found in Brazil and Tanzania, although the color change is not so pronounced and therefore they are less expensive.

Although no experiments have been done with this stone, I am sure that it's ability to change from the element of Water to the element of Fire must hold enchantment.

See Fake stones.

Amber (white (osseous), golden, brown, black, rarely green, blue and red)

Amber's most striking quality is it's weight, it has none! When you first pick up a piece of Amber you can be forgiven for thinking it plastic. It is almost sticky and is very soft, you can shape it with a nail file. It is a poor conductor of heat and so always feels warm to the touch. It was thought that if you held a ball of Amber you would be cool on the hottest of days. If Amber is rubbed on silk or wool, it emanates a negative electric charge that magnetizes the Amber and enabling it to pick up a small piece of paper. Professional polishers of this stone were often in the past, seized with wrist or arm tremors due to the static electrical charge in Amber. The word Electron comes from the Greek name for Amber. Because Amber is very easy to work into beads, it has been worn since Neolithic times. It originally came from sub-tropical forests and a now extinct Pine tree called Pinus Succinifers, 30-90 million years ago. Amber can be up to 125 million years old! But it structure breaks down the older Amber gets and so only microscopic fragments remain from this age.

Pinus Succinifers, produced copious quantities of resin, as the sap ran down from the trees, often small plants or insects became trapped in these globules. Which we can now see today incased in the harden resin which became Amber.

As the millennia passed so the resin slowly turned to Amber, first by polymerization and over the millenium by evaporation of the volatile oils.

As the ice melted after the last Ice Age, the resin was carried South by two great rivers and the Amber was deposited on the seabed. Autumn and Spring storms stir the seabed and release its precious cargo trapped under layers of silt. Most Amber is picked from the seashore after the high tide has withdrawn but it is also acquired by "fishing" with nets, deep sea diving and there are even Amber mines.

In earlier times Amber was often mistaken for Ambergris, which is a secretion from the intestinal tract of a Sperm Whale that is also found on the seashore and so its popular name of Amber was given to the tree resin we value today.

As with the Silk Road that took silk to the West from China, so a similar trade route developed called the Amber Road that took these valuable items from the Baltic to Ancient Greece and later to Turkey and farther. This is still the area that supplies 80% of all the Amber to the world. When we get to the Christian era in th early sixth century Caesarius of Arles in Southern Gaul and Eligius of Noyon, condemned the use of Amber as an amulet, complaining that women wear it round their necks.

We in the West prefer clear dark brown toffee colored Amber, while in the Middle East they will not even class this as Amber. Their preference is for a yellow egg colored- opaque Amber, quite possibly this is the type of Amber referred to in legends, as most stories of Amber originate from the Mediterranean Area. It is still used by Muslims today as prayer beads, carried with them at all times running between the fingers at every available moment. Although this is also confused with "African Amber" this is a modern resin collected by tribesman formed into balls while still sticky; polished when hard and sold, although not very heavy it is much heavier than true amber. This is not to disparage African Amber in the least, as it does have a use in healing but it is not 60 million years old and does not have the same vibrations. Any stone can work for you, if it feels right for healing or casting spells it is right for you, but be-aware of what you are buying.

Since amber has become fashionable, more high quality amber is needed to supply the demand. Less perfect amber is being treated to enhance its appearance for use in jewelry. By heating the stone it becomes the popular sparkling amber called "Crackled Amber" in the trade, caused by popped air bubbles within the stone, this clarifies and enhances the appearance. Nature uses the same means whenever Amber is heated naturally, so it's not as bad practice it may it first sound, in gemology, this is not considered a falsification of the gem. But whether you consider this an honorable practice or not is debatable. Different colored Amber in various shades of red, green and blue are also produced, by heating real Amber but these are a subtle variations of color and actually very pretty.

Amber comes not only in white-yellow-brown, but under fluorescent light some Amber, from the southern state of Chiapas in Mexico glows prettily and other forms of Amber turn bright green, blue and red by included air bubbles. Enclosures of pyrites commonly called fools gold may give Amber a bluish color. There is an interesting color change Amber that comes from the Dominican Republic. This is blue if you hold it so that the Sunlight falls on the nugget but yellow if you hold it up for the Sun to shine through or in artificial light. Under ultraviolet light this same Amber will glow a bright milky-blue, this is due to its strong fluorescence.

A young lady bought an Amber ring in a shop a few years back, with an insect with in. She took it to a Museum for identification, after research they found it to be an unknown species of insect and very rare, they bought it for £30,000! Shades of science fiction, no less. Though there are lots of faked insects in Amber on the market, some good, some with household flies with in and very bad.

Stories that are associated with stones are meant to tell us about the character and properties of that gem, most seem to be sad and Ambers' stories are no exception. In Greek myth when Phaethon, son of the Sun God Helios, was killed by lightning, intense grief turned his sisters to Popular trees (Popular trees are feminine and associated with death); their tears were tears of Amber. So we learn that Amber is associated with the Sun, not unsurprisingly with its wonderful color. But as His sisters cry the tears not His father Helios, we have a strong female connection to Amber. The Sun Goddess Saule from Latvia also weeps tears of Amber.

Although the Athenian, Nicias mentions that the heat of the Sun was so great in some regions of the Earth that the Earth began to perspire Amber. Early Chinese thought that the souls of tigers on their death, became lumps of amber. Amber was very popular with the Celts and particularly with the Vikings, amulets of animals and small axes have been found carved in Amber in a tumuli grave in Norway.

Amber was called "Freya's Tears" by the Norse and Vikings, in legend the beautiful Goddess Freya whose dominion was love and fertility, owned a breathtaking necklace called Brisingamen. This wonderful necklace was intricately crafted of Amber and gold so some legends have it. Freya fell head over heels in love with it at a glance. However the only way to acquire this breathtaking necklace was to sleep with all the four dwarfs who created it. Loki (the God of pranks and mischief) had encouraged the dwarfs to make the necklace to embarrass Freya who He knew would have to have that necklace. Hiding in the darkness, once more Loki smiled.

In Russia in 1716 an entire room was clad from interracially carved panels of Ukrainian Amber, a present from Prussia's King Frederick William I, and presented as a gift to Tsar Peter the Great. This was a state treasure and was packed away for safety during the siege of Moscow in WW11. Unfortunately it was "lost" and has never been seen since. In 2002 a copy of the famed Amber Room was finished, using the many shades of amber from palest yellow to black to recreate beautiful glowing room. The reconstruction, which involved six tons of Amber, was made from old photos and the memories of those that had seen the original. This now forms part of The Hermitage a palace that is now a museum.

Should Amber have natural markings that take the shape of magical sigils or your initials this has special significance. A friend was given a beach pebble, sadly not amber, that his initials can be plainly seen in, but I can well imagine how special it would be, to find this in amber. This idea can be adapted, as Amber can be shaped with a nail file, it can be carved or a simple rune inscribed onto an Amber pendant yourself.

Even today most High Priestesses wear a necklace of Amber and Jet, as can be seen in Waterhouse's painting of "The Magic Circle".

It is said that as Amber is so closely associated with the Sun it should for best effect be set in gold, the Sun metal. Although, strangely Amber has a close association with the Moon as well, being good for fluid retention problems, which you would have thought to come under the influence of a Moon orientated stone, rather than a Sun stone? I was actually taught that it was a Moon orientated stone but I can find no connection historically except it's sexuality but I'm sure the Sun God would claim that as his own. Pliny records the opinion of Callistratus an Athenian who lived in 360BCE, he suggested its use against mental problems, perhaps its Sun connection nullifying the moons affect on this, as the moon historically has been associated with madness? Amber does have a strong feminine connection, it is soft, warming and gentle and has links to female Goddesses but until I can find more evidence either way; I will leave this to your own instinct.

Magic: A stone of great spirituality and of immortality, Amber increases your animal magnetism and voluptuous sexual love. Amber worn while casting enchantments renders its wearers irresistibly attractive. This is probably due to the electrical attraction mentioned earlier, attracting love in the same way as it attracts paper. Small pieces can be added to love bags to attract good energies and people to you. It can absorb negative energy and helps the body to heal itself. Pieces of Amber placed on the altar increase its effectiveness, and helps with regression work.

The palest opaque Amber is the best for use as incense, this has been burnt on altars from ancient times in Egypt, Rome and China.

Healing: Amber reduces fluid retention and helps to detoxify the urinary system. It also helps prevent rheumatism, skin problems, intestinal disorders, headaches, catarrh, womens problems, asthma, cured fevers, diseases of the mouth, throat, and jaws when worn as beads. A necklace of Amber beads was said to guard off chills, by its extreme warmth and the circle of electricity it maintains. Amber helps deal with mental problems. When powdered and mixed with honey and oil of roses it was a specific for deafness, and for dimness of sight (do not rub into your ears or eyes).

Amethyst (purple)

One of my own favorites of all the gem stones, its color will always typify the Goddess for me. The most highly prized form of quartz, both monetarily and spiritually with a beautiful glowing purple color. From palest Lavender, known as Rose de France to deep Imperial purple, the most expensive with rose flashes.

There is a beautiful apocryphal story associated with Amethyst. Amethyst was a nymph, of great beauty, one day she was out in the forest, on her way to Diana's shrine to place some flowers on the alter. When Bacchus, the Roman God of Wine spotted her, after awakening from a night's reverie; as Bacchus is an immortal we must assume no headache the morning after the night before! (Another version of this story has Him upset at some slight and sending two great tigers to devour the first human that He sees.) And so with an enormous "Morning Glory" on seeing the beautiful Amethyst, he gave chase to impose his will on the poor nymph. She was fleet of foot but he was fleeter, time began to tell on Amethyst and she began to slow her footfall, Bacchus was gaining! She cried out to Diana, the Goddess of Virgins to save her. This the Goddess did, by changing her into a beautiful pure crystal. On seeing this, Bacchus was so mortified by what he had done, he poured his purple wine over the crystal to remind him that all women must be honored and never taken by force. This is why Amethyst helps in dropping unwanted desires and is well known for protecting from drunkenness (still under intensive research!). Although some legends suggest that it should be worn under the tongue when drinking, I preferred the stories of wearing it in your navel, so much easier to drink like that. I can understand where the idea of the wine soaking into the stone came from; Amethyst have deep coloring at the tip of the crystal flowing to pure crystal at the base, 'uncontaminated' by wine. Amethyst has become a token exchanged by true lovers. You can see from this delightful if somewhat sad story, how the Amethyst crystal is so intrinsically feminine, made from a female nymph by the Goddess Diana. It is the quintessence of femininity, a gem to communicate directly with the Goddess.

With the return of Goddess worship Amethyst has become more and more prized. New finds of Amethyst have brought the price tumbling down, allowing all to wear the gems formally only worn by Royalty.

Magic: Both men and women to deepen their relationship with the Goddess, by wearing amethyst, a wonderful gem for meditation or divination. If you stare into its depths it is easy to get lost with in its beauty. A gem of the Moon reveling in its gentle light, an Amethyst will fade in strong Sunlight, proving it to be the Goddess' own gem stone. Said by no lesser person than Leonardo Da Vinci to have the power to control evil thoughts and quicken the intelligence. Amethyst protects soldiers going into battle, giving them victory.

Light a purple candle and place some Amethyst tumble stones into your bath, particularly good to do before circle or for meditation.

In its role in helping to heal unwanted desires and grief, project your hurt or fear into the amethyst tumblestone- bury the stone and leave your pain behind. The Earth will cleanse the stone in time; it will cause it no harm.

So according to the Witches of Tuscany Amethyst will also aid memory.

Healing: Amethyst enhances all magic, and speeds all healing, physical, mental and emotional. Amethyst increasing energy, lifting depression, increases spirituality, stimulates enlightenment and relaxing stress. It promotes calmness and emotional balance, which helps relieve headaches, insomnia, neuralgia, grief and asthma. It is also good for the throat, lungs and helps tackle blood diseases. Place an Amethyst crystal under your pillow at night for a good nights sleep or an Amethyst geode in your bedroom or sitting room, to help you relax after a hard day. Amethyst works very well with Lavender oil, if you are suffering from stress, wear an amethyst and rub a drop or two of lavender oil on your chest, this will rebalance your system very quickly. In short, Amethyst is good for all healing.

Ametrine (purple and yellow)

This gem is a rare natural formation of Citrine and Amethyst. With careful cutting the beauty and power of both are present in the one stone. The male half of the stone the Citrine and the female half the Amethyst, God and Goddess united. So you can see, that it has opposing yet complementary energies like a married couple, some find it difficult to work with but I find it to be stronger than the Amethyst or Citrine alone. Although only discovered in 1977, this not a well-known gem, it is wonderful set into a ring for either a H.P or H.Ps to wear in circle or for a marriage gift.

Although we sometimes have these for sale, I came across one recently that I did not want to part with having an unusually dark coloring, unfortunately more Citrine and not a lot of Amethyst within, but I have found that it changes color! During the day under the light of the sun it is strongly Citrine (God) and at night by Moonlight, candlelight or electric light it is strongly Amethyst (Goddess)! Perfect!

Apache Tear (black)

In the 1870's the Apache fought bravely against the US Army at

Superior, Arizona. Eventually, running out of arrows they were backed farther and farther toward what has now become Apache Leap Mountain in Arizona, as one they turned and rode their horses off the cliff. When the squaws went to retrieve their bodies the next day, their tears turned to stone and became Apache Tears in the sand. Apache Tears are a form of obsidian, a natural volcanic glass, if you hold it up to the light you can see light through the stone.

Magic: Apache Tears are carried for the hope of better things to come and are a good luck charm.

Aquamarine (pale blue to green)

Cleanse the stone quickly in sea water at a full moon, if possible. Ideal to wear whilst casting water magic spells, for happiness.

Magic: A feminine stone Aquamarine instills peace of mind and increases the ability to love. This stone also preserves youth and health; this stone has always been closely associated with water. Helps calm storms at sea when worn so therefore may help with seasickness. Problems tend to flow around you, leaving you unmarked as within the eye of the whirlpool.

Healing: Aquamarine aids eyesight and relieves headaches. Alleviates fluid retention and kidney problems. It also cools fevers and relieves toothache.

Aventurine (green)

Carry a piece in your purse or place in you till or with your paying in book to the bank. I cannot promise anything but it's always fun to put your lottery tickets under one, but with so many magic workers all working for their lottery tickets you don't stand much chance.

Magic: Aventurine is well known stone for luck with money and health, vigor and cheerfulness.

Azurite (deep blue)

Place a piece of Azurite on your forehead during meditation, it will help you to awaken your third eye. Then use this to hold in your hand during divination work. Helps you to choose friends that will be true and strengthens existing friendships.

Healing: Helps those faced by degenerative disorders, wear on a long cord over the stomach area.

Azurite with Malachite (bright blue and bright green)

An almost synthetic colors it is so bright. Patches of bright blue and bright green looking like the land and sea, as seen from space. This is a strong stone for healing and good as a meditative aid.

Beryl (clear)

Some old Grimoires, which are books on Ceremonial Magic, give clear Beryl as the best stone for scrying. Dr Dee who was Queen Elizabeth's Astrologer, had a crystal ball made from Beryl. I have an old book describing the virtues of scrying in a large Beryl crystal, but if you think crystal balls are expensive, forget a beryl ball or a large beryl crystal!

Golden Beryl The clear yellow of Beryl attracts hope and friendship reported to give eternal youth and happiness. Beryl gives enjoyment in work and heightens the intellect. It is also a meditative aid and can help invoke familiar spirits. Beryl also guards against manipulation.

Healing: Good for hysteria and jaundice and helpful for mouth and throat problems.

Bloodstone (dark green, red spots)

This stone is a form of Jasper, without its red spots of Iron Oxide it is Green Jasper not Bloodstone; look for lots of blood! Some call this stone Heliotrope, but no one knows which stone the Ancients were referring to when they spoke of Heliotrope or Bloodstone, it may have been Ruby, Garnet, Red Spinal or what we now think of as being Bloodstone. In the Middle Ages this stone acquired the reputation of having been spattered with the blood of Jesus at the crucifixion.

Magic: It promotes eloquence, trust, loyalty, courage and happiness and also increases the will power, to do noble deeds.

Healing: Stimulates the flow of energy for general healing. Helps the blood supply and relieves digestive disorders, strengthening recuperative powers. It was carried in ancient times by solders to bind onto wounds to stop blood flow, although I would not doubt its magical ability to do this, I also realize that pressure on the wound would also help. It is used as medicine and an aphrodisiac in India.

Boji Stones Very popular now a days but Boji stones have only been used as healing stones for a few years now. They come in pairs one smooth and female, one with cubic crystals, which is male and heavier than the female stone. They must never touch but sit very close to one another always. Discovered, patented and marketed by a farmer in America on whose land they "grow". Farmers in the district are now also finding and marketing these strange rocks calling them Pop Rocks, there is no difference between them, only a few miles of origin. It is true to say however that Boji stones are better matched and of a better shape but twice the price, although Pop rocks can be much larger, use your instincts to help you decide which is for you, as with everything in magic.

Magic: Hold one in each hand the male in the right and female in the left, to strengthen and balance your system.

Carnelian (red)

Carnelian comes from the Latin word Carne, meaning flesh, due to its superb red coloring. For the Buddhists in Tibet, China and India the practice of setting Carnelian with turquoise, which is still practiced today, stems from the Ancient Egyptian belief that setting the two stones side by side enhances the power of both.

It was also known as Sadoine or Mecca stone and has a deep religious significance for Muslims, balancing creativity and mental processes and protecting against the 'Evil Eye'.

The best stones to chose with Carnelian are the semi-translucent stones, light passes through them when worn and is absorbed into the skin, taking with it the energy of this beautiful warming stone.

Magic: This stone gives courage to speak boldly and well and protection both at home and while travelling. Keeps the Evil Eye averted, by stopping jealousy from attaching itself to you.

So the old rhyme says-

Carnelian is a talisman,
It brings good luck to child and man;
If resting on an onyx ground,
A sacred kiss imprint when found.
It drives away all evil things;
To thee and thine protection brings.

Healing: Increases energy levels, arouses sexual energy and helps when courage is needed. Not recommended for those with high blood pressure or nervous disorders.

Catseye (grey yellow)

This stone is often confused with Tigereye, but they are two quite different stones, Catseye being far more valuable.

Magic: Catseye has wonderful moving eyes that moves to and fro across the stone. Encourages success in speculative ventures or competition in sport, love and home. Catseye is particularly good at protecting your family from danger.

Healing: Strengthens the voice and respiratory system. Helps rheumatism, depression and neuralgia. Helps with problems your eyesight.

Celestite (clear sky blue) or Strontium Sulphate.

Another of the hidden color stones, appearing a clear blue when it is in actuality a strong red if ground and burnt. These crystals are water soluble, just dust, don't wash it or leave it in a storm, certainly don't use it for elixirs. Celestite is far too soft to be set in rings or pendants.

Healing: With its colors interchanging it makes a lively stone for meditation.

Chrysophase (apple green)
Legend says that if a thief sentenced to be hung or beheaded places one in his mouth, he will be immediately escape from his execution by becoming invisible. Some legends are just legends.

Magic: Chrysophase has long been carried for victory in battle, bringing gaiety, joy and it also rewards initiative.

Healing: Used to help overcome addictions helping with diet control and thyroid problems. Chrysoprase is also good for rheumatism and all water retention problems.

Citrine (yellow to brown)
A very neglected stone, I feel due to yellow not being a fashionable color but Citrine is a stone of the Sun and therefore the God. Bringing both good luck and energy. Citrine is quite a rare stone, most on the market is heat-treated Amethyst, true Citrine is pale yellow with no trace of red. The darker colored Citrine crystals, named Madeira for their color's resemblance to Madeira wines, are generally more valuable.

Magic: Citrine increases energy, lifting depression. When worn enhances communication with the God, encourages luck, victory, boldness, and courage. Citrine also energizes clearer communications and is good for travel.

Healing: Particularly effective for men. It strengthens the body and gives energy. Aids digestion and general health.

Coral (red)
Coral is a small part of the dead remains of a coral reef, but in the past it was not thought to die but if washed up on the beach to still be a living spirit. If, however, after being used as a talisman it was broken, it's life and spirit was thought to have left and the separate pieces have no value. Red Coral is thought of as primarily a woman's stone,

mixing its birth in water, with the red color of menstrual blood and the Moon's dominance over both, used to regulate the menstrual cycle. Its color changing with the menstrual cycle, deepening during blood flow, if worn for this purpose it must be hidden, if worn for any other purpose, proudly worn on show. In Victorian times, red Coral was often given to a child for protection against becoming a changeling, a human child swapped for a fairy child and is the reason red coral was incorporated into antique silver rattles.

Magic: It is said to ward off evil influences and protects from lightning, whirlwinds and storms.

Healing: Helps with bladder and bowel problems. Coral helps with menstrual cycle; also a pick-me-up and. it also stanches blood flow from wounds

Brown Coral Brown coral gives wisdom and helps mental illness. It helps with sterility. Enables travelers to cross broad rivers safely.

White Coral Wards off nightmares and helps fight the panic of phobias, helping with all mental illnesses.

Black Coral Protection, very strong with magic against the Evil Eye, demons, and in the last century has been used as protection against the Furies (the Roman female avenging angel), succubi, incubi and phantasma.

Diamond (white)

A Diamond is a gem that transcends gender and is neither male nor female, although you may feel that an individual stone has characteristics of one or the other. Diamonds represent Spirit, pure and perfect. Plato wrote about diamonds as living beings, embodying celestial spirits.

Light hitting a diamond is split into the many colors of the rainbow and so holds all secrets within its heart.

From a poem written in the second century
The Evil Eye shall have no power to harm
Him that shall wear the diamond as a charm,
No monarch shall attempt to thwart his will,

And e'em (even) the gods his wishes shall fulfil.

Diamonds are made from carbon, the same substance as forms on my toast when I burn it. At the dawn of the world, the Goddess played with heat and pressure in the cauldron of boiling magma that lay deep below the surface of the Earth, from this She brewed carbon into diamonds.

The word Diamond comes from the Greek *adamas* meaning "invincible" and is the hardest substance known. The Diamonds atoms are arranged in such away that four bond very tightly together, known as "crystal habits" this makes diamonds very dense material. A Diamond's desirability stems from its luster and brilliance, their shine is caused by their ability to refract or bend light. This is the source of the colors or "fire" that radiates from the Diamond. They also have the highest measure of reflectance of any transparent material. All of this adds up to Diamond having what is commonly known as the "wow factor".

Some ancients thought that diamonds were born when lightning strikes the Earth and that if you water them they will grow (diamonds do grow but very slowly and only within the Earth's crust). The ancient Greeks and Romans believed diamonds were tears of the Gods and others thought that diamonds were splinters from falling stars (microscopic diamonds have been found in fallen meteors, so not so far from the truth). Pliny, wrote that swallowing a diamond would neutralize poison and guard against insanity (with the price of Diamonds its insanity to do this, please don't try this).

Another legend says that there was an inaccessible valley in Central Asia carpeted with diamonds. It was said to be *'patrolled by birds of prey in the air and guarded by snakes of murderous gaze on the ground.'* Diamonds were considered so precious by Hindus, that many large gems were placed in the eyes of statues of their Gods.

In China, diamonds are carried to thwart evil spirits and are regarded as a talisman of strength, courage and invincibility.

St Hildegarde in the early Christian era used diamonds to treat illness, by holding a diamond in her hand while making the sign of the cross over a wound or a diseased person.

A diamond is said to dim in the presence of lies and to shine brilliantly in the presence of truth. Due to diamonds dislike of lies and deceit, it brings bad luck if stolen, as most gems do, but diamonds seem to dislike it more than most. Large famous diamonds seem to prefer to be owned by women, perhaps the inner spirit feels more conformable with a female guardian (note I don't say owner) rather than a male. Spirits are like children and perhaps men do not appreciate them enough? Thinking more of their monetary value rather than of their beauty. The men even if they haven't stolen the diamond, having a tendency to drop dead, with great frequency. Leaving women owners or wives with very nice presents, living long and happy lives.

Diamond also promotes fidelity and so is given as the traditional engagement ring.

The tradition of giving a diamond as an engagement ring first started when Archduke Maximilian of Austria gave a ring to Mary of Burgundy in 1477. Placing the engagement ring on the third finger of the left hand, dates back to the early Roman belief that the Vena Amors, the vein of love, runs directly from the heart to the tip of the third finger.

Diamonds, when used in engagement rings, have the following meanings:

> One diamond – 'You, alone, I love'
> Two diamonds – 'You and I together'
> Three diamonds – 'I love you'

Diamonds were first used for their hardness, to polish other diamonds and to engrave other hard stones. Diamonds perfect form is an octahedron, many people consider the pyramid to be a magical shape and of course an octahedron is two pyramids back to back. As raw octahedron diamonds were set into rings in ancient Rome as amulets of protection. For centuries, rough diamonds were kept as talismans, and often not worn at all.

The cutting of diamonds into the faceted gems, is a relatively recent practice. At first diamonds were cleaved through the center of the octahedron and the five sides were polished. Later small facets were polished all over the pyramid side of the stone, making the diamond to a dome shape with a flat bottom, this was known as a Rose Cut. As people became more proficient at the cutting of gems they wanted to maximizes the area of finished gem produced from a rough stone this new cut became known as the Miners Cut and the

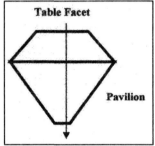

appearance that we are so familiar with begins to take shape. By the early 1900's. Marcel Tolkowski a mathematician, established the "ideal cut" now known as the Brilliant cut and was created to reveal the brightest gem, rather than the largest gem when cut.

I prefer a miner's cut stone, it has more character, than a regimented Brilliant cut gem with precisely 57 facets all perfect, all in exactly the same place, as every other Diamond cut this way. A miners cut gem has the same amount of facets but more haphazardly placed making each diamond a little personality. However, there are some Miners Cut gems that, probably, through bad cutting or chipping over the years, have a slice off the pavilion point this can appear as a hole in the stone, as seen though the table facet, this does not look so good.

Some diamonds fluoresce, under exposure to ultraviolet light they can be placed on photographic paper and a bright splash of light obtained.

The legend goes that while in South Africa a member of the De Beer's family discovered diamonds near the Orange River, South Africa, in a Shamans pouch. Buying them for a few coins, he then proceeded to purchase all the land around. The family still controls all diamond mining in the area and the price of diamonds on the world market to this day.

Diamonds were weighed, in early times, against the seeds of the carob tree; hence the size of a diamond is still measured in carats. A carat is a unit of weight and not size, one carat is divided into 100 points, a quarter carat is a 25 point stone. If a diamond is called flawless, it means that it has no flaws or inclusions as seen by a x10 magnification eyeglass. Inclusions are bits of non-crystallized carbon and internal stresses, these greatly affect the value of a diamond. Inclusions absorb the light and affect the way light passes through a diamond, rather than reflecting the light back through the top facet, as it should. If the inclusion is in the center of the diamond, the flaw can be reflected around the inside of the stone! Lots of flaws for the price of one!

How big do you think the biggest diamond is? Perhaps, the largest rough diamond ever found the Cullinan or Star of Africa, (3106 carats, or about 1 1/3 pounds) which was discovered in 1905 in South Africa?

The biggest ever diamond has been found floating in space. The gem, estimated at close to 10 billion trillion trillion carats! It is at the core of a dead star BPM 37093 now known as the Diamond Star - a crystallized white dwarf.

Unfortunately is floats 50 light-years from the Earth in the constellation Centaurus and just a tad too large for my finger, being a little bigger than our Moon. Although the star has been given a nickname of "Lucy" by astronomers, in memory of the Beatles' song. The star joins in the song and rings like a gigantic gong, undergoing constant pulsations. Many White Dwarf stars may have diamonds at their heart although Lucy is the only one known of at the moment. One day in the far distant future some 5 billion years our Sun too may become a White Dwarf with a singing Diamond for a heart.

Magic: Diamonds give purity and peace of mind; they attract abundance and prosperity, both material and spiritual. A diamond promotes fearlessness, power, protects from evil and drives away nocturnal demons. It is worn in battle for victory and promotes physical strength.

Healing: Purifying and magnifies the properties of other stones.

Fancy Diamonds (yellow, blue, green, pink, brown, red, violet) It is very rare to come across colored diamonds and most of us can only view them in Geological Museums but they do exist.

Fancy Diamonds are formed when trace elements such as Nitrogen are present within the gem; this can cause a yellow diamond, while others, like Boron, can cause a blue color.

There are few legends regarding colored diamonds, bright red and saffron yellow were thought to be exclusively for royalty in India, for these colors are thought of as blessed in India. Although most colored diamonds found have only subtle shades. The rarest colors are red, green and purple.

Each colored Diamond must be examined individually and an understanding of the gem's properties explored. If you are lucky enough to own a colored Diamond, you must do the groundbreaking work of working to understand its qualities for yourself.

Carbonado (black) Black diamonds where used at one time only for industrial drilling, being hard but tough under stress. Recently however black diamonds have become a fashion statement. To look at, they are rarely exciting, being from grey to black and looking like, to my eye, a polished version of pencil lead.

Black diamonds don't adhere to the rules of diamond mineralogy, having no inclusions from the Earth's core within and a strong luminescence which has attracted intense speculation as to their origin. They are mined as far apart as Brazil and Central African Republic, but at one time in the far distant past these two countries were joined. The latest theory is that Black diamonds were not formed on the Earth but near a Carbon Star. Picked up and riding to Earth within a meteor, crashing into our world and depositing its cargo at the dawn of our history.

For curiosity's sake, I would love to experiment with this very ancient gem with its unique properties.

Emerald (green)

Emeralds are another of the precious gems and were traded in Babylon 4000 years ago. Emeralds are rarely without inclusions and yet despite this it is one of the most expensive gems you can buy, even today. Luckily as nature does not provide perfect Emeralds, you don't need the best quality work magic with. Emeralds inclusions are romantically called Jardin, French for garden, deep bright green with only a few weeds in the Jardin of the Emerald is the best quality. Although to see the best Emeralds you will ever see, go to the Topkapi Palace in Turkey, they are simply magnificent. I have always loved Emeralds but these are massive and of the deepest green.

King Solomon the Wise who was given a ring made from Brass and Iron by the Jewish god Jehovah which represented the cardinal points and the four elements. Emerald as the gem representing water, Sapphire- air, Ruby- fire, unfortunately it is not recorded what gem he used for Earth, possibly Imperial brown Topaz. The ring was said to give Solomon dominion over all four Elementals Quarters, allowing him to command them to do his bidding.

Emeralds are well known for protecting the eyes. The Emperor Nero looked through a large emerald to watch the Gladiatorial combat, to protect his eyes from the sun, the first sunglasses no less. Perhaps it was a thin sheet of emerald cut from a gem as large as those at the Topkapi Palace, which were up to nine inches. But cut as thin as the wonderful boxes that the Turkish Sultans had made from a single Emerald, and then held up to his face? But all this is speculation, as no details are given.

In Peru at the time of the Spanish conquests, there was an immense Emerald the size of an ostrich egg, known as the Emerald Goddess Umina. The people gave smaller Emeralds to the priests in the hope of favors from the Goddess, as they thought that these were the Goddess's daughters and wished to return them to their Mother. The Spanish took most of the small Emeralds, but they did not find the Emerald Goddess, where is She now, I wonder.

Magic: As with all Beryl (Emerald, Morganite, Aquamarine, Yellow Beryl), Emeralds enable the wearer to forecast events. In Europe the Emerald is dedicated to Venus and so enchants true love, used as a gift between lovers, ensuring they will never part. Venus rose from the waves and so her special stone not only brings love but also protects you from drowning.

Enchanters, to be assured that spells were not cast on them and frighten away any demons sent to do harm, would wear an emerald ring.

The Egyptians used an Emerald amulet to ensure resurrection in the afterlife but then most amulets in Egypt are for that purpose.

The Emerald enables you to give love to others, strengthens the memory and shows honesty. Protects from drowning. Emeralds should always be set in silver to improve their qualities. Occasionally Star and Cats Eye Emerald are found on Brazil.

Healing: Emeralds gives relief in neurological diseases. Strengthens bones, spine and teeth. Cool fevers and improves eyesight.

Fossilstone (various)

Its old name is Toadstone, thought to come from the head of a toad. It gives protection for newborn children and their mothers from the power of the fairies. Worn to increase your natural defenses. Fossilstone is used by shaman all over the world and placed on altars to enhance their power. Experiment by holding one when attempting past life regression.

Fossilised Wood (browns)

Magic: Native Americans used it as a protective amulet against accidents, injuries and infections. Fossilised Wood increases longevity.

Healing: Gives energy and so eases physical and mental stress. Helps arthritis and strengthens bone and also promotes longevity.

Fluorite (purple, clear, green, yellow)

As you might expect with a name like Fluorite (fluorescent is derived from the word Fluorite) some stones glow when exposed to ultra-violet light, great to wear when out for the evening! As the Suns rays have ultra violet within, when exposed to the light of the Sun, it glows silently the entire time even though we can't, with our eyes see it. Some seem to look like green glowing coals and as you may guess a very powerful stone. This stone is rather soft and scratches easily, best not to use it for rings but keep it for pendants.

Magic: Fluorite aids assimilation of knowledge.

Healing: Helps cure impotence and enhances fertility.

Garnet (red)

Garnet increases faithfulness, yet still acts as a sexual stimulant. It guards while travelling and promotes loyalty, good humor and physical fitness. It works by creating a shield of positive vibrations. The name Garnet comes from the Latin word for grain or seed granatus, due to its resemblance to a Pomegranate and is also called the Pomegranate stone. When found garnet is in small clumps, as you tap it, the garnet breaks into a great many small stones, looking like a pomegranate fruit's many segments. As with the story of Persephone and her abduction into the Underworld by Hades. In the Underworld she took three bites of the pomegranate that Hades offered, tying Her to Him and the underworld for the three months of each year. This then became winter, without her presence upon the face of the Earth, all became cold and desolate, the plants wilted at Her absence. In Ancient Rome Garnets and particularly those set in jewelry that represented pomegranates, were given as gifts of love and of healing for a broken heart.

Exquisite, meticulously cut, Garnet jewelry of outstanding workmanship can be found in the Saxon finds from the ship burial at Sutton Hoo, England. Garnets also have an unhappier association, they were used as bullets during the India rebellion of 1892, as it was thought that Garnets caused more damage than normal bullets.

Healing: Documents dating from the Middle Ages agree that Garnets protect from poisons and were thought effective in dealing with problems with the blood and infection. Many hospitals in medieval times were believed to have Garnets hidden within, too radiate healing.

Garnet (green)

Mother Nature is truly wonderful, Garnet also grows in a wonderful shade of green although green Garnets are rare, and this adds a wonderful calmness to its usual get-up and go. Get ahead without stress!

Demantoid Garnet is another green Garnet, found in the Ural Mountains and is sparkler even than diamonds and needless to say very expensive. Before long, the workshops of Carl Fabergé were crafting stunning pavé set jewelry for the Czars. The outbreak of the revolution stopped both his craft and the production of gems in Russia.

A new supply was found in 1996 in Namibia and in 2002 in Russia, both producing better qualities than formally. Demantoid Garnets have dropped slightly in price, due to the new supplies being discovered.

Haematite (dark gray)

This is the old spelling of Haematite, you will notice the ae as in haemoglobin a constituent of blood, this gives away its secret. For if you rub it across rough white porcelain it will leave a red line, hence its old name- The Stone That Bleeds. Due to it's secret red color it has an association with Mars, the God of War and some Haematite jewelry is still engraved with a warrior, this enhances its potency the tradition has lasted from Ancient Rome to modern day, most wearers these days being ignorant of its meaning.

Haemetite contains iron and is a very good substitute for iron in magic, as iron these days is very hard to find. Some Haematite is magnetic.

When powdered Haematite becomes red ochre, which was

sprinkled over the dead, in Neolithic times to help them, it is thought, to life in the next world.

Magic: It promotes alertness and stimulates sexual potency. Success with litigation and all forms of battle

Healing: Improves circulation and eases nervous disorders and magnetic Haematite bracelets are also good for arthritis.

Herkimer Diamond (clear)

These are not diamonds at all but a type of very clear, sparkly quartz, naturally polished with a high degree of brilliance. Herkimer Diamonds start life in a free flowing suspension and so form double terminations, growing from the center in all directions simultaneously; unlike most quartz crystals that grow from their tip. This gives them a different character than quartz crystals. Some even have water bubbles inside, that links them closely to the Roman theory of crystals being strangely frozen water. Herkimer Diamonds, although always small, have a high degree of brilliance and perfection given to them by nature. The best natural substitute for diamonds in magic, much cheaper.

Jade (white, grey, yellow, orange, red, all shades of green, violet, brown and black)

The name Jade covers two gems Nephrite and Jadeite both are very similar and only in the beginning of the 19th century did it became possible to tell them apart. New Jade has just come on to the market but that is a gem quality Serpentine, not truly Jade.

Jade has been used for 7000 years, not at first for its beauty but for its strength. Jade surprisingly is stronger than steel, used for axes, knives and later in China as ornamental swords for their Talisman and Amuletic magic. To the Chinese, Imperial Jade (apple green) is the most precious stone and was used exclusively for the Royal Family. Legend tells us that it is the sperm of dragons (a creature of abundant luck) and so contains the concentrated essence of love and luck which it will pass on to the wearer and is often given as a love gift. The Chinese Empress and Emperor were buried in suits of Jade thought to protect the bodies from decomposition; many amulets are made from Jade in China, featuring Dragons, Bats and all auspicious animals. Though be careful in China, as they do not have the same laws of descriptions of goods as we do; I saw many other stones labeled as Jade (Rose Quarts as pink Jade), that obviously were not. "All precious gems are Jade" we were eventually told on querying this.

Maoris of New Zealand also venerate Jade as very precious, calling it just, Green Stone. They don't call it carving Jade as we would, but feeling and knowing what spirit is hidden within that piece of Jade and *"revealing the truth that lies within the stone"*.

Magic: Jade is useful when problem solving and for love and luck. This magical gem protects and balances the bodies energy and life force. Jade also favors artistic and musical endeavors. It is a symbol of good fortune and ensures high rank and authority.

Healing: Comforts the stomach, liver and kidneys and eases eyestrain. Jade dulls pain, induces sleep, which improves memory. It is calming and promotes good health.

Jasper (various)

Magic: Spells cast with consecrated green Jasper brings rain.

Helps to lightly ground after meditation, focuses the mind, calms emotions and relieves pain. Brings joy and happiness, defends the home and family, protecting from harm. A charm drawn or written on a piece of parchment can be set under a Jasper stone in a ring, or put with a tumble stone into a charm bag and it will increase its potency. If placed on a snakebite it will draw out the poison, this same belief is behind the idea of placing a piece a parchment under a jasper set within a ring or pendant, that it will draw to it, the object of the spell.

Healing: Promotes healing of the digestive system and helps with epilepsy. Improves the sense of smell, discourages depression and unwanted pregnancies.

Jet (black)

Jet is fully fossilized coal, used since Neolithic times for success, determination and drive. In Roman times it was considered a protection from disease and evil spirits, often engraved with the Medusa head of protection. In Anglo-Saxon times it was thought that Jet savings, myrrh, white frankincense in wine 'against elf and unknown sidra' causing illness, though I would not sugest that you use it today. Better to keep a piece of Jet in the house that no evil spirt or lightening can harm any whithin. In Victorian times it was the height of fashion as mourning jewelry. Jet is a highly magical stone sometimes called Witch's Amber and has been found in graves worn with Amber and even in modern times alternating beads of Amber and Jet form the High Priestess's necklace.

Magic: Protection from disease, evil spirits, for success and is also a good protection for travelers Burnt it drives away snakes..

Throw Jet onto the fire to make wishes.

Healing: Eases childbirth and dispels fever.

Kunzite (pink)

Smoothing over irritations to form unconditional love and forgiveness.

Healing: Improves eyesight and hearing.

Lapis Lazuli (blue)

This stone has the most wonderful midnight blue color, speckled with Pyrite and sometimes with white Calcite, like stars in the midnight sky. Good to wear when meditating as Lapis Lazuli, known as Stone of the Gods, was believed to contain a deity within that would help you in your magical work.

In the "Book of the Divine Cow", tells how Ra, the Egyptian God of the Sun, over heard the Egyptian people laughing at Him.

"The people of Egypt saw how old and frail their king had become Look at Ra! His bones are like silver, his flesh like gold, his hair is the color of lapis lazuli!"

I can only think that they meant that the Sun was so dim that His hair looked like midnight. He became upset and sent Hathor-Sekhmet to eat all humanity; glad he changed His mind (for the full story see mandrake).

In the 140th chapter of the Book of the Dead, it describes how Ra on the last day of each month places on his forehead an eye made of Lapis Lazuli, while His priests make offerings to a similar eye on the Earthly plane of existence.

Lapis Lazuli was used by the Egyptians not only for amulets and wonderful jewelry but also for eye makeup, probably using the same pigment for creating their breathtaking wall art. Certainly by the Medieval Period Lapis was used for pigment in paint called ultra-marine, which was reserved for the wonderful depictions of the Virgin Mary. I always thing of the Virgin Mary as our own Virgin Goddess. This expensive coloring was nearly always employed, to paint Mary's glowing robes, while gold leaf was used for her halo, it would be and still is, an impressive sight in a dusty church. Farmers used to only the sky and mud must have been deeply awed by the sight, as Mary glowed in the candlelight.

Magic: A highly prized amulet said to ward off all troubles.

Strengthens the physical body during spiritual awakening. Promotes love and courage and wisdom, giving protection from psychic attack.

Healing: Helps with hormone balancing and PMT.

Labradorite (peacock colors on a dark silvery blue ground)

Labradorite has a wonderful flash of color, called Labradoresance or shiller, as you move the stone and it catches the light. The colors may not all be present with in one stone, some are predominantly blue, green or yellow. Some yellow can be fluorescent under UV light. In the 18th century Labradorite was very fashionable, with pendants and rings being very popular and is returning to popularity.

Magic: The predominately blue Labradorite is sacred to Odin. It is a stone of transformation, brings prophetic visions and expands consciousness and energies the spirit.

Healing: Helps digestive disorders and nervous conditions.

Lodestone Lodestone is magnetite.

Magnetite (black-silver-red)

A natural magnetic stone used to produce iron axes, swords and knives. This also comes in octohdra shaped crystals as well as raw lumps. Lodestone is also used to magnetize an Athame Blade, this lines up all the particles with in the metal to face in one direction.

The history of magnetism and the lodestone started in Ancient Egypt where they referred to lodestone as the bone of Haroeri, grandson of the Goddess of the Earth. The Greek historian Pliny tells a wonderfully exaggerated myth of Magnes whose iron shod staff and iron nails in his sandals were held tight by natural magnetic rock. From Rome comes another intriguing legend of a statue of Mars made of Iron and one made of lodestone representing Venus. They were kept far apart, except for one ceremony, when they were pushed closer together, as soon as they came near one another they were magnetically attracted and crashed together, the mating of God and Goddess! I don't know if it is true but it sounds wonderful and the Greeks and Romans did build massive and technically advanced monuments like the Colossus of Rhodes, so it is possible.

In China BCE 221 magnetized iron was used for Taoist method of Feng-Shui, in which the propitious placing of rooms and furniture is used for a health, prosperity and a happy life. The Chinese called their Lodestone 'The Loving Stone' as two rocks would be drawn together, with a kiss. As far back as 83 Common Era (AD) 'Pointing Spoons' were mentioned in Chinese writings as a means of finding your way home. Certainly by the 8th century the Chinese were using the magnetic compass for navigation. In 1175 Alexander Neckem an English monk of St. Albans describes the workings of a compass. Whether the compass was developed independently of China or not, the same magic was being used in Europe by 1400 century, even before Marco Polo had returned from his remarkable adventures in China. I say magic, as even as late as the 17th cent an English sea captain would not allow his sailors to eat onions, in case the odor upset the compass.

In Central America, there are also Mayan legends of magnets dating back to pre-Colombian times. Many doctors during the time of Queen Elizabeth I of England experimented with magnetism and it has returned to favor today with many wearing magnet bracelets to relieve the pain of arthritis.

In the first factories to produce magnets, the iron was shaped and then taken to a special room where it was kept over night in secret, coming out from the room next morning as magnets, only added to its mystery. What happened in the mystical room? The average worker would not be allowed to see that the iron shapes being stroked in one direction with another magnet to create magnetized iron, as with the athame, so simple, so effective. But the secret as with many trade or guild secrets were kept in select group or with families.

Magic: Used to draw luck, love and business success into your life. It can also be used to repel bad luck from you, drawing the problem into the stone and away from you. Lodestone is also used as far away as Peru, to draw good luck into the home. Ensure that you wash your magnetite in saltwater every fullmoon to rid the stone of the bad luck that is has accumulated through the month. Lodestone should also be fed with iron filings to strengthen it. In Hoodoo (African-American magic) it is believed that it should be carried as a pair, one to draw good fortune towards you and one to draw bad luck from you. Lodestone is a good substitute for Iron in ritual, as it contains iron naturally within.

'Placed on the pillow of a guilty wife, it would make her confess her iniquities as she slept. It could be used for the treatment of many ailments, and as a contraceptive.' **Please don't put all your faith in this form of contraception.**

Malachite (green)

The green that you see on any copper surface, is in fact malachite. It grows on the surface of the metal, much as rust does on iron but with more usable and prettier results. Malachite contains copper and has all the attributes of that metal which is sacred to Aphrodite, the Goddess of Love. Aphrodite rose from the water, malachite swirls like water caught in a whirlpool and is believed to make spells more powerful. The priests of Aphrodite supervised works in the copper mines of Cyprus, Aphrodite's birthplace. In Cyprus and Greece, Malachite is always set in copper.

Ancient Egyptians used ground Malachite as eye makeup and it was also sacred to Hathor the Egyptian Goddess of Love.

Magic: Its best known attribute is of course love but malachite also brings with it Venus's other qualities of healing, patience, luck and protection from accidents.

Healing: Helps prevent infection, improves fertility and eyesight. Copper is a well known remedy for rheumatism and so too is malachite. Good for labor pains.

Mangango (pale pink)

A strange stone, very pale pink in both natural and artificial light but under Ultraviolet light it glows hot fiery pink. No historical uses but see what you feel from it.

Moonstone (white)

White Moonstone must have a mobile reflective eye that runs across the stone. You will know it when you see it.

Moonstone is exactly that, a Moon stone, good for women and men who wish to get in touch with the female Goddesses, she awards success to artistic and creative efforts. This stone changes character with the waxing and waning moon. When waxing, it enhances love; when waning, it helps divination and healing.

Moonstone is considered particularly sacred in India, it brings good fortune and is always displayed on a yellow cloth, in India a sacred color.

Magic: Love, healing and divination.

Healing: Good for women's swings of emotions.

Eagle Moonstone (dark grey)

Sometimes known as Black Moonstone, in the charge of the Dark Goddess and so therefore highly protective. Carried by women to protect against miscarriages and to secure an easy delivery. Woman wore them around their necks in a little bag during pregnancy and tied to their thigh in labor.

Its name of 'eagle' comes from the legend that eagles will always find and place a black moonstone in their nest, to protect their young. A Sufi priest used to come into my shop, who owned a mountain in Afghanistan on which his family farmed. He came bustling into the shop one day to tell me that there had been a storm at the farm and an eagle's nest had been knocked from its erie. So convinced was he that he was flying back to Afghanistan to be the first to find the eagle moonstone and if it was not there he felt sure that, one of his family had found it first!

Magic: Protection

Healing: Moonstone is a general healer and good for growth in children. Reduces PMT, regulates and eases periods, improves digestion and concentration. Moonstone must be washed in saltwater once a month, preferably at the full moon, to cleanse it.

Moldervite (dark green)

Moldervite either comes from outer space carried within a meteor or is formed by the meteors collision with the Earth. No one really knows. A very interesting stone, use in meditation and connect with the concept of the universe.

Morganite (pink)

Morganite was discovered in the early 20th century and named after John Pierpont Morgan and is part of the beryl family. It color is gentle pink and has no history behind it, so play with it, hear and feel what it has to tell you. General consensus of opinion is that it is a general healer, which gives strength.

Opal (white or black background with many colors playing across its surface)

Brings mental or physical harm if given and so has a reputation as an unlucky stone, though thought to protect against poison. Opals absorb water easily and so swell, when the air is dry they shrink, making them loose in their settings. All Opals given time, some within a short span of years lose their coloring. This I think goes some way to explaining their reputation, although from my own experience not all of the Opal reputation can be explained away so easily. Opals were called Eyestones in the Middle Ages and indeed, the cheaper ones do look like the blind eyes that I have always called them since childhood. The rainbow of colors locked within the best Opals were thought by the Arabs to be given to the stone as it fell through the air in a lightning storm. But as with everything, expensive stones can be very beautiful with a wonderful play of sparkly and fiery colors, making a wonderful amulet of the first order.

Magic: Opal aids meditation and prophetic sight.

Healing: Improves memory, intellect and vision, helping with digestion and stress.

Fire Opal (yellow- orange-red) or Girasol, Fire Opal is not like opal at all to look at, being a translucent to semi-opaque stone that is generally yellow to bright orange sometimes nearly red and as you turn the stone it can display different colors at certain angles. Fire Opal looking more like an orange Garnet than an Opal but is a far softer gem than Garnet and therefore scratching and marking of the stone can easily occurs.

Onyx (black)

This is its commercial name but it is really black agate, real onyx is the multi-colored stone of coffee tables and lamp stands. Black Agate attributes are protection and clairvoyance. Helps with contacting spirits as all black stones are under the rule of Saturn and The Dark Goddess.

Magic: The Dark Goddess (Crone) area of influence-Protection.

Healing: Onyx has always been used for tired feet.

Striped Onyx (black & white) If worn over the heart, it is said in India to cool love, it may be due to the distinct and separate bands of black and white.

Obsidian (black)

Encourages boldness, vigor and personal achievement. Helps with contacting spirits, as all black stones are under the rule of Saturn and The Dark Goddess. Dr Dee, Queen Elizabeth I court magician, had a wonderful Black Mirror cut from a piece of black Obsidian.

Magic: Protection and excellent for magic mirrors.

Healing: Strengthens flagging spirits and tired muscles.

Pearl (iridescent) many colors.

A Pearl is formed from a piece of grit that has inadvertently made its way into an oyster. The oyster is irritated by the grit and covers it in many layers of nectar until a pearl is formed. It takes three years for 1mm of nectar to be laid down.

Cleopatra was famous, amongst other things, for her pearl earrings. She owned a pair of fabulous matching drops pearls worth as much as an entire country. Cleopatra bet Mark Anthony who could spend the most money on one party. He provided gold plates set with precious gems, giving these as a gift to all his guests and only the best in lavish food and entertainment. She gave a party with fine food and good entertainment but not as fine as Mark Anthony at which, he claimed the prize. She then took a glass of wine (probably vinegar), took off one of her famous pearls and dropped it into the cup. After waiting a few moments, she drank it, and won the prize, Pearls dissolve in vinegar.

One very interesting use of gems historically, is the use of peridot, amethyst and pearl as a means of showing support for the suffragette movement. Spelling out *"Give votes to women"*, in gems.

Peridot- (Green) Give

Amethyst - (Violet)   Votes

Pearl- (White)   Women

By the wearing of a brooch or pendant of these stones, women would show their solidarity with their sisters in the fight for the ability to cast votes. No one else however would understand the meaning of the code.

Magic: Pearls come in most colors of the rainbow as well as black but the pearl the most desired for magic is the white pearl of the Virgin Goddess. Although I am sure that should you be the proud owner of a coal black pearl, the Crone Goddess would appreciate it dedicated to Her.

White pearls give faithfulness in love, if worn next to the heart, also rewards charitable deeds and selfless actions. As water is the pearl's special element, it protects across the sea and symbolizes purity.

Healing: A beauty aid, improving hair, teeth, nails and skin. Eases muscular tension relieving pain and lifting depression.

Mother of Pearl is a less expensive version of pearl for magical workings. Mother of Pearl is made from nectar the same material which creates a pearl in an oyster. Mother of Pearl is laid down on the inside of the shell like a cushion, to stop irritation and make the shell more comfortable for the animal within.

Peridot (olive green)

Both the Egyptians and the Romans loved Peridot. The Romans calling Peridot 'Evening Emerald' and the name in Greek means 'giving plenty'.

Magic: Peridot helps you walk a spiritual path, preserves marital fidelity and negates envy. It protects the wearer from illusion and promotes friendship and health.

Healing: Boosts energy levels, strengthens lower back and the skeleton, cools fevers cures mental and physical weakness.

Pyrite (golden)

This is what is referred to in the Old American West as 'Fool's Gold'. Pyrite is said to keep dragons away, which must be true as I have never seen a dragon near my home and I have several pieces of Pyrite. Probably, a dragons love of pure gold, is the reason that they shun Pyrite, although Pyrite has a sparkly beauty of its own.

Pyrite produces sparks if struck by iron.

Magic: It guards your home against lightning, also attracts vitality and lifts depression, tension and pain as well as giving sound business sense and success. This stone also restrains anger.

Healing: A general tonic.

Quartz Crystal (clear)

Its old name is Shewstone and it is a stone of the Moon and water. From early times rock crystal was thought to be a strange form of frozen ice. The Roman Claudius, 370-404BCE said, *"This piece of ice bears the trace of its original nature, in part it is crystallized, but it has resisted the cold. It is a game or trick played by winter,"* -this idea persisted until as late as the 17th century.

Necklaces of quartz have been found in graves dating to BCE 1200, many Stone Circles in Europe have a high quartz content. Wealthy Romans would purchase very large crystal balls, to rest their hands on during the long hot summers to cool the blood. In the Lithica from Ancient Greece, it states that the Gods love those that entre the temple with a crystal ball in their hands. Smaller crystal balls were used by doctors to cauterize wounds and by priests in the temples to light sacred fires by amplifying the Suns rays. Anglo-Saxon times faceted crystal beads were worn on a chatelaine one was found in a grave at Petersfinger, Wifts that was 40mm with 24 facets cut into it. Later quartz was thought to increase nursing mother's milk. In the 12th century crystal beads were especially cut in London for each purchaser to protect from the Evil Eye. Crystals have been used for healing since at least BCE 500 in Peru, with wonderful crystal necklaces coming from the Mochica period. Eventually the

Mochica culture was assimilated into the Inca Empire and their love of crystals was also adopted with the rest of their traditions, before the Spanish attempted to smash the South American cultures of Inca and Aztec. Shamans in Peru to this day still use crystals, and the Desana Indians of Columbia still see crystals as a *'means of communication between the visible and invisible worlds, a crystallization of energy, or the Sun Father's semen which can be used in esoteric undertakings.'*

Quartz Crystals were used by the Aztecs and Mayans who carved quartz into magnificent skulls, some measuring up to 8¼ inches, holding untold mysteries. This is not an easy undertaking without metal tools; it must have taken years of patient work to produce these magnificent magical artifacts. There true use is still is unknown but we all can appreciate there artistic skill and undoubted connection with the Gods

The Mayans dropped small pieces of quartz into mead and used this to read the future. In Native American culture, Crystals were known as Grandfather and Grandmother Crystals as they were aged and to be respected.

In Greaco-Scythian area of the Black Sea in the 4th and 3rd century BCE Quartz Crystal balls set in silver were worn, hanging from a woman's waist on a long chain.

In the late 5th century to late 6th century, Anglo-Saxon women proudly wore very similar Crystal balls. Most are found in graves sat on ornate silver spoons, which have holes in an equal armed cross pattern, some set with Garnets, that can only be a sieve of some kind. As they sat together in death, like a knife and fork would today, would that mean that they were used together? Strainers were used in Greece and Rome to strain wine and this practise was still in use in the Christian church, so possibly we could assume Rome influenced the Anglo-Saxon ladies.

From Beowulf we learn that the lady of the house served to wine and I assume she wore her crystal ball and sieve out of pride that she was mistress of her house. In relatively modern times, crystal balls looking remarkably like the Anglo-Saxon style were dipped into water to cure cattle. Did she bless the wine with the crystal ball or add healing for all present or was it used to start a magical fire or all three? Crystal ball became fashionable again in the Renaissance for divination.

You can see from the two genuine adverts, Quartz Crystal were very sought after in America during WW11 for radio and radar use.

Quartz Crystal balls are very expensive; not to be confused with lead glass also known as crystal, make sure when you buy you get what you want, be specific. Glass is an insulator of electrical impulses and crystal is not. Quartz enhances other gems placed with it, therefore does it do the same for the mind when concentrating on it? Does a Quartz Crystal ball magnify your psychic ability? Glass does not. Quartz Crystal balls are not easy to use, but the results are dramatic. Even today, with modern technology, it takes weeks to polish a crystal into

its ball shape but by hand it would have taken years; or the crystal skulls of the Aztecs an entire lifetimes work, and so are truly to be prized.

Double terminated crystals are slightly different as their energy comes out at both ends of the crystal at once. I tend to use these for giving healing and balancing laying them on the site of the pain placing my hand on the crystal and directing my energy down through the crystal into the problem. Always down from you to the pain, rather than drawing out the pain or this will then be trapped in you and is very difficult to remove.

Magic: Divination and energy enhancing. The moon has a great affect on tides and as quartz was thought to be frozen water, so rock crystal can be used to bring rain, quench thirst and afford protection for travelers on the sea. Crystal is a meditative aid and energy amplifier, which helps increase your clairvoyant ability, and placed with any other stone it increases that stone's energy and the strength of the altar it is placed upon. Given as a gift at birth, the purity of the Quartz Crystal protects the child.

It is said to be a component in spells of invisibility and if held or worn during astral travelling, it protects the individual from harm.

Healing: Brilliant all round healers and especially promoting skin rejuvenation.

Ruby (red)

The most valuable variety of corundum, the unromantic family name, is the stunning red Ruby.

They brought me Rubies from the mine,
And held them to the Sun:
I said "they are drops of frozen wine
From Eden's vats that run" by Ralph Waldo Emerson

Ruby can only be red, not even dark pink, any other shade and they are classified as Sapphires. The red hues of ruby result from traces of chromium within the gem. The Ruby in India is called the "King of Precious Stones" and it was thought that an inextinguishable flame burnt within each stone and you can understand why. The Burmese believed that gemstones ripened like fruit. The redder the color, the riper the ruby. A very flawed ruby was considered over mature.

They have a marked florescence and under ultraviolet light they glow like burning coals, even in direct sunlight the ultraviolet in the atmosphere enhances their color. I assume it's the florescence in the stones that makes them glow so much that a good colored stone will leave a memory print on your retina for some considerable time after you remove your gaze. The Mogok region of Burma is where the very finest of Rubies are mined called Pigeon Blood Red and costing thousands of pounds to buy and can cost more than diamonds. Ruby is very rarely found without inclusions, and is discovered normally as small stones.

Magic: They ensure love, passion and self worth, they prolong youthfulness, giving peace of mind and strengthen the will to love. Old legends suggest that Rubies change color, to warn against poison. Rubies also help traders when selling or buying and farmers by protecting their crops from damage. In India the first purchase a businessman makes is to buy a ruby for prosperity, before even his stock, it is considered that important. Rubies preserve health of the wearer, they remove all evil thoughts, "dissipate pestilential vapors" and heal disputes. To be truly invulnerable to harm the ruby must be inserted under the skin. But in any case whether worn under the skin or in a ring or brooch, Rubies must be worn on the left side, your receiving hand, to take their energy into yourself. Dark rubies are considered male stones and light and bright rubies are considered female but all rubies must be kept from other stones particularly poorer quality rubies as this is said to contaminate them.

Healing: Helps with low blood pressure and stimulates the heart.

Star Ruby (red) The special attribute of a Star Ruby is the distinctive six pointed star of light arranged in perfect symmetry, that plays across its surface, shifting it's center as the stone is moved, this is called Asterism. A Star Ruby is one of the most exquisite of stones; the star is caused by very fine needles of Rutile trapped within each stone is thought to hold a deity (a higher being or spirit) contained within the gem, who will work, protect and do it's best for you. The star represents the hexagram and so is said to control angels, demons and elementals.

Magic: Protection.

Healing: Helps those with low blood pressure and stimulates the heart.

Rhodenite (pink with black matrix)
Healing: Good for the skeletal system. Rhodonite relieves mental unrest, confusion and anxiety.

Rose Quartz (pink)
Rose Quartz is one of the most popular stones used to draw love and

friendship to you. It helps to heal a broken heart, giving gentleness and peace of mind, adding extra energy if heart shaped. The best rose quartz is a deep almost translucent pink that can glow with light, not very easy to find I'm afraid.

I never believed that stones changed color, believing it very fanciful, until I gave a friend a very large crystal-shaped Rose Quartz. They wore it for many months, slowly it began to change color, deepening in color and becoming more translucent, I found it astonishing to watch, that a stone formed over millions of years, could change its color due to being worn constantly. I am afraid I am skeptical until proved otherwise, but this can be very healthy, not accepting ideas until convinced of there worth.

Healing: Gentle stimulant for the heart. Helps skin rejuvenation and stops water retention. Rose quartz also has a calming effect.

Rutilated Quartz (clear + gold needles)
The old name for this strange stone, Venus Hair Stone is due to the golden needles of rutile within, looking like strands of blond hair trapped forever in crystal.

Magic: Rutilated Quartz brings light and love into your life.

Healing: Helps to heal wounds. Helps digestion and aids the immune system.

Sodalite (blue and white)
It helps clear away-outdated ideas and bad habits; it also awakens the third eye and enhances intuitiveness. This stone looks a little like Lapis Lazuli but without Lapis's glow, although Sodalite is harder and therefore better wearing than Lapis.

Healing: Sodalite prolongs physical endurance, so aids athletes and improves eyesight.

Smokey Quartz (beige to black)
Smoky Quartz gives pride in oneself and oneness with the Earth. Drew mental and physical energy from the Earth by the use of this

stone, also attributed unsurprisingly to the Dark Goddess. Comes in many shades of brown, some have been artificially enhanced, these are surprisingly the paler brown stones I love the dark, almost black stones from Brazil, they have such a deep connection to the Earth. Black Smoky Quartz are called Morian Quartz.

Healing: Gives mental and physical energy.

Snowflake Obsidian (black and white)
This stone sharpens both external and internal vision.

Sapphire (blue)
Sapphire and Rubies are only second to diamonds in hardness. Rarely do they scratch or mark and so with only a small degree of care, they will last for many thousands of years, being recycled from crowns to rings and back. Although Sapphire is traditionally thought of as blue, pure sapphire is colorless (pure aluminium oxide), the added chemicals of iron and chrome that the Goddess dripped into the gem as it was forming and so colors it to Her needs. A Sapphire can be any color and if not blue are usually called "fancy-color sapphire" and can be any color but red, as this is gem is called Ruby. The greater the concentration of naturally added minerals, the deeper the color.

Sapphire is considered one of the great gems of the world, along with diamond, ruby and emerald. This is not only due to sapphires' wonderful color, many gems have a brilliant blue color (the color most associated with Sapphire), or its cost, which is higher than other blue gems but its traditional association with magic. It was for that reason it was so highly prized and still is, in many parts of the world.

Sapphire's color comes from heat deep within the Earth, heating an almost colorless stone with needles of Rutile within, to high temperatures and then slowly cooling. The Titanium of the Rutile reacts with any traces of iron in the sapphire producing the breath-taking blue color of the Sapphire.

Sapphire also supposedly changes color if near poison, as with ruby, understandable as both jewels are part of the same mineral family.

Black Sapphire under the auspices of the Dark Goddess, comes from Australia. It is the least expensive shade of sapphire, not costing more than a shirt or skirt and so can be afforded by all and it will last far longer than the any piece of clothing.

Sapphire has many delightful stories attached to it, the Greeks associated sapphires with the God Apollo, patron of the Arts. Legend has it that sapphire was the stone on which the Ten Commandments were written. Strangely I saw a documentary about the tablets of Mount Sinai, suggesting that they may be a lot smaller than previously thought, if so, this fits with his legend.

Another delightful story of sapphire comes from Ancient Persia. They believed that the Earth rested on a colossal sapphire and the sky reflected its stunning color. The wonderful name of "gem of heaven" was long ago given to sapphire. Due to its beautiful color and its renown ability to give wisdom, sapphire is used in many crown jewels, in the hope that wisdom and justice will prevail in the kingdom.

In the middle ages the Roman Catholic Church decided that all gems held the devil within and the only way to exorcise them was to give them to the safe keeping of the church. Many years' later sapphires in particular were favored as Bishop's rings, bringing wisdom- hopefully.

Bartolomaes tells us *"Also wytches love well this stone (sapphire), for they wene that they may werke certen wondres by vertue of this stone."*

Magical properties- Sapphires great attribute is wisdom and hidden knowledge; from blue of air to black the color of the Dark Goddess, sapphire enhances clarity of mind and wisdom and promotes health and strength. Thought to clarify knowledge given in visions.

Star Sapphire (blue) The special attribute of a Star Sapphire as with the Star Ruby is the distinctive six-pointed star of light that plays across its surface, representing the hexagram. Each stone is thought to hold a deity within that will work, protect and do its best for you. The three bars that make up the six pointed star are meant to represent Faith, Hope and Charity, and even to look at the asteria (star) on the stone, is meant to bring great good luck.

Magic: It gives freedom from enchantment and offers protection.

Fancy Color Sapphires comes in all colors other than blood red, but almost any other color of the rainbow can be found from pink, yellow, purple, clear to browns each having a slightly different energy.

Pink Sapphire A Pink Sapphire is not an easily obtainable stone and is a beautiful sparkling shade of pale to deep pink. Within its facets it holds the wisdom to value true love and release unwanted love.

Padparadscha Sapphire is a rare and expensive orange-pink and comes from the Sinahalese word meaning "lotus colored".

Healing: It is said to increases the levels of potassium, magnesium and calcium in the body.

Sardonyx (brown and white layered)

The sardonyx protects from incantations and sorcery. The red hue of the stone sharpens the wits making you fearless, victorious and happy. This stone brings love, romance, vitality, confidence and fitness.

Healing: A physical stimulant. Sardonyx helps ward off infectious diseases, improves vision and speeds recovers from illness.

Satin Spar (Pure white)

It is a form of Gypsum, with long straight grain, very popular today and very cheap, although it is very soft and can be carved with a fingernail. When carved into a ball or any round shape it shows a wonderful moving eye which give its qualities of protection and brings good fortune. Large balls of this stone can be purchased quite cheaply.

Star Diopside (aka Black Moonstone or Black Star of India)

Diopside derives from the Greek word 'di' meaning two, and 'opsis', meaning vision. Although not part of the moonstone family, this is a wonderful stone. It has only just been discovered for use in magic and therefore has no long history. I'm sure when you hold it you will feel the power of the Dark Goddess (Crone Goddess), as the light catches it, it splits into a four pointed star, the only stone to do this! Which brings the power of the elements to any ring or pendant it is set. When Star Diopside contains lodestone (magnetite) it is easily attracted by a magnet, adding the power of Lodestone to this gem.

Magic: Protection

Sunstone (orange)

A stone of the Sun, (related to Moonstone) a male stone it bringing happiness and joy.

Tigereye (golden brown)

Tigereye has a wonderful play across the stone which is always cut cabochon, this is known as chatoyancy. Not always an eye, but often having bands of color. Tigereye is well known for averting the Evil Eye. Focuses negative energy drawn into the stone and channeling it into success in ventures. It also helps you to think more clearly.

Hawkeye (blue) Like Tigereye, so choose which of the two stones draws your attention, are you a brown or a blue person?

Dragon or Bulleye (red) As with Tigereye and Hawkeye, all having the same energy.

Healing: Reduces headaches and nervous tensions, increases the body's capacity to resist infection.

Topaz (blue, orange, brown, green, pink, beige and red)

The Golden Orangey Brown gem also called Imperial Topaz, has long been associated with royalty and nobility it promises friendship and faithfulness. Brown Topaz is very grounding (including mental health) and is a good sexual stimulant. It improves physical fitness, joy and prosperity, courage and wisdom. Topaz to the Egyptians typified the golden glow of the mighty Sun God Ra. To the Romans, Topaz belonged to Jupiter, King of the of Gods and dispelled enchantment.

To the Greeks it gave strength and in times of need made the wearer invisible. Topaz is another of the stones that change color near poison.

Healing: Topaz fights kidney and bladder ailments and is good for vitamin assimilation. Helps with mental health problems and prevents sleepwalking. Rheumatism and Arthritis responds very well to Topaz.

Blue Topaz (blue both light- Sky Blue and dark- London Blue)

Topaz is rarely naturally blue, most blue stones are irradiated by man, it is possible to get a natural Blue Topaz but it is impossible to tell from the irradiated stones. Irradiating the gems does not negate their energies but does change them from that of a clear or muddy colored Topaz to the energies of a blue Topaz, I have found them to be more ethereal, giving wisdom and a good meditative aid.

Pink Topaz New on the scene the exquisite pink Topaz is rarely natural, again mostly irradiated.

Tourmaline

When heated or rubbed creates an electric charge becoming a crystal magnet for lightweight objects, it is used to clean ash from pipes in industry. Now known as piezoelectricity and is used in computers, musical keyboards, cellular phones and other hi-tech devices.

Tourmaline (pink) Pink Tourmaline attracts inspiration, goodwill and friendship.

Tourmaline (green) Green Tourmaline improves the three bodies of physical, mental and spiritual to balance.

Tourmaline (blue) Blue Tourmaline sharpens mental accuracy.

Tourmaline (purple) Purple Tourmaline gives greater self-confidence.

Healing: Helps to prevent lymphatic diseases, fights anemia and is good for the intestinal tract.

Tourmelated Quartz (clear quartz with black needles of Tourmaline)

Increases mental awareness and enhances psychic ability. This stone keeps fears at bay.

Healing: Alleviates depression and nervous exhaustion.

Turquoise (blue, sometimes green)

The Egyptians have used turquoise since BCE 6000 in jewelry. True, it is a soft stone and easy to work but it is also a very magical stone. Its sky blue color comes from the presence of copper, making it a good conductor or both electricity and magic.

If Lapis is the midnight sky, then Turquoise is midday, much paler but most with a depth of color that speaks of shimmering heat in the desert. As an Amulet, Turquoise must be the best known stone in the world, from ancient Egypt to modern Greece and to the far flung Americas.

Magic: In the East, Turquoise is called the Horseman's Talisman, protecting from falls and injuries. Aids astral travel, gives ancient wisdom and opens energy channels to the third eye. Turquoise is a powerful help in physical and psychic harm. The deep blue of Turquoise draws love and passion and these help the artist in his search for creativity and imagination. This gem also gives the courage to speak the truth and relaxes stress.

An old spell to obtain good fortune is to see the reflection of the Virgin Moon in a Turquoise stone.

To the ancient Egyptians, both Lapis Lazuli and Turquoise, had the same healing powers.

Healing: Relaxes the body and helps prevent headaches. Turquoise is also good for the respiratory system.

Zircon (brown, green and red, yellow, blue, black, and colorless)

Zircon is naturally found as green and brown but changed artificially to the other colors mentioned above. The colorless versions were up to the invention of Cubic Zirconia used instead of diamond. Zircon is sometimes fluorescent and darker crystals may be radioactive due to impurities of rare Earth elements.

Magic: Zircon protects from enchantment.

Healing: Zircon helps ease childbirth, strengthens the body and restores the appetite.

Fake Stones

Personally, I don't work with fake stones but if you can then that's great. I would rather choose a cheaper stone, than a piece of glass that looks like an expensive stone. Rose quartz for love is very inexpensive where as an Emerald can be very expensive, both will get similar results and far better than green glass. Unfortunately not many New Age shops know the difference between the fake and real. Go to a shop that can advise you properly, I've been working with gems for many years now. I make sure I investigate all new gems that come onto the market.

Alexandrite Fake Alexandrite is the only stone you are liable to find, it is a form of synthetic corundum, violet with very little change in color. This is always without exception fake; easily distinguished from the real Alexandrite with its red to green or at worst brown, color change. Although some purple to green color change has just been found, but like all Alexandrite these are always small, but expensive stones. Unlike fake Alexandrite which will be a very large stone.

Amber Small pieces that are cut from stones to shape them for rings and pendants can be reformed into larger pieces, by heat and pressure this is called Ambroid. It is very cheap and can easily be identified, by an experienced eye. It is usually made into pyramids or statues by placing in the mould whilst still hot, and is only rarely used for jewelry. Sometimes with a hideous bluebottle fly added, to simulate the insects in Amber from so many millions of years ago. Black Amber is either amber with many inclusions of foreign debris or Jet, which also described as Black Amber. Another way of making black amber is to bake it; even in a kitchen oven about 200 degrees C for a couple of hours will do nicely.

Of course the worst way to fake Amber is with plastic or glass, once you have felt Amber, you will know instantly that glass is to heavy. But plastic on the other hand does need an expert eye. Luckily in England you are unlikely to be sold plastic for Amber in a shop, but I have seen it on market stalls being sold as Amber, be aware of what you are buying.

Blue Obsidian Very pretty but man-made glass not natural Obsidian.

Cat's eye Less easy to tell from the real thing, usually great fun colors of bright orange, pink, green, blue and red, are the give away, this can be colored Icelandic Spar, very soft.

Cubic Zirconia or C.Z. Invented to simulate diamonds, Cubic Zirconia does a good job, very difficult to tell by eye, a small diamond tester was invented to help. But with the newer synthetic diamonds, a more advanced diamond tester yet more complex had to be invented. Even this has difficulty with very fluorescent diamonds, it tends to read them as C.Z. Now there is yet another new man-made gem on the market, Moissanite, this sparkles more than diamonds and can withstand higher temperatures, needing yet another device to tell it from diamonds; when does a synthetic diamond become a real diamond? And yes the scientists can make diamonds in a lab now, but at the moment only small and very expensive but who know what tomorrow will bring?

Coloured C.Z. come in all colors now, as pretty stones for modern jewelry, they are superb. It is easy to confuse these with real stone, real amethyst or aquamarine but there is one way to tell a C.Z. it is too sparkly to be any thing but a diamond and you won't get a diamond for the same price as a C.Z.

Faux There are lots of names for fake stones and this is one, Nature Identical, Simulate, Lab Grown Gems, Created, these are just some of the words used in advertising to the public.

French Jet Right color but real Jet is very light, like plastic, French Jet is far too heavy, glass again.

Goldstone Glass (can be brown or blue) with brass or copper fillings with in. This has been used since Egyptian times, Egyptians were great fakers of jewelry. Thin gold coats over pottery for beads, glass to imitate Lapis, Turquoise or Carnelian.

Moodstone (Not Moonstone) Totally synthetic, predicts your moods, BUT I KNOW WHEN I'M ANGREE!!

Opal Triplet Black Opal is very expensive and there are many simulants on the market. This is a very thin slice of fine opal set on a bed of either plastic or onyx with a slice of quarts crystal glued on top, known as an Opal Triplet in the trade. An Opal Triplet will not work magically in the same way as a fine Opal, too much glue and plastic.

Quick Gem Guide

Courage-   Citrine, Garnet, Haematite, Lapis
                        Lazuli,

Energy-   Citrine, Haematite, Garnet, Ruby,
                        Smoke Quartz, Sodalite,

Divination-   Aquamarine, Beryl, Emerald,
                        Moonstone, Onyx, Opal, Quartz
                        Crystal, Sodalite Tourmalated
                        Quartz, Turquoise, Labradorite.

Happiness-   Blue Lace Agate, Yellow Beryl,
                        Bloodstone, Diamond, Jasper,
                        Ruby, Sunstone, Imperial Topaz,
                        Pink Tourmaline,

Healing-

Amethyst, Aventurine, Blue Agate, Aquamarine, Coral, Fluorite, Mangano, Jade, Jasper, Malachite, Moonstone, Opal, Peridot, Pyrite, Quartz Crystal, Imperial Topaz, Green Tourmaline, Tourmalated Quartz, Zircon.

Love-

Amethyst, Ametrine, Diamond, Emerald, Lapis Lazuli, Lodestone, Malachite, Moonstone, Pearl, Peridot, Rose Quartz, Rutilated Quartz, Turquoise.

Luck-

Apache Tear, Lodestone,

Money-

Aventurine, Green Agate, Diamond, Lodestone, Ruby,

Protection-

Catseye, Coral, Carnelian, Fossil Stone, Fossilized Wood, Garnet, Hawkseye, Tigereye, Jasper, Lodestone, Malachite, Eagle Moonstone, Onyx, Turquoise.

Protection with travelling-

Agate, Carnelian, Citrine, Fluorite, Jet, Eagle Moonstone, Quartz Crystal,

Psychic Protection-

Amber, Amethyst, Coral, Diamond, Diopside, Fossil Stone, Lapis Lazuli, Lodestone, Eagle Moonstone, Star Ruby, Star

Sapphire,

Self Esteem-
Brown to Red Agate, Jade, Jet, Sapphire, Smoke Quartz, Sodalite, Ruby, Imperial Topaz, Blue and Purple Tourmaline,

Sexuality-
Amber, Carnelian, Haematite, Garnet, Ruby, Imperial Topaz,

Spirituality-
Amethyst, Ametrine, Azurite, Citrine, Lapis Lazuli, Peridot, Quartz Crystal, Sapphire,

Legendary Mystical Qualities of Metals

Many metals can only be made in the heart of a star; a star must die throwing itself into the Universe millions of years before our sun was born, for you to hold it in your hands.

Gold and silver along with platinum are considered precious metals. Many countries around the world, Britain among them, insist by law that precious metals are stamped- hallmarked. This is a applied by the government to assure the buyer that their purchase is genuine.

Gold Sacred to The Sun (color yellow)

Raw gold, when taken from the earth, is a shiny metal of a deep yellow color, regardless of where in the world the metal is mined. Gold is a very heavy metal and is a good conductor of both heat and electricity and is unchanging, unaffected by moisture, heat, and most corrosive chemicals. Gold in its purest form is very soft and easily worked and along with silver, was one of the first metals to be made into jewelry and artifacts.

Gold is measured in Carats, 24 carats (ct) or parts are pure gold. The more carats the heavier and more expensive an item becomes.

Although 24 carat gold is too soft to be used as jewelry (unless you are an Egyptian Pharaoh or an Inca King with nothing to do all day but look powerful and godlike). In my grandmothers time only 22ct gold was ever considered good enough for wedding rings, just a little other metals are mixed with the gold a touch of silver brass or copper, to fortify the wedding ring to made it last a lifetime. This is still true in India and surrounding areas, the other metals mixed with gold can be affected by sweat and discolor and so in hot countries the higher the carat the better. The more metals that are mixed with the pure gold the less caret the gold has, other grades 18ct, 14ct, 9ct and due to the Common Market even 8ct is now accepted in England.

Quantities of other metals are added to gold that strengthens it, this is normally brass copper and silver. The proportions change, if yellow, red or white gold is being produced. Red gold has proportionally more copper in the molten mix; with more copper the deeper red the gold becomes. White gold has the addition of silver to the gold, the more silver is added the whiter it becomes. Mixing different metals can even produce green gold! Although this is very expensive, due to such a small quantity produced.

All the gold ever mined from the Earth is still in circulation, your wedding ring may contain gold that once adorned an Inca King or a Russian Princess.

Magic: Gold is the metal of the Gods, it shines like the sun, invigorates the mind and body of the warrior. Gold stands for immortality, chosen for wedding rings, due to its brightness never to be dimmed by time. Good for blessings, happiness and good luck charms.

It's cheaper alternative for magic is Brass.

Healing: Helps with Rheumatism, and invigorates the mind and body.

Mercury - Sacred to Mercury, (Silver color) for news.

Mercury's is named after the Roman God (the Greek Hermes), its old name is Quicksilver, the metal is liquid in our atmosphere and is indeed a wonderful silver color but very heavy for it's volume. Like

Mercury with his winged heels and hat, who was the messenger of the Greek Gods and Mercury the planet closest to the Sun and flying around and around, careering across the sky, a quick mover. The metal Mercury is also an accumulative poison absorbed through the skin, be VERY careful if you choose to use it. There is a Spell from the Caribbean, using Nutmeg that I would not recommend. Mercury being liquid, is difficult to use, take a nutmeg and hollow it out, fill this with Mercury drip wax in the top to seal and carry it round with you for luck. As Mercury is a poison that is absorbed by the skin, if it were to leak, you might not have much luck with this spell. This very poisonous substance was used as a medicine, not that many years ago.

Copper Sacred to Venus and Aphrodite (the color of the metal is a red/ brown, however green malachite grows on copper, so its other color is green) The Goddess of love, healing and wealth.

Copper has been used for 10,000 years and later with a little added tin makes bronze, useful for swords and all manor of vessels.

Copper is sacred to Venus / Aphrodite (Romans and Greeks shared the same Goddess under different names), well known for answering Her love spells. The priests of Aphrodite supervised works in the copper mines of Cyprus, Aphrodite's birthplace.

Magic: Use Copper in Love spells.

Healing: Copper helps with arthritis control.

Electrum (pale gold)

Used in Ancient Egypt to cover the caps of needle monuments and for amulets and talisman it is a mixture of at least 20% Silver and Gold. Silver and gold are often found together, perhaps this gave the ancients inspiration to create Electrum. Today we consider this a mixture of God and Goddess within one metal; it is a creamy color and has the attributes of both.

Silver - Sacred to the Moon (color silver)

Silver is the highest electrical and thermal conductor of any metal and this is the reason that it conducts magic so beautifully. Silver like gold is easily worked and used in jewelry almost pure 92.5%, again just enough extra metal to give silver strength.

Magic: Silver is imbued with magic and protection, a good metal to use for magical Talisman and Amulets. It is attributed to the Goddess and the night, gleaming by the gentle light of the moon, funnily it does not like sunlight and will discolor if left for any period in the light of the sun, turning black.

Silver was highly prized in the ancient world, twice the price of gold but today we have found extra silver deposits and its price has tumbled. This makes it affordable by all, not just the rich.

Healing: As far back as Hippocrates, the father of medicine from whom we get the Hippocratic Oath that doctors swear on taking up their profession, silver has been used speed wound healing and alleviate disease. Phoeniciens used to store wine, vinegar and water in silver. Silver compounds predated antibiotics during WW1 for the treatment of burns. Today we are able to confirm that silver does kill a broad spectrum of bacteria and fungi. In England to stop "witches" turning the milk sour, a silver coin was place into the container and in America a similar idea was used.

Iron - Sacred to Mars (Iron is a dark silvery color not unlike heamatite but rust grows on iron and so its color is red)

Iron is used in courage magic and is a talisman against evil. Whereas magnetized iron will work to attract your wish to you, as in the Hoodoo Mojo bags, which contain two pieces one to attract and one to repel.

The first Iron used was meteoric iron, dropping from the home of the Gods it was thought to be particularly potent for magic. The Ancient Sumerians called it 'sky metal' as can well be imagined. The Egyptian Was scepter is always made from meteoric iron. Meteoric Iron would have never been touched by human fire being beaten into shape, the only heat it would have been touched by would be the hand of the Gods. But wrought iron must first be heated to remove it from the iron ore, so has had some degree of human interference. Evil spirits, ghosts or demons (and some stories add witches to the list and this I think may be the origin of some covens not using iron within circle derive. But what of the iron cauldron, surly a must within all circles?) do not like to be in the vicinity of iron. Many folklore traditions around the world use iron, many to do with coffin nails. In parts of Scotland in the 1800's, when a death occurred within a family, the custom was to hammer an iron nail into all the food and the whisky barrel to stop the dead from entering it. Horseshoes are made from iron, which roughly resembles the moon, add to this the power of the horse, and you can see why horseshoes became such a potent protection symbol.

A Pentagram made from handmade iron Horseshoe nails

Iron is now days difficult to get, and so we look back and use the iron our forefathers first used- meteoric iron. Cheaper still is Magnetite rock, or Haematite tumble stones that contain Iron.

Tin - Sacred to Jupiter (again a silvery color but Jupiter's color is purple, sometimes royal blue). Tin draws luck to you, a very expensive metal, needless to say tin cans are not made from tin but steel and have a fine spray of tin on them to stop them rusting. It is impossible to get hold of pure tin and to add to the confusion, some tin cans now days are Aluminum.

Lead - Sacred to Saturn (who's color is black)
Wisdom.

Lead like Mercury and Gold is very heavy, difficult but not impossible to get hold of. Not much used in magic it is a very sedentary metal. Thin sheets were used in Ancient Rome to write curses on. Then rolled and placed within the property of the recipient of the curse.

Smiths are metal workers, in the early days smiths did not specialize as they did later, becoming Blacksmiths, Swordsmiths, silversmiths or goldsmiths but tended to make whatever the community wanted or could afford. Smiths and Farriers (people that shoe horses) have always been connected with magic. The first iron tools were made from meteoric iron that fell from the sky, the home of the Gods. The Smiths transformed this gift of the Gods into a magical tool of great power by the use of another great and powerful energy- fire. Later Farriers shaped iron into horseshoes for this magical beast and so horseshoes took on the energy of both Smith and horse, bringing luck. The water that Farriers use to douse their work, would be drunk by the family and only someone very privileged outside the family would be allowed a sip. The water was considered have very magical properties due to the Iron content and the words of power whispered into the Smiths work. On a more prosaic note, if in a community that was poorly fed, the iron within the Smiths quenching water would provide much needed addition to a diet, helping to stop anemia.

Many Goddesses possess Smithing as one of their qualities - Brigit, Athena who taught Daedalus, the builder of the labyrinth, as well as some Gods - Wayland, Hephaestus, Luno, and Gobine were all Smiths. Merlin forged Arthur's magic armor, in some stories of the Arthurian cycle. Goddesses as smiths may have came about by fire and cooking, being the preserve of the woman and so of female Goddesses. Coupled with a war Goddess, copied from nature, female and hunter and defender of the family. Egyptian priests of Isis were smiths, as were priests of Aphrodite in the copper mines of Cyprus.

Smiths have long been linked with witches. Exorcisms attributed to St. Patrick *"against incantations of false prophets, against black laws of hereticians, against surroundings of idolism, against spells of women, and of smiths, and of Druids. Thinking them to use all knowledge that is forbidden the human soul".*

It was thought that a Smith could heal, prophesy and work magic. Some were Blood Charmers and could staunch the flow of blood, by a wave or two of the hand. The Guild of the Smith was considered too strong by the Medieval church and were banned.

Until only a short time ago, it was still possible to be married in Gretna Green over the anvil by a smith. A Celtic scepter has been unearthed at Farley Heath, Albury, Surrey, on it is- a wheel (a Sun symbol), Boars, ravens, stags and hammer and tongs, which are Smiths tools of the trade. This links Smiths to the most prestigious of the sacred animals of the Celts.

Smiths were also in charge of brewing, using the same magic chanted over the making of a sword to enchant both beer and wine. This was brewed especially for occasions such as Yule and Handfastings. Each festival had its own special recipes, but unfortunately this practice had died out since the Second World War and the demise of small family breweries. Happily it is being revived by those demanding real beer, although the words have been lost. I hope they also keep up the practice that the smith must be served first at all banquets! This was to ensure that any magic he had placed within the brews was for the good of the company gathered and that the wine or beer was fit to be drunk, a bit like a poison taster really.

Smiths in times past had many secrets. Up until recently if a Smith died, Smiths would travel from far and wide to meet and say good bye to their colleague. At a point during the funeral, all would be asked to leave including the widow and Vicar, leaving only the body and the Smiths present, at which time a secret ceremony was conducted. After the funeral a donation would be given to the widow. I am sure only the very oldest smiths will remember this now.

Birthstones

Astronomy, as we know it, began to be devised in Before Common Era 2300, in Babylon. Slowly Babylonians began to understand the movement of the planets and stars, predicting eclipses and plotting the Moons appearances. This started firstly as a calendar to plot the year, to understand when to plant the corn or harvest the wheat. Gradually Astronomy began to develop into Astrology to help people to control their environment and future. The earliest horoscopes that we have written records for were plotted in Before Common Era 410. Such a wondrous invention then spread to all the countries around and about. Astrology then travelled to Ancient Greece translating the Gods of the Babylonian pantheon to the Gods and Goddess of the Greek. There, Alexander the Great was instructed in astrology by Aristotle his tutor, from here it spread to all the lands that Alexander conquered. Egypt was the country of learning and although they were experts in Astronomy, it was thought that they never developed this into Astrology, as it was only during the Roman occupation of Egypt that the Zodiac appeared on temple walls. But the Assyrians (a sister-state to Babylon) under their King Sardanapalus concurred Egypt in BCE670 and would surely have brought with them there court Astronomers? Back then, Astronomy and Astrology were one and the same thing, so Egyptian priests would have had access to this information many years earlier than was first though. Egypt added to the teaching, until we have the system that we have today. If you look at the ceiling painting of the Zodiac at Denderah Egypt, it's great fun to find our zodiac that we know and love mixed in with many other signs.

Originally, gems were assigned to each of the Zodiac signs, set into a ring that you changed every month as the year progressed to take into your life the positive aspects of each Zodiac sign and working as an amulet of protection against the negative aspects. But now we wear our birth sign throughout the year, to bring the good aspects of our sign into our lives and negate the bad aspects.

There are two types of gem lists; one shows the temperament of the sign and are called Starstones and the other the gem for the person to wear, this is called a Birthstone. As a Starstone Leo is repre-sented by a Citrine, a Sunstone showing its fiery temperament. As a

Birthstone, Leo should wear a Peridot as an amulet, for its calming effect on its wearer, if Leo's were to wear Citrine they would take over the Earth! I jest.... I think.

Aries March 21st to April 20th **Diamond or Clear Quartz**

Aries starts the procession of the Zodiac, as long ago the Spring Equinox, then considered the start of the year, was situated within Aries, now it sits on the cusp and is not always within Aries

With its passionate and violent temperament, Aries is hasty and rude as well as positive and energetic Aries is the warrior of the Zodiac with Mars as its ruling planet. It has no bright stars in its constellation, could this be the reason that dim Aries has been given the brightest jewel, diamond as its gem? Diamond or clear Quartz Crystal protects from evil and promotes fearlessness.

Taurus April 21st to May 21st **Emerald, Malachite** (which Hathor shares with Venus) under the power of Venus. **Lapis Lazuli and Turquoise** under the power of Hathor.

Taurus loves to give and except love, they are the lovers of the Zodiac it's ruling planet after all is Venus and Emerald is the stone for this.

The name Taurus comes from the Indo-European word for bull. The star sign has been depicted as this animal for hundreds of years but this does not make sense with the interpretation of the character of this sign. If however we interpret the bull as Hathor the Egyptian Horned Cow Goddess (see Hathor in Amulets and Talisman) of fertility, festivity, healing, birth, wealth, happiness and love the equivalent of Venus and Aphrodite (love, wealth and healing) which is the ruling planet of Taurus, everything then drops into place. Hathor the cow, fits the character of Taurus far better than a bull, Taurus loves beauty whether it be in gems, music, dance or food which often makes them too chubby, laughter and happiness are there gift to the world and all are the provenience of Hathor.

In the sky, the constellation of Taurus is depicted as only the front half of the animal and so no conformation can be drawn from this, no udders or penis to choose from. On Her back Taurus, in the Temple at Dendarah, She carries a Fullmoon or a Sun, Hathor is entitled to carry either.

If almost to confirm my theory the large red star Aldebaran (the star is fifty times more luminous than our Sun) is the right eye of the bull/cow constellation of Taurus, it is twice the size of the left eye. If Taurus is indeed Hathor, the right eye is the Eye of Ra. The Sun is the Eye during the day and as Hathor crosses the horizon and charges across the sky at night, She still looks down. Aldebaran may have been the reason that the Egyptians chose the right eye, rather than the left, they saw it in the sky. Most Egyptians would have been more familiar with the night sky and the constellations than we are. Light pollution wipes out the stars for us but for them the constellations were old friends returning. The Eye of Ra was given to Hathor to guard and protect Ra, as with Hathor-Sekhmet's culling of (see mandrake and Eye of Horus) mankind, at Ra's demand. This then became an amulet of protection, travelling across the world and through time and is still used to this day. Aldebaran, as The Eye of Ra stares down from the sky reminding all Egyptians that Hathor watched over them.

The Milky Way was considered the milk of the Cow Goddess Hathor; one of Her names was 'great flood' bringing nourishment and fertility, flowing from the udder of heaven over the world below. Hathor (and later Isis too) was identified as responsible for the yearly inundation of the Nile, bringing much needed fertility to the land and with it happiness, the gift of Hathor. Beside the constellation of Taurus flows the Milky Way, even several thousand years later it is still remembered.

There are also The Seven Hathors, who see the future and know at your birth the date of your death. These are represented by the Pleiades or Seven Sisters, a small but very noticeably bright cluster of stars that just happen to be on Taurus's shoulder, like a brooch.

Hathor was married to Horus and a great festival took place at this time. Where in the merry month of May, the month of Taurus, a Sacred Marriage was performed.

The Assyrian star map or planisphere, which was recovered from the library of King Assurbanipal in Nineveh and is dated to 800 BCE and has only eight, star signs and so eight months in a year. Possibly one month and star sign for each of the solstices, equinox and cross quarter days. Here the Pleiades or the Seven Hathors, features as a star sign but not Taurus. So possibly Taurus does not have as long a history as a star sign as was thought.

Aries may well be another Egyptian concept added to the Zodiac, Amun-Ra the Ram headed Sun God and the most powerful of the Gods, now starts the Zodiac. The ram as a Zodiac sign, seems to be unknown in Mesopotamia.

Hathor's special gems were Lapis Lazuli, Turquoise, once more small but interesting parts of the puzzle fall into place, blue is a Tauruian colour, and both of these gems are blue. Taurus is considered a "feminine" sign, which obviously does not suit a bull. An Earth sign and a negative sign, both of these were considered female not male traits in the middle ages and possibly earlier.

For me Taurus will always be under the guardianship of Hathor, Aphrodite and Venus.

Gemini May 22nd to June 20th Agate or Pearl

Gemini are the heavenly twins Castor and Polux if you were Greek and Romulus and Remus if you were Roman. The two bright stars that feature in the constellation of Gemini probably were the inspiration for the legend of the twins.

A nice thought to honor Gemini would be to carry or wear two stone one for each twin. If you decide on the gem Agate, choose a color that appeals, your body will guide your choice. Pearl on the other hand aids a beautiful skin, teeth and hair, and as Gemini is the sign of communication in the Zodiac, presentation goes hand in hand.

Cancer June 21st to July 20th Ruby, Carnelian, Pearl or Moonstone

Cancer means crab and that sums up a Cancarian, the hard outer shell hiding the soft inner sensitive personality. The Moon rules Cancer with its watery symboligy and it governs the house and home, so in witchcraft terms look to the Mother Goddess if you are born under the sign of Cancer.

Cancarians are fine for planning and dreaming but Ruby or Carnelian will help put plans into action for wealth and success. Moonstone or pearl will leave them forever dreaming and planning, never living life to the full.

Leo July 21st to August 21st **Peridot**

Leo either births selfless leaders or destructive dictators. Leo does not understand the word "neutral". When the ego dominates a force-fulness of the will results and Leo stamps their foot and demands obedience. Leo is of the fire elements and is hot and dry, this makes Leo according to Medieval magic a masculine sign.

It is said that the stars in the neck and back bring trouble, disgrace and sickness affecting the part of the body ruled by the sign, especially if they happen to be in conjunction with the Moon.

According to the Greeks, the star sign Leo is the lion that Hercules slew in the first of his labours. In some stories Leo was the spawn of the monster Typhon or other stories its parent as the two-headed dog Orthrus. Hercules strangled the lion with his bare hands and then ramming his fist down its throat for good measure. It is this lion's pelt that you see thrown over Hercules' shoulder and worn as a cloak with the head as a helmet, in many depictions of him.

Peridot helps to calm and balance this volatile sign.

Virgo August 22nd to September 22nd **Lapis Lazuli or Sapphire**

Sapphire's efficiency and wisdom makes Virgo use its time effectively. Lapis protects and guards the highly-strung Virgo. This is the only sign that is shown differently at The Temple of Denderah in Egypt, Virgo is depicted as two snakes but then, snakes very often represent the Goddess, so is this an early representation of the Virgin

Goddess?

Libra September 23rd to October 22nd **Opal**
Due to the Procession of the Equinox originally the Autumn Equinox, when day and night are of equal length, fell in Libra and so the scales of balance were most appropriate.

Opal, tradition says that if used as a Birthstone its negative aspects vanish.

The noble Libra of justice and honor, the scales in Ancient Egypt belonged to Ma'at the Goddess of Justice. You must place your heart on Her scales and weigh it against Her feather, at your death. But in modern times Libra comes under the auspices of Venus.

Scorpio October 23rd to November 22nd **Topaz**
Scorpio's are determined creatures and never change their mind Topaz's nobility helps when Scorpio tends to think jealous or secretive thoughts. Smokey Quartz is sometimes used as cheaper substitute, but only because it is a brown stone of similar appearance.

Sagittarius November 23rd to December 20th **Turquoise**
Sagittarius is the centaur Chiron, half man and half horse Chiron was tutored by Apollo and Artemis in the art of the medicine (which is why people born under this star sign are such good healers) and hunting (Chiron carries a bow). In a practice session Chiron was pierced by an arrow soaked in the blood of the Hydra, which left him in agony. He chose gave away his immortality, rather than suffer for eternity and so became the constellation of Sagittarius.

Turquoise for Sagittarians gives wisdom when they tend to put their foot firmly in their mouths.

Capricorn December 22nd to January 19th **Garnet or Tigereye**
Although very determined, they can be very cautious. Garnet gets Capricorn moving, Tigereye protects them while they move.

Capricornus is perhaps one of the first constellation to have been recognized The sea-goat that is the true emblem for this sign (sometimes wrongly depicted as a goat) had its ancient origins 3,000 years ago in Babylon and is the God Suhur Mas. Originally the Winter Solstice fell in Capricorn, then the first day of the year. The Sun stops decreasing the length of the days and for a few days it seems to remain stationary thinking whether to lengthen the days and move towards Summer or remain in everlasting Winter. In this period everyone waited with baited breath, for perpetual Winter would mean no crops and therefore- death.

Suhur Mas (the Sun - goat) is depicted transforming as he rises from the sea of chaos (his fishy lower half). Storms at sea and flooding on land are of course bad at this time of the year, I never understood why Turkish boats had bull and goat horns in the rigging, perhaps it was to ask Suhur Mas blessing? Many Amulets have a long history.

Aquarius January 20th to February 18th Amethyst
In the Greek version of the flood myth so much older than the bible Aquarius pours the water that drowns the Earth. Aquarians can be very independent, tending to be obstinate. Amethyst softens their temperament and is calming for this nervous sign.

Pisces February 19th to March 20th Aquamarine
Pisces is another of the oldest of the Zodiac signs.

Pisces people are very caring, although they try hard not show it. Aquamarine is calming to this highly-strung sign. Bloodstone, although not traditionally given for this sign, gives them the courage in a difficult situation to see it through.

It gives strength to give up addictions and situations to which Pisces will hang on to past their sell by date.

Anniversary Gifts
Although gifts have been given for wedding anniversaries at least since Medieval times, the list that is usually given is not very old. It

was devised in 1922 by an American, Mrs Emily Post in her book on etiquette and revised in 1957 to include more years, as it had become so popular. She envisioned that in the early years, an amusing gift should be given and only the couple having been together for a long time, do the gifts become more memorable. But are they outdated for today and particularly for Witches and Pagans? I've included Mrs Post's list but have had great fun inventing a Handfasting list, I hope you feel it is of some use.

Mrs Post's Wedding Anniversary Gifts	Handfasting Anniversary Gifts
Paper	The Handfasting Cord
Cotton	His and Her Cotton Aprons
Leather	Something kinky in leather
Linen (Table or Bed)	*Something* for the bedroom
Wood	Wood
Iron (Cooking Pot)	Iron Cauldron
Copper	Malachite
Bronze	Citrene
Pottery	Amethyst
Tin (Automaton?- adults wind-up tin toy)	Moonstone or a toy more unconventional?
Steel	Amber
Silk	Silk undies
Lace	Lace undies
Ivory	Jade
Crystal (Glass vase, decanter)	Crystal Ball
20 China (Dinner Set)	Backpack around China

(If you have been together for 20 years, you deserve it!)

25 Silver	Silver
30 Pearls	Pearl
35 Coral	Topaz
40 Ruby	Ruby
45 Sapphire	Sapphire
50 Gold	Gold

| 55 Emerald | Emerald |
| 60 Diamonds | Diamonds |

How to use a Crystal Ball

Old Grimoires suggest that to read the future or to see and hear the secrets of the universe, you must use either a quartz crystal ball or a ball of beryl. Unfortunately, as yet I have not even seen a ball of beryl available to buy, the only one I have seen is in the British Museum and belonged to Dr Dee. All of this makes the price that you may be asked for a rock quartz crystal ball seem inexpensive.

First, find your crystal ball! This may not be as easy as it seems, they are all individuals, and little personalities that need to find their owners.

Lead Crystal Glass, is not Quartz Crystal; although they may look similar to the naked eye they are very dissimilar in structure. Objects in the crystalline state have different sequencing of atoms in the various directions of the crystal, glass always displays equality in all directions. Quartz is a good conductor of electricity, glass is not. Many people tell me that they get very good results from lead glass (some erroneously described as crystal). Follow the same procedure either way, but be sure that you know which it is you are buying. Also on the market now are reconstituted crystal balls, off cuts of crystal fused under heat and pressure with acrylic filler (plastic) plugging the holes, as you can imagine I am none too enamoured of this practice, let the buyer beware!

Some people feel best using quartz crystal balls that have inclusions and cleavage plains within, these look like planes of light and form pictures. Strangely, these change from hour to hour. Sometimes clearly you can see a witch on a broomstick, the very next day the witch is no more and in her place is a tree; no matter how hard you look and turn the ball, the witch may never be seen again. These pictures need to be interpreted like teacup readings, as to their meanings.

A clear crystal ball is even harder to find and harder to use, but all are used in the same way.

Old Grimoires suggest that you engrave your crystal ball around the middle with names of angels and stand it in a cup of 24ct. gold on a pedestal of ivory or ebony. When I become a millionairess, I will tell you how it works, but this simple way I have always found adequate.

Wash your crystal ball or use any of the ways previously mentioned to clear it.

Make a tea with Mugwort (pour boiling water on the herb, allow it to cool, then strain).Wash the crystal in the Mugwort tea and dry, then store it in a bag of this herb. This awakens its individual powers.

Keep it near to you for at least a week under your pillow and even when watching television. Then do a ceremony of dedication upon on your crystal ball. You must attune it to your brain, making it a part of you. If you have any magical tools, put it with them when you cannot be with it. Do not allow anyone else to touch it.

Now you are ready to use it, but do not expect it to work first time, it may take weeks of practice.

Have ready:

Your quartz crystal ball
A white candle
Divination or sight incense
A black cloth
A charcoal block
A silver pentagram, or parchment and Dragon's Blood ink
Mugwort
A notebook and pen

First, cast a circle as this holding in the magic, concentrating it on your work.

Meditate for a while on what you are about to do.

Draw a pentagram on the parchment in black or use a silver pentagram. Place a black cloth over this and balance your crystal ball upon it or place the pentagram under the stand if the ball comes with one.

Light the charcoal block. When lit, add half a teaspoon of incense.

Cast a circle around you with your Athame if you have one or your finger.

Light the white candle.

Place the candle so that the light falls on the crystal ball, but not in the line of sight of your eye. It is traditional to wear a pentagram or Seal of Solomon, while scrying with a crystal ball.

Call upon your deity to help you with your work.

Gaze into your crystal ball, allowing your eyes to become unfocused but blinking whenever necessary to be comfortable. Blank your mind. Do not think of work or that you need to buy teabags tomorrow.

If you have a crystal ball with inclusions, turn it slowly; use your imagination to see pictures in the patterns of light that appear and disappear as you turn it.

If you have chosen a clear ball, the trick is the same as the all over patterns that you stare at and then suddenly a picture jumps out at you in 3D. Allow your mind to become unfocused, is the only way I can describe it, at first you may see smoke roll around inside. It may even roll out of the ball and onto the table. Don't worry, you are doing well, slowly a picture will form in the smoke, perhaps only fleetingly at first. Do not work longer than half an hour the first time, as it will be very tiring, recording in your notebook all that you see.

Put your athame or hand out and cut the circle of light you have created. Do not blow out the candle. Snuff it with fingers or a snuffer; never use one element against another. You may decide after practice that you do not feel the need to cast a circle, but it does help to strengthen the magic so don't be quick to do without it.

After every session, wash your crystal ball in a Mugwort tea. Later when you get more practiced and read for someone other than yourself, wash it in water first and then in the Mugwort.

Lithomancy

Whenever you see the word 'mancy' you know that it is a form of divination, as with Cartomancy divination by playing cards. Necromancy is divination by calling up and speaking to the dead, although this is a divination we mainly leave to our Christian brother and sisters, in their Spiritualist Churches. Strangely Necromancy is what the Christians accuse us of, I wonder if they know what it means?

Stone divination or Lithomancy (From *lithos* meaning stone and *manteia* meaning divination) is a very old form of divination, the art of casting stones to tell the future, to gauge the forces acting on a problem. There are many ways to do this, you can use tumble stones as I have described here or stones that you have picked up from the garden. The difficulty with the latter form of Lithomancy, which I was taught as a child, is remembering what each stone is meant to signify. Using tumble stones can help you to remember the meaning of each of the stones used. It is by far the easiest of the types of divination, use your own judgement and instinct to find the answer. Some people will suggest that you should not read the future for yourself. No harm will come from reading for yourself, the knack is to be impartial, as if reading for another person.

First wash your stones in water to clean them from every other influence or person who may have handled them. Rub them with Anointing oil to increase their magical qualities and keep them with you at all times and place them under your pillow or under the bed at night to pick up influences from your aura.

There is one stone for each energy that might affect the question you may want to ask:

STONE	COLOUR	INFLUENCE
Quartz Crystal	Clear	Significator
Rose Quartz	Pink	Love
Aventurine	Green	Money
Haematite	Grey	Sex

Tigereye	Brown	Protection
Onyx	Black	Negativity
Lepardskin Jasper	Multi-colored	Creativity
Moss Agate	Green and white	Home and Garden
Amethyst	Purple	Health
Fluorite	Purple and White	Wisdom
Rhodonite	Pink and Black	News
Carnelian	Orange	Energy
Turquoise	Blue	Luck

You will also need the cord that you use around your waist in circle, place this in a circle, loosely tying the ends.

Take the stones in your two hands, warming them for a moment, and direct your energy into them. Blow lightly onto them to help the flow of energy, from you to them.

If you are doing a reading for somebody else, ask them to blow onto the stone, placing their energy with in.

Hold them over the cord opposite you and circle the stone three times around the edge of the cord.

Concentrate on the question to be asked, or ask the person you are reading for to do so.

Move them to the center of the circle and allow the stones to fall.

Remove all stones that fall outside the circle, for they have no bearing on the question.

The Quartz Crystal is the Significator, this will tell you by its placement what you wish to know. It is in essence you or the person for whom the reading is to be done, where this falls, the stones around it are the strongest influence, the further away the stones, the dimmer the influence. The Significator between the Rose Quartz and the Haematite would give a positive answer to a question of love, for example.

Use your intuition to interpret the fall of the stones.

One last point, if the Significator falls outside the circle, this is not a premonition of disaster. If you are reading for someone else who is not used to divination, please make sure they understand this. It means only that the Gods do not wish to answer you at this time, the problem will disappear or that it is too far in the future to be answerable at this moment, try again in a month.

Wash the stones in water after every reading and re-anoint with oil.

Exercise
Assemble your own Crystal Prediction kit from tumble stones. Tumble stone are very inexpensive. See what the future holds for you.

CHAPTER 8

Herbs and their Magical Uses

Plants have been used in magic and for healing since time began. Almost every plant or tree has wonderful folk tales attached to them, telling us a little more about the plant and how they work. Healing and magic were one and the same thing until very recently and with herbs, healing and magic are possibly at their closest. Herbs do form the basis of most drugs that we use today, but they also have great magical energy locked within. The energy of the Sun God with His might and power, the energy of the Moon Goddess with Her magic and mysticism, these mix within the plant, that has its roots within the deep dark nourishing Earth Goddess. Herbs can be used as medicine, as incense or as a spell component. Within your magical circle the built-up energies of the herbs are released to fight the problem, whether it be illness, love, protection or lack of money. To separate these two, healing and magic, would be alien to our ancestors of the long dead past. They would see them as one science-the science called magic.

The first time a Crabapple branch or a big bunch of rosemary or sage gathered for firewood was consumed by flames and a beautiful smell arose, it triggered the same memories or altered states, way back then, as incense does today. Incense is a weaver of enchantment with the power to elevate the spirit allowing us to touch the Gods. It is a mixture of many items from the world of plants and can be so evocative of past times, past places and for some past loves. As I passing a sweet shop one day, a smell came wafting out, a particular smell, like lemon but not quite, softer and more flowery. Instantly I was transported back to when I was ten. My family had driven to Plymouth for a day out. Did I remember the ships? No. Plymouth Hoe? No. I remembered a garden of a Tudor House that we visited; there was an enormous flower almost 12 inches across, just one, like a giant white tulip but growing on a heavy old vine with only a few sparse leaves. The vine grew on the back wall of the house in a very small courtyard. I remember gently cupping the flower in my two hands and deeply smelling the wonderful scent. Even now too many years later I can still smell that flower. Smell can be one of the most evocative senses. Had it not been for the sweet shop, that memory would have lain dormant in my mind, possible forever. Incense too can work in the same way, transporting you back to wonderful days in your childhood, to other planes of existence, to meet your God and Goddess or if you are lucky past lives.

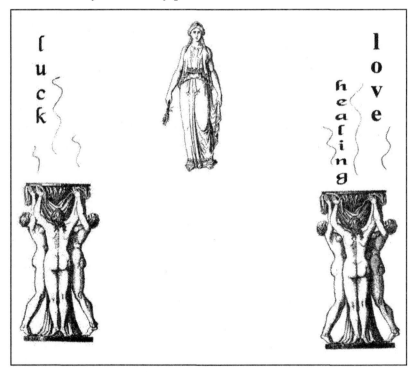

Herbs that smell sweet are used to call good spirits, never use anything that smells offensive, as this will call darker energies that you don't want to a circle.

Each herb has within it, like each crystal and tree, a spirit. If you contact the spirit of the herb, you understand it better and therefore it will work for you better. Start by choosing an herb, smell it; how does it smell in its natural form? Place quarter of a teaspoon onto a lit charcoal block, does its smell change? Has it changed the atmosphere with in the room? Does the herb make you think of anything? Lay down, relax and breathe in the smells, drift, allow the herb to speak to you. Plants are very primitive intelligent forms, so be gentle and await its knowledge.

Make notes on what you have felt.

If you do this meditation before bed, make notes on your dreams, as well.

Never do this with more than one herb at a time, as the atmosphere will become too confusing.

Which herbs to use in spells are a little more difficult to define, the smell is important but it is the psychic vibration that they set up that brings the spell to fruition. Herbs like Eucalyptus for purification and Rose for love are easily understood by their smell alone. Rose has a warm soft inviting smell; Eucalyptus on the other hand is hard and catches your breath. Both have good uses in incense but both are very different energies.

The old Anglo- Saxon name for herb was wort, as in St Johns Wort. To use worts to heal was known as wort cunning, the people using herbs and magic openly were called Cunning Men or Cunning Women. In times past Cunning men and women had bundles of herbs hung around their house, like doctors of today displaying their certificates of education but as all gardeners know, the best way to dry herbs is to hang them up and let them dry naturally. Now days we can use an airing cupboard or as in days of old just hang them up in a warm dry room or near the fire as our ancestors did. Of course we can buy packets of herbs from all over the world but it was not always like that. Herb bundles drying around the home, does add a wonderful smell to the house that commercial sprays can not compete with and of course is far cheaper. Grow as many herbs as you can; you can then plant on a waxing moon. Rosemary is a good herb to start with, easy to grow and it doesn't spread all over the garden. Once established you can cut as much as you like from it without injury to the plant and every time you brush past Rosemary in the garden a wonderful smell fills the air. It also has the advantage that fresh rosemary tastes wonderful stuffed into lamb, before roasting.

When walking in the country or your local park pick berries and leaves that you safely use, dry them and add to incense, ask the tree or bush first. You can use Rowan Berries, Elder Berries (use in Dark Goddess incense), wild garlic, yarrow or many more can be harvested free. Or pick rose petals to dry or try Rose hips (scrape out the itching powder, first while wearing gloves) from your own garden.

Use a Pestle and Mortar to grind herbs and gums. It may seem a good idea at the time but only use your coffee grinder with seeds, never Frankincense or Myrrh or it will get clogged up and may never work again. I know.

Thanks to Theophrastus, Pliny and Ancient Egyptian papyrus' we know so much about Egypt and the Classical world. Their knowledge was recorded by Dioscorides a Greek, who lived in Rome during the times of Nero and is thought of as the father of pharmacology. He translated the Ancient Egyptian knowledge of plants, perfumes and incenses into Greek. His writings were then further translated into Arabic, at this time great treaties began to be written on magic. This knowledge traveled the trade routes of the near east and west entering into folk legend, Witchcraft and into the great European Grimoires, his work was used until the 1600 century. Without their written work, it would be impossible to take a look at how the ancient world used their herbs today.

Doctrine of Signatures

The Doctrine of Signatures is the European, very fancy name, for a worldwide practice. It first appeared as a title of a book and was original called Signatura Rerum- "The Signature of all Things" by Jokob Bohme 1575-1624 a German shoemaker. The idea though is far older and merely means that the herb that will cure the problem, in some way resembles the problem.

The Lungwort, so called because the mottled leaves resemble lungs, is still used by herbalists to treat lung-related ailments today. Another example, although there are many, is Devil's claw root, used to treat Arthritis. As you can imagine old ladies hands crippled with arthritis and unable to cut her very thick and yellowing nails, would have resembled devil's claws. What effect does Devil's Claw have on the human system? It is anti-inflammatory and so still used to treat arthritis.

In the Amazon there is a leaf that is used to cure men's inability to produce an erection. How do the natives know? When you bend and crack the leaf and then let it go, it slowly becomes erect and re-joins back up again!

It's better not to use incense or to ingest any herbs during pregnancy, as some herbs can be abortificants, best to keep far away from anything that could harm your unborn baby.

Secret names of Herbs

Some herbs in old spells have secret names to protect the spell from being used by the general populace and to frighten and confuse. They stated that you might need a Hares Foot or graveyard dust, this is a form of code and only the initiated would know how to make the spell work.

Here are some of the code words and their translation, to give you an idea-

Blood of Hephaistos-	Wormwood
Blood of Hestia-	Chamomile
Blood from a Head-	Lupine
Eagle-	Wild Garlic
Graveyard Dirt-	Patchouli and Valerian
Lion Semen-	Human Semen
Man's Bile-	Turnip Sap
Tears of a Baboon-	Dill Juice

Titan's Blood-	Wild Lettuce
Semen of Helios-	White Hellebore (Christmas Rose)
Semen of Hephaistos-	Fleabane
Fat from the foot-	Leek

These are only some of the ones that I have come across. Every area will have their own variations. It illustrates that not all of the old spells that you may find, use the ingredients you think they are. Our forbears did use animal parts in magic, but not in the quantities you think and what you read about may not be what they used. Although I haven't found one called eye of newt.. ....yet.

These below are true names of herbs just to confuse the unwary yet more.

Adders tongue

Colts Foot

Deer's tongue

Crowfoot

Doves Foot

Hares Foot

Hares Ear

The Best Time to Pick Herbs

The Eve of the Summer Solstice at midnight is the best time to pick herbs for magical work. The yellow petal flowers of St Johns Wort are particularly associated with Mid Summer Solstice. Witches and fairies are great friends, so no need for you to wear a crown of herbs (see Wheel of the Year) to protect you from their influence, leave that for the general public.

Cutting Herbs or Wood for magical purposes

Herbs and woods should not be just hacked off the tree or wrenched from the ground. Knock on the branch or run your fingers through the herb and ask it if it minds you taking a piece of the tree or bush. Obviously you should as much as possible, try not to take the whole plant. Wait for the reply, this can be the wind or a bird-call or just a warm feeling. This way, the plant or tree will leave some of its energy behind for your work. Its like going to the doctor for a blood test, you offer your arm and he takes your blood with your life force within. If he were to just jab your arm, just after you walked through the door, you would automatically pull your arm way- no blood- no life force.

The Language of Flowers

The language of the flowers was called Floriography in Victorian times. It has been used in folklore and witchcraft, without its fancy name for many hundred of years, coming originally from the East. Flowers would be given as a gift and the meaning of the flower would portray a secret message to its recipient. In witchcraft a flower was added to a spell to bring that same energy. The lasting version of this is of course the red rose added to love spells, but there are many more. There is also a darker side to this art, with flowers and weeds hung by doors to give warnings to those within.

Almond Flowers- Hope

Bluebell- Love everlasting

Camellia- Go away, I don't love you

Clover- Maiden, Mother, Crone

Chrysanthemum- My love be stronger

Carnations- I am longing for you

Daffodil- Respect

Daisy- Innocence

Dandelion- vanity

Freesia- Trust Red

For get me not- Remember me

Heliotrope- Devotion

Hollyhock- Ambition

Honeysuckle- Generosity

Hyacinth- Friendship

Hydrangea- Think of me

Ivy- Fidelity

Lily- Purity

Mimosa- Sensitivity

Marigolds- Jealousy

Peony- Bashfulness

Pink Rose- Grace

Rose- Passionate Love

Rhododendron- Danger

Snowdrops- eternal

Sweet Pea- Thank You

White Heather- Good Luck

White Rose- Pure Love and Beauty

Herbs and their use in Witchcraft

The modern definition of herbs is any plant with a use, be it culinary, medicinal, household or magical. Which is why we look at the magic of herbs, trees, gums and spices in this chapter. It would be very involved and complicated to place the bay which is a tree and thyme which is a bush in different lists, so please forgive me for my clumsy grouping which is not scientifically correct but possible more understandable to most of us.

Although some herbs can be used for cooking, some on this list are poisonous and are for use in incense and spell bags only, not for ingestion. Some can be used for potions and lotions but these days, with the litigious society we live in, potions and lotions may not be advisable.

Amber - Spirituality

You will find Amber in the chapter on gem magic as well as herbs and oils, as Amber doesn't belong solely to one chapter or the other. Amber is the sap from a tree millions of years ago and is therefore an herb, of sorts. It has hardened over the years and is now set in pendants, and so is also a gem. Many ancient peoples including the Romans used Amber as incense. This fossil amber resin is found on the shores of the Baltic Sea and even England. So scour the beaches when you are there and look for well scratched and very light weight pebbles.

Aniseed - Protection, purification.

Aniseed is famous for averting the Evil Eye and all harmful spirits. Aniseed was used as a slimming aid in Roman times chewed like tobacco as it suppresses the appetite.

Basil - Love, money, exorcism and stimulant.

Called the King of the herbs by the Greeks and Herb Royal by the French. In Persia Malaysia, Greece and Egypt, it was planted on graves and in India placed on the head of a dead person, to ensure a safe journey into the next world. The Romans thought Basil a herb of poverty that when planting Basil you should shout and abuse the plant, the more you shout the better grows the herb. Culpepper thought basil poisonous and that the leaves gave off a deadly miasma. He tells us.........

> *'Galen and Dioscorides hold it is not fitting to be taken inwardly and Chrysippus rails at it. Pliny and the Arabians defend it. Something is the matter, this herb and rue will not grow together, no, nor near one another, and we know rue is as great an enemy to poison as any that grows.'* And
>
> *'Hilarius, a French physician, affirms upon his own knowledge, that an acquaintance of his, by common smelling basil to it, had a scorpion breed in his brain.'*

But in Italy it is given as a love token. In Haiti Basil comes under the domain of Erzulie the Goddess of Love. In Mexico Basil is carried in the pocket to attract money and a lovers roving eye!

In the Middle Ages it was used as a strewing herb to make the house smell sweet.

Bay leaf - Protection, psychic awareness, money and healing.

Bay is known as a herb but is actually a tree, which brings good luck and protects from lightning, if planted near the house. Sacred to Apollo and Aesculapius, the God of Medicine it has always been considered a fortunate plant both for medicine and driving away evil, thought of as is male plant. The Bay is a cousin to the Laurel that was used for victory wreaths in Ancient Rome, and Laurel is still used to make the Jack-in-the-Green in May Day parades around England, used for its long lasting properties.

Write a wish on a Bay Leaf and burn it in a flame. In its natural leaf form, it can be used for divination, place a leaf beneath your pillow for physic dreams or carry for good luck. Because Bay is a cooking herb, it can be added to potions to attract any of the above qualities without harm. Wear as an Amulet to ward of negativity and evil. Drop a few chopped leaves onto charcoal and from the copious smoke that issues, see a prophecy as the priestesses of Delphi saw thousands of years ago.

Balm of Gilead - Healing, love, wisdom and protection.

The strange name of this herb comes from the caravan carrying Balm to Gilead that Joseph of the coat of many colors fame, was sold to. The herb is also mentioned in Edgar Alan Poe's poem "The Raven" to heal a broken heart. Legend tells us that it was taken by the Queen of Sheba to King Solomon as a gift.

This is a strange herb, they are buds that have been pickled in rum and you can smell it quite strongly. It catches the throat in incense, use it in spell bags instead.

Benzoin Gum - Purification, astral projection, protection, money

Benzoin's old name is Flowers of Benjamin and it is a resin that is added to incense to draw spirit to your ritual. Good to burn in a public place before any magical ritual takes place. It has a strong sweet vanilla like smell when burnt.

Birth or Beth Root - Pregnancy, Birth and Menstrual pains

The flower of this plant has three distinct petals, one for each of the Maiden, Mother and Crone. Make a tea by pour boiling water onto a couple of tablespoonfuls of powdered root, when the tea is cold and sprinkle around the bed during childbirth.

Boldo - Purification

Make a tea by pour boiling water onto a couple of tablespoonfuls of leaves and sprinkle around your house, when the tea is cold.

Buchu - Psychic powers.

Has a very strong smell of blackcurrants. Burn with frankincense in the bedroom for physic dreams.

Calmus Bark (Sweet Flag or Sedge) - healing, love, protection, money (poisonous) Associated with Algiz rune of protection (see runes in the chapter on charms).

Calmus like mandrake is poison, it was still used for its hallucinogenic effects, but I certainly do not recommend it.

Small pieces placed in the corners of the kitchen protect from hunger.

String pieces of calmus into a circle and place it around the area to be healed, chant then blow healing incense onto the area, do not do this with open wounds. Use in Bags of protection, for its strong energies.

Catmint - Happiness, psychic powers and love.

Before China tea was brought into this country, people would use Catmint and *"more flavoursome it was"*, so they swore. It is meant to be stimulating and the root when chewed gives courage. As much as cats love it, rats hate it. Grown near the home catmint attracts good spirits. Add to love bags, it attracts love like cats.

Add to Bast incense to please the Cat Goddesses.

Carraway seed - protection, health, mental powers and love.

Thought to protect valuables and lovers from theft. Good to add to love potions and carried to ward off evil. Added to cakes, will spice up a marriage.

Cardamon - health, courage, sexuality, strength.

Also chewed for bad breath, aids digestion and stimulates the appetite. Add to cakes or wine for a potency potion.

Carnation Petals - love, healing, protection, Mother/ Seductress Goddess.

Use in spell bags and incenses for love.

Cedar Leaf - Purification.

Burn to purify after sickness or if an unpleasant guest has entered the house.

Cedar Wood - Spiritual, healing, purification, protection, and money.

Burn to stop bad dreams. Cedar sticks with three limbs, as with the rune of protection Algiz, can be stuck in the ground near the home, for protection.

A wood much used in ancient times for its wonderful smell, boxes that store clothes would be made of this and Temples would be built of Cedar of Lebanon. Used in incense in Tibet. I have looked high and low over the years for a source of Cedar Wood; I found it in a most unusual shop. Go to a place selling Archery equipment, some arrow shafts are made of Cedar, use a pencil sharpener to get fine wood shavings for incenses.

Centaury - protection, binding, God energy.

Used by the centaur Chiron, who was a famed herbalist, to heal himself from an arrow poisoned with the blood of the Hydra. If burnt with oil in a lamp, all about will think themselves witches! Well there's a surprise it worked in my house!

It is also powerful against wicked spirits, so old tales tell.

Cherry bark - love

Put in a pink bag under your pillow, to dream of your true love.

Chamomile Flowers - money, love, purification, protection and healing.

Wonderful for all healing spells of all types, spell bags or mix into the wax of a blue candle when making healing candles or into green candles for wealth. Rub some into your hands when you need to attract money.

Also said to be the plant's doctor, plant Roman Chamomile to heal vegetation growing near by.

Chocolate - Love and sexuality.

Cocoa is of course a herb, beloved of the Maya and Aztecs, called "Theobroma cacao" or "food of the gods" by Europeans on first tasting this wondrous gift of nature. Moctezuma 11, the last ruler of the Aztecs, was said to only drink hot chocolate flavored with vanilla and spices, whipped to froth that dissolved in the mouth and served in a gold goblet and eaten with a gold spoon.

Although it's introduction to Europe has been only a short time in the great scheme of things, the population of the world has taken it to their heart or at least stomachs. When eaten is releases endorphins that make people feel happy, which apart from its wonderful flavor, is the reason for its popularity.

It is now considered sacred to all love Goddesses, Venus particularly (to please Venus feed your lady chocolate, champagne and give her red roses) and I am sure that Hathor would take exception if left from the list although obviously, chocolate was never made in Egypt either.

Cinnamon (powdered or sticks) - astral projection, sexuality, money, protection

Cinnamon has a very strong vibration to magic it is hot and spicy, and adds that energy wherever you use it. Add to a green Money spell bags for a quick result.

Clove - Divination, courage, protection, love and an aphrodisiac.

Make a tea with cloves, when cool rub on your hands and then on your partner, for love.

The Clove tea is used to relieve sickness.

Coriander - health, aggression, sexuality and strength

The seeds of coriander were found in the tomb of Rameses 11, this may have been to strengthen him in the afterlife. The Chinese attribute this spice with the ability to confer immortality.

Add to wine for a sexy potion, Mulled wine has all the spices necessary for a nice evening in.

Copal gum - protection, purification, exorcism
Burn when you have unwelcome spirits in the house.

Cumin - love, good in potions, hots up the magic of love, fidelity and protection.
A spice found in most curries, so cook him a curry for a sexy evening.

Mix with frankincense for protection, in incense not curry!

Damiana - love, visions
Damiana is an aphrodisiac, scatter around the bed on anniversaries or burn to see your future.

Damar Gum - clearing, healing, knowledge
Very good to burn when studying for an exam.

Dittony of Crete - astral protection, luck
Add to incense when you feel uneasy in a new house.

Dragon's Blood - adds power and protection.
This resin comes from only one island in the Caribbean, the trees weep red sap from the bark. A great favorite of mine, Dragon's Blood is wonderful for that extra energy in incense, for whatever purpose you need it.

Elmi Gum - love, spirituality.
This gum is like chewing gum to work with; you can't work in other ingredients. I suggest you give it a miss, unlike me that just had to have ago.

Frankincense Gum (Olibanum Gum) - protection, visualization, spirituality, God energy.

Perhaps the most popular and possibly the oldest incense, used all over the world. The earliest recorded use of frankincense as incense is in Egypt and is found in an inscription on the tomb of a 1500 BCE Queen Hatshepsut. After burning they ground the charred resin into a powder called kohl, this was used to make the distinctive black eyeliner seen in Egyptian art.

Frankincense's irresistible fragrance helps expand consciousness through a deepening of theta wave brain states. Frankincense is sacred to the God, as Myrrh is to the Goddess. Its light bright smell aligns it to Sun energies and therefore the Sun God but the Sun God is also a warrior and so his gift is protection.

Fennel Seeds - Protection, sexuality, luck, happiness, money, strength, courage, said to lengthen life and have Goddess energy.

Longfellow was rather enamoured of this plant

Above the lower plants it towers,
The fennel with its yellow flowers.
And in an earlier age than ours,
Was gifted with wondrous powers,
Lost vision to restore.

Fennel Seeds work on the womb, having a mild estrogenic quality and so are therefore in the charge of the Mother Goddess. Fennel also stimulates milk production of breast-feeding. But don't use fennel if you have been advised not to take the contraceptive pill or have any form of blood clotting problem.

Branches or pouches of seeds were hung over doors and eaten at Midsummer to keep evil spirits and the fairies at bay. It was said to give strength, courage and lengthen life, being used as a slimming aid in classical times as not only does it suppress the appetite but also helps the weight put on with 'The Pill'. You can also, chew fennel seeds to clear the breath of garlic.

Fumitory - Exorcism
Add to the wash water when spring cleaning, if you feel you have any problems from unwanted spirits.

Galangal - Sexuality, luck, happiness, money, healing and to break spells.
Chewing John or Low John is the Hoodoo (African-American) name for this herb, in that tradition you boil it in sugar, chew and swallow the juice and surreptitiously spit the remains onto the floor of any court case you are involved in; but I prefer to add Galangal to spell bags.

Grains of Paradise - Sexuality, luck, happiness, money
Place in small bags and hang from windows under the curtains, the Sun will warm them and happiness will radiate into your rooms.

Guacium wood - healing, love, protection
There is also a Guacium resin but that is very expensive, use the wood in its place.

Gum Mastic - love, power, success, psychic power.
Gum Mastic is getting difficult to obtain and has always been expensive; if you decide you need it, only use a little.

Gum Arabic (Acacia) - wealth, happiness, healing
A strange tree Gum Arabic is only produced from trees in a poor state of health or damaged trees, the best Gum Arabic is harvested in the Sudan, as the soil is poor and weather conditions extreme. The bark is removed from the tree and long 'tears' of gum are produced by the tree.

High John the Conquer Root - Luck, money and protection

High John is also known as Jalap Root and is a climber, with wonderful red flowers but the part of the plant used is the hard woody root. This herb is not available in Europe, so unless you have a friend travelling to the Americas it will be difficult to obtain but a very interesting plant with deep roots in magic. Only perfect roots are used, any other roots are placed in a mixture of essential oils where it dissolves to give a magical oil. Jalap Root is poisonous and is never taken internally. It is part of the Morning Glory and Sweet Potato family, originally only found in Mexico, Louisiana and Florida. To the local Iroquois Indians, High (not Hi John as I have seen it called) John is known as 'Man Root' or 'Man in the Earth Root' and is greatly respected. This is the Mandrake of Mexico and the deep south of America and has been successfully transported to the Caribbean Islands.

I'm sure that slaves coming over from Africa, deprived of the plants that they know, for magic, would have learnt from the local Indians the plant that best approximated its use. Add to this any knowledge that may have been available from Europeans about Mandrake and you have very strong magical root. High John the Conquer Root has been sung of in many Blues Songs before WW11.

High John the Conquer Root brings good luck, power, money, love and protection from magical attack. Very powerful root from our Hoodoo sisters, I have two large roots that I was given as a gift. One I keep in our sitting room and one with the bankbooks! Anointing with High John oil every fullmoon. I placed some of the small broken bits that are used for making an oil into a jar started to add the required Essential oil and like Mandrake torn from the Earth it screamed. Not an audible scream, but a psychic scream, I don't think I went mad but you can never tell yourself. But it was a very interesting phenomenon. I use this root very sparingly as it is very difficult to get, but it is extremely good to place in spell bags for good luck and money or to rub for luck. Both Jalap and White Bryony (English Mandrake) are climbers clinging tightly to trees and bushes, they help you to cling and hold on to money and luck in the same way.

Holy Thistle - purification, hex breaking

Honesty - Brings love into the home.
Its other name is Moon Wort as its seed are held on a translucent circle, resembling the full moon.

Hyssop - Purification and banishing.
In the Bible it tells to *'purge me with Hyssop'*, got no reason to argue.

Jasmine flowers - healing, love, Mother/Seductress Goddess energy.
Very good for love Spell Bags or indeed any love spells.

Juniper wood and berries - psychic power, purification, exorcism, love, healing.
Juniper was used in both mummification in and dyeing cloth Ancient Egypt. The berries are used in incenses and spell bags.

Smoke rising from the burning Juniper wood was thought to keep away demons. Twigs were tied to farm buildings to protect from the Evil Eye.

The Wood not the berries are used in the famous Fire of Azrael which enables you to see the past, present and future. On the beach at midnight, light a fire allowing it to burn down then add, juniper wood, cedar wood and sandalwood in the same quantities. Allow this to burn down and then look into the embers, for the answers to your questions. Due to the impossibility of getting sandalwood in quantities sufficient for this ritual, it is unlikely that this ritual is ever performed again.

Kava-Kava - psychic, stress relief
In the Pacific Islands Kava-Kava root is prepared by the women only, it is chewed and spat out mixed with coconut milk and drunk communally, it gives an euphoric, relaxed effect.

Lavender - Protection, purification, calming, healing.
Lavender is derived from a verb to wash and so, as you might guess, is wonderfully relaxing in the bath, having been used since Roman times. Use in Spell Bags for almost anything especially peace or healing. In England it was burnt to drive out evil spirits and was sprinkled around the home for a peaceful life. Shake over clothing that is being stored, to keep away moths. If you grow lavender yourself, also use the leaves and stalks as well as the flowers. They don't contain quite as much oil but it is a shame to waste them. You can also chop up the stalks and scatter them on your carpet, leave for an hour and then vacuum; it gives off a wonderful smell, better by far than synthetic fresh air sprays.

Lemon Verbena - purification.

Lemon Grass - psychic power

Lemon Peel - purification, Moon, Virgin Goddess energy.
Easy one to prepare yourself, after using a lemon in cooking slice the skin in thin bits for drying, use in spell bags. If you wish to use Lemon in incense, it is better to use just the zest or use lemon oil.

Lily (Madonna)
A beautiful but strange flower, the Madonna Lily with a deep and superb perfume. This white lily is the flower of the Virgin Goddess,

yet used extensively in funerals, which is the Crone Goddess of course. For me it is the flower that joins the Crone to the Virgin, when She changes back, at the time of the Dark Moon.

Mandrake (Mandragora Officinarum)
Mandrake root is used for love, sexuality, fertility protection, power, healing and DEATH!

Mandrake, the famous Witch Herb, which from the far distant past has been kept in the home to bring, love, wealth and protection, as it drives out all evil. It is also one of the oldest healing herbs, it has been used as a painkiller, sedative, soporific, aphrodisiac, trance mediator, anaesthetic and a virulent poison.

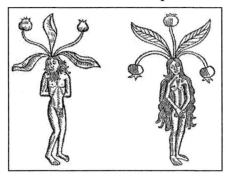

Mandrake is considered far too dangerous to be taken internally today.

The name Mandrake is made up of two words, the root can have a resemblance to a man and 'drake' is derived from dragon, as you can see from its Latin name Mandragora, which refers to Mandrake's magical, powers and is originally from North Africa. Its great power derives from the root having a human like shape. Around the world the roots with a human like shape are attributed the same power, in China its ginseng, in both North and South America, the same shaped root is thought to have the same power. If you can procure a root of Mandrake, it has always been very difficult to come by and it is reputed to have a very strong magical effect. At some periods of history you could be burnt at the stake for owning one, one of the charges against Joan of Arc was of owning a Mandrake. As an amulet, Mandrake should be placed on the mantelpiece, the hearth being the heart of the home, to avert misfortune and bring peace and prosperity to the household and if it grows in the garden it brings wealth.

The human shaped Mandrake or Womandrakes must be treated with great reverence, washed and dressed every morning and put to bed every evening. It was thought to have a very strong spirit inside that would, if you looked after it properly, help to bring happiness to the home.

In Ancient times and still today in the Far East everything magical is carved into a phallus and Mandrake is no exemption, worn on a lady's left arm, it will help her to conceive. If you can bring yourself to cut a root (not a human shaped one of course) you can use pieces in and incenses, best to use leftovers from carvings. Juice from the root is known as blood.

The best mandrake root is shaped like a person, with arms and legs and a head. Although it is very possible that the human shaped Mandrakes have had a little human help to take their shape. The soil can be gently removed from them and with the aid of a sharp blade cuts were made into the root, sometimes wedges of wood are pushed into the cuts to enhance the human appearance. The root then heals itself, taking on a man or woman like form, if cleverly done the incisions are not noticeable. The more human the Mandrake looked, the higher the price it could command.

Mandrake has many names, the Moors of Andalusia of Spain call it "The Lamp of the Elves" which is perhaps the prettiest, it seems that Mandrake attracts glow-worms and so shines at night. Aphrodite was known as the "Lady of the Mandragora", for its fertility and aphrodisiac qualities. The name "Devils Apples" however, is not so nice, the first the Arabs and then the Christians gave this name to Mandrake, again due to its aphrodisiac qualities and that it is a virulent poison.

How to remove the mandrake from the earth- safely.

The oldest way to safely dig a Mandrake comes from Theophrastus of Greece in 230BCE, although he no doubt, was documenting a method that had been practiced for sometime.

You were advised to...

1. On Mid Summers Eve (a popular day to gather herbs) or the day

after, failing this the day of Venus (Friday).

2. At night before dawn

3. Stand facing West in honor of the Chthonic Gods, the plant at that time is thought to be at its most potent and the guardian spirit still asleep.

4. Anoint your exposed skin

5. Fill your ears with wax (he gives no reason for this but it is further elaborated on in the Christian era)

6. Stand down wind.

7. Now draw a circle three times around the plant with a double-edged sword, which had only been used for magic.

8. Dance around the Mandrake telling it of the mysteries of love. The verse has not survived, perhaps something like this, while circle and chanting...

Mandrake, Mandrake,
Come to me,
Bring me love and fertility!
Mandrake, Mandrake,
Unlock for me,
Of passion and wealth that special key.

9. No birds must be in the sky; eagles were considered a very bad omen.

10. Leave bread and wine in place of the Mandrake, as a thank you to Ceres the Earth Goddess, for allowing you to take Her Mandrake.

11. Wash the Mandrake in human milk.

12. Then wrap it in clean linen

13. Place on your altar. Before putting it in a warm place to dry (airing cupboard or windowsill).

Mandrake is not the only plant that rituals were performed on its release from the Earth. Hellebore, which again is a narcotic and virulent poison, is another that a circle should be cast but this time you must stand facing the rising Sun.

Later the early Christians and Arabs thought the spirit within the Mandrake was a demon, and would pass into the human when it was dug from the earth. The only way to avoid this, it was said, was to attach a long piece of string a dog and the other end to the Mandrake. Then encouraging the dog to come to you, pulling the Mandrake from the earth. In Shakespeare's Romeo and Juliet, Juliet describes what would happen if you didn't do this. *"And shrieks like mandrakes torn from the earth. That living mortals, hearing them, run like mad dogs."* By using a dog the man was saved and the dog was given an honorable funeral, as it had given its life to save a human.

By the 15th –16th century the legend had grown still further. The only place to find a Mandrake, so the legend now goes, was under a gallows, as the sperm and urine that was ejaculated by the dying man, became the Mandrake. At this time in Germany and Austria, they were known as Galgemannlein, 'little gallows man'. They must be well treated, bathed in red wine every day of Venus and dressed in a clean white shirt every new moon. And on death, must pass to the youngest son.

But Mandrake's legend goes back much farther than Ancient Greece, to at least the New Kingdom in Ancient Egypt 1500 BCE. Strangely, here it was not its extraordinary root that intrigued but the apples it produces. Ladies hold the mandrake apples to their noses, presumable to smell the perfume. As the only other depictions that seem to show this act, in the banquet scenes painted on the walls of the tombs, are with Blue Lotus flowers that are narcotic, can we assume that the apples were used for their narcotic smell but also for there aphrodisiac qualities...

"Surely, she would make me bring
A bowl of mandrake fruits,
And when she holds it in her hand,
She would breathe from it,

Thus offering me her entire body".

Thus runs the Ancient Egyptian love poem, so even the smell of the apples is enough to make them an aphrodisiac, it seems.

Mandrake is also used in the legend of the Sun God Ra. Ra overhears humanity whispering that He has grown old and frail. He tears out his eye and throws it toward the Earth- "The Eye of Ra" the Lion Headed Goddess Sekhmet is born. Sekhmet is sent on a rampage to destroy humanity, She lays waste His people with teeth and claw. Ra becomes horrified at what He had done in a fit of anger but unable now to control Her. Ra conceives a plan; He mixes red Ochre and Mandrake apples with seven thousand measures of beer. He pours this into pools near where Sekhmet rested for the night. She awoke thirsty and drunk deeply of what She thought was blood from yesterdays slaughter. She fell into a deep sleep that lasted for several days. According to some legends when She awoke She had transformed into the gentle Cow Goddess Hathor.

After this Mandrake was known as "Giver of Life" and the name was later transferred to Hathor Herself. As a result, soldiers also prayed to Hathor-Sekhmet to give them her strength and focus in battle.

In the Bacchanalian orgies held to honor the Roman God of Wine, Bacchus, Mandrake was added to the wine, to improve the effect. Being an aphrodisiac, it would be well suited to orgies.

Mandrake wine was used in warfare as well as love. Hannibal is said to have used it against a large army of African rebels. He feigning retreat and leaving jars of wine mixed with Mandrake for the enemy to drunk, returning when they were unconscious to slaughter them with ease. Julius Caesar used the same ploy, when captured by Cicilian pirates. When the wine is made with a strong infusion of mandrake it can imitate death, this is known as "Death Wine". As in Shakespeare's Romeo and Juliet, Friar Laurence gives Mandrake to Juliet and describes in detail its affect. This then fakes her death and fools her family. Unfortunately it fools Romeo as well, starting the chain of events leading to both their deaths.

"Death Wine" was also secretly given to prisoners being crucified, they fell into a death like sleep, the Romans thinking them dead, removed them from the cross. So many "mysteriously" recovered that the Roman solders were given orders to decapitate the bodies, before releasing them to loved ones. Could this explain Jesus' crucifixion?

An Egyptian papyrus of the 3rd century BCE describes a potion including mandrake henbane and ivy, preserved in wine, to make a man sleep for two days. It allows rest in times of great pain. Don't try this at home, he may sleep for a lot longer.

Bartholomew Anglicus's in his 13th-century herbal wrote *"the rind there of medled in wine....gene them to drink that shall be cut in their body, for they should slepe and not fele the sore knitting"*

By the 2nd century AD, a Syrian monk mentions that Mandrake deadens feelings, relieves pain and induces sleep and is much more cautious in his use of the plant. Saying that it causes coldness and quenches the natural warmth of the body but he does suggest a use for even the leaves of the plant, to be mixed with barley flour and rose oil to cool an inflamed stomach, when applied as a poultice, externally.

In Syria they would press Mandrake into a mould and then leave it to dry, preferring it prepared this way, rather than a natural root. I bought something similar in Thailand, a he and a she, it could be a Mandrake root or some type of fruit placed in a mould, but no one spoke English to give me a little more information.

Mandrake followed the trade routes from North Africa to Europe. With so far to travel and so rare, Mandrake was very expensive and very difficult to obtain in the Middle Ages. So, much so that the King of Bohemia had 'his and hers' Mandrakes as part of the crown jewels. He personally dressing them every morning and sitting them on mini thrones, undressing them every night and putting them to bed, by this maintaining the power and protection of the crown with in the country.

I'm sure that poor witches could never have been able to afford this herb, however, we do know that White Bryony was sold in this country as English Mandrake. Many educated people at the time believed that it was a confidence trick, but I prefer to think that it was just fitting the pocket of their customers.

I use White Bryony in incenses to add power to the blend and find it very potent. I also have a wand made from a dried root of White Bryony and I add precious lumps to Spell Bags and this works very well.

Mandrake of course has its famous root, this can be single, double or triple pronged, straight from the root grow several dark green leaves of about foot, lying flat on the earth. Mandrake has whitish/purple bell shaped flowers; this matures into a fruit, about the size of an apple changing as it ripens from green to a deep yellow color, full of pulp with a strong scent. Many Herbalists throughout history have commented on its smell, some suggesting that it is wonderfully sexy and other that it stinks. It has taken me a long time to work this conundrum out; smells can be very subjective. Both smell and taste can very markedly from country to country plus the climate and soil makes a lot of difference to the smell of the Mandrake apples. Warmer climates produce a better, sweeter smelling crop, but

then this is probably true of many fruits.

As with Deadly Nightshade's berries the unripe apples eaten with the seeds are deadly, it burns the mouth and tongue, leaving it numb and heats the skin to bright red color. The antidote is supposedly wormwood, rue, scorduim, mustard, origanum, caster with wine and vinegar but I would not like to trust it to work.

Healing: The whole plant has uses in folk medicine.

Mandrake **roots** were dried and used as Amulets or pulped, the juice this was allowed to thicken in the sun, infused in water, wine was then added as a preservative; this was used as a painkiller, soporific, anaesthetic and as a love potion. This mixture was also dabbed on the eyes and joints; this remedy was used until the at least 19th century.

The **bark** was sometimes striped from the roots and hung out to dry, pounded and dissolved in water then mixed with wine as a sleep inducer.

The **leaves** were used externally in ointments and poultices, to relieve stomach pains and for inflammation of the eyes and external ulcers mixed with Polenta as a poultice and if used on scars it is said will lesson them in 5-6 days.

From the **apples,** as they are known, a little of the juice or even just the smell is an aphrodisiac and narcotic, more induces sleep. Doesn't this remind you of the story of Snow White?

The **seed** of the apples is a purgative and when powdered and rubbed on it stimulates a woman's blood flow and extracts a still birth.

In 1490 the sleeping sponge was invented by Hugo de Lucca, who was the chief of the school of surgeons in Tuscany. This was an inhalational anaesthetic, using a mixture of herbs, mandrake, hemlock, opium, mulberry, water hemlock, dock and the seeds of lettuce, to induce sleep for operations.

In 1888, Benjamin Ward Richardson took the first scientific look at the plant. Reproducing the ancient recipe he found this tincture would anaesthetize cats and dogs. Due to the dilation of the pupils, the mandrake must contain an alkaloid similar to hyosine. Unwisely, he finally tried a small dose on himself and found a dryness of the mouth, numbness of the tongue, confused vision, sensitivity to sound and restlessness.

But I must reiterate this is for your legendary knowledge and not use. Mandrakes and White Bryony if eaten, even just a little too much, is a deadly poison!

Mistletoe - Protection, healing and love.

The Golden Bough of legend, Mistletoe beloved of Druids according to Pliny, though how much is legend and how is true we may never know. The Chief Druid was taken by a vision to go forth and seek out mistletoe, which is a parasite growing on trees. It must only be cut at the Summer and Winter Solstice and on a waning moon. If the mistletoe fell to the ground it was considered a bad omen for the nation. It was always cut with a gold scythe from the sacred Oak and caught before it touched to Earth. They then danced around the oak waving the mistletoe with the song *"Hey, derry down, down, down derry"*. The Druids would then go around waving the mistletoe and announcing the New Year. Oaks in some parts of the country are still called the derrys.

Mistletoe does however also have a sadder story. The Heathen legend of Balder the Good, shot with an arrow made of mistletoe in a silly game that was engineered for darker purposes by Loki. Mistletoe was given to the Goddess of Love and everyone that walks under the herb at the Midwinter Solstice should receive a kiss to show that mistletoe was forgiven. A lovely story but probably, the tradition of kissing under the mistletoe comes from mistletoes shape, two leaves joined with a milky berry that oozes white sap.

Although in our tradition the white berries of the mistletoe represent the Virgin Goddess.

The Celts believed that it protected the owner from evil and that the oaks that it grew on were to be respected and used for healing. But in truth is very difficult to grow on oaks and grows far better on Apple, not that I have managed to get it to grow on that tree either.

Its use in Churches at Christmas is banned, as too Pagan.

Used to attract customers to your place of business, position under the carpet by the door. Also acts to allow friendly people into the house and not allow foes to enter.

Research is being done in connection with a treatment for cancer at the moment.

Mugwort - psychic power, protection, Crone Goddess energy.
Its old name is Crone Wort and was seen as women's plant, used for problems of the womb. It likes to grow by the door of healers and was used in Europe as a protective charm against evil and danger. Medieval travelers thought that if they carried Mugwort in their shoes, they would never tire on their journey and of course turn away the Evil Eye, according to the Herbarium of Apuleius of the 11th century. It is said that if you dig up Mugwort on Midsummer Eve you will find there a piece of coal buried under the roots that will save you from all manor of evils.

Mugwort is considered a precious ingredient in folk religious rituals all over the world due to its dream inducing ability. This herb can be used to increase your psychic ability as a tea or to wash your crystals, altar or temple. Do not use too frequently. In the Middle ages, St Johns Wort would be hung over the door and a crown of Mugwort would be made to wear at the Summer solstice to protect the Christians from fairies.

In Europe the leaves were used compressed and burnt to stimulate the body with heat to relieve gout and rheumatism, much as they do in the East.

Marigold petals - Sun, happiness, money, luck.
Marigolds close their petals as the Sun goes down and opens them at dawn and so are considered disciples of the Sun God, with eyes only for Him.

They can be added to soups and stews to "gladden the heart".

Makes a good poultice to apply to insect bites.

Myrrh - psychic power, blessings, Goddess energy.
As Frankincense is the Sun and the God, so the dark and mysterious Myrrh is the Moon Goddess. Used in incense from early times, especially the famous Egyptian incense Kyphi. Ground it was used to perfume clothes, of those that could afford it.

'Place Myrrh upon your head, dress yourself in expensive linens.'
Egyptian Poem

Myrrh was a common analgesic in ancient times, it was often mixed with wine to make the drink more potent.

Mace - psychic power, Crone Goddess energy.
Mace is the very fine web around the Nutmeg and was very expensive years ago, now it is much cheaper.

Marjoram - Protection and love.
Called the Herb of Sobek the Egyptian crocodile God.

When marjoram grew on a grave the Greeks and Romans, were assured that the dead loved one was happy. Young couples were crowned with marjoram. Milkmaids would place marjoram and thyme near milk to stop it souring, when thunder rolled.

Mint - money, sexuality, healing, travel, exorcism, and protection.
Mint Tea is brilliant for indigestion; perhaps the reason restaurants give mint sweets after dinner?

Nutmeg - psychic power, money, Crone Goddess energy.
This is the spice reputed to have been used by Nostradamus in his famous visions. I have heard stories of people finishing the nice nutty bits at the bottom of mulled wine and needing an ambulance. Use in incense only and don't eat too much of the nutty bits of mulled wine!

Opoponex - aggression, courage, Mars.
Although herbs are used for their energies not smells, there are some you might think not worth the bother of tracking down, when many other herbs that you can use smell sweeter: this is one.

Orris - protection
Orris is used in pomanders to hold the smell.

Orange Peel - Sun, happiness, money and luck.
Easy to make yourself by cutting the skin of the orange into thin strips and drying it but I prefer to use Orange Essential Oil for incense. The smell is stronger, it is not expensive and has more power. Orange peel can be used in spell bags, successfully.

Oak Moss - Earth, wealth, luck.
This is wonderful cross between a herb and thick oil; it smells of the very Earth itself.

Oregano - healing, love, protection

Patchouli money, fertility, sexuality, psychic power, Mother/Crone Goddess energy.

Pine - Life, purification.
Used in washing water and baths to clear negativity and for fresh starts. If using in a bath, tie in a little bag of muslin or any fine fabric you may have and hang under a tap.

Keep old Yule tree needles; they conveniently dry on the tree ready to pick them off, rather than vacuuming them and throwing them away.

Poppy Seeds - Psychic, healing and money
The only part of the poppy that is not hallucinogenic is the seed, which is why it is used in cooking. It still however, carries the energies of Goddess and is a good substitute for any ingredient that you may come across in old incense recipes that you don't choose to use.

Rose - Healing, love, spirituality, psychic, protection, Seductress/ Mother Goddess energy.

Roses are older than human hands that first cared for them and later were to share their life, love and gardens with this beautiful flower Forty million years ago, a rose left its imprint on a slate deposit and Rose fossils have also been found in Germany and in Yugoslavia. Long before humans ever existed, their beauty shone and the superb perfume filled the air. Roses grow wild up to the snow line and as far South as the equator but no wild rose has ever been found growing in the Southern Hemisphere. The celebrated Lydian poetess Sappho called the rose " the queen of flowers".

The earliest depiction of roses in art comes from the Indus Valley were the Goddess wears a crown of roses 6000 years ago, the same Mother Goddess that was worshiped with the antlered Horned God Pashupati.

Amytis the wife of Nebuchadnezzar loved roses above all other flowers and so no doubt they would have flowed down the walls of the famous Hanging Gardens of Babylon.

The rose was sacred to Venus, Cupid and Baccus, both Egyptians and Romans would cover the floor of their banqueting halls with rose petals. The Emperor Nero held banquets where he cascaded rose petals on his guests suffocating only a few in the display. Cleopatra covered her royal barge to a depth of 18 inches with roses when she wished seduce Mark Anthony.

The rose was celebrated in festivals in classical Rome, the Rosalia, this took place whenever the roses burst into bloom. During the Roman occupation of Egypt roses became a symbol of Isis, as well as Venus. Romans covered themselves in roses, they were used in jellies, honey, bath essences, and medicines, as prizes for victories and scattered on tombs. The Romans floated rose petals in their wine and strew them before the wheels of their victorious heroes chariots. Rose scented canopies hung over the Coliseum in Rome, as it dried in the sun, the air was beautifully perfumed, drowning the scent of blood.

Roses were originally white according to one legend of Ancient

Greeks surrounding the birth of the rose. One day while Aphrodite the Goddess of Love was chasing Her lover Adonis, she caught Her finger on a rose thorn and Her blood turned the white rose blood red, and ever on they would be the flower of love.

Sub Rosa comes from the Latin, meaning a secret meeting, held originally in a rose arbor or "under the roses". In a later development in Rome, a rose was painted on ceilings, as a symbol of secrecy and also to remind senators and politicians, *Sub Vino*, "under the wine" loosens tongues. The legend that inspired this practice comes from Cupid giving Harpacrates, the God of Silence, a rose to encourage him to keep the secrets of his mother Venus. The ornament around a light fitting on ceilings even today is still called a rose.

Because the Romans loved the rose the early Christians thought it a symbol of debauchery and extravagance but after a lapse of four or five hundred years the Rose in its purer white color, with out any trace of Aphrodite's blood became the symbol of the Virgin Mary, Sancta Rosa. Rose Sunday was a festival in the Middle Ages, commemorating the belief that the tomb of the Virgin Mary was found full of roses and lilies after she ascended to heaven. The first Rosaries were probably made from rose-shaped beads or rose hips.

The Rose was a symbol of chivalry in the Medieval Age and of courtly love.

In the East, Rose Water was used in the Middle Ages to mix mortar for temples and sprinkled on guests as they arrived at the house or temple.

Nostradamus used red rose pills made from petals to help fight the Plague in France. It fortifies and strengthens the body against germs.

When Emperor Napoleon was at war with England, the war was stopped so that the boat carrying Empress Josephine's new Tea Rose from China could get through the blockade and her new rose be delivered to her garden.

Rose Hips are the fruit of wild roses, as with rose petals they draw love but a more mature, fruitful love. Sew with strong cotton when fresh as a necklace at lease 24 inches long and hang up your house to dry. They are also a great source of vitamin C. For the ancients, mixed with honey to sweeten it becomes Rose Hip syrup, with ten times more vitamin C than apples, Rose hip syrup would have been thought of as a magical red liquid. Use Rose Hips in spell bags for love and luck.

Many of the older verities of rose had only five petals and are therefore associated with the pentagram, add to this its wonderful perfume and you have a flower fit for a Goddess. The double rose is the Western magical version of the Lotus, with it's many layers into the heart of the Goddess. Choose the color of the rose to match the Goddess, you wish to call to your circle, white for the Virgin, red for the Seductress and as dark as you can get for the Crone. There is now a lavender colored rose, as the color lavender is half mourning, it makes a good addition to an altar or incense for the Crone. There is nothing wrong with modern innovations being added to magic. Don't think that the ancient ones would have turned down any herb or symboligy that worked well. I'm sure the Crone would be delighted with your thoughtfulness.

Rose petals are wonderful in love spells or use sprinkled on salads for a loved one, they taste like roses smell.

For a Handfasting gift, I take a pretty bottle push some red rose petals in add a pinch of ginger, to spice up the love life, then fill with mead. Finally tie a red bow on the bottle, this can either be drunk or just kept as a good luck talisman.

On Valentine's night or to give its old name the Roman wolf (wolves were sacred to Romans feeding the abandoned twins Romulas and Remulas the founders of the city) fertility Feast of Lupercalia and Christianised in 469CE Pope Gelasius. Make or buy from your local Turkish grocers rose jam, make little heart shaped tarts and serve with cream for your loved one, most of us have a sweet tooth on the odd occasion. Remember the old witches tale, a way to a persons heart is through their stomach! Don't forget rose water in Persian Cooking to add love to your meal.

With our modern technology rose perfume has been tested and is in fact a mild aphrodisiac and has the same chemical as chocolate but less fattening.

A nice idea for your own incenses is to dry any rose petals that you are given for Valentine's day. I always used to leave them in the vase until the last petal had fallen; now I dry them and use them in love incenses and spell bags. I can't think of a better use for them, to pass love on and it is far better than putting them in the bin, which always seems so uncaring.

Rosemary - purification, banishing, remembrance and love.

Said to strengthen the memory and bonds of love. It was used at weddings and funerals, tied with ribbons in the bridle bouquet, dipped in sweet scented water or sprinkled with oil, it drove evil away from the happy couple. A branch of rosemary was tied with ribbons of all colors and given to wedding guests, not to forget the wedding and remember the young couple in there prayers. A sprig of rosemary was given to mourners at a funeral before leaving the house to throw into the grave. Rosemary is not truly a love herb but a remembrance herb, reminding us both in life and death.

Rosemary only grows where the lady rules the home and it was said in Victorian times that husbands would sneak secretly into the garden and damage the plant.

In France its old name is *Incensier,* as it was used in place of more expensive ingredients in incenses and is good at driving away evil from the home.

Place with clothing and books to repel insects and moths.

Place a sprig under your bed to get rid of nightmares.

Bind a sprig to your right arm in a linen cloth and you will be light and merry.

Boil the leaves in white wine, when cool and wash your face for good skin.

Send to a loved one, when separated that they will always be reminded of you.

If you have dark hair, boil the leaves, when cool use as a final rinse for your hair, promoting for shine and helps prevent dandruff.

Rue - Healing, Protection and Purification

Rue has a strong disagreeable smell known to keep way fleas, carried by judges to ward of pestilence from the goals and has a very bitter taste. Widely used in magic in protection formularies and spell bags mixed with lavender. Its fruit is eye shaped, this makes it a superb protector against the Evil Eye.

Ruta from the Greek "to set free" of disease and evil. To be used for healing it must be picked in the morning. Blessed water is sprinkled around the home with a branch of Rue during exorcism and is therefore called "the herb of grace".

The famous herbalist Gerard 1583 says: *"If a man be anointed with the juice of rue, the poison of wolf's bane, mushrooms, or toadstools, the biting of serpents, stinging of scorpions, spiders, bees, hornets and wasps will not hurt him."*

Pliny says, *"Every species of rue, employed by itself, has the effect of an antidote if the leaves are bruised and taken in wine."* Curing the stings of all serpents – *"so much so, in fact, that weasels when about to attack them, take the precaution first of protecting themselves by eating rue."* It is good too for *"stings by scorpions, spiders, bees, hornets and wasps, the noxious effects produced by cantharides and salamanders, and the bites of mad dogs"* altogether he mentions Rue as being a remedy for eighty-four diseases or ailments.

It strengthens both the sight and second sight and is one of the reasons it is worn around the neck in the beautiful Cimaruta charm of Italy.

Sandorac Gum - psychic powers

Star Anise protection, purification, adds power

Make a tea and sprinkle this into the bath and around the altar. Choose perfect stars, like the illustration top right, to add to spell bags, for the best results.

Salt Petre - Mars- courage.
Add sparingly to Mars incense and you will get a small firework display or add energy to other incenses but be careful what you add the energy of Mars to or you'll get strife instead.

Salt - protection and purification
Of course salt is a mineral rather than an herb or resin, but it is easier to deal with it in this chapter.

Star Anise

A little Salt is needed for life. Salt has been used since ancient times to preserve and purify food and was considered very precious. The word salary is derived from salt, as Roman soldiers were paid in salt. Arab traders trekked thousands of miles to export salt to the west, remember that when you shake the salt on your chips! Sprinkle around the home if you feel threatened or add to the cleaning water. Add to your bath pre circle or to your bath for healing wounds.

Add to Exorcism incenses.

Sage - protection, purification, healing.
Sage grows best for the wise. Eat sage in May, just before it blooms and you will live forever or so the old proverb says (no guarantee given).

Also wonderful to gargle with sage tea, if you have a sore throat. Sage tea is also used to bring a shine to brunette hair, when cool pouring over your hair after washing and it is supposed to whiten teeth.

Sanderswood (red) - aggression, courage, sexuality
Carry in your pocket for courage if in need.

Sandalwood - healing, protection, spirituality, love, Mother/Seductress Goddess energy.
Sandalwood and Sanderswood are spoken about in old Grimoires as red and white sandalwood. I love the smell of sandalwood, sadly now becoming rare.

Spelani
Spelani comes from India and is used to drive away evil spirits and encourage good spirits. Not as nice a smell as sandalwood, but does the job very well.

St John's (Baldr's) Wort - Calming, happiness, healing
St John's (Baldr's) Wort, adopted the name that we know it by, from St John of Jerusalem, a doctor in the Crusades who found a cooled tea made from the herb wonderful for bathing wounds, burns and ulcers. It became associated with John the Baptist; the red resin that flows from the flowers signified the blood that flowed when John the Baptist was beheaded.

For centuries, northern European women wore St Johns (Baldr's) Wort to ease night phobias and repel demon lovers. For them it was sacred to Baldr the God of sunshine and Summer, the golden yellow flowers of St Johns (Baldr's) Wort tell us clearly and here the red resins signified the blood of the slain God. The herb can be carried to protect from evil spirits. Hung in the home St John's (Baldr's) Wort protects from fire and engenders a peaceful atmosphere.

If you take St John's Wort it is brilliant for depression but there are certain drugs you must avoid so check on these, and your contraceptive pill won't work too efficiently, so beware. There are also some foods to avoid, anything aged, dried, fermented, salted, smoked or pickled. Watch out especially for Soya sauce, pepperoni, salami and liverwurst.

Yellow and red dyes are obtained from St John's Wort, depending on the mordant used.

Sunflower Petals - Sun, happiness, money, luck, wishes, health, wisdom

Sunflowers are meant to follow the sun across the sky each day. In Peru the sunflower was held in high esteem by the Incas, priestesses were crowned with sunflowers and carried them in their hands. The Spanish found many representations of these flowers in pure gold, before melting them into bullion.

Tonka Beans - love, money, courage, protection and wishes.

These are wonderful; their smell is somewhat like vanilla. I love to add these to spell bags, as they are very tactile as well as adding such a wonderful smell. When you give a spell bag, the first thing most people do is rub it between their fingers, trying to workout what you have placed within. Tonka beans being quite large are easily felt but difficult to identify adding to the mystery. Their eye shaped bean makes Tonka beans another of the many preventatives of the Evil Eye.

Thyme - Courage, purification

Purifies the temple and objects, crush leaves against your third eye to enhance your psychic powers. It was customary for a lady to embroider a favor to be given to a knight before battle or tourney. A bee meaning immortality, over a sprig of thyme meaning courage and purification, for if a knight was not pure of heart he would lose in battle.

Used in cooking meat in particular, for its preservation qualities.

Vanilla Pods - happiness, aphrodisiac.

The juice of the crushed leaves rubbed onto the hair produce healthy thick hair.

Valerian - protection, calming and Astral travel.

Its name in Medieval times was All Heal, so highly was it valued. It is an aid to Astral travel. Not only used for its medicinal value but also as a spice and perfume, cut roots were laid between their stored clothing. Valerian is beloved of cats and rats. It was used by rat-catchers to bait their traps and perhaps by the Pied Piper of Hamlin to affect his miraculous feats. By tucking valerian roots in to his pockets the rats were bound to follow him easily. The Anglo-Saxons used it in salads. Valerian tablets can be taken when you can't sleep, or tea if you have no sense of smell as to human noses this herb stinks of sweaty feet!

Vervain - love, protection, money, healing, exorcism, adds power.

Old names for Vervain are Herb of grace, Holy herb, Enchanter's plant.

You grow this in your garden for a steady flow of money into the home. The traditional time that Vervain should be gathered is 2nd May, go barefooted to the plant, dressed in a clean white robe and ask your Goddess if you may take this herb. No cold iron may be used to remove it from the earth, it is best if you dig it from the Earth with a stags horn. Leave it attached to the earth by a small root, lay it upon the earth and leave it until the next day, only then can Vervain be removed, leave bread and wine in its place. Wash it in human milk, wrap it in clean linen and leave it on your altar. In the Middle Ages Vervain would then be made into a necklace to be worn to protect from the Evil Eye, the bite of snakes and to draw good luck.

Vervain is sacred to Diana add endive seed to make a good love potion.

Violet Leaves - Luck, healing, love and Crone Goddess.

The heart shaped leaves should be worn in the shoe to attract a new lover. Most lavender colored flowers come under the domain of the Dark Goddess as this color was considered half mourning. Full mourning was worn the first five years after a loved one died; this was only black, white or purple. For the next five years, lavender, grey and combinations of the black, white or purple were allowed.

Witchazel - Use to fix broken heart and protection

Woodruff - Enhances psychic and money
In the Middle Ages Woodruff, part of the Artimesia family along with Mugwort and Wormwood, was used to flavor wine, but is now considered too strong. Woodruff was used, as a strewing herb to make the home smell sweet and no doubt for its ability to attract money didn't hurt.

Wild Lettuce - psychic powers, Crone Goddess energy
Has been used for centuries in medicine and smoked as an aid to Altered states.

Wormwood - psychic powers, Crone Goddess energy.
This herb is used to make the famous French liqueur Absinthe, that was banned in France about 45 years ago, as it was said to rot the brain, I believe it is now on sale again. It was also adulterated with copper to just add that little extra brain rot.

White Bryony *(Bryonia alba L.)* - Luck and protection.
Also known as English Mandrake (see mandrake) there are two species of White Bryony both are climbers, very like Jalap root another plant used in magic. One has red berries but it is only the plant that bears black berry that is used in magic. White in the name refers to the root, this being a creamy color, the plant has tendrils to help it climb and with large with five pointed leaves.

There is also a Black Bryony, the root being creamy but with a black coating, the leaves on the Black Bryony is heart shaped and very glossy.

Strangely it is only the White Bryony that has a use in magic.

White Bryony should never be taken internally as it is a virulent poison. Augustus Caesar used to wear a wreath of Bryony to protect himself from lightning and hide his hairless head. White Bryony was also used as a wand, gather the root in May, in the Middle Ages prayers would be said whilst doing this. Ask your Goddess if She wishes you to take the plant. Cut the root to the desired length and shape (you may wish to round off the ends) and dry the root in an airing cupboard or in a sunny spot on a window seal. Use the dried left over small bits for Spell Bags and any very small bits to add to incense.

White Bryony during the fourteenth century was thought of as a cure for leprosy.

Yarrow - love, exorcism, divination, clears negativity.
Also used as a wound poultice, old name was Solders Wound Wort.

Ingredients for incenses that you may come across in old Grimoires (books on Jewdian/Christian magic), that are not available today.

Ambergris Not a herb but a product of the Sperm Whale, which excretes Ambergris in its intestinal tract, to soothe the passing of its main food, cuttlefish, through its body. Ambergris was always obtained from whaling, which are luckily no longer hunted and is unlikely to be available outside Japan where whale hunting is still legal, unfortunately. Ambergris is sometimes washed up on the beach, if you're very lucky and know what it looks like you might be able find some or it is collected from the surface of the ocean by fishermen. Ambergris, as you can imagine, was always a rare and expensive commodity and far more expensive and difficult to aquire now. It has been used for thousands of years for it's wonderful smell, which is said to be the most sensuous smell in the world.

Mandrake True mandrake is becoming easier to find with plant nurseries now growing it. White Bryony still grows wild in the England so find out what it looks like and keep an eye out for it on your country walks.

Musk Of course not a herb but musk is from the Musk deer, a secretion from his rear glands, that were milked for it's evil smelling secretion but in VERY small doses it smelt wonderful. A little going a very long way, it was the base of all expensive perfumes until about forty years ago. Musk is never used today and is the reason that perfumes do not last on the skin now.

Sandalwood Sadly, this has recently become in very short supply, like the oil (fuller explanation with the oil).

Strange that a witch used to carry herbs (worts) with them to heal and they are nowadays depicted as having warts, in all old charactures?

Quick Herb Reference

To make your own incense choose herbs from a category love or healing; you don't need them all. Mix together and add appropriate oils into a gum base. If the list does not include a gum for the incense you wish to make, add frankincense (God) or Myrrh (Goddess) energy or both, which ever you consider to be more appropriate.

Adds Power- Dragons Blood, Gum Mastic, High John the Conquer Root, White Briony, Star Anise, Vervain,
Astral Progection- Benzoin Gum, Cinnamon, Valerian Root
Binding- Centaury
Calming- Kava-Kava, Lavender, Valerian,
Clears Negativity- Basil, Coriander, Copal Gum, Fumitory, Hyssop, Holy Thistle, Juniper berries, Mint, Rosemary, Vervain, Yarrow.

Courage- Cardamon, Chilli, Coriander, Opoponex, Salt Petre, Sanderswood, Tonka Beans,

Elemental Energies-

Earth- High John the Conqueror Root, Oak Moss, Patchouli, Vervain, White Bryony.

Air- Honeysuckle, Damar Gum, Benzoin, Mace,

Fire- Opoponex, Salt Petre, Sanderswood, Cardamon, Coriander, Chilli, Rosemary

Water- Catmint, Gum Arabic(Acacia), Vanilla Pods, Jasmine Petals, Lavender, Willow Bark.

Exorcism- Basil, Coriander, Copal gum, Fumitory, Hyssop, Holy Thistle, Juniper berries, Mint, Rosemary, Vervain, Yarrow.

God Energy- Frankincense Gum, Centaury, Marigold petals, Sunflower petals

Goddess Energy- Fennel Seeds, Myrrh, Sandalwood, Rose petals, Sweet Violet Leaf, Lavender, Carnation Petals, Jasmine flowers,

Happiness- Catmint, Galangal, Gum Arabic(Acacia), High John the Conquer Root, Marigold petals, Orange Peel, Sunflower Petals, Vanilla Pods,

Healing- Basil, Bay leaf, Balm of Gilead, Calmus Bark, Carraway seed, Cedarwood, Cardamon, Carnation Petals, Chamomile Flowers, Coriander, Damar Gum, Galangal, Grains of Paradise, Guacium wood, Gum Arabic(Acacia), Jasmine flowers, Juniper berries, Lavender, Mistletoe, Marigold petals, Mint, Origano, Rue, Sage, Sandalwood, Sunflower Petals, Sweet Violet Leaf, Vervain, Willow Bark,

Knowledge- Damar Gum, White Bryony,

Mental Powers- Carraway seed, Rue, Sunflower Petals,

Money- Basil, Bay leaf, Balm of Gilead, Benzoin Gum, Calmus Bark, Cedarwood, Chamomile Flowers, Cinnamon, Fennel Seeds, Galangal, Grains of Paradise, Gum Arabic(Acacia), High John the Conquer Root, Mistletoe, Marigold petals, Mint, Nutmeg, Orange Peel, Oak Moss, Patchouli, Sunflower Petals, Tonka Beans, Vervain, Woodruff,

Moon Goddess

Many books show the herbs for the moon but do not split them into Virgin , Mother and Crone.

Virgin Goddess- Lemon Peel, Eucalypyus, Camphor, Lemon Verbena,

Mother/Seductress Goddess- Rose Petals, Carnation Petals, Jasmine flowers, Sandalwood,

Crone Goddess- White Bryony, Mugwort, Mace, Nutmeg, Patchouli, Wild Lettuce, Wormwood, Sweet Violet Leaf, Lavender.

Love- Bay leaf, Calmus Bark, Carnation Petals, Cherry bark, Chamomile Flowers, Catmint, Damiana, Elmi Gum, Guacium wood, Gum Mastic, High John the Conquer Root, Juniper berries, Marjoram, Origano, Patchouli, Rose Petals, Rue, Sandalwood, Sweet Violet Leaf, Tonka Beans, Vervain, Yarrow

Luck- Basil, Dittony of Crete, Fennel Seeds, Galangal, Grains of Paradise, High John the Conquer Root, White Bryony, Marigold petals, Myrrh, Orange Peel, Oak Moss, Spelani, Sunflower Petals, Tonka Beans,

Psychic Powers- Bay leaf, Buchu, Catmint, Damiana, Gum Mastic, Juniper berries, Kava-Kava, Lemon Grass, White Bryony, Mugwort, Myrrh, Mace, Nutmeg, Rose Petals, Patchouli, Sandorac Gum, Woodruff, Wild Lettuce, Wormwood.

Protection- Aniseed, Bay leaf, Balm of Gilead, Calmus Bark, Carraway seed, Carnation Petals, Chamomile Flowers, Centaury, Cinnamon, Coriander, Cedarwood, Copal gum, Dittony of Crete, Dragons Blood, Fennel seeds, Frankincense Gum, Guacium wood, Southern Root, White Bryony, Mistletoe, Mugwort, Marjoram, Mint, Orris, Origano, Star Anise, Salt, Sage, Spelani, Sandalwood, Vervain, Valerian, Witchazel,

Purification- Aniseed, Boldo, Benzoin Gum, Cedar Leaf, Chamomile Flowers, Cedarwood, Coriander, Copal gum, Damar Gum, Hyssop, Holy Thistle, Juniper berries, Lemon Verbena, Lemon Peel, Lavender, Rosemary, Star Anise, Salt, Sage,

Spirituality- Cedar Wood, Elmi Gum, Frankincense Gum, Rose

Petals, Sandalwood,

Spell Breaking- Galangal, Holy Thistle.

Sexuality- Cardamon, Cinnamon, Coriander, Fennel Seeds, Galangal, Grains of Paradise, White Bryony, Mint, Patchouli, Rose Petals, Sanderswood,

Strength- Cardamon, Coriander,

Success- Gum Mastic,

Travel- Mint,

Nine Sacred Anglo-Saxon Herbs – to repel evil attacks.
The Lacnunga, a 11th century manuscript

> *'A worm came creeping, he tore asunder a man.*
> *Then took Woden Nine Magic Twigs*
> *and then smote the serpent that he in nine dispersed.*
> *Now these nine herbs have power against nine magic outcasts*
> *against nine venoms and against nine flying things*
> *against the loathed things that over land rove.'*

An Adder Snake tried to attack Woden (Odin), He chopped the snake into nine pieces. These then turned into nine poisons, Woden then changed them into nine healing and magical herbs. He then tells us how the nine herbs will cure all mannor of disease, from the air, land and sea.

Mugwort *'Remember, Mugwort, what you made known, what you arranged. You were called Una, the oldest of herbs, you have power against three and against thirty, you have power against poison and against infection, you have power against the loathsome serpent encircling the Middle Garth.'*

Mugwort valued for its effect on the nervous system and stomach. It was also said to help with fatigue, sunstroke and protect against wild beasts, snakes and evil spirits. Mugwort should be picked before Sunrise, for best efficiency. It gives energy for those travelling longs distances. Mugwort tea is also a psychic enhancer, an aid in the second sight and Seidh working.

Waybroed (Plantain - from the same family that produces the bananas) '*And you, Waybroed, mother of herbs, open from the east, mighty inside. Over you chariots creaked, over you queens rode, over you brides cried out, over you bulls snorted. You withstood all of them, you dashed against them. May you likewise withstand poison and infection, and the loathsome serpent encircling the Middle Garth.*'

Shades of Lord of the Rings no less, Tolkien was an expert in Saxon history. Waybroed's other name is Englishman's Foot, as it was said to follow everywhere that the European explorers went and became Snake Weed in America where it is thought to cure snake bites. In Europe Waybroed was thought to cure insect bites, mad dog bites and was bound onto a wound to staunch the flow of blood and was considered an "All Heal". Also used in Anglo-Saxon flying potions

"*Take a handful of Hammer Wort and a handful of Maythe (Chamomile) and a handful of Waybroed and roots of Water Dock, seek those which will float, and one eggshell of clean honey, then take clean butter, let him who will help to work up a salve, melt it thrice: let one sing a chant over the worts, before they are put together and the salve is wrought up.*"

Pick Waybroed before Sunrise and tie with a red ribbon to your head, to relieve headaches and look silly.

Watercress '*Stune is the name of this herb, it grew on a stone, it stands up against poison, it dashes against pain. Unyielding it is called, it drives out the hostile one, it casts out poison, it has the power against infection. This is the herb that fought against the world serpent*'.

The Persians would eat large quantities of watercress before heavy work to increase their energy levels. High in many vitamins, calcium and iron, making a wonderful addition to diets and I'm sure this applied to earlier societies too. Beneficial to be eaten in Spring to aid the system after Winter, helpful for arthritis, rheumatism and good for the skin.

Atterlothe '*Put to flight now, Venom-loather, the greater poisons, though you are the lesser, you the mightier, conquer the lesser poisons, until*

he is cured of both.'

There is no known interpretation for this herb. Scholars have done their best to guess at what it could be, but no answer is yet definitive, until now, possibly. The latest theory states that Vipers Bugloss the missing herb, a wonderful theory that fits all the facts. Culpeper's Complete Herbal written in the 17th century describes the herb

"It is a most gallant herb of the Sun; it is a pity it is no more in use than it is. It is an especial remedy against the biting of the Viper, and all other venomous beasts, or serpents; as also against poison, or poisonous herbs. Discorides and others say, That whosoever shall take of the herb or root before they be bitten, they shall not be hurt by the poison of any serpent."

Maythe *'Remember Chamomile, what you made known, what you accomplished at Alorford, that never a man should lose his life from infection, after Chamomile was prepared for his food.'* Roman Chamomile is very calming and a tea made with the flowers is anti-inflammatory. The tea is good to be drunk for nervous stomach and nausea.

Nettle, *'This is the herb that is called Wergulu. A seal sent it across the sea-ridge, a vexation to poison, a help to others. It stands against pain, it dashes against poison, it has power against three and against thirty, against the hand of a fiend and against mighty devices, against the spell of mean creatures.'*

Nettle is used as a young plant in the Spring for food and beer, the old plant in the Autumn for weaving. Also an old use of nettles was Urtication or flogging with nettles, for rheumatism and loss of muscular power. This was used by the Romans legions stationed in England against the cold, anyone who has ever fallen into a bed of nettles can thank the Roman Legions for introducing them into country.

Crabapple *'There the Apple accomplished it against poison that she (the loathsome serpent) would never dwell in the Middle Garth.'*

Crabapples are small, very bitter fruit, but these are the basis of the wonderful variety of apples that we have today. A crabapple tree wood burns with a magnificent fragrance so useful in incenses to bring happiness and the wood is wonderful to carve. Also used to make crabapple jam and mead, full of vitamins. For such an esteemed 'herb' there seems to be very few legends attached to it. However, there is archaeological evidence for their use in Early England, and compensation if a Crabapple tree should be cut down in Anglo-Saxon times was 30d (30 pennies), a lot of money back then.

Fennel *'Chervil and Fennel, two very mighty ones. They were created by the wise one-eyed Lord, holy in Asgard as he hung on the tree; He set and sent them to the nine worlds, to the wretched and the fortunate, as a help to all.'*

Fennel was used both as in cooking and medicine, the thick globular stems are eaten, the fine feathery leaves and the seeds are used in medicine, fennel had twenty-two uses to the Romans. Thought by the Greeks "for those that have grown fat". An infusion of the leaves or crushed seeds will ease flatulence. Culpeper mentions a common use of fennel, its seed or leaves boiled in barley water and then drunk by nursing mothers to increase their milk and its quality. Fennel is used in charms against all that wish bad luck and was another of the herbs that were used to protect against fairies at the Mid Summer Solstice and even used in early societies against insanity.

Chervil, the whole plant can be eaten in salads at the beginning of Spring as a tonic and used against scurvy. Chervil comforts the heart and increases a lust for life,

it is also used to encourage menstruation and has a similar smell to myrrh.

These Nine Sacred Herbs are used in a Charm to rid you of pain and disease.
To work the charm, first stand facing the rising Sun.

Sing a chant three times (sorry, no one knows what the chant was, I'm sure your own work will be happily received) over each of the herbs and the Crab Apple before you prepare them.

Take Mugwort and Plantain (Waybroed), Lamb's (Watercress) cress, Atterlothe, Chamomile, Nettle, Chervil and soap: pound the herbs together mix them with the soap and the juice of Crabapple. Then mix a paste of water and ashes, take fennel and boil it in the paste. Stir with both mixtures together. Sing the charm into the mouth, into both ears and the area of the body of the person to be healed, three times. Wash the area to be cleansed with beaten egg, apply the salve to unbroken skin, wash again with the beaten egg.

Sacred Trees

Of all the trees that grow so fair,
Old England to adorn,
Greater are none beneath the Sun
Than Oak and Ash and Thorn.
Puck of Pook's Hill, by Rudyard Kipling, 1906

The tree is the largest plant on the planet and if only due to this, is considered magical. Before books and therefore knowledge was readily available, when young, a person would look up at a mature tree, so tall above them. When they died at a ripe old age, the tree had not changed and so was thought immortal. Groves of trees formed the first temples, to worship the trees and then later the Gods. Trees protect from wind and sun, provide heat in the depths of winter and a fire to cook on. Trees provide clothing from their bark, fruit to eat and wood for shelter. Primitive man was not so far wrong, trees are also the lungs of the Earth. They breath in carbon dioxide and breath out oxygen, without trees the Earth could not sustain life. What we see is only half of the story of a tree. Many trees spread up as high as their roots reach down into the rich dark earth. All stones, gems and herbs have a spirit within and a tree is no exception to this. Each species of tree has a personality and within that family each tree is an individual. In Greek mythology the spirit of the Oak tree were called Dryads and the spirit of the Ash were called Meliai. To the Greeks they were beautiful women, some were able to wander around, others only lived within the tree. In Europe, Wood- Folk or Moss-Folk, are small and grey-green in color, old looking and over grown with moss. Yet others tell of stick like deigns, with long twig-like fingers and twig hair, that sit in trees. Tree Folk live half in this world and half in the land of the Gods, they are not seen by all. A belief in their existence is needed first, for them to bother visiting this world. Leaves carry all the knowledge from its tree and many magical working requires a crown of leaves of a special tree. Fire was thought of as a gift from the trees, possibly a lightning strike would have first given birth to this idea.

Please ask the tree spirit before taking any wood from the trees. The wood will be happily given and some of the magic of the tree remains within. If the wood is taken without asking, you can understand where the magic of the wood will be withdrawn leaving a wand or staff that is "dead" with no power to help your magical work.

But what of the magic of a group of trees – a wood?

Like a coven, the group energy of a wood is very strong, all the roots knitting together beneath the soil creating one unit. A wood is a very special place.

There is a type of tree in Africa that if the animals over graze just one tree on the edge of a grove, then whole group will develop a poison. The trees, even those a mile away from the affected tree, will be influenced. The poison in the trees will then kill any animal unlucky enough to eat from the leaves of any tree within that area. The trees will return to normal when the over grazing has subsided. There has to be some form of communication between these trees, for this to be able to come about.

In the Middle Ages, woods abounded with activity, hurdles were made from the supple twigs of Hazel, Charcoal burners were busy and people needed to collect large quantities of firewood. But as night fell, it was thought that elves and fairies came out to play, best to be around your fire safe at home, far away from harm. If you must be out and about, protection needed to be carried, or they would whisk you away. Much as it is believed by some, that Aliens abduct people today.

Today, many Witches hold their rituals in woods at night, our coven being one. We have only had friendly interest from 'The 'Little People', this may be due to the old custom of bringing evergreen into the house at Yule. In pre-Christian times it encouraged the fairy folk to share your house in the depth of the coldest part of the year and so be friendly to you. Possibly this is the reason that in the Christian Middle Ages people didn't get on too well with the Fairy Folk. Now with Pagan rituals returning and evergreens being brought into the house at Yule once more, the old relationships between people and the fairy folk are at last returning.

One of the oldest magical uses for wood is for Divining. Since at least the eleventh century Diving has been one of the many practices of the local Witch. A forked branch of Hazel, Alder, Beech or Apple is the most favored. Hold one fork in each hand palm up, with the main branch held out horizontal before you. Walk slowly towards where you feel water will be. If water is present the branch dips toward the Earth with great force. Once practiced on water other things can be tried, buried treasure or mines, divining was also used to divine thieves and murders. In England it was thought that Elves helped your divining rod to work... or not! The Earth was in their care, if they wanted you to find what you were looking for, you found it, if not no amount of looking would uncover it.

Some forests are Ancient, the ancestors of the trees standing there, were among the first to colonize the soil after the Ice Age ended in England. Newer woods were planted in neat rows; many of these are pines for a quick crop. Even ancient forest, have been managed, copicing trees every fifteen years for straight staffs for fighting or building. When not copiced many trees were pollarded, which is to cut the staves about 10 foot above the heads of the pigs, boars and deer that would graze the forest floor. When left to grow wild, this produced the wonderful twisted trees of fairy tales, with thick short trunks and later forming heavy low boughs.

In Winter the forest is bleak still and empty and then from around a tree a Mont Jac deer will run too fast for my camera to catch. Under a coating of snow, deep within the Earth the roots are growing and awaiting the gentle rain of Spring.

In Spring the wood stirs, and begins to stretch, buds grow, trees flower and squirrels wake from their long sleep. All becomes active once again.

In Summer the wood abounds with flowers, first bluebells then foxgloves, said to only bloom where fairies dance. At Fullmoon and twilight bats fly over ponds, between the trees, catching insects for their dinner. Late Summer the flowers have dropped and many berries ripen in the sunshine turning from red to black filled with rich sweet juice, for animals, birds and people.

And then to Autumn, when trees turn golden and red, starting to gently float back to Mother Earth. Nuts, mushrooms and toadstools of all shapes and colors bedeck the woodland floor and grow from the trees. The pure white mushroom, the most dangerous of all 'The Death Angel' grows silently in the darkest shade.

The wood is in constant change, but the magic remains, at any time of year.

All trees are of course sacred and have uses in magic, this is but a small selection of the most popular.

Apple- Love, fertility and wisdom. The Apple is related to the rose. This shows best in its blossom, it is so similar to that of the Dog Rose. Sacred to both the Celts and later to the Norse tribes and the apple was associated with immortality. Place an apple on your altar as an offering to all Fertility Goddesses.

Idunna "the renewing one" a beautiful Goddess who grew apples, to keep the Norse Gods and Hero's forever youthful. As they kept the Gods forever young, the same idea may be behind the saying "An apple a day keeps the doctor away." Apples were also used as grave goods, from the Bronze Age onwards, giving immortality to the dead.

The Apple when cut around the middle has a pentagram within

 and so is considered the fruit of the Goddess. If peeled complete and thrown over the left shoulder it will form the initial of your future partner in life. The last apple should always be left on the tree for the fairies to insure a good harvest of the following year. Apples can be made into apple jam with honey and will keep through the winter, providing an invaluable source of vitamin C for our ancestors. Not forgetting Cider of course, a wonderful drink still enjoyed today. Cider is a great way to use the windfalls and not so perfect apples that could not be stored, in the past nothing could be allowed to go to waste. I hate to throw away food and like to be as ecological with my food, as well as my rubbish. Apple trees are wassailed and a little Spiced Cider poured at their roots in winter, to bless the trees, possible in honor of the Goddess Idunna.

If an apple tree blossoms in the Autumn, it was said that death will visit the house. Both the fruit and bark of the Apple tree was used for tanning.

Apple is a female wood.

Ash- Protection, love and healing, are the properties of this tree. Used to make fighting staves, as it grows straight and tall. Sacred to both the Celts and the Norsemen, who thought of the Ash as the great world tree called Yggdrasil. In Norse mythology the first man was created from an Ash tree, his name was Ask. The Ash tree was considered too dangerous to cut down, as it was considered sacred and the spirit of the Ash the Meliai, were known to be very protective of it. It was also used in healing a child with rickets. Ash is a very straight wood used for staves. A branch would be split and the child passed though nine times. It would be passed from father to another man and from West to East, Widdershins the way of the Moon. The branch was then bound up, as it healed so the child's rickets healed as well, if the tree was damaged or cut down the problem was thought to reoccur. This may add to the thoughts of not cutting down an Ash tree.

If cattle were thought to be 'overlooked' or had the Evil Eye (see Amulets and Talisman) placed on them a branch of Ash was twisted around its horns, as protection. The serpent feared the mere shadow of the Ash tree, and to escape from the Ash a serpent was thought to even crawl into fire. The first cuttings of hair and nails of a child should be buried under an Ash for the child to be a great singer. But don't hide from lighting under its branches as it was thought to attract strikes to it. An Ash is a healing tree, carry a bit of a branch or leaf with you for protection from chest problems and serpents. An Ash tree produces bunches of 'Ash Keys' which are its seeds.

Love Divination Verse
'Even-ash, even-ash, I pluck thee,
This night my own true love to see,
Neither in his bed nor in the bare,
But in the clothes he does every day wear.'

If you find an Ash tree leaf, keep it for good luck.
Ash is a male wood.

Beech- If growing alone in a field Beech is a tall and wide, an imposing tree. But growing within a Beech wood, the tree will grow thinner and to a great height, struggling up to the Sun.

Not many plants can grow beneath their thick canopy, Holly though is quite happy to grow in the shade of its high sisters. The nuts on the Beech are called masts and are used as animal fodder. There was a Temple to Zeus at Dodona, in Epirus, Ancient Greece, that was built in the middle of a grove of Beech trees, by listening to the sound of the leaves in the wind, Zeus whispered secrets to His followers. As Zeus was a God of Thunder and Lightning, so Beech protects from lightning, and was carried for this purpose.

Birch – Used for protection, purification and exorcisms, carried or utilized in a spell, at the start of a journey or project, often inscribed with the Berkana rune or the B Ogham letter. Place a branch above your door for protection from Evil spirits. The bark of the Birch tree rolls off in thin sheets and flaps in the breeze, making it easy to remove. The name of the tree comes from this, meaning 'to write upon'. Birch was also used for shelters and boats and as tinder to light fires. Coleridge speaks of 'The Lady of the Woods', as Birch is a tall and elegant tree, one you will recognize by the bark, as the leaves are often too high to see. After rain is has a delightful perfume. The Silver Birch and Fly-Agaric (as in flying, not insect) or Amanita Muscaria mushroom (which are the bright red fairy mushrooms of childhood stories) have a symbiotic relationship, combining with the roots of the tree and feeding it minerals and taking sugars. This beautiful mushroom, which is as large as a dinner plate, has been used by the earliest people all round the world for its hallucinogenic magical experiences. Called 'Flesh of the Gods', or 'Food of the Gods', as it was thought to connect you to the Gods themselves. The mushrooms of the Fly-Agaric that you see are only the 'fruit' of the mushroom, the same organism can spread for a large area around and live up to 1000 years old.

But be warned Fly-Agaric is also poisonous and illegal in England

and many other countries.

Birch is another of the twigs used to make Besoms and the characteristic smell of leather, comes from the use of Birch Tar in its tanning. Birch fungus, so the old wives tale goes, is good instead of plasters on a cut.

Birch sap is tapped in March, 16-18 gallons that does no harm to the tree, it's very good to drink or can be made into birch beer or wine. For wine, add honey, cloves, lemon fermented with yeast. It is high in vitamin C and is being tested as an anti- cancer drug. Birch appears to have large bird's nests hanging in the branches, best seen in winter, when no leaves obscure the view. These are galls, which are untidy bundles of twigs caused when the leaf buds are attacked by a fungus or tiny mite, the country peoples name for these are Witches.

Birch is a female wood

Blackthorn- It is more of a shrub than a tree, said to grow no more than thirteen feet, with long wicked thorns. It gets its name from its black bark and the strong air of magic that surrounds this wood.

Blackthorn, is full of magic and tradition, in Ireland the wood is considered protective, and a small twig should carried with you. If chased it can be thrown behind you as you run. This will root and form an impenetrable boundary that none can cross. In fairy tales it grows around Sleeping Beauty's Castle protecting her until her prince comes to save her. The famous Irish Shillelagh carried as a walking stick and defensive weapon is made from Blackthorn or Oak. A thorn rune can be carved on to a Blackthorn Shillelagh to increase its potency. It is also used in many other forms of protection magic. Sacred to The Morrigan, this woods' special time is between Samhain and Imbolc, the dark time. It is a wood of transformation, from the Dark Goddess of Halloween to the Virgin Goddess of Spring. After the first frosts it berries turn sweet, they are called Sloe (Mother of the Wood, Wild Plum or Wishing Thorn) and are used to make all manner of medicines, preserves, wine and mixed with gin, become Sloe Gin (see recipe at the end of the chapter). In early Spring it bursts into small delicate white star shaped flowers, musk scented in honor of the Virgin Goddess.

It is said in Scotland that Winter begins when the Dark Goddess strikes the ground with Her Blackthorn staff, and a long hard Winter in England was known as a Blackthorn Winter.

In the English Parliament, Black Rod's famous staff is made from Blackthorn. Major Weir, a self-confessed witch, was burned in Edinburgh in 1670 and his Blackthorn staff was burnt with him.

Medieval Christians were frightened by the Blackthorn, thinking it evil. But in the Craft we know the Dark Goddess well, chatting to Her at least once a month. We understand that death is but another step on the path, that we all must take, which only leads to another path. Witches do not fear death in the same way as Christians used to fear their Hell and Purgatory.

Blackthorn is a Female wood

Elm-Its old name is Elvenwood, it is used for love and protection, this tree is beloved of the fairy folk. Thought to be under the protection of the Gods and so not struck by lightning. Sprinkle Elm sawdust around the ritual area for protection. In Norse mythology woman was created from an Elm tree, her name was Embla.

The Greeks planted Elm to honor dead heroes and traditionally used in England for coffins. Elm was the fleet footed Mercury's special tree.

Perhaps because the Elm was so beloved of fairy folk, Christian didn't seem to like the Elm. Dante Alighieri wrote in 1300 in his poem *The Divine Comedy* of the vestibule of Hell where he has Virgil speak the lines...........

"In the midst a gloomy Elm displays its boughs and aged arms, which seat vain dream are commonly said to haunt, and under every leaf they dwell".

From this the Elm was called the Tree of Dreams or The

Morpheus Tree.

Unfortunately the Elm trees no longer sit and dream in England, as Dutch Elm disease destroyed most of our Elm trees.

Wych Elm Wych is the Anglo-Saxon word for bending, as its boughs bend down towards the Earth. It is one of the hardest woods, used for the keel of boats. It was thought that pigs teeth stuck into a Wych Elm tree will give the bark the power to cure toothache.

Elm is a Female wood

Hazel- Poetry, love, fertility and childbirth, known as the Tree of Knowledge. Twigs placed in the hair or around a hat to make a 'Wishing Cap'. Twigs of Hazel are also used for water divining; staffs, wattle for building and the nuts, are

the gifts of this tree. A Hazel is a good tree to make wands from. A Hazel nut carried in the pocket in Ireland was thought to ward off aches and pains, brought on by the fairy folk. A double Hazel nut was thought to cure toothache in Devon and defend against evil in Scotland. Hazel is one of the magical trees associated with May Day, along with Hawthorn in England and Rowan in Scotland. Oil from one Hazelnut should be rubbed over a walking stick for a superb glow to the wood and to give you protection from falls.

Hazel is a female wood.

Holly- Holly is used for its Timber, the grain is very fine like ivory. The female trees being covered in berries, and represent in our tradition, the Mother Goddess. Caution as the berries from the Holly are poisonous to humans. The Holly is another of the trees brought into the house at Yule to remind us that Spring will soon be here and green will return to the brown Earth once more.

The dried leaves was then transferred to the barn to protect the animals within. A branch if thrown at an animal, even if it doesn't touch it, will make him obedient and strangely a coach drivers whip is made from Holly. A branch of old leaves from a male tree Holly tree was hung in the home and is used as protection from magic and from lightning or a tree planted in your garden will defend against poison and evil. Steep nine leaves in boiling water, when cold; sprinkle around the home as protection, particularly around a baby's cot.

Holly is both male and female wood

Oak- Protection, healing, luck. Oak is considered to be one of England's special trees, living to a ripe old age of 800 years and was even at one time part of the design of coins. The Druids held the Oak Groves sacred, as did the Greeks and the Romans dedicating it to Jupiter and later it was dedicated to Thor, both are Thunder Gods and therefore thought to protect from lightning strikes. Oak branches or acorns were hung in homes and worn for the purpose and acorns on blind pulls even today are related to this. Pagan marriages were celebrated under some Oak trees. Wreaths of oak leaves were used in fertility ceremonies. Acorns were carried to preserve youthfulness and deaths were announced to the Oak tree. Holes in the Oak are considered to be door to the fairy realm. Dryads live their whole lives in a Oak tree and therefore it is considered very unlucky to cut an Oak tree down it is said that it shriek when cut. The more so if it contained Mistletoe, because of this Oak trees were used as boundaries markers to property.

Common Oak   **English Oak**

The Oak tree provided acorns for pigs to eat, bark for dyeing and wood for timber. Drive a nail into an Oak tree was thought to cure tooth ache. You can make a very dry wine from young oak leaves. Jays and squirrels bury acorns far from the wood that they were harvested from and then after all the work, forget where they were buried, leaving the acorn to carry on growing into a mighty oak tree.

Oak is a male wood

Rowan (the name in America is Mountain Ash)- Protection and healing, are its attributes, it is sometimes called "The Lady of the Mountain" or Dragon Tree in Germany. Rowan is strangely unrelated to the Ash tree that it so closely resembles, but is bizarrely related to the Rose tree instead.

The Greek Goddess Hebe whose chalice of youth was stolen, sent an eagle to recover the magical cup and the droplets of blood of the eagle that were lost in the fight fell to Earth as Rowan trees. So that no one would forget the eagle's bravery, Hebe made the leaves of the Rowan in the shape of the eagle's feathers and the Rowan's berries are the drops of the eagle's blood.

In many places Rowan became known as the Witch Tree and used for divination, healing, psychic powers, success and protection. Staves with runes carved on them and magic wands were often made

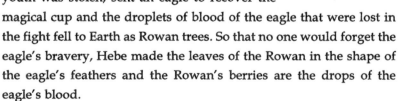

from this magical wood. Rowan is also sacred to the Celtic Goddess Brigitte of Smithing, the arts and healing. Nothing from this tree may be cut and used, the exception being for sacred purposes, which I can but assume applied to spindles and spinning wheels, which were traditionally made of Rowan in Scotland and Ireland. Druids considered the Rowan, a tree of inspiration calling it "Tree of Bards", but it was also used as wood for funeral pyres, as it was the tree of death and rebirth. Coffins were rested under Rowan trees while those carrying it had a little refreshment, before finishing their procession to the graveyard. Rowan was also burnt in fires of divination, to invoke spirits and was one of the nine sacred woods to be burnt at Beltane. Necklaces of the berries are worn for protection and ease in childbirth. The berries were fed to cows and mares to ensure uncomplicated births. Rowan Day is the 3rd May, a day to cut the Rowan to place over the door and to carry in our pockets, as the Rowan would be in blossom at that time. If crossed twigs were tied with red thread and placed over stables or home no human or horse could be hag-rid at night. To be hag-rid was to have an evil spirit sit on your shoulders and make you run them to their destination. In the morning you would wake in your bed with no memory, but hot and sweaty or find your horse in his stable in the same condition. This was also tied to animals left in the fields, as protection against fairies on May Eve. Riders, who had no choice but to be out and about on that day, wore sprigs of Rowan in their hats for protection. A churn staff should be made from Rowan to stop any evil thoughts from stopping the cream turning to butter. In the Christian Middle Ages Rowan was thought to protect from Witchcraft. In that period, Witchcraft was synonymous with evil, anyone who didn't worship their god, be they Witch, Jew or Muslim qualified as evil. **Rowan is a female wood.**

White Willow (not Weeping Willow) - Love, Divination, Protection, Calming and Healing are this trees special gifts. White Willow Bark is very bitter and is the tree that Aspirin was originally extracted from. Willows are sacred to the Moon Goddess, in the Celtic world the Willow was associated with life and death. Willow's are also known as the 'Tree of Enchantment' and 'Witches Aspirin'. Those wishing to develop their artistic skills should sit under a Willow Tree at night. Willow is also considered a Guardian Tree so carry some part or place it in your home. Ask the tree to protect you from accidents by tapping on the trunk. As Willow is so closely related to water, it was used as a divining rod to find this. **Willow is a Female Tree.**

Yew- Yew is a wood of protection and of remarkable power, living to a great age over 1000 years, a tree of life and death.

On a Summer day the yew tree will give off a gas, it is not advisable to fall asleep under its branches, or you may never wake;

a wood of the Dark Goddess. Because the Yew is so poisonous, it was grown in churchyards with a wall around to keep away animals and to impart immortality to those buried within and handy to line the newly dug graves.. As churches were often placed on old Pagan sites, it may have been a long standing tradition that the Yew had always been grown there and this just carried on through the Christian period. Yew makes the best Longbows; both the sapwood and grain are used forming a natural composite bow.

Yew is a female wood.

The Tree Alphabet or Ogham
No chapter on the magic of trees would be complete without looking at Ogham often called the Tree Alphabet. Many magical trees have a letter associated with Ogham, only four are very old, namely Birch, Alder, Willow and Oak the others were added later, that is before 1390, so it still has a strong magical build up of energy! But in truth Ogham is not only a Tree Alphabet but has versions for birds, food,

pigs, ox, water, even art and many more.

Ogham may be as old as the 4th century but at that time it would have been written on wood or other perishable substances. Later Ogham was carved into stone and mainly used as territorial markers and grave stones.

Ogham is written above, under and across a base line. This line would normally be the corner of the stone to be carved. The text is read from the bottom left-hand side of the stone, around the edge, across the top and down the right-hand side.

yourgoddessgowith

Y	Y
A	O
M	U

Ogham was the first known sign language, using the fingers for the strokes and the leg, hand or nose for the base line. In this way it kept its secrets from all but those who could read the mystic language and in the middle of a crowd two people could have a secret conversation all in Ogham undisturbed.

The *Auraicept na n-Éces* ("The Scholars' Primer") is a manuscript describing Irish Grammar written in the 7th century. The only surviving copy of the Auraicept is preserved within the Book of Ballymote compiled in 1390. Also within the Book of Ballymote is a copy of *In Lebor Ogaim* another of the sources of information on this intriguing subject, this speaks of 92 "secret" variations of Ogham. With such strange names as "Finns Window" an Ogham of ever decreasing circles, "The Secret Ogham of Warriors" a very cursive variation and even claiming the runic Younger Futhark as the "Ogham of the Norsemen". All we know of how to decipher Ogham comes from the Book Of Ballymote and luckily like the Rosetta Stone of Egypt the (but not the Irish) English stones have a Latin translation inscribed on their surface.

There are many secret ways of writing Ogham, one is to start in the middle of a name with the first letter, writing half and then write backwards from the first letter to the beginning (called Serpent about the head).

ettejean

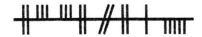

If you wish to make your herb book secret according to Longarad, the writer of the Auraicept, take the first letter of your herb (in Gaelic of course) and substitute a single Ogham letter instead. This works as long as you don't have two herbs starting with the same letter, Basil and Bay, for example, but of course just use the first and second letters.

Ogham inscriptions are found all over Ireland but are especially concentrated in the South, around Kerry. In Britain, they have been found across the North Sea facing Ireland in South- West Scotland, Wales, Cornwall, Devon, the Isle of Man and one lone exception excavated in Silchester, Southern England.

I have arranged two poems and the Ogham of the birds and colors together, as you can see from the following not all the ancient writings on Ogham agree.

Auraicept na N-Éces (a short excerpt from the original words)
What are the place, time, person, and cause of the invention of the Ogham. Not hard. Its place the island of Ireland where we Irish live, In the time of Bres son of Elatha King of Ireland it was invented. Its person Ogma son' of Elatha son of Delbaeth brother to Bres, for Bres, Ogma and Delbaeth are the three sons of Elatha son of Delbaeth there. Now Ogma, a man well skilled in speech and in poetry, invented the Ogham.

It is from the trees of the forest that names were given to the Ogham letters metaphorically.

T Moreover *Beithe*, **B**, is from the **Birch** *of the forest for the first letter on the path of the Ogham alphabet.*

Feocus foltchain, faded trunk and fair hair, that is for birch, b, in the Word Ogham, because names which Morann gave of himself to the Ogham letters, these are they which take the effect of letters in the Word Ogham. Feocus foltchain for b, for these are two aspects of the Birch, and it was hence put for the Ogham letter which has taken a name from it.

Bird- Pheasant

Color- white

Π *Luis*, **L**, that is **Rowan**, or **Elm** in the forests.

Li sula, delight of eye, that is luis, Quicken Tree, l, to wit, the flame.

Bird- duck

Color- grey

Π *Fern*, **F**, that is, **Alder** in the forest.

Airinach Fian, i.e., shield of warrior-bands, i.e., shield for fern, f, with him owing to their redness in the same respect: or because the Alder, the material of the shield was from fernae given to the Ogham letter which has taken a name from it. Airenach Fian, i.e., shield, that is fern, f, with him.

Bird- gull

Color- red

ΠΙΙ *Sail*, **S**, of the Ogham, that is, **Willow**, again, in the forest.

Li' n-aimbi', hue of the lifeless, i.e., hue of one dead, to wit, am for denial, so that he is not living but is dead. Li' n-aimbi', again, to wit, that is sail, Willo', s with him, and hence it was put for the Ogham letter.

Bird- hawk

Color- fine color (?)

ΠΙΙΙ *Nin*, **N**, of the Ogham, to wit, maw of spear **(Ash)**, or **Nettles** in the woods.

Cosdad sida, checking of peace, that is nin, Ash, n: it is the maw of a weaver's beam as applied to wood: a sign of peace is that. A checking of peace with him is that from the ash of the weaver's beam.

    Bird- snipe

    Color- clear

⌐   *Uath,* **H,** *of the Ogham, that is, test-tree or* **White Thorn** *on account of its thorniness.*

Conal cuan, pack of wolves, that is uath, Thorn, h, for a terror to any one is a pack of wolves. Conal cuan said of the Ogham h, owing to the affinity of the name, for they are a thorn, in the same way.

    Bird- Night Raven

    Color- Terrible (?)

⊔⊔   *Dur,* **D,** *of the Ogham is* **Oak,** *again, in the forest.*

Ardam dossaibh, highest of bushes, that is dur, Oak, d, with respect to its wood in the forest.

    Bird- wren

    Color- black

⊔⊔⊔   *Tinne,* **T,** *of the Ogham,* **Holly** *or* **Elderberry** *in the forest.*

Trian, t, another thing the meaning of that today.

    Bird- starling

    Color- dark grey

⊔⊔⊔⊔   *Coll, C, of the Ogham,* **Hazel** *in the forest.*

Cainin fedaib, fairest of trees, that is Hazel, c, owing to its beauty in woods.

    Bird- hen

    Color- brown

⊔⊔⊔⊔⊔   *Quert,* **Q,** *of the Ogham is* **Holly** *in the forest, or* **Apple** *or* **Aspen.**

Clithar mbaiscaill, shelter of a hind, i.e., a fold: to wit, boscell, lunatic, that is bas-ceall, death sense, it is then his sense comes to him when he goes to his death. *Clithar boscell*, again, that is an apple tree: or *boscell*, that is, hinds, to wit, they are light. *Clithar boiscell*, again, i.e., lunatics or hinds: quert, an apple tree, q, with reference to its letter.

Bird- *(no bird is recorded here)*
Color- *mouse colored*

Muin, **Vine, M**, mead (from it).
Tresim fedma, *strongest of effort, that is muin, Vine, m, with him, i.e., owing to identity of name with muin, back of man or ox, for it is they that are the strongest in existence as regards effort.*

Bird- *titmouse*
Color- *variegated*

Gort, **Cornfield, G, Fir.**
Millsin feraib, *sweeter than grasses, that is gort, ivy, g, with him owing to the identity of the name with the cornfield. When it is in the blade, sweeter than any grass is that grass, to wit, the cornfield.*

Bird- *swan*
Color- *blue*

Getal, **NG, Broom.**
Hence for that letter in Ogham owing to the complete identity of the name between them Luth legha, *a physician's strength; that is broom, ng, because it is strength with the physicians, and there is an affinity between cath, battle (the sharp thorns on broom), and getal, broom.*

Etiud midach, *robe of physicians, cath, panacea. Hence it was put for getal, broom, ng.*

Bird- *goose*
Color- *green*

Straif, **Z, Willowbrake (Blackthorn)** in the forest.
Tresim ruamna, *strongest of red, that is str with him in Ogham.*
Straif, Sloe, *according to fact; for in the sloe red for dyeing the things is stronger, for it is it that makes the pale silver become azure, making*

it genuine silver. It is it which is boiled through the urine into the white gold so as to make it red. Tresim ruamna is the sloe according to fact. Hence it was put in the letter named z, owing to identity of name between them, i.e., straif is the name of each of them.

Bird- thrush
Color- small rook

Ruis, **Elderberry, R**

Tinnem ruccae, intensest of blushes, that is ruis, **Elderberry, R,** *from the reddenirig or shame according to fact, for by r it is written, and it is a reddening that grows in a man's face 'through the juice of the herb being rubbed under it. Tindi ruccae, an ingot of a blush, again, said of the ruis, elder-berry, from shame or from reddening, for it is by r that it is itself written.*

Bird- small rook
Color- red

Ailm, **Fir, A,**

Ardam iachtadh, loudest of groanings, that is wondering, that is ailm, **Fir, A,** *with him; for it is ailm or 'a' a man says while groaning in disease, or wondering, that is, marveling at whatever circumstance*

Bird- lapwing
Color- piebald

Onn, **O, Ash**

Congnamaid echraide, helper of horses, the onnaid of the chariot, i.e. the wheels, that is onn, furze, with him, for it is by onn, o, that the wheels of the chariot are written. Also, comguinidech, equally wounding, i.e. whin. Hence it was put for that letter which is named onn, o, owing to identity between them, for onn is a name for each of them; and it is from whin that the name onn was put for the Ogham letter o.

Bird- scrat(?)
Color- dun color

Ur, U, Thorn.

Uaraib adbaib, in cold dwellings, that is ur, fresh, with him, for from uir, the mould of the earth is the name uaraib adbaib. Hence it was put for the letter named ur, Heath, in Ogham, owing to identity of name between them, each of them is ur, and it is written by u.

Bird- lark

Color- resinous

Edad, E, Yew (Aspen?)

Snamchain feda, most buoyant of wood, that is ebad, aspen, with him, for fair swimming is wood; that is a name for the great raven. Hence it was put for the letter named the Ogham ebad, for e is a name for salmon, and it is written by ea like the alphabet of the fauna: i.e., by stag (deer), eo by eonasc (ousel).

Bird- swan

Color- red

Ida, I, Yew.

Siniu fedaib, oldest of woods, that is idad, Yew, with him; for siniu fedaib is a name for service-tree. Hence it was given to that letter in Ogham named idad, yew, i, for hence the name idad was put for it; for idad, yew, is a name for ibur, service-tree.

Bird- eaglet

Color- very white

(These last five symbols were added at some time between the 7th century and when the Book of Ballymote was compiled)

Ebad, EA, Elecampane. (Aspen)

Ergnaid fid, distinguished wood, that is Aspen with him, for ergnaid fid is a name for the trembling tree. Hence it was put for the Ogham letter named edad, aspen, for hence was edad, e, put for it.

Oir, **OI, Spindle Tree.**
Sruitem aicdi, most venerable of structures, i.e., oir, oi, spindle tree, according to fact. Hence it was put for the letter owing to the identity of the name that is between them, to wit, oir is the name of each of them.

Uilleann, **UI, Ivy (Woodbine , Honeysuckle).**
Tutmur fid uilleann, juicy wood is woodbine, that is woodbine with him, for it is a name for honeysuckle. Hence it was put for the Ogham named woodbine, ui; for hence was woodbine put for it, for it is a name for honeysuckle.

Pin, **IO,** of the Ogham, **Pine,** again, in the forest. Hence are named *caera pinne,* **Gooseberries;** *ifin,* again is the name of that letter.
Millsem feda, sweetest of wood, that is gooseberry with him, for a name for the tree called pin is millsem feda. Gooseberries are hence named. Hence it was put for the letter named pin, for hence pin, or ifin, io, was put for it.

Emancoll, **Witch Hazel, AE,** again, c doubled according to fact or according to form, c across c in its form.
Luad soethaig, expression of a weary one, i.e., ach, ah! uch, alas! that is emancoll, ae, with him, for emancoll is taken for ach, though it may be taken for something else.
Finit Word-Ogham of Morann.

Of course the best way to understand trees is to sit with them. Do visualization and let them tell you of their sacred secrets.

Incenses
Incense creates a powerful background to all magical workings and prayers. For at least five thousand years they have burnt, rising from altars to the skies, from ancient Egypt, Babylon, Mexico and Rome

(both Pagan and Christian). It both purifies the atmosphere and stimulates the mind.

Incenses are not joss sticks, commercial joss sticks are mostly made of synthetic oils. Incenses are mixtures of resins, woods, herbs and oils that you can easily make yourself. This adds an extra strength to the incense, that like anything in witchcraft, if you make it yourself you add extra power to it. You are also more in control of what herbs and spices the incense was made from. Incenses are used not only for their smell, which in ancient days masked the smell of burnt offerings, but when burnt they release vibrations and attract intelligences that enhance all magical workings. It stimulates the Jungian collective unconscious, tapping us into a basic mind that understands the meaning of smell, far better than our modern thinking mind, with all its over-analysis of subjects. Cutting through to the Id or our basic instincts of love, sex, anger and flight. It also connects us to the Gods and Goddesses, sending a message of love and an offering. It calls to them that a circle is to be cast.

Over-laying this is a personal sense of what smell means to you.

Does a smell of roses remind you of your mother?

Or a lover?

Or for you has it a darker connotation?

Or just simply the smell of baby's plastic pants, that are impregnated with the synthetic smell of roses?

Incense helps with all forms of divination, relaxation when meditating, spell workings and protection.

Incense is a mixture of many different things.

A mixture of resins that might include exotic names like Frankincense, Myrrh, Benzoin, Mastic and Dragons blood.

Woods- In the incense I make for sale, I only use Sandalwood, Sanderswood and Cedar wood but you can also use pine, apple wood and oak chips are great to add. Add them also to commercial incenses to make them go farther, remembering to add the wood that is right for the magic of the incense bought (oak- protection, apple- love, etc).

Herbs- Balm of Gilead, Grains of Paradise, many exotic names all with different attributes, or herbs that you can grow in your garden like Rosemary, Thyme or dried Rose petals.

Essential oils to enhance their long burning qualities, add just enough to dampen the mixture and provide the top note. Neroli, Patchouli, Cedarwood, or Rosemary, choose from an extensive list nowadays. We are so lucky today to be able to buy so many.

Making incense is an Art Magical, how to make incense may be as old as how to make bread. Each herb, wood, oil or resin must be added one at a time rather than all added together and just stirred. The last items you add are the most important. Like making a cake the order that you mix it makes a difference to the finished product and the cherry on top of the icing, is the ingredient that attracts the eye. But it's when you bite into the cake that its full flavor is revealed. To use only one herb would be like serving the Goddess cabbage for dinner, it's boring, you need to enchant and delight Her attention. Each herb and spice has its own vibration and energy, by choosing a selection of herbs with the right powers you refine your wish to a fine point. Your wish may be a spell or a celebration as at a Sabbat but for it to work your need the attention of the Gods and the quarter elementals and a fine blended incense will do that. You may need a pestle and mortar to pound up some of the ingredients, benzoin, cloves or some roots, for example. Funnily, the best pestle I have ever seen I do not own, was in the Museum of London and was from Roman London, with small pieces of quartz cast into the bottom to help with the grinding. I have never seen a modern one to match it. Keep a special bowl to mix your incense in, I use a small cast iron cauldron but choose what feels best to you.

An incense is never designed for its smell, if you want a pretty smell use joss sticks. It is designed for its magical content, this makes it sound as if all incenses smell foul; they don't, the Goddess is kind with Her magic. You will fill your house with the smell of enchantment.

How to burn incense.

For this you will need charcoal blocks from your occult suppler, unfortunately these can't be made but they are cheap. You will also need something to burn the incense in, for your first attempt a flowerpot or something similar will do. Get some dry earth or sand to place in the bottom of the container. The charcoal blocks generate a lot of heat the sand will absorb it. When I first experimented with charcoal blocks I had no idea how hot it would get, the saucer I used smashed and I burnt the kitchen work surface, don't make my mistake.

Light the block of charcoal, a sparkling line will cross the block, this is the salt peter burning. The charcoal will get very hot very quickly, put it down onto the sand with the concave side up and let the line of sparkles finish, it may still look black and dead but believe me it isn't. Wait a few moments and then place quarter of a teaspoon of incense onto the block. A wonderful smell of magic will arise and fill your room, just as it has always done from the beginning of time.

Knock off any burnt incense before re-applying every now and then, the blocks last for about two hours, which is plenty for your ritual. Replenish with incense as necessary.

Be careful if you are asthmatic, perhaps you could experiment with mixing essential oils and drop onto the charcoal block, this does not give off so much smoke and will be easier on your chest. Another thought would be to use Colts Foot herb as this was proscribed for chest problems in the last century.

The Ancient Egyptians had a room within some of their temples adorned with recipes for incenses, where the ingredients were stored. Used in all their rituals one lovely poem runs…

'The incense comes, the incense comes,
The scent is over thee,
The scent of the eye of Horus is over thee.
The perfume of the Goddess Nekbet
It cleanses thee, it adores thee,

It makes its place upon they two hands
Hail to thee, oh incense!
Take to thyself the Eye of Horus (Protection).
Its perfume is over thee.'

How an incense is constructed

Let's take general Sabbat incense as an example

Sabbat: An incense for all quarter days and cross quarter days (Witch festivals) an absolute must.

Frankincense -	God
Myrrh-	Goddess
Benzoin-	Astral protection
Cinnamon-	Astral Projection
Rose Petals-	Love, Goddess
Wild Thyme-	Love, Happiness
Red Sanderswood-	Courage and God
Juniper Berries-	Love, Healing, Psychic ability
Mugwort-	Psychic

Add a little Ylang-Ylang oil to mix

All potions, incenses and oils will need a spell to charge them up. Cast circle, call quarters and say your words of power. This is only an example, far better to write your own.

Mugwort, Mandrake and Rose (change the herbs to that of the Spell)
I blend,

Magic powers on the wind I send,
I ask of Earth, Air, Fire and Water their magic to agree,
And of the Lady, Blessed BE!!

Incense Formulary

To act separates the scholar from the mystic, you can read but it is only in the doing that you truly understand.

Here are some formulas to get you going, as with blending your own incenses always keep a note of your recipes.

And then have fun!

Astral Projection: Use Astral Projection incense, when practicing out of body experiences or for meditation.

Frankincense

Myrrh

Benzoin

Mugwort

Dittany of Create

Business Success: Burn in your place of business to increase customers or use with Business Success oil on the till and around the door.

Benzoin

Mastic

Cinnamon

Oak Moss

Ginger

Grains of Paradise

Patchouli

Tonka Beans

White Bryony

Add Orange oil

Banishing: Use to clear an area of negative vibrations.

Frankincense

Myrrh

Hyssop

Cedar

Add Eucalyptus oil

Bast: An Egyptian Cat Goddess. Used for harmony in marriage, happiness and fruitfulness.

Myrrh

Gum Arabic

Calamus

Cinnamon

Catmint

Add The Egyptian (see oils) you don't have to wait 8 years, three months will do.

Bee: This incense deals with all wealth and money spells and to the mother Goddess.

Use at the full moon.

Myrrh

Dammar Gum

Nutmeg

Ginger

Chamomile

Cinnamon

Mace

Clover

Add a little Honey and Lavender oil

Crone: For all divination, work with the Dark Goddess, her sphere of influence is to take away pain, problems or illness. Use on the waning moon.

Myrrh

Pine Resin

Damiana

Wormwood

Cinnamon

Nutmeg

Mugwort

Juniper

Charcoal (loose, just enough to darken the mixture)

Add Vetivert oil

Consecration: To bless new tools and magical instruments.

Frankincense

Myrrh

Benzoin

Marjoram

Lemon

TonkaBean

Grains of Paradise

Centaury

Poppy Seeds

Mace

Add Rose Geranium oil

Curse breaking: I have been asked to make an incense to clear the evil eye, this is very strong and should clear all hexes and problems sent against you. Try keeping a Tigereye stone in the jar for a week with some of the incense and carry the Tigerye with you for added protection.

Frankincense

Myrrh

Bay

Rosemary

Dragons Blood

Clove

Cinnamon

Add Juniper oil

Divination: For all work with Tarot, Runes, Crystal balls or any form of divination.

Frankincense

Myrrh

Nutmeg

Cinnamon

Nutmeg

Mugwort

Bay

Wormwood

Add Nutmeg oil
Myrrh oil

Earth: Good for all Earth magic and nature conservation.
Myrrh
Benzoin
Nutmeg
Rosemary
Patchouli
Basil
Chamomile Flowers
Bay
Cardoman
Cinnamon
Juniper
Add Oak Moss
Patchouli Oil

Esbat: For all Full Moon workings.
Myrrh
Benzoin
Rose Petals
Fennel Seeds
Patchouli
Wild Lettice
Add Rose Geranium Oil

Exorcism: Used for only the most difficult cases of ghosts or poltergeists in the home. Burn on nine consecutive days and carry around your entire house each time.
Frankincense
Myrrh
Lavender
Salt (pinch)

Hyssop
Rue
Vervain
Add
Lavender Oil
Hyssop Oil

Greenman: For outdoor workings or to bring the outdoors, indoors. This incense is particularly good at Beltane.

Frankincense
Benzoin
Damiana
Juniper
Clove
Patchouli
Add Oak Moss
Patchouli Oil

House of Anubis: The Egyptian guardian of the dead under whose auspices incenses belong, in the Egyptian Pantheon. This incense is designed to be burnt when someone you love has died.

Attracts all good spirits to your ritual workspace and increases psychic power.

This incense is based on the Kyphi formula,
then add to the your ready made Kyphi
Rosemary
Sandalwood
Grains of Paradise
Gum Mastic
Oak Moss
Add Vetivert and Ylang Ylang oil

House Blessing: Burn House Blessing incense to bring a warm happy atmosphere into your home.

Hyssop
Basil
Juniper
Frankincense
Myrrh
Dragons Blood
Mistletoe
Chamomile Flowers
Add Orange oil

Handfasting: Handfasting is an old name for wedding.
Frankincense
Myrrh
Rose petals
Rosemary
Patchouli
Bay
Tonka bean
Add Orange Oil
A little Neroli Oil

Horned God: Cernunnos and Herne are antler horned Gods of the forest. To honor them and the Earth, burn this incense within your circle.
Frankincense
Benzoin
Centinery
Calamus
Origano
Sunflower petals
Vervain
Horn (Pinch)
Add Orange oil
Patchouli oil

Healing: A good healing incense triggering the centers of the brain that deal with magic, to send out waves of healing for yourself, or for any that are ill.

Frankincense
Myrrh
Dammar Gum
Cedar
White Willow Bark
Coriander
Nutmeg
Juniper
Rosemary
Chamomile
Poppy
Add Lavender Oil

Initiation: For something special at this special time.

Frankincense
Myrrh
Hyssop
Juniper Berries
Sandalwood
Horn (pinch)
Fennel Seeds
Grains of Paradise
Bay Leaves
Wormwood
Dragons Blood
Rose Petals
Mix with Amber oil or Benzoin
3 drips of Rose oil or Rose Geranium

Isis: An Egyptian mother Goddess, the Romans called her the Goddess of a thousand names, a strong Goddess, with a deep love for all who worship her. A protection incense.

Myrrh

Juniper

Bay

Rose Petals

Mugwort

Clove

Calamus

Chamomile

Add Ylang-Ylang oil

Although not from Egypt it has the similar vibrations as the Lotus flower and makes a good substitute.

Kyphi: Many Egyptian Temples have an incense room in which incense ingredients were stored, on the walls was written in Hieroglyphics the recipes for Kyphi. Use it to celebrate festivals if you work with Egyptian Gods.

Frankincense was burnt in Egyptian temples at dawn to welcome the Sun God Ra.

Myrrh was burnt at noon when the Sun was at its height.

And Kyphi was burnt, at the going down of the Sun into the underworld, according to Plutarch, that He may return safe and well at dawn. Its effects are soporific and intoxicating, it was taken as a medicine and applied externally as a treatment for wounds. Kyphi is not recommended to treat any illness, except magically today, never eat Kyphi! Burn the incense and ask for Ra's help to be restored to health.

There is a story of a wife that mixed together Frankincense, Myrrh and Kyphi to raise the Sun God Ra, to speak through her dead husband. Effectively mixing morning, noon and evening in one magic spell.

Speaking of Kyphi Plutarch says " *Without drunkenness it relaxes and loosens the chain-like sorrows and tensions of daily cares. It polishes and purifies like a mirror the faculty which is imagination and reception to dreams, like the notes of the lyre which the Pythagorean used before sleep, to charm and heal the emotive and irrational or the soul. For odours often recall the power of perception when it is failing, while often they obscure and calm it since the exhalations penetrate the body by reason of their smooth softness."*

Dioscoides a Greek philosopher writing in the first century ACE called Kyphi a perfume most welcome to the Gods.

Among many exotic ingredients, Kyphi contains wine, honey and raisins and takes three months to make.

Raisins
Honey
Sweet thick Wine
Myrrh
Soak the above ingredients together for a week.
Mastic
Pine Resin
Camel grass (Ginger Grass) or use ginger instead
Juniper berries
Calamus
Cinnamon
Saffron
Chant while mixing to add power to the incense and sing the vowels as Egyptian Priests did.

Store for a further 11 weeks at least before use.

Love: To attract all kinds of love, mother love, popularity, a partner or sexual love.

Frankincense
Myrrh
Benzoin
Dragons Blood
Orris
Cinnamon

Rose Petals

Grains of Paradise

Ginger

Damiania

Add Patchouli oil and if you would like, synthetic rose, just for its smell as of course synthetic oils have no magical energy.

Luck Incense

Frankincense

Nutmeg

Calamus

Grains of Paradise

Tonka

Cinnamon

Verbena

Oak Moss

Vetivert oil

Ylang- Ylang oil

Morgana's Brew: A good power and protection incense for any ceremony, highly recommended by our customers "Hideously good stuff".

Frankincense

Myrrh

Benzoin

Ginger

Cinnamen

Bucho leaf

Boldo leaf

Orris

Add Orange oil

Lemon oil

Moon A full moon incense like Esbat.

Myrrh

Jasmine

Calamus

Poppy seeds

Fennel

Wormwood

Wild Lettice

Chamomile

Add Lavender oil

Ntyw burnt by the King of Ur the put the Gods and Goddesses in a good mood. Not all incenses have a long list of ingredients.

Cedar wood

Myrrh

Old Dorothy's sight incense: A excellent divination and visualization incense. I named this incense after Dorothy Clutterbuck of Wiccan fame.

Myrrh

Gum Mastic

Cinnamen Bark

Juniper

Sandalwood (if you can get it)

Patchouli

Add Patchouli Oil

Vetivert oil

Protection: For use when protection is of the utmost importance, stops all bad feelings sent against you. Burn and carry around the house.

Frankincense

Myrrh

Juniper

Rosemary
Mugwort
Anerseed
Sage
Angelica
Calamus
Add Juniper oil

Pan: God of the forest. To bring him into your temple area, not for the newcomer to magic as Pan is a notorious prankster.

Frankincense
Benzoin
Patchouli
Pine
Vervain
Wormwood
Bay
Red Wine
Add Oakmoss
Pine oil

Pathworking: To allow the mind the freedom to roam, on the astral plane.

Myrrh
Sage
Dragons Blood
Frankincense
Cedar
Juniper
Thyme
Mace
Mugwort
Add Myrrh oil
A little Nutmeg oil

Peace and Protection: Burn in a home where strife is prevalent. For calming a situation, can be used in a wider context for peace.

Frankincense
Myrrh
Vervain
Basil
Jasmine Flowers
Rue (pinch)
Add Lavender oil

Purification: For cleansing second-hand items that you wish to use as ritual equipment and for places with a negative atmosphere.

Frankincense
Copal
Thyme
Juniper
Lemon
Salt
Aniseed
Fennel
Yarrow
Basil
Add Lemon Oil
Eucalyptus oil

Success: For success in all endeavors, good luck incense brings a change of fortune into your life.

Frankincense
Myrrh
Dragons Blood
Patchouli
Marigold petals
Add Ylang-Ylang oil

Sun: For all happiness, luck and God spells

Frankincense

Benzoin

Gum Arabic

Colophany

Marigold petals

Sunflower petals

Cinnamon

Add Orange oil

Triple Goddess: In all her aspects, an all round incense for use in the temple or on your altar.

For the Virgin add

Willow bark

Lemon verbena

and mix sing or chant to the virgin. We find the child's nursery rhyme "Twinkle, twinkle little star" works wonders.

For the Mother

Rose petals

Dragons Blood

Mix separately chanting

For the Crone

White Bryony

Myrrh

Mix separately chanting. Add to the Virgin mix, the mother mix and then the crone.

Add a few drops of three oils Lemon, Ylang Ylang and Myrrh

Unicorn: To be used in luck ceremonies, to draw luck towards yourself. If you have a specific wish, burn the incense and imagine the Virgin Goddess and the unicorn. See yourself walking towards the unicorn and ask the Goddess to rub its horn while you state your wish.

Benzoin

Damar Gum
Galangal
Clove
Bay
Damiana
Aletris Root (also known as True Unicorn
Add Patchouli oil

Wealth: To draw wealth into your life. This may come as a pay rise or some good luck with gambling, but it will never make you very rich, only help you pay the bills.

Frankincense
Bay (lots)
Sandalwood
Basil
Pine Resin
Patchouli
Add Blue Chamomile oil
Patchouli oil
Orange oil
The orange oil and Blue Chamomile will turn the incense Green, the color of Money.

Potions and Lotions
Egyptian The
This is a perfume, greatly esteemed throughout the ancient world and worn by women in ancient times.
Soak Myrrh granules
Cinnamon sticks
In sweet wine.
Leave to mature for up to 8 years, but at least three months.

Hangovers
Feverfew Tea (Feverfew contains Aspirin, hence it's bitter taste.)

Happiness
St John's Wort Tea once a day (not if you are taking other drugs for depression or are on the Pill as it will negate it).

OCCULT INKS for writing Amulets and Talisman

Invisible Ink
Lemon Juice

Hold the paper or velum near a heat source to see the writing appear, not too close!

Dove's Blood Ink - Good Spells
I use standard Ink for spells with essential oils added. If you use the old recipes they make very poor ink, the other ingredients are there only to carry the oils, I can't see the point. It's quicker and better to use commercial ink, but please remember to consecrate it.

1 part dragons blood resin

2 drops cinnamon oil

2 drops bay oil

2 drops rose oil

10mls Red Ink

Dragon's Blood Ink -Protection Spells
1 part dragons blood resin

2 drops Myrrh Oil

2 Drops Frankincense Oil

10mls Red Ink

It is best, whether using these traditional inks or commercial inks, to consecrate them. To do this, draw a pentagram in the air and say:

"Out of thee goes all that is impure, leaving only the might of the Great Goddess remaining."

Bats Blood Ink- for cursing magic

You won't be cursing so no need to give the formula here.

Love

Love Potion 1

A small pretty bottle

Add Rose Petals

SMALL pinch of Chili

Ginger

Cumin

Fill with Mead; give it a good shake.

Tie with red and pink ribbon

A good gift to those to be Handfasted.

Love Potion 2

A tea made from Hibiscus Petals

Honey

This wonderful tea made from Hibiscus and is a wonderful blood red color, the color of passion. Give it to the one you love, as often as possible!

Keeps in the fridge for a week.

Love Spell

Place a handful of yarrow wrapped in a new hanky and place under your pillow.

Say *"Thou pretty herb of Venus's tree,*

Thy true name is yarrow,

Now who my bosom friend must be,

Prey tell me on the morrow".

Love Necklace

To be given as a lovers gift.

Pick rose hips in early autumn, thread on strong thread with a needle. Tie into a necklace at least 24" long and hang up to dry.

Love Cakes

Not a spell I would recommend for more than one reason, practically this comes too close to controlling magic. But if does have a historical interest.

Get sweaty,

Clean off sweat with flour

Mix with oil, egg, sugar,

And ashes of pubic hair and bake!!

Give to the one you love

(Yuk!!)

Brides Cake this one is far nicer by adding roses you bring all of the energy of that beautiful flower of love into the wedding.

1lb of flour

1lb of sugar

½ lb butter

Whites of 6 eggs, beaten to a stuff froth

Flavor with Rose Water

I'm sure you can see the difference in these spells.

Luck Potion

Brew together

Pinch each of Nutmeg

Ginger

Cinnamon

Juice and peel of one Orange

1 bay leaf

With half a pint of water.

A pretty looking bottle or chalice (this will only keep in the fridge for a few days).

Flying Potion (Do not Try!!)

Contains aconite, which slows the heart rate, decreases blood pressure and numbs pain. This would have been boiled in a little water and mixed with the goose fat. Then rubbed into the body, this gave the illusion of flying. Please do not try this, it is very dangerous, the herbs in this recipe are absorbed through the skin and are very strong. This could easily kill. I give it here only as a curio of times past.

Aconite or Monkshood as all herbalists know comes of course from Cerberus spittle, closely related to Fluffy of Harry Potter fame, but older!

Quick Brews

The first three are fine to use in circle but its not traditional to use spirits. Having said that, if I have opened the cupboard and the cupboard was bare, I have used spirits and the Goddess didn't say She disapproved.

Mulled Wine, very good at Yule.

Cinnamen

Cloves

Nutmeg

1 oranges

Bottle of cheap red wine

Water to the same quantity as wine

Lots of sugar

Heat, don't boil and serve. You do need the water, as liquid will come off the mulled wine as steam, it then becomes too strong and bitter.

Mulled Cider, delicious at Yule.

Cinnamon

Cloves

Nutmeg

1 oranges

Bottle of Cider

Sugar to taste

Heat, don't boil and serve.

Merlin's Manky Minute Mead (or known as 4M Mead)

4 ltrs of Cider,

I bottle sweet sherry

I lemon

Jar of honey

Mix out froth, drink!

Should there be any over this can be bottled for 2 years for superb proper mead.

Sloe Gin

Sloe Berries are from the Blackthorn, which is the same tree that provides the wood for the Stang. It is a wood full of magic and the berries are no different. Sloe Gin was thought to cure many problems, indigestion, tonic, eczema, colds, weak heart, catarrh and many more. In the 17th century it was used to treat flatulence and wind pains in the stomach. A gift of the Dark Goddess as Sloe berries grow freely on bushes just waiting the knowledgeable to pick. Made into a potion, a small glass of Sloe Gin is good to drink before a Calling Down of the Dark Goddess or before divination. It is also used in protection magic.

The Sloes must be ripe when picked and are best after the first frosts. This is one of the few fruit that can be picked after Samhain and at which time the Pooka wees everywhere. I can but assume that he makes Sloe Gin too, and doesn't like to wee on Sloe berries.

Traditionally no iron must be used to prick the berries, only silver or a thorn from the bush can be used, be very careful of the thorns which if pricked, the wound can turn septic.

Fill half a bottle with Sloe berries (they are related to plums).

Add lots of sugar. The sugar extracts the juice from the Sloes.

Fill with cheap Supermarket Gin

Shake everyday, until it turns a deep purple, about two weeks.

As you shake the potion, call the Dark Goddess to empower your brew.

Then shake every week for two and a half months, until-

Sloe Gin, magnificent!

Sloe Gin Wine

Pour off the Sloe Gin into another clean bottle, fill the original bottle still with the Sloes in with white wine, and shake every day for a few days. This washes off the Sloe Gin into the wine, and you have a very unusual rose wine.

Throw the Sloes out for the birds, but not too many at once!

Blackberry Vodka

Both Sloe Gin and Blackberry Vodka are the cordial of the 18th century, drunk after dinner by the ladies in tall stemmed glasses with small bowls, a little goes a long way.

Nuke (microwave) your blackberries (no water) and then sieve.

Add to vodka, when cool, with lots of sugar, about half and half –

This can be drunk immediately, isn't nature wonderful.

Eat sieved remains with icecream or cream, too good to waste.

Love Rum

Add Cinnamon sticks to a bottle of rum with lots of sugar, keep for a month or two, give small glass to your loved one!

Samuel Pepy's Hot Chocolate

And just for the fun of it, after all chocolate is made from a herb and dedicated to Venus at that. Some how I think she would approve of this recipe, try it on Valentines Night on your partner, if you can bear to part with it.

Chocolate

Sugar

Hot Port (not boiled)

Whip together (The drink! The drink!)

Exercises:

Design incenses for all the Sabbats separately eight in total. This can be on paper you don't have to make them or make them as the different festivals come round; you will only need a small amount of each. Remember which is God and which is Goddess festival, is it Summer or Winter? Add in all the information that you have about a festival or can find out about.

CHAPTER 9

Essential Oils and their Uses

He would now study perfumes and the secrets of their manufacture, distilling heavily scented gums from the East. He saw that there was no mood of the mind that had not its counterpart in the sensuous life, and set himself the task to discover their true relation, wondering what there was in frankincense that made one mystical, and in ambergris that stirred one's passions, and violets that woke memory of dead romance, and in musk that troubled the brain, and champak (the sacred Frangipanni tree) *that strained the imagination; and seeking often to estimate the several influences of sweet-smelling, and scented pollen-laden flowers or aromatic balms.*

Oscar Wild from the story The Picture of Dorian Gray

The energy and essences distilled from leaves, flowers, roots and berries are known as essential oils. There are about 300 essential oils made, although not all are on general sale, as some are controlled substances and are deadly poisonous, they may be natural but not all that is natural is good for you. Prices vary extensively for oils; Otto of Roses is distilled from 60,000 rose blossoms to produce one ounce of oil. It takes 8,000,000 hand picked Jasmine blossoms to produce 1 kilo of Jasmine oil. These therefore are the most expensive oils in the world, and have the most beautiful smell. Luckily not all oils take this amount of materials or essential oils would be too expensive to use.

The plant draws energy from the Sun, Moon and from the very Earth, growing leaves and then flowers, fruits or berries, from which we can extract the curative and magical qualities of essential oils. Hypocrites, from whom we get the doctors Hippocratic Oath, prescribed macerated perfumed oils to be massaged into the skin once a day to maintain health. So oils, if not essential oils, have been used for hundreds of years.

Essential oils are similar to highly concentrated herbs. The most basic form of oil and obviously the oldest are cold pressed oil. This form of oil is still produced in many countries around the world in the same way as our distant ancestors produced the oil. Farmers load their wooden press with produce from the farm, be this olives, linseed or caster beans, and with the aid of heavy stones or screw thread, pressure is applied and the oil extracted. Although only cold pressed oils and macerated oils, in which flowers or leaves are immersed in a base oil, would have been available in the past. No Cunning person worth their Earth salt would have ignored a helpful idea. So had Essential Oils been available, and as cheap as they are now, our ancestors would have been happy to use them.

Macerated oils are fun to make yourself, pick fresh herbs on a dry sunny day, not easy in England. Tightly pack a glass jar with the herbs and pour over Sweet Almond oil, screw the lid on tight and leave it in the sun for two weeks, shaking every day. Replace the herbs every two weeks until you have the desired strength of oil. The most spectacular herb to do this with is wild St. John's Wort petals, these are a beautiful yellow color, there is no need to replace the petals, one day when you shake it will turn a spectacular shade of blood red, isn't nature magic! Other useful flowers to try are Red Rose, Violet or Chamomile, very expensive to buy, so well worth making yourself. These will never be as good as the commercial products but it is better to have home made rose oil for instance for your spells, than to use a substitute.

Not all medical problems can be tackled with essential oils but many minor problems can. Dandruff, menstrual pains, smelly feet, stress and arthritic pain, all of these can be better treated with essential oils than with conventional medicine. For more serious conditions, get the advice of your doctor first. My own doctor now recommends essential oils for many problems, but it is best to be sure you have the right diagnosis if you are treating yourself, you don't want to treat a minor symptom of a bigger problem. Another advantage of any essential oils, is the price- a little goes a long way. A bottle of essential oil for example Tea tree or Cedarwood can be mixed with a cheap shampoo base to cure dandruff, it is more effective than expensive branded shampoos and you will have enough oil to last for a long time.

Essential oils not only have medical uses but also have magical. When growing flowers, trees and herbs, trap the energies of the Sun, Moon and Earth Goddess. Drawing the vitality into the plants, later to be released into the different oils to work for you, in their own special ways. When burning oils, the perfume of the oil is released into the air and absorbed by the skin of the nasal passage, the olfactory epithelium which contains up to fifty million odor receptors in five square centimeters of microscopic hair-like cilia which are connected directly to the brain. This can then react immediately, recalling smells of childhood, past lives and other dimensions. The most well known use for essential oils is anointing oil, use this to anoint the third eye, wrists and feet, tools, spells and ceremonial jewelry. Add two drops of purification oil into a bath before a ceremony, or a protection oil if you are feeling vulnerable. Don't be too heavy handed, these are very strong and can cause irritation or allergic reaction, test first. Remember, more oil is not more purification or protection, its just more active ingredient that will upset the skin.

Always consecrate talisman or amulets with oil or incense before you use them, as is awakens their powers and imprints them with your personality. Candle magic also uses essential oil (See the Chapter on Esbats).

The magical blends I have listed, I have refined over many years but do not be worried about mixing your own. Choose oils that please you and have the right properties, mixing and empowering them with your will. When you mix oils, you can tune the properties that you want to a fine point. Be guided by your feelings, if you feel the need for certain oil, add it. You may not find the reason for many months, but the answer will come. It always does. Always keep a record of your blends; if a formula works with spectacular results, you will want to be able to recreate it.

It may cost a little to stock yourself with oils but the mixing is great fun, you learn a lot about yourself and magic. Whether a dab of something you feel should be there comes from the Gods or from a past life, it is an uplifting pastime.

A Quick History of Perfume

The word perfume is derived from the Latin word *per fumum* which means 'through the smoke'. So originally this referred to incense rather than any sweet smelling plant extract placed on the skin.

As long ago as 5500 years, within the boundaries of the great bustling city of Nineveh that was situated on the banks of the Tigris River in Assyria, great vats were used for a simple form of distillation according to Dr Jean Valnet. Water was poured into large clay pots over plant material, woven woolen fabric was then laid over the openings. The great pots of water were brought to the boil, the steam passed through the cloth carrying the essential oil and depositing onto the woolen fabric. This was later washed, with the precious oil floating to the surface.

In Ancient Egypt, it is thought the same process was used to make fragrant oils. The Egyptian was the first to anoint their bodies with a mixture of cinnamon and honey, which would have made them smell sweet I am sure but would have attracted the flies too. The sacred waters of the Nile fed great gardens of exotic plants gathered from all over the known world, some were destined to produce the wondrous oil. Not enough could be grown to supply demand by the rich and famous and so all manore of herbs, spices and flowers were imported, from far distant countries. For thousands of years the Egyptians had been the guardians of knowledge, too whom all turned for help. The great Library at Alexandria was the finest in the world had ever seen, the pride of the collection would have been the scrolls on medicine and magic, all catastrophically lost when the library burnt in the Battle of Actium. What great treatises were lost? Some we mourn over and yet some not even the knowledge of their existence survives.

The Greeks believed that Goddesses and Gods emanated a sweet smell and in Homer's Ulysses, one can read about the practice of anointing the dead with scented oils.

The Romans first celebrated scent around BCE 750 in religious ceremonies to celebrate the Goddess of Flora. The Romans were also known for their gardens, but the flowers were mainly used for garlands to be worn in maidens' hair. When the Roman's began their world conquest they, as Alexander the Great before them, began to adopt the use of perfume into their own culture. Greek influence was especially prominent in the use of perfume in religious ceremonies. In the famous baths of Ancient Rome people were rubbed with sweet smelling oils, a curved blunt blade known as a strigilla was then used to remove the oil and with it the dirt and sweat.

Rose is one of the oldest oils in the world, known for hundreds of years. The legend of its invention is one of love. After the wedding, of the Princess Nour-Djihan to the Mogul Emperor Dhihanguyr they sailed on their private lake, the Emperor had thrown thousands of rose petals on the lake to fill the air with the wonderful perfume for his new bride. They sailed around lazily all afternoon, with the magnificent smell of roses hanging heavily on the hot afternoon air. The beautiful young bride trailed her hand into the water, and found the water to be oily. The Sun had extracted the oil from the rose petals and the young bride by her discovery had increased the wealth of the country and given Rose oil to the world.

Once more the remaining knowledge of the Egyptians passed to the conquering Arabs and as with other inventions, the secrets of the distillation of oils. This information passed to Europe with the clash of cultures, the Crusades. By the 16th century in Italy, Marquis de Frangipani who traveled with Columbus on his voyage to the New World, where he smelled the beautiful flower that now bears his name. The perfume he created was made from almost every known spice and animal extracts- hint of Civet and musk, was to take Europe by storm.

Just a few don'ts,

Caution: the same rules apply to oils used in magic as for healing, always dilute them if they are to be placed on the skin, Lavender and Tea tree are the exception, they can be used neat.

Essential oils are flammable.

Avoid contact with the eyes.

Do not take internally.

Keep out of reach of children.

All essential oils should be used with care, as many can be toxic if used over long periods or in large doses.

Don't use any Essential oils if you are pregnant, its not worth taking any chances.

Don't use sage, clary sage, fennel and hyssop oils if you are Epileptic or you may not consider it worth taking any chances that an Essential oil will trigger an attack.

Don't use thyme, rosemary, sage or hyssop, if you have High Blood Pressure.

You could also be allergic to any oil so test first.

Only use if the skin is unbroken.

How to use Essential Oils.

A problem can be treated in many different ways.

Choose one or more methods that you feel comfortable with.

Massage- 20 to 60 drops of Essential oil in 100ml of Sweet Almond oil, almond keeps well and won't go rancid.

Face cream- A few drops of essential oil added to a pot.

To relive pain use a cream- A few drops of essential oil added to an inexpensive moisturizing cream.

Baths- 5-10 drops of Essential oil added to the bath after it is drawn.

Steam- in cases of Sinus or chest infections 5 drops in boiling water, place a towel over your head and breath the fumes.

Oil Burners- place a few drops with a little water on to an oil burner or neat on a lamp ring.

This list is intended as a guide. Allergic reactions may occur from using essential oils.

Don't over do the essential oils, they are very strong, more will not fix a problem quicker.

Synthetic Oils

Unless it says Essential oil it isn't essential oil. Synthetic Oils are given many fancy names perfume oil, flower oil, normally anything but synthetic. In magic it is strongly advised that you do not use synthetic oils. Their magical vibrations are not the same as true essential oils, no Sun or Moon has placed their energy within. However they can be used for their scent alone, this can add a traditional smell to a mixed blend. Perhaps using Patchouli Essential Oil, for love and a synthetic rose to give it a traditional smell?

Essential Oils Used in Magic and Healing

Always use diluted oils if they are to be placed on the skin.

Amber

Amber is a strange gem from which an oil can be extracted.

Genuine Amber oil is made from amber pieces unfit for jewelry as well as grindings from gem cutting. Heating Amber pieces to 200°C yields an Oil of Amber, this then leaves a black residue which is known as Amber Colophony.

But unfortunately in many cases Amber oil is being adulterated with many other products, which only become evident when the oils are analyzed. It's never possible to know whether you have true unadulterated Amber oil and what exactly went into the bottle that you have bought. A favorite way to produce a copy of Oil of Amber is to mix Clary Sage and Benzoine. There is also a tree called Liquidamber and so Amber oil can quite genuinely come from this source too. It poses a problem, as to quite what you are buying. One certain way of telling is if you are being offered synthetic Amber Oil, if it smells pretty it isn't Amber Oil. Which doesn't mean that Amber oil has an unpleasant smell, genuine Amber oil has the smell of the Earth and forests but lifts the spirit. Synthetic Amber oil smells of flowers and is very pretty, nothing wrong of course with burning it to perfume a room but for mystical rituals it is useless.

Magic: Amber oil is exceptional for spiritual work and protection, promoting courage, virility, and fertility. It can be used as purifier for any negative atmosphere. Amber's spirituality and protection energies are the reason why of course it is used in anointing oil.

Amber used to be very popular oil for business success or marital happiness, when more easily available.

Healing: Amber oil works wonders on headaches. I now have only a little left of the original I bought and I have no wish to sell it, as it does wonders for my sinus headaches and I use it in our anointing oil. What a contrast.

Sniff Amber for Catarrh or use as an inhalation and for digestive disorders.

Allspice (Pimento)
Allspice's name comes from the berries, which taste like a mixture of pepper, clove, juniper, and cinnamon. Rub a very week dilution of Allspice Oil on feet and navel to strengthen will power. It is also good for all business success.

Almond Sweet
Although not an essential oil but a fixed oil, I've added it the list, it is great to mix essential oils with to dilute them, and it will take years before it turns rancid. Just imagine making a wonderful, even expensive blend and then find that it has turned sour in a month. This happened to me, when I first started to use essential oils. I bought a 10% solution of rose, but did not enquire what it was diluted with; it turned sour quite quickly. That 10% rose was more expensive, in a way, than if I had bought a small quantity of full

strength. There is also an essential oil of Bitter Almond, this is deadly poison; you'll never come across available for sale. All traces of the poison, Prussic acid is removed before it is used as the flavoring and it becomes Almond Essence (knew there was a reason I didn't like it).

Healing: Almond is good to use neat obviously, on the hair and if your cat or dogs fur is looking a bit scruffy, dampen your hands with almond and stroke him, it will soon be gleaming again, if it is not indicative of a deeper health problem.

Aniseed

Magic: Aniseed is for clairvoyant abilities; anoint your crystal ball, Tarot cards or table. If Aniseed is burnt in the bedroom or sprinkled on the pillow, it will protect from nightmares.

Healing: Burn Aniseed to relieve coughs, catarrh and bronchitis. It helps to relieve cramp, rub a diluted solution on the affected areas. For nervous indigestion, rub a diluted solution on the stomach area.

Basil (French)

Magic: Basil improves relationships between two people. The essential oil is useful to encourage happiness and stimulate the mind. It is also a money attractant; this is why Spanish prostitutes once wore it as perfume to attract customers.

Healing: A mind and body stimulant that eases fatigue, good to burn when studying, as it improves blood circulation to the brain (not to be used on the skin).

Bay

Magic: Bay can be used to draw happiness to you; it is also extensively used to enhance psychic powers. Use Bay oil with green candles or on your purse or till to encourage it to fill with money.

Bergamot

Magic: Bergamot is highly protective and also a good money magnet. Not to be rubbed on the skin as it is can cause skin pigmentation changes.

Healing: An anti-depressant, used in the making of Earl Grey Tea.

Benzoin

Magic: This oil is used for purification, driving away evil spirits and to increase mental powers, for astral projection, and prosperity or success.

Because of its purification and success properties, it is one of the ingredients used in the Coronation anointing oil in England, when a new monarch is crowned. You can use it to anoint your feet and hands before ritual work.

Black pepper

Magic: Protects and promotes bravery. Use very well diluted in carrier oil.

Healing: A stimulant, it also aids digestion if the oil is breathed. My Gran used to tell me pepper aided digestion and liberally sprinkled her dinner with lots of it. Some old wives tales are true.

Cajeput: A respiratory tonic, for colds and flu, also a pain reducer and stimulant.

Camphor (white)

Magic: Purification oil. Warning: Can encourage celibacy!

Healing: A decongestant, inhale direct or put onto a tissue and breath deeply. Also you can add a little to hot water and while under a towel inhale the fumes.

Cardamom

Magic: Cardamom essential oil is the complete opposite of Camphor increasing sexual energy and love. Add its spiciness to love bags and use in healing bags or candle magic.

Healing: Helps nausea, coughs, headaches, Cardamom is also a digestive tonic and relieves flatulence. It is also used for treating anorexia, breathed on a tissue, it encourages the flow of gastric juices, while relieving any nausea.

Cedarwood

Magic: Increases spirituality. Use on a white candle, in candle magic when working with your Deity.

Healing: Cedarwood is calming and harmonizing, (too strong for children) inhale or burn for coughs or bronchitis. Add a few drops to your shampoo if you have oily hair or dandruff.

Chamomile

This oil comes in various varieties.

Chamomile Roman is very distinct in scent and different healing effects from the German (blue) Chamomile, it has a pale yellow color sometimes with a hint of green. Roman Chamomile has been used for at least 2000 years, in recent tests it has been found that macerated Chamomile oil was used to wash out the body of the Egyptian Pharaoh Ramesses 11, so we know that it was used at least that far back in history. Later used by the Moors who were also great doctors as well as magic users. Roman Chamomile is one of the sacred Anglo Saxon herbs.

Magic: Chamomile essential oil is used for protection, meditation and relaxation.

Healing: Roman Chamomile is extensively used to treat overwrought and highly strung temperaments. Roman Chamomile can be used to treat asthma attacks until help arrives. Children's temper tantrums are sometimes difficult to control; Chamomile is excellent for this. Often used to calm mental problems, burn on an oil burner for all of the above, being careful to place it in a safe place.

Chamomile German has the same uses as Roman although not one of the sacred herbs in England but it has the most wonderful blue almost black color, very potent but expensive. This is the Chamomile from which Chamomile tea is made. The deep blue color of this oil comes from chamazulene, which is a chemical naturally found within German Chamomile and is the reason for its superb anti-inflammatory ability.

Magic: Chamomile essential oil is used for protection, healing and meditation.

Healing: Due to German Chamomiles expense and anti-inflammatory ability, it is mainly used to treat physical problems, rather than mental. It is very soothing and relieves swelling, when rubbed on unbroken skin.

Chamomile Moroccan this Chamomile is fairly new and does not have a long history in magic.

Healing: Any of the Chamomile mixed with Lavender compliment each other, being stronger than either separately.

Cinnamon

Magic: Cinnamon is oil of happiness and attracts money (very necessary for happiness!) Use very well diluted. Add to floor wash for luck at home and work.

Healing: Never use on the skin.

Citronella

Magic: Citronella is a purification and clearing oil, add it to the wash water around the house to clear all negative vibrations.

Healing: Tonic, stimulant and insecticide. Add to a dried flower arrangement to give the room a lovely fresh smell and give a stimulant for work but not in the bedroom. Add a few drops of real Citronella to cheap candles to drive away insects. Citronella should never be used on the skin, as it can make it light sensitive.

Clove

Magic: Is used to promote courage and protection. You are supposed to rub clove on thighs and neck for seduction in magical herbalism but I think it would put me off, smelling like a dentist but then perhaps that's only me.

Healing: An antiseptic. It has a numbing effect on gums and relieves toothache, use clove oil well diluted mixed with Sweet Almond oil.

Coriander

Magic: Coriander is used in love and healing, blends.

Healing: Rub diluted to help diarrhoea, indigestion, fatigue and rheumatism. After a long day at work, rub the back of your neck with a very dilute amount of Coriander oil to lift you for the evening.

Cypress

Magic: This oil can also be used to heal both mind and body.

Healing: A skin cleanser and deodorant. Cypress also helps to relieve cramp.

Clary Sage

Relaxing, warming, useful for high blood pressure and relieves cramp (add a little salt to your diet as well), but it is habit forming so be careful with this one. Do not use when drinking alcohol since it can induce a narcotic effect. A few drops added to your shampoo helps to clear dandruff.

An abortificant do not go anywhere near if pregnant.

Evening Primrose

Although not an essential oil, it has many uses. Use in the bath for softer skin, add a few drops of Evening Primrose to a cheap moisturizer to make it into very expensive one and add to footbaths to improve sweaty feet.

Eucalyptus

Magic: Excellent for health and purification blends. To be used on the Waxing moon, as it is an oil of the Maiden Goddess, this oil is sometimes wrongly attributed to the Full Moon, as it promotes celibacy it would not be appreciated by the Seductress/ Mother

Goddess. Rub onto your wrists and temples for general healing.

Healing: Inhale direct or from a tissue to relieve colds and catarrh. Rub into Rheumatic joints or tired muscles. Rub diluted onto skin as a deodorant or insect repellent.

Frankincense (Olibanum oil)

In 1981 it was found by scientists in Germany that when Frankincense was burned, it produced trahydrocannabinole, a psycho-active substance, known to produce deep trance.

Magic: Rub on the third eye for spirituality and meditation. Frankincense lowers and deepens the breathing, relaxing the body and therefore helping with meditation. You can use it to anoint ritual tools and spell bags to draw spirituality.

Healing: Frankincense is very calming and slows and deepens the breathing and use to relieve stress.

Although in Ancient Egypt according to Ebers Medical Papyrus

'To remove wrinkles: frankincense gum, wax, fresh balanites oil and rush-nut should be finely ground and applied to the face every day. Make it and you will see! '

But I still think in this instance, I'll stick to modern methods.

Fennel

Magic: Longevity, courage and strength, used to ward off evil spirits.

Healing: Fennel lessens PMT and is brilliant for relieving period pains. Just rub diluted on your tummy to relieve even very bad pains, re-apply as necessary. Also relieves the swollen feeling where the body retains too much water at this time of the month. A few drops of fennel oil in boiling water (be careful) and breath the fumes to help a chill.

Geranium Rose

Magic: Geranium Rose has a delightful smell that promotes happiness and love. Can by used as a substitute for pricey Rose oil.

Healing: With its delightful rose like perfume it makes a good antidepressant and hormone balancer with mild diuretic. Geranium helps poor circulation and so helps with chilblains and puts a glow on the skin. It is also an antiseptic.

Ginger

Magic: Ginger's up the situation in a spell, including your business and love life.

Rub a little diluted Ginger oil on your hands before casting spells to enhance your ability. Apply to knees, elbows and behind the ears for a happy and exciting day.

Healing: Alleviates rheumatism, muscular aches and pains, sprains, nausea and diarrhea. Ginger oil applied to a kitchen paper towel can be sniffed to keep travel sickness at bay.

Grapefruit

Magic: Purification.

Healing: A tonic and used against obesity, an aid in drug addiction, kidney and liver problems. It also helps with migraines. Add two drops to a bottle of your shampoo to help with hair growth and greasiness.

Hyacinth

Magic: This oil is the exclusive property of the Dark Goddess, to smell it is to visualize Her, deep and mysterious, guardian of hidden knowledge, also used to invoke Her protection.

Hyacinth is a great oil to use for stress relief and meditation, promoting the creative side of the brain.

Hyssop

Magic: Purification. Hyssop is a good anointing oil for candles, altars and all magical tools.

Add two drops to your bath before magical rites to clear all negativity and sprinkle around the area where the magical rites are to be performed.

Add to water and sprinkle around a home that has Poltergeist activity.

Healing: A tonic to ease breathing and also a laxative if rubbed diluted on the skin. Hyssop eases fatigue.

Jasmine

Magic: A very expensive oil, but one drop can go a long way. Used to attract love, happiness and money. Promotes meditative calm; its beautiful smell attracts good spirits.

Healing : The wonderful smell of Jasmine makes it obviously an aphrodisiac. It also lifts the spirits on depressive days but unfortunately it is very expensive, as it takes a field of flowers to make a small quantity of this oil. Used in past times to 'warm the womb and facilitate birth,' and was through to be good for cold humors but not for hot. As in medieval times it was thought that men were hot and women cold, this seems to tell us it is the Goddess's oil.

Juniper

Magic: Highly protective. Combines well with Rosemary for purification. Use with a blue candle for healing magic. In Ancient Egypt, Juniper Oil was used to anoint the dead given the name "the life of him that is dead".

Healing: Juniper oil rubbed into knees is also very good for those days when you feel swollen through rheumatic pain. Massage into the skin to reduce cellulite.

Never use in pregnancy this plant is an abortificant.

Lavender:

Magic: Lavender is liquid Amethyst, if Amethyst had a smell it would smell like Lavender, liquid Goddess!

Lavender's greatest benefit is as a peacemaker, calming a situation. Healing, wealth, and happiness are also powers locked with in its oil. Use in a bath for meditation.

Healing: If you only have one oil make it Lavender, it can be used for so many things, I keep a bottle in the first aid box, one in the car, everywhere.

Use neat for burns (place Lavender oil on the burn and then place a packet from the freezer on top to cool the burn) or insect bites, use diluted on temples for headaches.

Lavender's main attribute is its ability to calm stress, use on the pillow for a good night's sleep.

Lemon

Magic: Lemon oil is good for purification and healing and should be burnt during the waxing moon to attune with the Virgin Goddess powers. Apply to the corners of an old pillow (it might stain) at night only, as this oil is attributed to the moon and does not react well in the sunshine. Do not place your skin in contact with this oil, this ritual should not be repeated frequently.

Healing: Burn lemon oil or place on a hankie, for colds, flu or high blood pressure.

Lemon oil should not to be used on the skin in healing.

Lemongrass

Magic: This essential oil purifies the mind and enhances psychic awareness.

Healing: A general tonic and antiseptic.

Lime

Magic: Protection and purification, place on window and doorframes to guard the home.

Healing: Freshens rooms.

Mandarin

Magic: A Sun oil very much as orange, bringing happiness.

Healing: Insomnia, nervousness, liver problems, obesity and digestive problems can all be helped with Mandarin oil.

Marjoram

Healing: Meaning 'joy of the mountains', used by the Ancient Greeks in fragrances, cosmetics and medicines. It mixes well with Lavender to relieve stress and is anti-rheumatic. Good for headaches, colds, bruises, and menstrual pains, rub onto warm radiators to release the oil into the air while a child is having a temper tantrum or is upset in any way.

Melissa

Melissa is very difficult to obtain like amber oil, what you buy may not be true Melissa oil but a mixture of lemongrass, lemon and citronella. If the Melissa oil is genuine then like Marjoram, Melissa has a calming effect and helps lower high blood pressure. (May cause severe irritation on the skin.)

Myrrh

Magic: This oil is attributed to the Goddess and is an excellent aid to spirituality. It has been used for at least 3700 years for magic and healing. In the past Frankincense and Myrrh were very expensive and sought after. Fortunately, both are now readily available and far less expensive than they used to be but more expensive than some oils.

Healing: Myrrh is excellent for healing chapped skin. This oil is antifungal, being very good for dandruff and athletes foot. It also helps to relieve catarrh, and has been used to treat leprosy in the past.

Neroli

(Orange Flower oil). The oil is named after a Princess of Nerola in Italy, who always wore it as a perfume.

When in Turkey we were lucky enough to catch the first few days of the orange blossoms season, the smell was breathtaking; you could never be depressed if you lived there, during orange blossom time.

Magic: A bringer of happiness; wear on your wedding day for a long and happy life together but it is used surprisingly on wreaths, perhaps to relieve grief.

Healing: Neroli is an anti-depressant, PMT and an aphrodisiac. Add to an inexpensive moisturizer to enhance your skin.

Niaouli

Magic: Highly protective and purifying.

Healing: Powerful antiseptic. Use dilute in water for skin cleansing,

Nutmeg

Magic: Sharpens the senses and is used in many psychic incenses and oil mixes. Nostradamus, the famous French psychic used nutmeg to predict his quatrains (four lined poems of predictions), in which he describes many events that have come to pass.

Healing: An aphrodisiac. Add a little to your bathwater to help with rheumatism.

Oak Moss

Not truly an Essential Oil, but I could not leave out this wonderful oil, even though there was no category for it. It is a thick treacly, black liquid that smells of the Earth after a thunderstorm. It is extracted from light green lichen found growing on oak trees.

Magic: Oak Moss is a money and luck attractant and works for wealth wonderfully, the epitome of the Earth.

Wonderful in oil mixes and incenses but do not use this oil on the skin.

Orange

Magic: Orange is an oil of the Sun and therefore of the God. It imbues the Suns qualities of bleaching purity and happiness. Mix with cinnamon for a wonderful Yule scent.

Orange flowers are used as a symbol of weddings and as such, Orange oil is the fruit of the flowers of love. Burn neat to bring happiness, luck, fertility and success into your life and a delightful smell into your home that will lift your spirits.

Healing: Burn to relieve depression, anxiety, constipation, muscular spasms can be helped with Orange oil.

Oregano

Magic: Healing, love, protection, should never be used on the skin.

Parsley

Magic: Parsley has been used for protection and purification since Roman times. Two drops into baths for purification with the added bonus as a skin softener.

Healing: Parsley oil is used extensively for nervous conditions also helpful in menstrual or menopausal problems and is good for hair growth. Use well diluted or burn to calm the nerves.

Palmarosa

Magic: Palmarosa smells of Lemons and Roses, this oil therefore has the qualities of both, healing and love. Useful in lost love oil blends, to acclimatize to the situation.

Patchouli

Patchouli is very individualistic smelling oil, you either love it or hate it. If you love it, use it liberally as a powerful aphrodisiac. It is also one of the few oils that improve with age, becoming more expensive the longer it has been stored. Please, please do not buy synthetic patchouli, it has no magic within it and smells foul, very hard and aggressive. The price of the Patchouli Essential Oil and synthetic oil is not much different, its not worth using the synthetic.

Magic: For love, virility and for increasing sexual prowess. Patchouli is a powerful money magnet, aids physic ability and an excellent protector. Anoint your doorknob to cause troublemakers to be unable to enter your home.

Healing: It is also anti-fungal, so a few drops in your shampoo will clear your dandruff and attract a partner to rub their nose into your hair, can't be bad!

Peppermint

Magic: Purification. Add to your floor wash to bring happiness to your home.

Healing: It reduces fever and has a cooling effect on the body when the oil is rubbed on the skin. Good for shock, headaches and travel sickness; sprinkle it on your handkerchief and breath deeply. Put in a foot-bath for tired feet and into a bath to ease fatigue.

Pine

Magic: Very good for use in Earth magic, also for healing, money, purification and protection.

Healing: An antiseptic, use in steam baths for blocked sinus. Be careful it can be irritating on the skin.

Rose

There are over 10,000 types of cultivated rose.

There are two types of rose oil, Otto of Roses and Rose Absolute (not counting synthetic of course). Otto of Roses is distilled from newly opened flowers, picked at dawn before the sun has had a chance to evaporate their precious oils. Rose Absolute is extracted from the petals with an alcohol solvent. They both smell completely different, Otto of Roses is by far the better, deeper richer smell and far the more expensive. Even in tiny amounts, Otto of Roses will contribute a sweet, natural radiance to any perfume or magical oil.

This is a very old way to make rose oil and one of the simplest. Fill a jar with as many dry, sweet smelling rose petals as you can, add salt and almond or olive oil. You may choose to add some alkanet to tint it rose red, stand it in the sun for forty days. Shake or pound the petals to get out every possible particle of perfume and magic. You can then strain off the oil and repeat with fresh petals.

Magic: The pure scent of love, luck and happiness. The rose is the flower of the Seductress/ Mother Goddess, the archetypal woman. Expensive but beautiful!

Healing: Rose oil is used by women as an aphrodisiac, as a hormonal balancer, a tonic and astringent for sensitive skin. Culpepper wrote that roses streangthan the heart, I'm sure he meant both mentally and physically and is used for headaches and tired eyes. Don't rub the oil on your eyes, just sniff rose oil or a smear under your nose so that you smell it continuously, as rose oil is far too expensive to burn.

Rosewood

Healing: Use in the bath and as massage oil, to relieve fatigue and muscular cramps. Rub on the feet and underarms as a deodorant; this has the added advantage of relieving stress.

Rosemary

Magic: One of the earliest plants to be used for food, medicine and magic. Healing, love remembrance and clearing. Rosemary is beloved of Elves and other friendly spirits.

Healing: Rosemary is a good pain reducer, very good for rheumatism and when you have over stressed your muscles, use in the bath for stiffness or poor circulation. Use with your conditioner for hair care, rub on your skin for your cellulite, and inhale from a tissue for flu (not for people with high blood pressure).

Spikenard:

Burnt in Tutankhamen's tomb and still retaining its fragrance years later when Howard Carter opened the crypt, so the story goes. It is also mentioned in the Bible, in the Song of Solomon and Mary Magdalene uses a pound of Spikenard to anoint Jesus' feet and dry them with her hair.

Sometimes known as Nard, not very easy to obtain, smells a little like valerian oil, not very pretty. Used by the Mughal Empress Nur

Jehan in her rejuvenating cosmetics and by Roman perfumers in the preparation of Nardinum one of the most celebrated aromatic oils.

Magic: Used first in ancient Egypt for purification and to enhance spirituality. Spikenard means holiness, use it to anoint the altar, the incense burner, and to wear it as a perfume to enhance spirituality.

Sandalwood

Sandalwood has a deep musky woody smell, one of my most favorite perfumes. It has the most wonderful smell! The oil and wood from the trees have been used for 4 thousand years for sacred temple decoration and incense. Solomon built his temple from Sandalwood due to its spirituality. In China there is a statue of Buddha twenty-seven feet high, carved entirely of sandalwood.

Unfortunately Mysore Sandalwood oil, the best, is becoming very rare, the heartwood and roots of the trees are used to make the oil. Regrettably it is being cut faster that it is being grown. In some countries sandalwood oil is more precious than gold. Sandalwood trees have been planted outside India but they do not grow with the same wonderful fragrance and do not contain the same rich healing qualities or magic. A mixture of Sandalwood and Rose oils are one of the oldest aphrodisiac perfumes in the world.

Magic: Sandalwood is a deeply spiritual oil, its properties are love and protection which always go hand in hand but it also is a strong sexual attractant and healer.

This wonderful perfume is dedicated to the Seductress/ Mother Goddess of the Fullmoon.

Healing: A perfume with this aroma obviously relieves stress and depression with an added bonus of an aphrodisiac. Place on a tissue for catarrh and dry coughs but watch for members of the opposite sex clustering around you, the sexiest cold you have ever had! Add to your moisturizer and use at night to improve your skin and your love life.

Sage (Spanish)

Common Sage oil is toxic best to use Spanish Sage but even this is being considered too strong for home use.

Magic: Protection and purification.

Healing: Relieves pain and the puffy feeling caused by water retention, too strong for children.

Sesame

Again not an Essential oil, Sesame brings better job expectations and opportunities to travel, you will find sesame oil in your local super-market.

St Johns (Baldr's) Wort (See history under herbs)

Magic: This macerated oil protects from evil spirits and fire, also helpful at engendering a peaceful atmosphere.

Healing: The oil of St John's (Baldr's) Wort is used by herbalists in massage oils for minor aches, pains.

Storax is a lucky oil, called for in many old medieval formulas. Hopefully making luck stick to your fingers

Tagette Rub onto dry or chapped skin, as Tagette is anti-inflammatory and healing.

Tangerine The power of the sun. See Manderin.

Thyme

Macerated Thyme oil was used by the Ancient Egyptians in the embalming process.

Magic: Love, Happiness and Success.

Healing: Rub on to chilblains and on to legs with poor circulation. Add two drops to a tissue and inhale its fumes to relieve colds.

Tea Tree:

When Captain Cooke first discovered Australia, having run out of tea aboard ship, they found this tree a perfect substitute - hence its name. Used by the Native Australians for hundreds of years.

Magic: Purification.

Healing: Tea tree is anti-fungal and so helps Herpes, Ringworm and athletes foot. (Do a patch test on your skin before using this oil, as it can cause irritation in sensitive skin.)

Vanilla brings happiness into the home. Carry two Tonka beans in a bag and anoint with Vanilla oil once a week.

Vetiver

Magic: Known as 'the oil of tranquillity' very good for meditation. Anoint purse to keep it ever full. Use with all money magic, Vetiver overcomes all bad luck.

Healing: Nervousness, insomnia, rheumatism, acne, oily hair and skin are helped by Vetiver. It is an antiseptic and is also used as a relaxant. Can be too strong for some people.

Verbena: Used to remove hexes and curses.

Violet

Magic: Promotes love, healing and peace. Drop a little into water for the famous Voodoo Love Water to sprinkle around the house to attract these properties into your life.

Healing: Another of the rare and expensive oils can be used for acne, eczema, thread veins, fibrosis, poor circulation, rheumatism, dizziness, headaches, insomnia, stress, bronchitis and catarrh.

Ylang Ylang

Magic: Use in love magic as it brings good out of bad situations. As with all stress relieving oils, it makes a good meditative oil.

Healing: Is very good for lowering blood pressure and sexual anxiety, helping to relax and relieve stress. This oil is a general anti-depressant and sedative.

Yarrow

Magic: Courage, love, self-awareness, psychic powers and exorcism.

Yarrow is used in exorcism spells. Sprinkle around the area that is in need of clearing. Yarrow stalks are used in I Ching divination.

The old name for Yarrow was Seven-year love. Anoint a pink candle with Yarrow oil for seven nights, starting in the waxing moon and working till the full moon. Perform a complete love spell on the full moon and repeat in seven years.

Healing: It helps relieve high blood pressure and menstrual problems. Helps with the inflammation due to rheumatoid arthritis and helps acne. Yarrow oil also promotes hair growth.

Magical Oil Formulary

All of the spells can be made with herbs instead of oils, if you prefer, just add the herbs to water and boil for half hour, strain. Keep them in the refrigerator but they will not keep very long.

All magical blends must be empowered so get your thinking cap on and write a rhyme.

Altar Oil

For private or communal altars. Place on the altar once per week and sprinkle around a room in which rites are to be held and place in a dish on the altar to increase the spirituality of the room to encourage the presence of higher beings.

Sandalwood

Myrrh

Frankincense

Almond

Only to be added to sanded wood not a polished table!

Anointing Oil

THE most important oil, to anoint during ceremonies, on third eye, hands and feet. For use on center altar candle at Imbolc or put three drops into the bath before rites.

Myrrh

Frankincense

Amber (If you can't get this oil don't worry, this recipe works perfectly well without it. Amber just adds to its strength.)

Sandalwood

Rose

Benzoin

Almond

Aphrodisiac Massage oil

Sandalwood

Ylang-Ylang

Lavender

Patchouli

A few drops of each to a 100m of Almond, you can be liberal with this recipe.

Banishing

Eliminates bad spirits.

Frankincense

Myrrh

Hyssop

Cedarwood

Salt

Almond

Business Success

Use on green or gold candles for success in business. Anoint doors and put 4 drops of oil (one on each corner) of the place of business.

Benzoin

Cinnamon

Ginger

Patchouli

Orange

Add to Almond

Cunnunnos

To call Cunnunnos into your ritual.

Patchouli

Oakmoss

Cedarwood

Nutmeg

Almond

Evil Eye Oil

Averts the Evil eye, spells and hexes.

Rose Geranium

Hyssop

Vetivert

Lemon

Almond

Take a white plate; draw an Eye of Horus in blue vegetable coloring or blue Chamomile oil.

Wash it off with a mixture of the oils above and bottle this in a small bottle or jar and ask Horus or your Goddess to bless it.

Rub a little on your hands for seven days.

Protection will last up to one year.

In this spell you have the power of the Eye of Horus in a jar, it is that you sprinkle.

Drawing a pentagram instead of an Eye of Horus is another version of the same spell, if you prefer that symbol.
Elemental Oil
Use on Elemental candles at Imbolc or for spell bags.

Earth Oil
  Oakmoss
  Patchouli
  Vetivert
  Almond

Air Oil
  Lavender
  Peppermint
  Few grains of Damar Gum in the bottle.
  Almond

Fire Oil
  Chilli
  Cinnamon
  Ginger
  Dragons Blood
  Almond

Water Oil
  Hyacinth
  Myrrh
  Ylang- Ylang
  Almond

Exorcism
Sprinkle around the room, altar, the person or place that you are

removing spell from. Only use in the presence of the person to be exorcised.

Lavender
Blessed Salt
Bay
Hyssop
Vervain
Almond

Greenman oil

To invoke the essence of Summer, can be used at Beltane and to help plants to grow.

Frankincense
Benzoin
Juniper
Sandalwood
Patchouli
Oakmoss
Almond

House Blessing oil

Place a drop of each in washing water when you move home or when you feel the need.

Lavender
Basil
Rosemary
Juniper
Frankincense

Hex (means spell) Breaking

Sprinkle across the doorway, around the doorframe and around all windows at the fullmoon to remove any hexs sent against you. Repeat if necessary every full moon.

Myrrh

Bay
Clove
Cinnamon

Handfasting

After the handfasting ceremony, the couple may be given two bottles of handfasting oil. For seven consecutive nights, each partner rubs the oil into the other. At the end of seven days, pour the remaining oil into one bottle. This is a spell for seven years. On your seventh anniversary, re-anoint each other for another seven years of love, leaving even just a little for a further seven years.

Lavender
Sandalwood
Red Rose Petals
Almond

Healing

Use to anoint talisman and blue candles for all healing spells.

Chamomile
Fennel (if for a woman)
Bay (for a man)
Juniper
Lavender
Almond

Love Oil

Patchouli
Ginger
Orange
One drop of Jasmine or Rose
Almond

Luck

To anoint talisman and gold or purple candles.

Nutmeg

Orange

Vetivert

Violet

Almond

Musk Oil Blend

It is impossible to get Musk Oil today, as it is painfully extracted from a musk deer- I don't want it. I have formulated this blend to replace it. The blend has the same love and sexual energies.

Rose Geranium

Sandalwood

Vetivert

Ylang-Ylang

Almond

Nine Mysteries

Composed of nine ingredients, the magical three by three of the Celts. Nine is also a mystic number in many magical traditions, burn while meditating or for candle magic, to gain secret knowledge. Sacred to the nine phase Goddesses or the nine planets. Lemon

Benzoin

Frankincense

Orange

Rose Geranium

Sandalwood

Myrrh

Violet

Wintergreen (this formula used to contain Wintergreen but it is now thought to be a a bio hazard replace with Camphor oil).

Place a drip of each and fill with Almond oil.

Peace

To bring peace of mind. To calm, sprinkle around the home, wear, or anoint white candles.

Lavender

Frankincense

Ylang-Ylang

Rose

Chamomile

Almond

Peace & Protection

To bring peace into the home and to protect from psychic harm.

Lavender

Vervain

Basil

Frankincense

Benzoin

Oakmoss

Almond

Planetary

For use with candle magic.

Sun: **Frankincense-** Physical energy, happiness and luck, use with a gold or orange candle.

Moon: **Sandalwood or Myrrh-** Psychic awareness, healing, fertility, peace, and family, use with a silver or white candle.

Mercury: **Thyme-** Intelligence, study, overcoming addictions and travel, use with a yellow candle.

Venus: **Rose or Ylang-Ylang-** Love, healing, beauty and fidelity, use with a green candle.

Mars: **Chilli Oil-** (either buy if ready made, or place chopped chillis in a bottle for a few weeks, Wash hands after use) Courage, healing after surgery, physical strength, sexual energy, use with a red candle.

Jupiter: **Bay-** The bringer of joy and success, use with a purple candle.

Saturn: **Aniseed-** Protection, longevity, exorcism, use with a black candle. Purification, to purify an area before work.

Success

Anoint green candles for success.

Benzoin

Patchouli

Sandalwood

Cinnamon

Frankincense

Chamomile

Almond

Sun Oil

Anoint gold candles for health, wealth and happiness.

Frankincense

Cinnamon

Rosemary

Orange

Bay

Add a few marigold petals to the oil.

Almond

Visualization

Apply to temples for a deeper mystical experience.

Cedar wood

Juniper

Frankincense

Nutmeg

Lavender

Almond

Wealth Oil

To anoint a talisman, green candles, till and purse.

Patchouli

Cedar wood

Vetiver

Ginger

Clove

Orange

Chamomile

Bay

Almond

Zodiac Oils

For healing a friend, use the oil associated with their Zodiac sign, or to bring in your life the positive aspects of your own sign. Mix with Almond.

Aries: **Frankincense-** Sweeping away old ideas and for creative projects, use with a red candle.

Taurus: **Rose-** Love, beauty, joy, and healing, use with a green candle.

Gemini: **Thyme-** Increase your intelligence and eloquence, use with a yellow candle

Cancer: **Jasmine-** Psychic forces, healing and to improve family matters, use with a silver candle.

Leo: **Cinnamon-** Healing, physical energy and sexuality use with a gold candle.

Virgo: **Ylang-Ylang-** Analytical abilities and a sense of self worth, use with a yellow candle.

Libra: **Violet-** Love and spirituality, use with a pink candle.

Scorpio: **Pine-** Psychic energy and physical strength, use with a red candle.

Sagittarius: **Lavender-** Better standing in the community and success, use with a purple candle.

Capricorn: **Patchouli-** Divination and success in legal matters, use with a dark blue candle.

Aquarius: **Peppermint-** Helps stop mood swings, use with a pale blue candle.

Pisces: **Clove-** Inspiration and safe travel over sea, use with a mauve candle.

Exercise- Make herb oil by filling a jar of Almond oil with a single herb or many, stand this on the window where the Sun can stream through. Refill with fresh herbs as necessary.

CHAPTER 10

Charms and their Meanings

Amulets are some of the earliest forms of magic. I can't help but think of a hunter thousands of years ago, at the start of a hunt, bending down to pick up a rock that caught his eye, nice shiny stone or a pebble with a hole in. After a successful hunt with no problems encountered, perhaps our hunter would keep his stone and remembered to take it with him next time. Is this how the first Amulet was used? Since the hunter's momentous invention, people have carried with them either natural or human made Amulets and Talisman, to bring them luck or to ward off evil. Every society on earth has had its charms but strangely they are all very similar. What is a charm against evil in one country, also prevents evil in another. But can a piece of silver protect you from harm or a baby in a walnut shell actually help to make you pregnant?

This begs the question, do amulets and talisman work and how? I tend to think that if you believe in magic then you must also believe in charms as a part of magic. But the question must be asked is it the shape of the charm that has innate ability or is it something in our subconscious that gives it power or does it link us to the divine? Or perhaps it is due to the accumulated power of centuries of belief? Personally I think that it is an amalgam of many of these reasons. The shape is definitely important. A pentagram for example, has a significant appearance in itself, the Greeks were the first to write about its significant shape, it forming one of the basic shapes- circle, square, triangle, equal armed cross, spiral, star, etc. These patterns form part of the basic building blocks of life, they are found in flowers, stars and shells, with the same patterns repeating and repeating down to the microscopic level. The patterns have a deep meaning for the primitive part of the brain. Add to this primary shape the power and energy acquired over the years of use. The Pentagram builds in power becoming a very potent symbol. Modern Pagans have adopted the Pentagram as a recognition symbol in every day life, as well as retaining its protection function. Pentagrams are consecrated and so form a spiritual link to the Goddess herself, through which She can send a blessing (or luck if you prefer the word) on a daily basis.

Most charms seem to have taken their shape very early in our history and changed very little with our wanderings from the rift valley of Africa. The hag stone, the Eye of Horus and the Moon all have their part to play in the life of the modern Witch. A star was thought of as a hole in the sky where celestial light poured in, you can not carry a piece of heaven with you, but you can take a representation, the Gods will understand your thoughts and so a star amulet is born. The world has not changed as much as we like to think, it is still a wild and dangerous place in many parts. I carry amulets and talisman wherever I travel; London is a dangerous place!

Amulets and Talisman can be an object or piece of jewelry; either natural or man-made that will draw or reflect magical power. Jewelry is not only pretty, but enhances status and is also a statement of who you are. Moreover it is also represents the armor we need to wear as protection in every day life. Did you know we are all knights or warriors under the skin? A necklace protects the neck, a very venerable point, while a bracelets acts like an iron gauntlets keeping safe our Radial artery from harm. Jewelry makes us feel secure on many levels, before even considering it as a talisman or amulet.

But what is a Talisman and what an Amulet? This question is almost as difficult to answer as how does it work. In truth, the answer has been lost over the years. The dictionary provides no assistance. There are numerous interpretations of the differences between Charms, Talisman and Amulets, so much so that the names are now almost interchangeable. I do not feel the difference is important, if it works does it matter what it is called?

Charm

Charm is derived from the French word *charme* meaning to chant. The local witch, shaman or wise person would sing or chant or utter an incantation to drive away evil spirits. Later it became possible to write down the spell and to give it a permanence, that chanting could not provide. Of course, still later charms developed into silver and gold Amulets and this is where the different interpretations start.

Amulet

The word Amulet is derived from 'amolior' to do away with or to baffle and was only ever used for protection. Boccaccio author of the Decameron who was born in 1313 in Italy tells us of

*"the skull of an ass set up on a pole in a cornfield as a potent **amulet** against blight"* or the ancient Greek Pliny, writing about the plant cyclamen

*"It ought to be grown in every house, if it be true that wherever it grows noxious spells can have no effect. This plant is also what is called an **amulet**."*

Talisman

Talisman coming from the Arabic word 'Tilsam' and is a sigil or charm engraved in stone, metal, wax or a gem and is used to attract love and to avert harm from its owner. A repellent talisman is called an Apotrapaic charm.

Amulets and Talisman are of four types,

    * Those that attract the Evil Eye (more later in the chapter) away from the owner of the charm or to grab the attention and so break the gaze of fascination, usually worn in plain sight. Amulets worn on the third eye are considered the most effective but today going to the local shops with some of the Amulets in this chapter, could attract unwanted attention.

    * Household objects displayed for the same purpose.

    * Thirdly, the written words of runes and other sacred writings or

formula considered so powerful or secret, that they too must be hidden away.

* Just to confuse matters still more, some Amulets and Talisman should be hidden under your clothing, you may not wish the world to see what you would like to come to pass.

Every time your eyes fall on the Amulet you enforce the magic with in.

Symbol

Originally the word Symbol meant the separate contribution of each person towards the cost of an Ancient Greek drinking party! Where each person would leave their signet rings as deposit for the wine. Gradually the signet ring became the symbol itself, rather than a form of payment.

All amulets and talisman must be consecrated, to be awakened. A pentagram is a special shape and in itself protective, but it far less effective before consecration. In fact I won't allow the wearing of any jewelry within circle that has not been consecrated.

Symbols may be worn on any part of the body, even attached to the collar of your animals, hung in the house or attached to the outside of the house. They can be large for a whole community, such as a Totem Pole or larger still for a country, like the statue of Liberty in America or the Statue on Sugarloaf Mountain of Christ in Brazil. Charms can be tied to the headboard of the bed of a sick person or given water in which the clean amulet made of silver and gold, has been allowed to stand. Some amulets should be in contact with the skin; others such as phallic amulets should be hung near the genitals to attract the Evil Eye from the real thing.

In Tibet there are special silver boxes that women wear that contain their charms, hidden away from prying eyes. Horsemen, all over the world, carry charms to prevent falls and injuries both for the horse and its rider, these would show very boldly. Camel-train drivers would place a string of turquoise or blue faience beads, pretending to be turquoise, on the forehead of their animals to avert the Evil Eye. Bells are worn on both camels and horses, to drive away evil; their pure note upsets demons.

Tribes and clans would share a common symbol, this would work on many levels, as an amulet, a symbol to bind them together, a confirmation of who was whom and important to each side in time of war.

These symbols later developed into Mascots, seen in many cars and on the football field, a design that would impart speed or strength to the car or the team. Some regiments may also have a goat or other animals as their mascot; some people are considered lucky and are mascots without whom a game will not be won.

You can wear Amulet or Talisman that might be a natural object such as a sprig of a herb, feather or even a drawn depiction placed in a locket. In many traditions a small bag made of leather, velvet or red flannel; are worn on the body. Perhaps the most popular way to wear an Amulet or Talisman is as a silver charm worn around the neck or wrist.

While in Thailand, a friend and I were visiting a Tiger Temple; there one of the Keepers was wearing many Buddhist Amulets about his neck. I asked if this was to protect him from the claws of the tigers "No, I am Thai, my amulets are for money!" he answered.

Amulets and Talisman take their time to start work, but have a steady trickle charge that will last as long as you need it.

Metal Amulets and Talisman

Many metals can be used for magic.

Though silver and gold are normally used for charms, as these are easily available and easy to work. This is no problem for a witch that works predominately with the Gold of the God and Silver of the Goddess.

If you would like to try to use other metals, you will need to be creative, see the chapter on gem and metal magic. Copper for Venus and love is by far the easiest to use.

Love Talisman- If you can get a small off cut of copper water pipe (copper is sacred to Venus/ Aphrodite) polish it. Plug one end with a cork sealing it with wax, fill with red rose petals and other appropriate herbs and symbols, possibly adding an incantation or a rolled up piece of parchment with a drawing of a heart, a shell, roses your initials birth sign or anything that you feel is applicable. Fill the other end with a cork and melted wax, you have an excellent talisman to draw love in general to you (see also Copper Love Spell in the chapter on Esbats and Spells).

Wax Tablets

Not all Talisman are made of metal, wax tablets are far easier to make. Find a suitable container, the smallest plastic storage box you can find not more than a few inches, heat wax of the appropriate color in a double boiler. Pour a little wax in to your container; allow it to cool a little. Place in suitable charms, herbs, feathers or parchment with words, anything that takes your fancy. Fill with remaining wax carefully; when cold and hard, place it in hot water for just long enough to loosen it from the container; using your burin (the scriber we spoke of in the chapter on magical equipment) or boline finish off the charm with any sigils that you wish to add. This should be engraved and passed through the elements of Earth, Air, Fire (be very careful wax melts easily) and Water, asking the Lord and Lady to place their energy within. Store (well wrapped so that one spell does not contaminate the other) in a spell box, which is a box that you keep for just such a spell.

Natural Charms

Many items from animals, herbs and inanimate objects, thought to have special energy, have been used over the years. A dear friend gave me a piece of wolf hair; collected at a wolf sanctuary, from a living wolf that I prize greatly. I must stress it would go against the Witches creed to kill an animal to use any parts of it but there are still things that can be used in this group. If you are a vegetarian this does limit you perhaps to antlers from a deer, that fall naturally each year, wood or birds feathers? But for the carnivores amongst us it is perfectly valid to use as much of an animal, which has been legally killed for food as possible. Although it isn't easy to get bits these days, beef bones after Sunday lunch are good. Cut into pieces scrape off all meat and fat, soak in bleach and water for a few days, re-scrape and use to carve runes or amulets. Horns from goats or bulls, teeth, tanned fur from animals killed for their meat not just for the fur, the fur being the by-product. But again I reiterate ONLY from an animal killed in a legal abattoir or shot by a huntsman's gun.

I have a friend that maintains a deer-park for a living. Part of his job is to shoot deer; this must be done to maintain the herd, if the herd gets too big, the deer will starve to death during the winter. The park that he works on can only support 200 deer, and with one new deer for every female, each year this would soon outstrip the available food. And so one hundred deers are killed every year, the flesh is eaten, the horns are sold, both he and I would like to say that the fur is used but unfortunately, now there are no places in England that you can have fur tanned. I have helped to tan a skin from the Deer Park in the traditional way, but it is very hard work without modern machinery. Although I treasure that skin especially, as a symbol of the Horned God, I will not be making a career as a furrier.

Deer are very skittish animals when not in the rutting season, a deer shot by a gun suffers far less than one that is rounded up and taken to an abattoir to be killed. When shot they just lay down, all the rest of the herd carry on eating as though nothing has happened, completely unaware of the death. The hunter stands, the deer run, like a wave across the field and the hunter retrieves the now dead animal, killed of course with one shot to the head, yes they are that good, every time, time after time.

Written Talisman there are charms that you can copy from old Grimoires but these are Ceremonial Magic not Witchcraft, but the idea is still very effective. You will however need to be a bit more inventive for your own needs. Preferably use parchment, or good quality paper, with Doves Blood ink for love and healing spells. Of course you don't take one dove; this is a blend of essential oil and herbs. For protection spells, Dragons Blood ink is used, which is how England lost all its dragons. But of course, again it's herbal ink and both recipes are in the Chapter on Herbs. Draw which ever symbols appeal to you and are appropriate for the spell- a pentagram of protection, a heart for love, a caduceus for healing or add a rune or three, but feel free to experiment. Any of the symbols below or an animal shown on the Familiar Chapter, can be drawn, there is no need to buy them in silver for them to be effective, the symbols merely need to be there to work. Lay them out in a neat design, the most important in the center, with initials, names or Sun signs of the person in question. You don't have to be a great artist; the Goddess knows what you are trying to express. But this is no excuse for slap dash work, take you time, draw as best as you can, at a time that you are in no hurry. Before you are about to cast circle or during circle is the best time to construct the spell. At the appropriate time of the moon, charge it with energy by taking it through the elemental quarters; anoint it with oil and throw your energy into it, before closing circle again.

This is a **very** small selection of Amulets and Talisman, from our Pagan ancestors. It is not meant to imply that all the charms featured here are from Witchcraft, but they are charms that you will see used. Some are well known, others are more obscure, but all work to attract or repel energies from your life and most importantly. Amulets and Talisman are not that fast workers, give them time and they will give you all the energies that you were looking for.

The list could go on forever, just a few to start you off.

Amulets and Talisman

Ammon's Stones
Ammonites were thought to be Ram's Horns turned to stone by the Egyptian God Amon and considered to bring good luck

423

and bring dreams of prophesy also known in England as Snakestones. Ammonites are sea creatures of the Palaeozoic to the end of the Cretaceous era, 65-70 million years ago.

Thunder stones or Eagle–Stones are fossiles too.

These are beautifully patterned Echinoids with stripes and between lines of spots. These were set in silver, kept or worn, as it was thought that lightening never strick twice in the same spot.

Amulet or Talisman Case

 A case made of silver or gold, to hold your Charms from prying eyes and from injury or contamination.

Draw what you need on a piece of paper, you can  use Virgin parchment if you choose, the traditional way, but I have used ordinary paper when I needed a quick spell and parchment for long lasting talisman, but the choice is yours. A Talisman Case can contain anything from a prayer; a bit of combed out fur, as my bit of fur from a live wolf, a drawn talisman, charms or/and some herbs. Any combination you feel the need for.

An ornamental leather bag from the Anglo-Saxon late Bronze Age burial, that was closed by a bronze pin contained....

A tail of an Adder,

A conch shell from the Mediterranean

A piece of red stone

A broken Amber bead

The Jaw of a young squirrel in a leather case (very delicate)

The claw of a Falcon

A piece of wood

A piece of red wool

A piece of pyrite

A stone spearhead wrapped in a piece of bladder

I give this list for your knowledge and I am not suggesting you go out and kill these creatures for a spell bag. As I feel that these things held with in this bag were found and there for considered a gift of the Gods.

Ankh

Ankh or Crux Ansata as it became known later in Coptic Christian times and continuing to the Middle ages. It promotes good health, knowledge, abundance, and power and is the Egyptian hieroglyph for life.

One of the oldest charms in the world, possibly originating with the or Knot of Isis (Tet) and is the symbol of life, carried by both Gods, Goddesses and Pharaohs, possibly meaning that they were both the givers and takers of human life. Another thought is that it originated from the hieroglyph for fish's mouth, which in legend gives birth to water and represents the key to the Nile, which floods the land with rich black soil, fertilizing the land and bringing both prosperity and life, which is the meaning of the Ankh. Also found surprisingly on some Celtic coins.

Royal Ankh My own name for this Ankh it is so different from any other Ankh I have seen. This Ankh, has a composite design. First,

the Ankh for life and abundance, on this rests the Djed pillar, the symbol of Osiris. Over this lies the Was Sceptre, a sign of power, protection, good health and prosperity. Above kneels Heh, 'God of a thousand years', this is an amulet for long life (Heh holds a staff in either hand this is a very popular symbole from many ancient civilisations although there is no exact meaning known. The same symbole turns up again in Egypt held by an Anubis type figure in the Leden papyrus 200 BCE. In England The Long

Man of Wilmington, a white chalk figure carved into Wendover hill, East Sussex echos the same stance and a few Viking figure hold a spear in each hand, one comes from the 7th century grave 7 at Valsgarde, Sweden.

This seems too much of a coninsidence, were they all desended from Heh I wonder? Is the Long Man of Wilmington actuly the Egyption God Heh, or at least his great grandson? Do the two staffs reprocent the beginning and the end of time? We may never know.

Combined, they form an amulet for a long, healthy, wealthy and protected life.

" Live long and prosper" now where have I heard that before?

Ashes

Ashes from a fire carry the magic of the fire itself. Ashes of the Sabbats are particularly good and more so if lit from need-fires. This is a new fire that you light with out the aid of matches and lighters but by rubbing or twisting sticks together. If you are working your Sabbats outside it brings especial good luck to light your fire in this way. No iron must be present or it is said the fire will never light. No fires must be present and so no smoking is allowed. The person to make the fire must be free from all crime and you must turn your sticks diesiel, the way of the Sun. In 742ADE the Church condemned need-fire making as a Pagan practice, so all the more reason to practice it! Although I can attest to Need fires not being an easy knack to acquire.

Acorn

Acorns are fruit of the great oak, bringing life, fruitfulness, youth, vigor and return of a lost lover.

Mighty Oak trees have been a symbol of power since the beginning of time. Standing tall for hundreds of years, having during this time acquired great knowledge, by carrying an acorn either real or as a symbol it will help to pass on this information.

Axe

The axe is the sign of power and success, as well as a symbol of Gods of thunder and lightening (this includes Thor's hammer).

Small jade axes as carried in China to protect from accident and injuries.

Labrys Axe the sacred Axe of Knossos in Crete. Labrys is not a Greek word but comes from Ancient Lydia. A double axe for the waxing and waning Moon, bestowing power and divinity and is now considered a symbol of the Goddess and matriarchal power.

Very small to very large Labrys Axes have been found, sometimes mounted between bull horns, adding to its strength. This same axe design was still going strong in Medieval times as a talisman to attract women.

Bell

The pure note of the bell protects from evil and as such are attached to horse's harnesses, Stangs and other items. Bells were rung to drive away thunderstorms. If bells ring of their own accord it means a death will follow shortly. Small bells were also rung around those who were ill to drive the illness away.

Bindrune

This Scandinavian Bindrune (more later in the chapter) is called "Helm of Awe" and robbed the enemy of its courage, has four runes of protection, joined at the center and forming a defensive guard on all sides, with two bars, further shielding the center, which is yourself.

This was painted on the third eye before battle, with the words " Helm of Awe I carry between my brows" to protect the warrior and cause fear in all that saw it, as they knew the warrior to be invincible.

Bractette

Viking - produced in Gotland in the 600ADE, but found in graves in England. Bractettes are protective.

a very stylized horse.

B. three ravens below a cauldron with labyrinth circling around and a stylized face below the jump ring

C. three ravens, the pattern is not symmetrical, so that not one particular raven is favored.

A   B   C

Caduceus

The symbol used by all healers.

The earliest Caduceus BCE 2350 dedicated to the Sumerian God Ningishzida where it was the emblem of life and death. The Caduceus in Roman times was carried by Mercury.

Apollo gave a staff surmounted with a pine cone and wings to Mercury the Messenger of the Gods help him on his journeys. Apollo added that who ever carried the wand would have the power of persuasive speech. Flying off, Mercury soon saw two serpents fighting, using his new powers he persuaded them to end the bitter feud. Two snakes were then added to the wand. Snakes slough their skins regularly and were thought of as immortal. By wearing the Caduceus as an amulet you move from the earth element- the snake, to the air- symbolized by the wings. Meaning to take wings and fly.

Asclepius, the God of Healing, also has a staff with one or two snakes on, according to different stories. In my favorite story, Asclepius acquired his Caduceus by placing his staff in the blood of the Medusa. Allowing the snakes representing both life and death that are depicted around the Medusa's waist to climb up his staff, giving him the power to both heal and to lay to rest. Asclepius staff was the symbol used in the healing temples of Hygeia and Panacea. In the 16th Century printers used both the staff of Mercury and Asclepius to illustrate books on magic and healing as these two subjects were so closely linked, they became confused and Mercury's magic wand became the symbol of healers. Coincidentally? the genetic pattern of the double helix, which are the very strands of life, twist in the same way as the snakes on the Caduceus.

Charm Necklace

A Charm necklace has been known since Ancient Egypt, combining the charms containing the energies you would like to draw into your life, onto one chain for convenient wear. Charm bracelets, became fashionable in 1900, but the general public did not understand the real meaning of what each charm represented, charms were collected from holiday resorts and all manor of strange items, instead of being used to draw good luck or banish bad. But a necklace or bracelet is still a good idea, if you can rise above the image the charm bracelet has given it. It brings together the small charms that have always been worn into a neat package. Perhaps a good example of a charm bracelet would be one collection for a new born child- choose one amulet at its birth. Traditionally this would be to stop the child from being taken by fairies and a fairy child left in its place, a changeling. One as a charm for travel, one as a charm for luck, one to draw love into its life and finally a amulet to ward off the Evil Eye. Held in place by a lock charm to bind all together. It won't help the child however if it is kept in its box in the drawer. If you are afraid that the child will swallow it, tie the charm securely under the cot where little fingers can't get to it or to the mobile above the child's head. But this is only one idea, perhaps add to the chain that you wear you pentagram on, an Eye of Horus, an Amethyst, a small dragon for power, the ideas are endless.

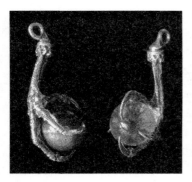

Claw

An eagle claw is carried for strength, cunning, ambition and is good for gambling as the claw clasps on to luck. Add to this the meaning of the gem carried by the claw. This is a crow claw and so you ask for knowledge from the Goddesses and Gods that use crows as messengers, The Morrigan and Odin to name but two. The Gems in this case either Tigereye for protection or Crystal to enhance the energy of the claw.

Celtic Knotwork

Celtic knotwork came into being about the 7th century CE, most examples you see are from Christian Bibles, the one below is from the Book of Kells. It may have developed from the Germanic Anglo-Saxon tradition or from Arabic knotwork; as yet no firm conclusion has been reached. True Celtic designs are plain spirals. What we now call Celtic knotwork has a few simple rules each path must flow over and then under the next, never over two paths and the ends must always be re-assimilated back into the design so that you have a line of infinity. Many like the example below are an animal or zoomorphic interlacing, here there are ends to the pattern and tongues, feet and such are twisted or spiraled to complete the design. Whether it was used as a protection from the Evil Eye, we may never know but it does work on the

same principle. When a jealous person casts the Evil Eye on you, it is thought that their eye gets trapped in the knotwork, following it round and round, with the original purpose forgotten. This is like the belief that the devil gets trapped in the lines of the pentagram running round for infinity trying to find the way out.

Champagne Bottles (miniature) and corks

If you have an event you would like to come true, and this then would be cause for celebration such as success in an examination or a competition. A small representation of a celebration symbol whether it be a winners cup or a bottle of bubbly, in silver or carve it yourself in wax, soap or clay.

You can also use a Champagne cork from an old celebration.

Being a frugal type, I bought in my local market several yards of black material with a decoration of Champagne bottles bursting, printed in silver. This is perfect for this type of spell, an oblong containing the Champagne bottle, can be easily cut out and used.

There is no need to spend a fortune for a

spell to work, be inventive.

Please remember that a spell for an exam will only help you to remember what you already know and calm exam nerves. It will not provide the answers, you still need to put in the work, for the spell to be effective.

Cimaruta

A charm of Italian folklore and modern Italian Witches, the Cimaruta or Cima di ruta, or in English "Sprig of Rue". It depicts the herb Rue (see Rue in Herbs for the meaning), no plant had more virtues attributed to it in ancient times than this herb, with various small symbols in its branches. The Cimaruta must only have three branches; this is of course the (see numbers in this chapter) magical number three. Historically it is used as protection charm against malevolent magic, fascination and the Evil Eye. Neville Rolfe of Naples first wrote about the Cimaruta in 1888 where at the time this charm was a common sight. Unhappily, today it is not very well known.

The Pitt Rivers museum in Oxford, sadly unfashionable with anthropologists these days, suggests that the Cimaruta is the remains of the worship of Diana (Artemis) into the modern era.

Diana is a Moon Goddess, traditionally known as the Eternal Virgin, looking after both the animals and children in Her care. The Virgin moon on this charm belongs to Her. As Aradia's mother and Diana of Ephesus, She is also the Mother/Seductress aspect of the Goddess; in this Diana was called the "Mother of the World". As Huntress, Diana is also crone and taker of life. This amulet which must only made of silver, Diana's metal, and was only acceptable in 1888 if stamped or hallmarked as such. Only children and women, who are in the Goddess Diana's special care, wore this charm.

Some of these charms are common to all Cimaruta; these are the Moon and snake, the key, which takes a prominent position. On the Cimaruta the bow of the key was always shaped like a heart, and so the key has many meanings.

The Cimaruta has various small symbols in its branches; there are many permutations of the charms, each Smith producing their own design but most commonly used are-

Virgin Crescent Moon - *Diana's Moon- fertility and increase.*

In the first charm of this type I saw, the Moon still had its small suspension ring on the top, this annoyed me. All Smiths would have removed it unless it had a meaning but what could it be? On seeing a very old charm I noticed the snake that curls around the moon has a coil of its body in the same place. With each generation the reproduction of the charm became worse until finally, the snake had been forgotten and why there must be a coil there, but the loop still remained.

Snake (curled around the moon) *with its healing power is sacred to Diana, Hygeia, Athena and Aesculapius.*

Fullmoon- *Diana as Mother love and healing.*

Waning Moon- *Diana as Crone Goddess of protection and psychic ability, the horns of the moon sending back all negative energy sent to you.*

Cock *sacred to Apollo the Sun God, Diana's twin, who sings its salutations to every morning at dawn.*

Five pointed Star or flower *the flower is probably Vervain, which draws money and represent the pentagram*

Fish- *Love, as the fish is a symbol of Aphrodite and Venus and remembering that wet charms protect from the Evil Eye, its no surprise that a fish turns up in the Cimaruta.*

Keys- *Hecate, the crone and therefore hidden knowledge. As a lock and key it stood for sexual intercourse, the key alone represented the phallus.*

Heart (on the Key)- *Love, Mother Goddess*

Hand- *holding knife, flower, snake or dragon.*

Horns- *Phallic, fertility*

Grapes- *Baccus, fertility and happiness*

Horned God Hand- *Fertility and protection*

The Cock, Key and Fish are all local slang for Phallus, which is a Pagan charm banned by the Vatican long ago.

Bologna Museum has the earliest version of this charm which points to it being Etruscan in origin. It clearly shows only the Rue branch with its "hand" type leaves that finishes each twig. My personal opinion is that the little hands invited something to hold. Strangely there is no trace of the charm throughout the Roman and Medieval period but the herb itself is hung round the neck, for both its Amuletic value and its lice control value. Possibly if the charm is only effective in Diana's metal, it would have been too expensive for the poor and a branch of the unpleasant smelling herb was worn instead. Gold and silver have a habit of being melted down or perhaps we just haven't found a Cimaruta of these periods yet (see phallic charm). To find one of anything can change our perception of history very easily.

To add my thoughts, the Cimaruta is very much a symbol of the Triple Moon Goddess and Sun God and represents the phallus banned by the church hundreds of years ago.

Cornucopia

The Cornucopia originally represented Amalthea the goat that fed Jupiter as a baby. Later many Roman Goddesses carried the Cornucopia or Horn of Plenty. The goat horn is a symbol of fertility, overflowing with flowers, corn and fruit, which can never be emptied. In Roman England the Cornucopia was best known carried

by the Goddesses known as the Three Mothers and the Celtic Horse Goddess Epona sitting side-saddle on Her horse with Her Cornucopia on Her lap. During the Middle Ages the Goddess was forgotten but the Cornucopia still remained a symbol of fertility and plenty.

The Cornucopia promotes business success and general prosperity and the charm was traditionally given to expectant mothers to insure healthy beautiful children. This developed into the Horn of Life a sort of shorthand for the Cornucopia.

Corno, Cornicello or Horn of Life, made in coral, silver or gold and said to cure impotence and bring luck into your life.

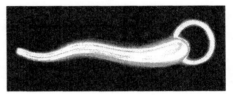

Cross

Crosses were not used by Christians until the 5th Century, before that, they were considered too Pagan. The oldest Pagan equal armed cross is in the British Museum and comes from Western Asia, is depicted on a cylinder seal dated about BCE 1750, with a prayer to the Sun God. Crosses have been used all over the world, they are a very simple design and so easily envisioned. Some equal armed crosses appear within a circle.

Even what we call today a Latin cross with one long arm, in pre-Christian times represented Apollo, also used in South America as a Sun Sign. The sign has always been used for breaking spells and protection from evil. The Roman Catholics took the Sun God's cross and used it as a symbol for their Son of God. Equal armed crosses can also represent the elemental quarters.

Celtic Circle and Cross The Celtic cross may be much older than Christianity, although it must be said that very little Celtic knowledge survived though the Christian period. There are many Christian Celtic Crosses in Ireland that have unknown Pagan legends mixed with Christian biblical stories carved onto them, which tends to make me think that the symbol is indeed much older. The Celtic Cross was adopted by the Christians as a symbol already known and loved.

For Pagans the cross in the center stands for the four elements with man in the center, protected by the circle of continuity.

To draw a Celtic Cross is like visualizing a Witchcraft ritual..........

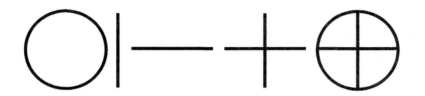

First cast your circle

In symbolism a single vertical straight line is movement.

This line connects the pentagram (the pentagram is also a shield) of the Northern quarter, to the sword of the Southern quarter and female to male. A single horizontal line is passive.

This line connects the chalice to the wand and again female to male.

To cross these lines you have an equal armed cross a very old Pagan symbol.

Place the equal armed cross within our circle, this then becomes the Sun symbol that can be found painted on Neolithic caves. Not that I am trying to implying that Witchcraft is that old, not by any means, but possibly the energies that we work with may be the same.

Sun Cross This is a sigil (the same as above) that extends into the past possibly as far as the Neolithic and its meaning is the Sun. Over the years its meaning began to change until it became as the Planetary Sigil for Earth. In Viking lands the Sun Cross was called Odin's Cross. The Sun with its powerful energies of health, healing and happiness or searing heat of purification embraced by the round of the Heavens, is its meaning.

Inverted Cross- The inverted cross so beloved of Hollywood as evil, is the Cross of St Peter, who was crucified upside down and has nothing to do with Witchcraft. Mamertine Prison in Rome where St Peter was held prisoner, which is now a  Roman Catholic chapel, has an inverted cross on the altar.

Solar Inca Cross The Tahuantinsuyo's Chakana - **Solar Inca Cross**

Most of the Inca Cross are carved from stone. The four points represent firstly the solstice and equinox and the cross quarter days.

Next the Inca principles- don't lie, don't be lazy, don't steal and learn, work and love. In the Inca world everything was thought to have a duality so one half would be good, the other bad, one day the other night. The left side female, the right male, which is strangely the same as in western magic. The Condor, was thought to represent the heavens, the Puma the Earth and the Snake the underworld. It also represents the four winds and therefore the entire universe. The Southern Cross-a star constellations that can only be seen from the Southern Hemisphere- and is thought to be the Inca cross hanging in the sky. The hole in the center of the cross is Cusco the navel of the Inca world and also yourself the center of your universe.

This design is certainly on Inca buildings, but whether it ever meant the same to the original Incas is unclear. It certainly means this now to people of the old Inca Empire in Peru. It is worn there very much like the pentagram is worn in western countries, as a statement of their beliefs. This one was given to be as a gift by a Shaman and is a prized possession.

Chinchaysuyo
(Winter Solstice)

Heaven

This World

Underworld

Don't Lie

Don't be lazy

Don't Steal

Contisuyo Antisuyo Centre-Cusco the navel of the world and your center.

Learn

Work

Love

Condor

Puma

Snake

Collasuyo
(Summer Solstice)

Crows Foot

The crow's foot also known as Witch's foot and were used to cast spells and worn as protection. It bares a close resemblance to the rune of protection Algiz.

Dearest

There is a type of ring which spells out a sentiment in gems, an example would be DEAREST, given between lovers.

D- Diamond
E- Emerald
Amethyst
Ruby
E- Emerald
Sapphire

Topaz

It would be a nice idea to carry the name of your Goddess or God.

Diamond, Iolite, Amethyst, Nephrite Jade, Amethyst. = DIANA

Beryl, Amethyst, Sapphire, Turquoise = BAST

Moonstone, Onyx, Ruby, Ruby, Iolite, Garnet, Amethyst, Nephrite Jade. = MORRIGAN

Djed Pillar

From Ancient Egypt and represents the Pharaoh's backbone or possible phallus. A charm of *'all protection, life, stability, domination and health'*. Its meaning is stability and has been associated since ancient times with the God of Creation and Craftsman Ptah, who called order out of chaos. Later, it was adopted by Osiris the resurrected God of the Underworld. When a new Pharaoh took the throne, there was a ceremony of raising the Djed Pillar, which would bring stability to the land.

In the great Pyramid of Cheops, is a room that holds an empty sarcophagus, and is now called the King's Chamber, if you look at the pyramid on a schematic of the pyramid, doesn't it look like the Djed Pillar?

Archaeologists tell us it is to relieve the weight of the pyramid, to enable the builders to place the room. I think the builders were quite clever enough to relieve the weight and build a Djed Pillar, if they chose or did the plan then become the Djed Pillar? Perhaps this gives us some clue as to the real use of the pyramids? Not for burying the dead but for ceremonial initiation of a new King?

Dragon (see familiars)

Durje

Known as the Thunderbolt of Jupiter and Buddha. It protects against the dear old Evil Eye once more and is thought to bring abundance and riches. It is a symbol of power and indestructibility, used to overcome the serpents Vrittra and Ahi, that in India and Tibet that are thought to swallow all the water causing draught and hunger. In the lower example, the same idea as the Icelandic Bindrune is used, crossing the Durje, hoping to double its power and protect from all directions.

Elf Shot

Elf shot was the term used in the Middle Ages for Neolithic Arrow heads. Some of them can be tiny which does explains the name. They were considered as gifts of the Gods making the finder into a Cunning Man or Woman. Used by dipping into a goblet of water and drinking the contents was said to cure all diseases.

Evil Eye Charm

In many countries it is said that people will casts an "Evil Eye" on you or yours. This is a form of extreme jealousy, not too far from a curse and must be averted at all costs. Many Amulets are designed to avert the Evil Eye, the name of these has been shortened over the years to just Evil Eye charms. These of course are not meant to cast the curse, but to avert it.

This charm's history starts in Ancient Egypt as the Eye of Horus, and it is possible to trace the Eye of Horus' progress and use, across Europe ending as the "Evil Eye" charm. Born in the North African Desert, the Evil Eye was thought to dry up what ever it looked at. A nursing mother's milk would dry up, the cows in the barn would stop producing milk and any young child would vomit causing dehydration. The only exception from the Evil Eye's influence was during the period of the Zodiac sign of Pisces (Feb 20th – March 20th) the two fishes; this was thought to be a safe time from the drying out effect of the Evil Eye. Many other charms also protected against the Evil Eye, any charm that was considered 'wet', fish, phallus, mermaids and mermen, seahorses and the Moon that controls the tides, to name only a few. Later to cast the Evil Eye became any problem that one suffered with, that had no known cause. It is thought that you must not call a child pretty or this may make a person with the Evil Eye turn and look at that child and it's beauty will quickly fade. To complicate matters fairies were said to take beautiful children and leave changelings in their place. So again no remarks, except derogatory ones are ever to be made.

In Rome and into Medieval Europe the eye still reigned supreme among charms, it is mentioned in Herbarium of Apuleius in the 11th century.

Many auspicious animals and other objects were sometimes added circling the eye. The animals had various meanings, in one seven animals surround the eye, one for each of the seven days of the week. In this one I have used animals of the four quarters to protect from all directions.

The Eye pendant is always blue as with The Eye of Horus, even in countries where the color of the eye would be naturally brown, showing its close relationship to The Eye of Horus. The Evil

Eye has quite a hold in most countries of Europe, although we in Modern English speaking countries seem to have forgotten it. In England and Scotland in the last century it was called "Overlooking" rather than casting the Evil Eye.

The best known of these charms is the blue glass eye of the Mediterranean, used everywhere to avert bad luck and to draw good luck. Still to this day very a popular amulet, with most people and even young children will wear one will one pinned to their clothing. My English friend married a Greek chap and joined him in his homeland; in due course they had a child. All the Greek relatives called round to see the child and bring evil eye charms to protect it. Everyone commented on the baby's beautiful skin. My English friend thought it to old fashioned to place these on her child, only days later he was covered in a terrible rash! The charms went on and the baby's skin cleared up.

There are many ways to cure the Evil Eye once cast, wash in holy water (your blessed water from your circle), break an egg (eggs are 'wet' and look like eyes) and leave it under the crib if the child is affected or in the animal barn if the problem lies there. In many countries the wise woman of the village will know a secret incantation that will remove the Evil Eye.

The Eye looks out at you from an American Dollar bill and from Masonic ritual regalia. This is the universal image of the Sun and wisdom, protecting from the evil *Eye of Horus* (Wadjet or Uadjet Eye) The blue eye has been a protection symbol from ancient Egypt to the

present day.

In the beginning, there was only the eye of the Goddess Wadjet this was the Sun and with this eye She watched all. Later Hathor absorbed the eye and it became Her symbol.

Seth plucked out Horus' left eye, (Horus plucked off Seth

testicles!) His wet nurse Hathor, using gazelle's milk or milk from the sycamore tree and her saliva mixed together, restored His sight.

This then became the symbol of protection par excellence. The Eye of Horus is always blue and has the markings of a Peregrine Falcon's cheek, as Horus is often depicted as a Falcon.

The Eye of Thoth (Moon) the left eye. It is Thoth the God of wisdom and magic, in some versions of the myth of Horus, it is Thoth rather than Hathor that restores Horus' sight. Egyptian history spans a long period of time and during that time inconsistencies have creep in to many of their legends. For the return of His sight Horus gives Thoth, His left eye. Thoth is a God of magic and magic was used to heal. The Eye of Thoth was used as a mathematical medical measure by the priests to brew medicines, adding the energy of the God Horus to the potions. The plucking out of the Eye of Horus, explained to the Egyptian why the Moon was missing from the sky for three days every month, the fullmoon is the restored eye.

To complicate matters, there is also right eye, which is called *The Eye of Ra* (Sun, see the story of Hathor in Mandrake) This can (but not always) be shown with the Goddess Wadjet (the Pharaoh wears this as the Uraeus) who by this time had become a cobra, rather than the eye itself. In some texts She is said to be able to spit fire, like the cobra spits venom. It is also the reason that Ra is shown with a snake wrapped around His Sun disk. Both Ra and Horus can be portrayed as a Falcon and this I feel is the reason the Eye of Ra and the Eye of Horus are confused in Egyptian mythology, both are protective.

Both eyes together represent the order and reason on the right and magic on the left.

Eye Agate or Endi Is another version of the Eye of Horus, and as such is protective. Especially cut from Agate with a white ground, blue, green or brown and a black pupil, the blue being considered the most effective.

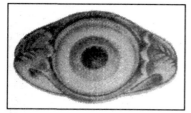

Glass "Evil Eye" Charms
Outside shops in Turkey the Evil Eye is set into the pavements and it hangs in every home and business.

In England, I bought some pasta from my local Turkish grocers, and

even this had a photo of two glass eyes to keep the pasta fresh, within the packet.

Fishermen paint blue eyes on boats, either side of the prow, both as protection and to see their way home on a dark and stormy night.

Feather

To wear a feather or a depiction of one, you borrow the attributes of the bird the feather comes from. So, with an eagle, you borrow bravery and farsightedness; with an owl you borrow wisdom; with a raven you borrow their skills at divination and knowledge.

Fish Tail (dried)

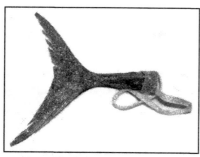

I bought this in a market in Tunisia. It is a real fish tail covered on one side by gold glitter. A full fish or a tail of the real fish helps ward off the Evil Eye. Although Tunisia is now an Arab country it was at one time a Roman province, fish are sacred to Venus and as such would bring health and love and due to its fertility a fish was thought to increase wealth and draw it into its owner's home. Old habits die hard.

But if you don't fancy a dried fish tail, any representation of a fish will do the same.

Four Leaf Clover

A variation on the normal three leafed verity, thought to bring great good luck if found and carried or worn in representation. Only if all four leaves are present, do they mean Hope, Faith, Love and the fourth Luck.

I remember spending hours as a child on a day out with my parents looking for a four leafed clover, so therefore I would also add, known to keep children quiet.

Now being especially grown by a company in Ireland.

Grapes and Vine Leaves

The wine of life, happiness and truth, sacred to Bacchus.

Gods and Goddesses

If as yet, you are not working with a particular God or Goddess you could choose to carry the depiction of one to draw their particular energy into your life. Perhaps using Bes when pregnant as the Egyptian did, or Janus over your door to bless your comings and goings. For some Goddesses and Gods no representation has come down to us, like my own Goddess The Morrigan, then choose to depict them as you see fit. The traditional representations have an energy that is built up over thousands of years but someone at some time decided on how they looked, you are no different and can choose how they appear for you.

Here is a very small example on the most popular Gods and Goddesses.

Anubis Jackal-headed Egyptian God of the dead. He weighed the hearts of the dead against Maat's feather, on the scales of death.

He is also the guardian of the gates of death. Anubis was thought to prowl the tombs of the Pharaohs to devour all caught stealing from their tombs.

Anubis is also depicted as embalmer of the dead, anointing with precious oils and incense to purify and empowering the corpse. He is worn mainly as protection and also for help with incense making.

Artemis/Diana 'Goddess of Wild Animals' Her title from the Iliad, Artemis is one of the oldest of the Greek Goddesses and was depicted as a winged Goddess in the 6th century BC. She is also, the Goddess of Childbirth.

Immediately after Her mother gave birth to Her, She helped to deliver Her twin brother Apollo. Mothers invoke Artemis to help them through pregnancy and childbirth, at this primal time.

She was also Goddess of Hunters and is both a giver and taker of life. In Rome She was called Diana and is sometimes depicted with a moon on Her forehead. Diana illuminates the dark night bringing us safely through our fears into Her brother's bright day.

Bes Probably originating from Syria and adopted as an Egyptian God. Bes is a mountain dwarf and guardian at childbirth, and is depicted in many 'House of Birth' attached to Egyptian Temples. A good charm to wear when pregnant and giving birth.

Green Man A Pagan symbol of nature and fertility, often depicted with leaves sprouting from His mouth sometimes from His eyes. He brings fertility and wealth.

Jack-in-the-Green The Greenman also shows his face as a dancing bush, known as The Jack-in- the-Green some times with horns sometimes with a crown and is the spirit of Summer. As seen in the Pagan Pride Parade in London (on the LAST weekend in May, Pagans like to party for a month) Jack is a fertility symbol and to dance with the jack will inevitably get ladies pregnant or tie a ribbon or rag on his branches for your spell to come true. The Jack is torn apart to release the spirit of Summer, with all present taking home a leaf or two for good luck, in the coming months. The leaves must be returned to the cauldron at Samhain that Summer may rest and return strong and well the following year.

There are two different thoughts about where Jack-in-the-Green origins lie. According to Fred Elworthy writing in 1892, He had His origins in ancient Greece at the marriage of Dionyses and Ariadne re-enacted every year in Crete. This is also acted out in the French Alps on the 1st May people dress in leaves as the spirit of vegetation, *"our Jack in the Green is his personification"*, in Germany small children accompany Him dressed in leaves, going from house to house, singing, dancing.

The other possibility of the origins of the Jack-in-the-Green is that in the 18th century the London sweeps would parade on the 1st May, to collect money for beer. Slowly over the years more and more greenery began to appear on their costumes.

Hathor So vast is the influence of Hathor, She existed for the entire three thousand year history of the ancient Egyptian culture as a powerful and influential deity. Due to such a great stretch of time there are many conflicting legends of Hathor.

The name Hathor means House of Horus the hieroglyph is a Falcon within a square. She was both the wife Horus (though this changes over the three thousand years of Egyptian history) and mother to another Horus, possibly it may also refer to the night sky in which Horus as a Falcon flies and both may represent Her womb.

Hathor was deeply loved by the population of ancient Egypt; She had more festivals in Her honour than any other God or Goddess. Amongst Her many titles are the Mistress of Heaven, Lady of the House of Jubilation, and The One Who Fills the Sanctuary with Joy.

She has been worshipped from the very earliest times in Ancient Egypt, a Goddess far older than Isis, from at least 2700 BCE. It is impossible to say when Her worship started for it is clouded in the mists of time and stretches into the far distant future.

In Her oldest form Hathor is depicted as a full cow with the Sun between Her horns and the markings on Her coat of stars, a Goddess of Midnight. Each of Hathor's legs are related to the four cardinal points of Egypt, at a stretch of the imagination we could call Her, Guardian of the Quarters of Egypt. There are even creation myths attached to Her legends in this form. Hathor rises from the sea of chaos to create the world, giving birth to Ra the Sun and holding Him aloft between Her horns.

But Hathor is best known as a Bovine headed Goddess with a disc usually gold or carnelian, between the horns of Her head-dress (later this is sometimes borrowed by Isis), in later times this was thought to be the 'Eye of Ra' (or 'the eye of Horus') the Sun God. She was sometimes depicted with a cow's head or later still, a Lady with cow ears. We tend to think rather dismissively of cows today, as a bit of an insult even. But in Egypt, even currently, they refer to a woman as having beautiful eyes or ears of a cow and as with the later Irish legends of The Morrigan, cows are also abundance and riches.

As a Sky Goddess, She is associated with the Milky Way, which is the milk from Her udders flowing across the sky to feed the world. The Milky Way was also thought to be a reflection in the heavens of the Nile below and therefore called The Nile in the Sky. As the Nile transported kings up and down their kingdom, so too did The Nile in the Sky transport Gods around the heavens. The Milky Way also represented the flooding of the Nile (this was transferred to Isis at a later date), in this aspect she was associated with the star Sothis whose rising above the horizon heralded the annual flooding of the Nile. As a midwife Hathor helps with the delivery of children, in this context the Milky Way may also have been thought of as Her own amniotic fluids flowing, at a moment prior to birth. She is the only Goddess, with Her companion the dwarf God Bes who protects mothers in childbirth, who were ever depicted full faced like the fullmoon itself, rather than in profile.

Occasionally Hathor is depicted as a Moon Goddess holding out Her crescent moon, which are also called horns of the moon, as shining arms to the dead. Hathor is also the Guardian of the Western Gate, the necropolis or city of the dead at Thebes. With Her kindly nature She greets the souls of the dead, offering them food and drink to sustain them on their journey through the underworld. But Hathor was life as well as death; Hathor was the incarnation of dance and sexuality and was given the title Hand of God (referring to the act of masturbation), Lady of the Vulva and the Mistress of the Tree of Life. One myth tells how Ra had become deeply depressed that He refused to speak to anyone. Hathor opened her robe and danced before Him skyclad, wiggling Her bits to make Him laugh out loud and return to a good mood.

Hathor is also the Eye of Ra and is Ra's spirit on Earth, doing His bidding, slaying (see mandrake for full story) at His command becoming Sekhmet, later these Goddesses separated becoming two distinct Goddesses. In Her hymns she is described as the Uraeus (a protecting cobra) on the horns of Ra.

She is also is the Goddess of fertility, agriculture and moisture, one of Hathor's symbols are the papyrus stems that grew in the Nile and which were fed to cows and the shade offered by the Lady of the Sycamore, that like cows weeps a milky sap. She is Goddess of all perfumes particularly myrrh, as well as gold, copper and Malachite. One of Her many titles was Lady of the Blue Stone referring to Turquoise and Lapis Lazuli, also sacred to Her. Both Lapis Lazuli and Malachite were used in eye make-up in Ancient Egypt, to apply eye make-up was an act of beauty and so an act of Hathor. Royal mirrors were decorated with Her face, as homage to Her.

As the Great Mother, She was the ideal woman and consequently She was also Goddess of Love, beauty, festivity and music.

Hymn to Hathor from the 18th Dynasty:

Ra says *The beauty of your face*
Glitters when you rise
Oh come in peace.
One is drunk
At your beautiful face,
O Gold, Hathor.

She has two instruments sacred to Her, the Sistrum a type of rattle, which originated as a handful of Papyrus stems shaken. According to the ancient Greek historian Plutarch, the sistrum's arch was the lunar cycle, the bars (which held the metal discs) were the elements, the twin Hathor's heads that often decorated the top were life and death and the cat, often included in the decoration, was the moon. The sistrum represented the Ankh the giver of life and may have been used, by the priestesses, in ceremonies of fertility. As a Goddess of beauty, which any woman knows includes your accessories, Hathor and Her priestesses shake a large and heavy Turquoise necklace called a Menat, as a second musical instrument.

Hathor was married to Horus and a great festival took place at this time. At the fullmoon the statue of Hathor was taken from Her temple at Denderah and sailed down the Nile on Her royal barge to the Temple of Edfu. The procession was magnificent, possibly blue sails Her sacred color billowed in the breeze. The glisten of gold and silver on the statue and the glint of gold on the tips of the red oars as they dipped and rose in the water, the sound of the drum keeping time for the oarsman. The priests sung Her name in praise and the priestess lining the sides of the boat, beating the sistrems in time. Apuleius the Roman philosopher described a procession where the rhythmic pattern was three beats followed by a pause on the fourth. People lined the Niles edge to watch and pay homage to their favourite Goddess, would they have thrown rose petals into the Nile? Hoping perhaps that She would bless them as She passed. On the way many craft joined the procession, the flotilla becoming longer and longer, gleaming under bright Egyptian Sun. Hathor arrived at Edfu at the dark of the Moon in May, where a Sacred Marriage was performed. May is of course the time when our God, Goddess and Witches are handfasted. Like Hathor and Horus their sacred marriage is renewed every year. For the next fourteen days, until the next fullmoon at Edfu it was party time! Her worship was unusual in that both priest and priestesses took part; they were dancers and musicians. Her rituals were spectacular with ochre colored beer (see mandrake). Food and drink was provided free by the Temple of Edfu, all kinds of bread, roast fowl, oryx, gazelle, oxen, and ibex with wine in abundance. The women wore garlands of flowers in their hair and the young girls danced with wreaths of flowers. On the fourth day after the marriage it was thought the child Harsomtus was conceived. The queens of Egypt were thought to be the Earthly incarnation of Hathor.

One story tells of seven Hathors that come to the birth of a prince to foretell his future, the story reminds me of many European folktales of the seven fairies come to give there blessings to the birth of princess.

To my mind Hathor is the archetypal Maiden, Mother and Crone, if you choose to wear Her pendant you ask for love, fertility and festivity in your life.

Herne or Cernunnos His worship traveled across Europe and

now even farther to many English speaking Witches across the world.

He has become the Stag horned God of the Witches and Pagans, a symbol of male fertility prosperity and well being.

Lord of Nature, beasts, fruit, corn and plenty symbolized by the money seen issuing from His mouth in some Romano-Celtic depictions. Rats are depicted in one Celtic representation of Cernunnos in Paris; this shows that He has some Underworld associations. And of course male rats have enormous testicals, which seems to point to a fertility connection!

That He is both life and death. Ask Him for fertility and the good things in life.

Herne's Pentagram This is a composite charm of my own

devising, although it has a basis in folklore. The stag was always a symbol of Paganism so the Church decided to Christianize it. The story is that of St Eustace, who was out hunting when he saw a white stag caught in a thicket, between its horns glowed the cross of Jesus. I merely replaced the cross with a Pagan pentagram returning it to its former Pagan iconography.

There are still many pubs named after The White Hart, in England.

Isis the Egyptian Goddess of life. As 'giver of life' Isis was thought of as the star Sirius, that rose above the horizon at the Egyptian New Year, foretelling that the Inundation of the Nile was imminent. This brought with it the life giving fertile soil onto the parched desert sands. The Romans called Isis 'The One that is All' and adopted Her, taking Her to the many lands they conquered. An altar to Isis has been found and is now on display at the Museum of London, England.

At one time Isis' religion balanced equal in popularity with Christianity, only by hairs breath did the world turn away from Paganism. The depiction of Mary with child is thought to have been originally Isis depicting suckling Horus.

In a beautifully written piece the Roman Apuleius tells us about the Goddess, in his work "The Golden Ass" - as translated by Robert Graves.

Isis speaks *"I am Nature, the universal Mother, mistress of all elements, primordial child of time, sovereign of all things spiritual, queen of the dead, queen also of the immortals, the single manifestation of all Gods and Goddesses that are. My nod governs the shining heights of Heaven, the wholesome sea breezes, the lamentable silences of the world below. Though I am worshipped in many aspects, known by countless names, and propitiated with all manner of different rites, yet the whole round earth venerates me. The primeval Phrygians call me Pessinuntica, Mother of the Gods, the Athenians sprung from their own soil, call me Cecropian Artemis; for the islanders of Cyprus I am Paphian. Aphrodite, for the archers of Crete I am Dictynna; for the trilingual Silicians, Stygian Prosperine; and for the Eleusinians their ancient Mother of Corn. Some know me as Juno, some as Belona of the Battles; others as Hecate, others again as Rhamnubia, but both races of Ethiopians, whose lands the morning sun first shines upon, and the Egyptians who excel in ancient learning worship me with ceremonies proper to my godhead, call me by my true name, namely Queen Isis ... "*

Isis can be recognised by the throne that She wears on Her head as a crown (Nephthys Her twin sister wears the Hieroglyph for gold as a crown). With the throne Isis bestows the right to rule on all pharaohs, this passed down the female line in Egypt from Isis Herself. In Her worship devotees were offered a chalice the shape of a breast, containing milk and bread the staff of life.

Isis is a Goddess of magic, magic of the whispered word, all names have power and to know the true name gives you great control. On one occasion Isis makes a serpent from dust and mixes it with the spittle of the God Ra and courses it to lie in His path and bite Him. As He lies dying Isis coerces out of Him His true and secret name which She uses later to bring Osiris back to life and to give Her a child, Horus.

The depiction of Isis here shows Her with outstretched winged arms, as She flies the length and breath of Egypt to reassemble Her beloved Osiris. We see Her sorrow by Her kneeling position, that of grief at Osiris' death. The out stretched wings became a gesture of protection and with a Hathor head-dress of abundance (this follows an old Egyptian tradition, Isis frequently borrows Hathor's head-dress). This makes a powerful charm, combining abundance, love, joy and protection in one.

Maat The plume worn by Maat is the feather of truth and justice, the plume being the hieroglyph for truth. When an Egyptian died he thought his heart would be weighed against Maat's feather.

Sometimes borrowed by Isis as the law giving mother. Be sure you are in the right if you choose to wear Maat.

Osiris Osiris, husband and brother to Isis was torn to pieces by Seth, Their brother, and scattered the length and breadth of Egypt. Isis searched the land flying hundreds of miles to bring all of the one She loved back together again. Isis whispered in Osiris's ear the magic words of power, She had learnt from Ra, to awaken Him in the Land of the Dead. To seal Their new union She fell pregnant with Horus.

The phallic looking Tamarind seed is sacred to Osiris and in some version of His story Isis finds Osiris within a Tamarind tree. He is always depicted with a green face, not the color of petrifaction but the color of new life and growing things.

Osiris is a sacrificed and resurrected God, (the tearing apart of His body represents the thrashing of the grain) whose body was eaten in the form of bread, by his worshipers, long before Christianity borrowed the idea.

Out of death and the dark Earth new life grows, an amulet of hope and fertility.

Pan The Greek and Roman Horned God of the Forest, known for His mischievous tricks and his music that can be used to warn wild animals of danger, where the work panic comes from.

Pan, God of Mischief! I had not

finished making the first one (called a Master) of these Pan pendants when it was time to go home.

In the middle of the night the burglar alarm went off and I were called back to the shop. No sign of any intruder but while waiting for the alarm company to come and re-set the alarm (several hours), I had time to finish this master of Pan!

Pan would be a perfect God of Ecological issues, He protecting the forests with His Pan Pipes and panic. Wear Pan to draw the forest and wild creatures into your life, but remember His prankster habits and He has a heavy fertility element, you have been warned!

Sekhmet Her name means "powerful" and a very powerful Goddess She is, the burning winds of the desert are Her breath and a glowing aura surrounds Her body. Sekhmet is the lioness Goddess of Memphis in Egypt; She has the body of a woman and the head of a lion, with a golden Sun disc on Her head and the Uraeus (Cobra Goddess) stands proudly before it. She is usually shown seated holding an Ankh meaning life or standing holding a scepter in the

shape of a papyrus stem.

She is the daughter of the Sun God Ra and the wife of the creator God Ptah and mother to Nerfertum the Lotus God. Sekhmet is very closely related to Hathor, even possibly Her stern alter ego and shares the same crown. In the story of Her rampage in Egypt, in some accounts it is Sekhmet and in others Hathor, that kills half of the population at Ra's order. For She is the vengeful "Eye of Ra" a title that at various times She has shared with both Bast and Hathor.

She is a Warrior Goddess that stands in the chariot behind the Pharaohs and guards his back with

"Flames" another of Her titles. She also has a far darker title "Lady of the Bright red Linen" which applies equally to the color of the soil of Her homeland and of bloody bandages. She is also "Lady of the Acacia". The red gum Acacia tree was slashed with 2 or 3 feet long gashes and an inch or two wide. The gum, like blood would run out filling the deep wound, which could be extracted when dry and used medicinally and for incense. Sekhmet was not originally a healer but a remover of plague and disease in this She is "Lady of Life", the giver and taker. Prayers still exist entreating Her to remove Her pestilence and return the patient to health. Her priests were later healers themselves, with a good knowledge of the workings of the heart. I hope I have portrayed even a glimmer of Her personality in this pendant I made of Her. Ask Her for inner strength or wear Her for the removal of an illness.

Sheela- Na- Gig One of the most intriguing historic puzzles are the Sheela-Na-Gigs. She stares at us across the years and shows Her favors to all, but who is she?

The entrance to the womb is a gate between life and death and as such has been recognized as a very magical and special place from early on in human history. It seems only right to place Sheela-Na-Gig above the gate, like Janus the Roman God of Doorways, guarding the comings and goings. She is a protection and I think a fertility charm, many that are placed with in reach are  shiny from touching, offering both protection and fertility over all aspects of life.

Strangely She (do I put a capital, is She a Goddess?) seems to first to appear above the entrance to Norman churches, but what is She doing there? It has been suggested that She was placed there as a reminder of the Sin of Lust, but if so, why are no other sins shown? You would have expected all seven to be as graphically displayed.

The Sheela-Na-Gig abounds across Europe in Britain, France, Spain, Switzerland, Norway, Belgium and in the Czech Republic but also on houses in the Palauan archipelago there She is called Dilukai. She is to be found in the same location as our own Sheela-Na-Gig, above the doors and protecting the house and its inhabitants. They are typically shown with legs splayed, sometimes sitting, very like our own Sheela-Na-Gig revealing a large, triangular pubic area; with the hands resting on Her thighs. How far in Asia does Her fame spread, I don't know.

Sheela-Na-Gig may have been even older. There is a gold pendant of the Egyptian Goddess Hathor in the shape of an inverted triangle,

it shows us just her essence, face with large ears as befits a Cow Goddess, but with human nipples and vulva at the point of the triangle. Is this the first concept of what was to become the Sheela-Na-Gig? Was She to travel from Africa to Asia and beyond or is She such a universal truth that She developed in many different places at different times?

Sheela-Na-Gig isn't even Her name, "gig" is Northern English slang word for a woman's genitalia and an Irish word is very similar. The oldest name recorded for Her is in 1781 by R Worsley "The Idol", referring to the Binstead carving on the Isle of Wight. This name crops up many times over the years, before the name Sheela-Na-Gig becomes popular. In county Cork in Ireland the local name for the Sheela-Na-Gig is 'the Hag' this is the same name they apply to the local Cunning woman, purveyor of herbal and magical cures. Johann Kohl, toured Ireland in the 1840s, noted that people often went to the wise woman if they wanted to avert 'evil eye' the method she used was to stare wildly and pull up her skirts, exposing herself to the victim!

Later the Sheela-Na-Gig wanders into the churches and can be found on many pillars, next to the altar, near a Green Man. Are The Greenman and the Sheela-Na-Gig providing fertility for the farming community, as Pachamumma and Pachapoppa do in Peru in Roman Catholic churches?

Perhaps the most famous English Sheela-Na-Gig is from a church in Kilpeck Hereford, the carving is very well preserved. This one doesn't sit over a door nor near the altar but is a gable end for the roof. She has a whole array of friends along the roof but one is missing. The story goes that a Victorian lady of the village, was so upset at this depiction that she had it smashed, but she left the Sheela-Na-Gig? I can only think that it must have been a male version with a large phallus that so upset her so much. It is even possible that she didn't understand the Sheela-Na-Gig. There are a few male versions of the Sheela-Na-Gig around Europe but none in Ireland, possible this is a continuation of the Roman phallus worship and could the Sheela-Na-Gig be a later female development?

Many churches have a Sheela-Na-Gig hidden away in the vaults ashamed to allow them to be seen and sadly many have been vandalized even in this century. If no one wants them, I'll volunteer to give any unloved Sheela-Na-Gig a good home.

The Triple Goddess

The three Goddesses –

Maiden, Mother and Crone. This can of course be represented in many ways, this is only one, Virgin is represented by Moonstone Mother is represented by Garnet Crone is represented by Onyx or Star Diopside All of The Triple Goddesses aspects and a quartz crystal to magnify the power.

Great Rite
Representing the sexual union of God and Goddess. A potent fertility charm, very much like a phallic charm, the athame is the God and the Chalice is the Goddess.

Griffin (see Familiars)

Hag Stone
A natural hole in a stone found on a beach or in the countryside or one either made or drilled for use as a hag stone. The Anglo- Saxons were happy to drill stones that they felt held magic within and wished to wear. The Romans as well as the Anglo-Saxons made glass beads to use as Hag stones. Perhaps they thought that by using the secret of making glass and taking the trouble to make them they were even more powerful.

Hag stones brings luck and gives protection, thread it through the hole and wear it or hang it in your home.

Spindle Whorls these may have been the origin of Hag stones, or Hag stones were the first Spindle Whorls. Used to hold wool when weaving and as mentioned in Knot Magic weaving was also a form of magic. Goddesses who wove where spinners of fate as well as cloth, in the same way spells could be woven into the cloth. In Anglo-Saxon times they began to appear on chatelaines worn by women, whether this was to announce them to be spinners or healers or homemakers we don't know. Some were used, as were hag stones as 'dipping stones' dipped into water they were used to cure both cattle and people.

Sword Beads, which are a form of Hag stone, were attached to swords, possibly on the 'peace strings' as mentioned in the Norse sagas. Which is a thin piece of leather used to hold the sword in its scabbard. When untied it was to draw the sword, when the 'peace string' was tied peace reigned. In the Roman period multi-coloured glass, Chalcedony and Nephrite Jade were used. In the Hun Kingdom 400-480 CE Crystal and Amber were added but in England 70% were made of green glass the rest being Amber and multi-colored glass. TheBeautifully crafted swords with brightly colored lumps of glass hanging from them, the owners must have felt them to be important amulets to add to such wonderous work.

Hand

The hand as a charm has many meanings, it can be raised in greeting or peace or it can hold a sword in protection, but it's best known as a charm against the dreaded Evil Eye.

From as far back as BCE 2100 hand amulets were very common. Hands finish the Sunrays on the wall paintings of Akhenaten and his God the Aten in Ancient Egypt, showing the benediction of the Sun falling on the Pharaoh and through him on Egypt. Arms and hands are added to many symbols in Egyptian art, such as an Ankh.

In Europe hands hold many items as charms against the Evil Eye, a rose, a sprig of rue, an arrow a dragon or a snake.

A very pretty one I saw, was made in the 17th century in 18ct gold, is a charm, within a charm. It depicted a hand enamelled in white, offering a pendant, which was set with three diamonds surrounding a ruby, with a pearl dropping from it. Its traditional meaning was "I love you (Pearl-Venus) passionately (Ruby) for ever (Diamond)"

Hand of Fatima also known as the *Hand of Miriam* or *Hamsa* meaning five.

A strange charm this, as it is equally treasured in a Jewish or an Arab home and is said to predate both religions.

Fatima is Mohammed's daughter

and is a hand of blessing.

Although in Islam, magic and talisman are banned, this sigil is found everywhere, on doors, hanging in taxis and bedecking Berber

women. The palm of this charm, can have many designs added, Hebrew (called The Hand of Miriam), an eye, six pointed stars, pentagram and moon, adding that magic to the Hand of Blessing.

Mano Fica Mano Fica is an unusual Amulet from Italy; the symbol is a hand that is closed; the thumb protruding between the fore and middle fingers. The name means fig and it is meant to represent the man inside the lady or the woman and is an excellent defense against the Evil Eye. These Amulets are made of bronze, silver, red coral or even red plastic

these days. Mano Fica replaced the Pagan Phallus, when banned by the Roman Catholic Church.

Sign of the Horned God (Mano Cornuta) To symbolize the Horned God's horns and horns on general.

A sign of dedication to him and as such a good luck symbol and inviting his protection, repelling the Evil Eye. If you point your hand or this charm at a mans head in some European countries, it is taken as an insult, meaning that the mans wife has

slept with others. I'm sure, as with banning the phallus, it was another attempt to wipe out the worship of the Horned God. Used by rock fans as a sign of the devil, but of course the original meaning had nothing to do with this.

Eye in the Hand This amulet is an eye and a hand, once more protecting from the dreaded Evil Eye. In this depiction the two fingers are raised in a blessing bringing good luck. In Tibet the amulet is known as *Phurbhu* and in Spanish

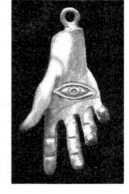

Mano Poderosa, it is also used by the Native Americans and throughout the Mediterranean and combined with the *Hamsa* hand in North African countries. The amulet is sometimes used prove pre-Colombian connections between cultures.

Hand of Power The right hand in benediction, which was placed

on an altar, with many added charms, pine cone, crested snake, lizard, tortoise, caduceus, sword, goat head, rue and a baby on the fingers and palm, to name but a few of the many variations. Is far older than the Christian Church, the oldest Hand of Power that has been found so far comes from Greece, 800 Before Common Era and is a charm against enchantment.

Horseshoe

Protective- Starting off as a crescent moon of the Goddess Diana and as horseshoes were invented, transferring the magic of the powerful magical horse to its footwear, bringing Earth Goddess power, wisdom of self, to the bearer.

A bringer of great good fortune if worn or hung with points up in England, where it was thought to hold luck for the family. But not on the continent particularly in Germany, where the horseshoe is thought to be only lucky when hung with the points down. In England only smiths may hang horseshoes this way, over the forge, to allow luck and magic to pour into their work.

The horseshoe seems at some point to get muddled with horseshoe magnets and are therefore said to attract luck. Now many other charms like dice are added to the Horseshoe, to draw luck with gambling. In the past horseshoes sometimes had an Evil Eye placed in the center.

If tied to an Ash tree and allowed to grow into the wood, it was thought a branch from the tree will cure all ills.

In Peru, two horseshoes are cemented into the doorstep, one facing out and one facing in, like the Roman God Janus protection for your coming and goings.

Small brass horseshoes that you see hanging by the fire in pubs now days have probably never seen a horse but are copies of charms that were hung on horse and carts to protect them. A full set of twenty pieces would have only been worn on special occasions. Normally one or two would be sufficient if working in the field. The earliest ever found to date is 2000 years old. The most primitive were very simple, handcut from sheet brass and then hammered to give them shape. The symbols that were used for human protection from the Evil Eye, Stars, Moons, wheels and rayed Suns, would of course work just as well on horses as humans and so all were adopted.

Key

A key is a sign of love locking the heart so that it can not escape. Older still the key was the symbol of life and wisdom, a foresight of things to come and remembrance of things past. Silver keys attached to finger rings belonged to the Roman Goddess Hecate, Crone Goddess of the Underworld, in her power as Guardian of the Gate of life and death. If hung upside down above your bed will protect you from evil while you sleep. The key was also the symbol of Frigg the wife of Odin and large keys were carried throughout the Middle Ages by married women as a status symbol, the more keys the more you owned the higher your wealth.

Knots

Knot Magic binds in good and is a hindrance to all evil, in itself it is a spell for longevity and averts the Evil Eye. As

with so much in magic, Egypt was one of the first to use knot magic. Our old friend Pliny had something, as usual, to say on the subject. His suggestion was to use the Knot of Hercules to tie wounds that made healing 'wonderfully more rapid'. Of course weaving, a very important female past -time, is closley assosiated with knots. Eligious of Noyon preached that woman should not 'name other unfortunate persons either at the loom or in dyeing or in any work with textiles.' In Anglo- Saxon times tie a spindle whorl to the cheek, with woolen thread, for skin prolems.

Knot of Isis or Thet (or Tet) Carried for wealth and health, this later may have developed into the Ankh. The original was carved from red carnelian or jasper and was called the Blood of Isis.

From the Book of the Dead (Ellis, Awakening Osiris – Incantation No. 55):

"At the ends of the universe is a blood red cord that ties life to death, man to woman, will to destiny. Let the knot of that red sash, which cradles the hips of the Goddess, bind in me the ends of life and dream … Give me magic, the fire of me beyond the borders of enchantment. Give me the spell of living well… I am the knot where two worlds meet. Red magic courses through me like the blood of Isis, magic of magic, spirit of spirit. I am proof of the power of Gods. I am water and dust walking."

Found in many Ancient Egyptian tombs, the Thet amulets of Carnelian, are sacred to Isis and was thought to give protection in ensuring the Ka's (the soul's) passage into the next world. Place on a Sycamore plinth (the Sycamore tree is sacred to Hathor and as Isis borrows much of Hathor's symbolism to Isis also) and soak in Ankhami flower water, the Thet was then placed on the mummified body saying.

"Let the Blood of Isis, and the magical powers of Isis, and the words of power of Isis, be mighty to protect and keep safely this great God (the

Pharaoh on who's mummy the Thet is to be put), and to guard him from him that would do unto him anything which he abominateth."

Tibetan Monastery with Knot of Eternity and Wheel flags

As the Thet was Isis symbol, so was the Djet Pillar Her consort Osiris, very often in tombs you can see the two symbols alternating, as a frieze around the room. Binding them both for eternity.

Knot of Eternity A protection sign from Tibet; can be used for meditation and thought to represent Buddha's entrails, very similar to Celtic and Viking knot work.

Aloe Vera tied with red ribbon, another variation again a protection, charm this time from Peru. Hung in every doorway, the Aloe Vera spikes and red ribbon, protect from enchantment.

Witches Knot or Magic Knot is a symbol of the four Elements or four winds under control of Spirit. It appears both as depicted and on its side, the circle varying in size from quite tight to the knot or too near the edge of the loops but this was only fashion and has no bearing on the power of its magic. The charm was carved on Celtic stonework and was used in exorcisms in the 12th century, eventually coming to be used in

protection magic and also functions as a love charm, binding passions. The same charm can also be seen in Tibet, as a symbol of protection.

Kris or Keris Knife

The Kris is an amuletic knife from the Indonesia, Bali, Malay and Java area, with many of the magical attributes of the Athame or Trigu a Tibetan ritual knife. Kris is the prized symbolic blade that was developed to the highest art form of

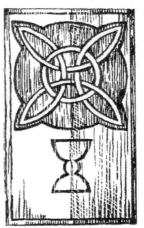

patterned damascene in the Majapahit Empire of Java which spanned the period of the 13th -15th century. The Kris was an established magical knife by the 7th century as carvings on stone temples are identical to the earliest known Kris.

The largest museum in the world for the Kris is in Jakarta, Indonesia which has a wonderful collection of these magical weapons.

Some Kris's have wonderful wavy blades with, most importantly, an uneven number, others have straight blades both have distinctive meanings. But all have meteoric iron twisted in by the Empus (Bali) or Mpu (Java) a Kris-Smith. Energy is placed within the blade as it is beaten between the anvil and the smith's hammer. The two metals are repeatedly beaten together and folded like a Japanese Katarna until at last a thin sheet of steel is formed containing layers and layers of alternating iron and meteorite and the Kris is born. The meteoric iron shows up distinctly in the blade as bright and shiny, where the earthly iron is dark and matt, as perhaps it should be. Meteoric iron was the first iron ever to be used for any weapon; it came as a gift from the Gods, a rare and priceless commodity.

According to Java lore to be called a Kris a blade must consist of two parts a *wilah* (blade) and the *ganja* (there is no word in English for this, it is sometimes referred to as a guard but this is not a fighting knife and so the word is incorrect) united they bring longlife, creativity, and prosperity. As with the Athame and the Chalice being a union of God and Goddess, the Kris is the union of mankind and Spirit. This is the only knife to have a two-part blade.

The Empus is not only a Smith but a form of Shaman and belong to an elite group of craftsmen who are highly respected in society, as were early European Smiths. They are held in great esteem, as they possess the knowledge of how to blend the elements of fire and metal. In Bali the Empus worship the volcano Gunung Batur where it is believed they draw their powers enabling them to craft their profession. The Empus forges each blade within ritual, placing into each a *'khodam'* or nature spirit, during the making, which makes all true sacred Kris alive with power and so legend goes, unable or unwilling to hurt its owner. As an amuletic knife, the Kris will help its owner if attacked magically.

Kris made by some Empus are highly sought after it is believed to have extra special powers of protecting the bearer's property from theft. It is thought the Kris has the power to nag at the conscience of any thief and can continue nagging and haunting the thief's dreams until the stolen goods are returned or the thief goes mad.

The most powerful *Tayuhan Kris* a true Amuletic knife, is kept secret and only an *Ageman Kris,* some very beautiful are used on dress occasions. Sadly not many Empus have the ability to produce *Tayuhan Kris* these days.

Beginning in the Great Depression in the 1920's-1930's and even more so during the times of the Second World war and the upheavals that followed it, the arsenic used in the cleaning of Kris became very expensive and impossible to acquire and so people began to *Cacam* their Kris blades. As many nasty venomous animals that could be found were placed in a bucket, venomous snakes, frogs, centipedes and scorpions. It was left to rot with the Kris blade firmly placed in the center. When all rotted and become slime, a film of that slime was allowed to dry and stick on to the blade, as the Kris was handed down from father to son or daughter with each adding to the treatment, many layers can be seen on some old Kris blades. This of course is not good for the blades and rust can develop unnoticed underneath the cacam. Unfortunately people do still use cacam daggers for fighting although it is not fashionable to cacam Kris blades now. This strange process is only an extension of an all cure that is sold in markets in many countries in the Orient. Only in the all cure the venomous creatures are placed into homebrewed whisky for a good while and then the small glasses of the whisky are drunk

The Kris will appreciate the curtsy of you take your time when handling a Kris (perhaps we could learn something on the handling of an Athame from our Javanese and Malay cousins), do not rush. Hold the hilt firmly with your right hand and slide the scabbard off fully with the left hand (scabbard and left hand does this mean female again?). As a sign of respect to the Empus who made the blade, hold it to your left ear and listen to it for a second before looking at it. After you have looked carefully at the knife draw the sheath over the blade.

Kris are not bought and sold like ordinary knives, swords or daggers. To purchase a Kris use the language of courtship and marriage, only during the day never at night. A Kris is not haggled over nor is it bought like a pound of fish. Instead you ask for the hand in marriage of the Kris and offer a dowry or *maskawin* meaning wedding gold. Custom has it that a token dowry must be paid even if someone gives a Kris as a gift to make the 'wedding' a beginning of a happy marriage between you and your Kris. This of course follows the rules of knifes in the west that must never be given as a gift or the two friends will part but must be paid for, if only with a token amount of money.

Blades- Straight blades are sought by politicians and midwives for the esoteric powers of the are associated with the process of birth.

Tilam Upih, meaning the bed of spittle or the tongue is a simple Kris with an uncomplicated blade is believed to be useful for those who make a living through speaking.

If the blade of a Kris is straight with a strong *ada-ada* (backbone) down the middle, this signifies that the bearer of this blade is blessed with steadfastness and faith.

There is a Kris with a design called a Jalak bird building its nest and this is believed to have the esoteric power to bring love and romance to the bearer. Some blades can not be used by certain occupations but this blade is not choosy and the esoteric powers associated with it are suitable to be used by anyone wishing for love.

A Kris with a small praying figure on the *gandhik* (where the blade juts out at the side) means that the bearer of this blade will be granted steadfastness, happiness, faith and protection.

A three lok'd (wave) blade represents passion, ardour and fire.

The Kris with five waves and small shiny patches down the blade, like sparks, is believed to have the power to shoot esoteric fire.

Five waves with no sparks in the blade symbolize the smith's prayers to the Spirit within the blade to give the bearer of this Kris eloquence in language.

If the Kris has eleven waves, the bearer of this Kris is given high spiritual and material aspirations and ambitions to the power to achieve them. If there should be a lion on the *gandhik* it is associated with the knowledge and bearing of kingship.

A Kris with thirteen waves is associated with stability and peace both materially and spiritually. This Kris would, in the past, have been only owned by people who were leaders and of noble birth. It was not thought a suitable Kris for someone of low or middle social status.

Some Kris are made with a very high meteorite content. It is supposed to be unsuitable for people who have not yet had children but it has the power to bring family happiness to married couples who already have children.

Patterns on the blade or *pamor*- The damascene is the pattern on the blade formed when the two metals are beaten together.

The pattern that looks like the rind of a watermelon is associated with prosperity and happiness This blade is believed to be beneficial to the family because its esoteric powers bring peace and happiness.

The pattern called the flow of water is believed to flow prosperity into your life, as with a raindrop blade and the scattered rice pattern is also associated with prosperity.

The bearer of a Kris with the difficult to make fern leaf *ron genduru* pattern, is blessed with the feelings of beauty and peace believed to be represented by the leaves of the fern.

Other determining factors of the quality of the Kris scabbard, the hilt and on the base of the handle there is sometimes the intricate ornament *selut*, sometimes studded with gems. The wood scabbard is usually protected with metal, called the *pendok*. A Kris may have up to three scabbards used for the same blade for different occasions of formal dress. As a Kris was passed down through the family often with time the wood will break or styles and social circumstance would change. It was also considered disrespectful to leave a Kris in an untidy condition and so many old blades are refurnish with new scabbards and hilts. The type of wood used in the hilts and scabbards sometimes has magical meaning, *awar-awar* wood is supposed to 'keep' the powers of the Kris fresh and strong. Certain marks on *timaha peled* wood can bring fame while a knot on the back of a *tayuman* wood handle will allow the owner to have more than one wife without trouble- so legend says.

A Kris should be passed throw the smoke of the incense at every fullmoon, offerings of flowers left by it and inspected and cleaned every year in the Java New Year. Traditionally to clean a Kris take the blade out of scabbard and remove the hilt and leave the Kris blade soaking in the milk from a fresh green coconut for 2-5 days. Pat dry with a clean cloth or paper towel let it stand awhile to dry. Once this is done you need a special type of small green orange (lime is the next best thing to use) clean the Kris with this to brighten the meteoric iron and use arsenic to react with the Earth iron to turn it black. Finaly brush on gun-oil mixed with a little sandalwood essential oil, to please the spirit within. Although personally I am always loath to touch a blade with liquid, so being a coward I miss this bit out and just oil, you can never go wrong with just oiling a blade. In both Malaya and Java there are professional Kris cleaners, so I am not the only one loath to take apart such an expensive antique.

There are also special holders for your Kris; there are carved boards that hang on the wall or my favourite a wonderful two-foot high statue of Hanoman a monkey general and leader of a large army. He cuddles the Kris and holds it safe.

Gerald Gardener the ancestor of Gardanarian Witches, was an expert on this weapon, having written 'Kris and other Malay weapons', still a standard work and a much sought after book.

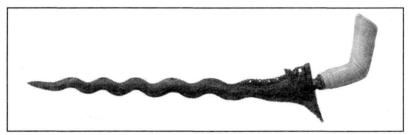

Labyrinth

A labyrinth is different from a maze; a maze is a fun and exciting game to get you lost. A labyrinth is a dedication of your time and patience to the Gods and a quest to find them. The designs of labyrinths themselves are made to confuse the Evil Eye or the Devil, so that they could run-around forever never finding the way in and so guarded Kings graves and as with the spirals patterns on New Grange in Ireland.

The Labyrinth has a strange power that has enchanted mystics the world over. They are cut into village greens in England, into stones in Rome and Aztec America. The Minotaur roamed the labyrinth of Crete in myth, although the maze does not exist under the Palace of Knossos, at least, not on this plane of existence. Even so, the Palace, has wonderful paintings of bull dancers and is a warren of rooms and passages. I am tempted to think the story was a form of Chinese whispers as the legend of the palace spreads, so the story expands and grows. The story itself becomes like the labyrinth winding.

Peru has it rightly famous Nazca Lines, which can not be seen from the ground, only from the air. Many wonderful patterns of birds, a monkey, a "spaceman" and a spider stride across the desert, unknown until fairly recently. No one knows their real purpose, but like the labyrinths in Europe, these may have been walked as a meditation or may have just marked the times for planting, or both.

There is a wonderful hidden maze in a woodland in Hampshire The Mizmaze near Breamore, it is of unknown date, but very old. legend has it that it was a prominent center for folk rituals in the past, and in the present I'm sure.

Near Tintagel Castle in Cornwall, England, in which according to legend King Arthur was conceived, stand two early Bronze Age (1800-1400 BCE) huts built of stone. Carved on them are two identical labyrinths, these have fascinated me since I discovered them at the age of ten, walking with my family on holiday. Next time we took pen and paper to copy the design, carefully numbering the coils so that we could trace how they wove round and round Years later, I was taught the trick to drawing the maze, which seems to make it

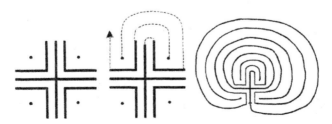

How to draw Tintagel Labyrinth

more magical than before. Just keep joining the dots and the labyrinth unfolds before your eyes.

Whilst in Egypt, I was walking around the temple of Sobek and "The Good Doctor", when I spotted a similar Labyrinth with other graffiti of the Roman period. In the temple the patients queued all night to see the Doctor some had got bored and carved this symbol onto the pavement. Possibly this was carved as a charm, so that they may hear good news from the priests, when they were finally allowed entrance or was it a game with counters, we will never truly know. To wear a labyrinth is a symbol of one's search for spiritual awakening and a protection symbol.

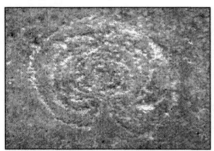 

Egyptian Temple   **Tintagel in Cornwall, England**

Lemon with nails

Lemon, a liquid filled eye shaped fruit, pierced with nine iron nails is used extensively in Europe through Spain to Peru placed above the door, to protect the house from the Evil Eye. Sending back all bad thoughts, with a bit of a kick to their owner, very much like an English Spell Bottle. Although in 1892, a cook in Italy throw up his hands in hysterics at the mere sight of the charm, vowing he would not stay in the house unless it was removed! Did he think it a curse? Or was he just frightened of magic?

Medusa

Used as an Amulet of protection across all the Greco-Roman world up to the Reformation. The Medusa one of the Gorgan sisterhood, would turn all to stone by a single glance. Perseus shines his shield like the sun and looks at Her face as in a mirror, enabling him to cut off Her head in safety. Perseus presented the terrible head to Athena Goddess of Wisdom, war, the arts, industry, justice and skill. She wore this on Her aegis. Originally the aegis was the skin of the divine goat Amaltheia worn as a protective garment but later it became a breastplate and afterwards a shield, called an aegis said to be fashioned by the Smith God Hephaestus. When Athena is depicted as a War Goddess, She always carries the Medusa's head emblazoned

upon Her shield or as a brooch forming an Amulet.

The Medusa or Gorgon starts Her journey as an amulet, as an evil and very ugly woman with huge tusks, tongue thrust out, and with snakes twining about the throat, stomach and hair.

"Some whisper from that horrid mouth
Of strange unearthly tone;
A wild infernal laugh to thrill
One's marrow to the bone.
But, no! it grins like horrid Death,
And silent as a stone." by Hesiod

Her face is emblazoned on lamps, bowls and graves as She turns all unwanted magic to stone. But as time moves on Her face changes and the Medusa's head becomes a beautiful woman but still that with snakes in Her hair and even small wings. Her history finishes with Her snakes turning to wet tendrils of hair as in the statue in the Villa Ludovisi. There is a Roman Talisman which is a small bottle that is emblazoned with the face of the Medusa and is called The Bulla, inside is tucked an invocation to the Gods to look after you.

The less scary rather sad Medusa with wings

Mermaids and Mermen

Charms depicting these were considered to have great healing powers, for respiratory disorders, impotence, general lethargy and pain. Mermaids and Mermen also due to their 'wetness' protected from the Evil Eye.

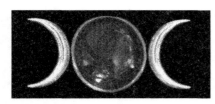

Moon

The Moon is revered in Witchcraft as the great Goddess, giver of magical wisdom. Good as a travel charm, particularly over the sea. The Moon and sea are very closely linked of course, as the moon produces the tides of both the sea and magic. The Moon is but one more of the charms to prevent the Evil Eye, due to the Moons control over water. This charm is beneficial for children and women, especially for self-expression and enhancing psychic powers.

It was always thought unlucky to point at the moon, when a new moon is first seen it must be bowed to and never seen through glass. Turn over your silver in your pocket or purse on seeing a new moon to make it grow, particularly if it is the first moon of the New Year.

Nothing in the garden must be cut at the time of the waning moon or the plants will never grow again (would the exception be the grass?) The tips of a quarter moon known as the horns, turn back negativity.

Crescent Moon Worn in ancient Rome and Greece to safeguard against danger; this charm changed and became a horseshoe, this guards against sickness and plague.

In the Middle Ages it was turned into an amulet against Witchcraft but I prefer to use the term evil.

Moon Maiden The waxing moon showing the face of the Maiden Goddess with flowers in her hair (my interpretation).

Good for children and for all growing projects and knowledge.

Moon and Star Used extensively in Muslim countries in North Africa, originally it repre-sented the Moon and 'The Morning and The Evening Star' which is Venus. You will find Venus if she chooses to show Herself, early evening or just before dawn, low near the horizon.

Moneybag

A depiction of a bag full of money or any symbol of money come to that, will show the Universe what you need and attract it to you, when working wealth spells.

In Lao when a stallholder makes a sale, the money is quickly rubbed over all the goods on display. In the hope that money will attract money, and the luck will infect all of their goods.

Mythical creatures See the chapter on Familiars

Nebra Sky Disc

A new and very exciting discovery in Millelberg Hill Bronze Age

Camp, near Nebra in Germany.

A gold and bronze disc said to be 3600 years old. It shows, possible the Sun or Fullmoon, Virgin Quarter Moon, possibly the Sun Bark and many star constellations.

It charts the Winter Sun rise and Sun set on the 21-12-1600 BCE at 9pm. It is far more complicated than first thought, being a calendar, a star chart, and a planting guide and blue prints for how to build a stone circle, no less. The Nebra Disk is an incredible piece of engineering. Although, not a traditional charm, it was used to venerate the sky, its age, subject matter and its magic, do give it the same traditional attributes as a charm.

Nine Wisdoms

Perhaps one of the oldest talisman and one of the most interesting amulets, coming from the Far East, it is of Hindu origin. Called Naoratna in India, translated this means Nine Wisdoms. It combines all of the influences that you could possibly need into one ring or pendant. In the center is a Ruby, at the top a Diamond crystal, clockwise, pearl, coral, imperial topaz, sapphire, cat's eye (not Tigereye), yellow beryl and emerald. In Thailand this combination is thought so powerful, that the King may, for deeds of outstanding valor, give "The Ancient and Auspicious order of the Nine Gems" and Royal Rings are set with these nine most precious stones. Nine being the perfect number and so combining all to draw all possible beneficial influences into your life. The gems don't quite touch the skin in a traditional setting but are set a little high. I noticed one day that you can see the light playing through the gems onto your finger like a stain-glass window. So by wearing this ring you absorb sunlight that has filtered through the gems, modifying the energy of the Sun, healing or attracting all the luck you need.

Numbers (Sacred)

There are countless ways of explaining the meaning of numbers, this is but one.

Even numbers are sacred to the God

1 (with this notable exception) is a phallic number and is a God number, a leader, giving honor and the number of success.

2 knowledge, harmony with nature and peacemaker

4 logicality, dexterity and agility

6 solidity, calmness and pride

8 balance, perseverance and truthfulness

10 the development of number 1, the leader into Kingship and wealth

12 the number of months in the Zodiac, through which the Sun passes

Uneven numbers are sacred to the Goddess.

These are the numbers most used in magic

0 the nothingness out of which the Goddess created all, the Goddess sacred womb, the Sheela- Na -Gig of the number world

3 leadership, energy, courage, luck, a Celtic magic number and the Triple Goddesses own number

5 inspiration, idealism and freedom

7 victory, ambition, honor and authority

9 self-sacrifice, sensitivity and completeness

Nine is the perfect number, the highest point before the sequence starts again. There is nine month in the human gestation period. Nine is also the magical 3 multiplied by itself, making nine a very special number. Nine also has a magical connection in Arabic numbers, the digits of every multiple of nine add up to nine.

$2 \times 9 = 18$ add $1 + 8 = 9$,

$3 \times 9 = 27$ add $2 + 7 = 9$,

$4 \times 9 = 36$ add $3 + 6 = 9$,

$5 \times 9 = 45$ add $4 + 5 = 9$

6x9=54, 7x9=63, 8x9=72, 9x9=81, 10x9=90 and so it goes on.

11 is a Master number (as with 22 and 33), a number of challenge and insight

13 is a variant of three, the old Celtic magic number. There are thirteen in a traditional witches' coven, thirteen lunar months in a year. Friday is the day of Freya (this is where the name Friday originates) and Venus so the church taught that it was very unlucky. The unluckiest day being of course Friday 13th! or for Witches perhaps the luckiest.

Nut

A nut is a fertility charm and as such should be carried by young ladies unable to conceive.

Ouroborus

The great world serpent who encircles the Earth, devouring its own tail to feed itself, an amulet of re-generation and eternity. It can also be depicted as half day and half night, dark and light neither good nor bad but both forming part of perfection.

It is one of the oldest symbols in the world, being found in ancient Egypt Before Common Era 1600 from where it passed to Phoenicians and then to the Greek philosophers, who gave it the name Ouroboros ("self-devourer"). The design is found in China, with the Aztec God Quetzalcoatl and in the Native American cultures. In Norse mythology it appears as the serpent Jormungandr one of the three children of Loki, who's children are doomed to bring about the end of the world as we know it.

Padlock

As on a charm bracelet, it secures the affection of the receiver and gives the blessings of long life and happiness. In China a chain with a padlock on is placed around the neck of the only boy child, this is made from the silver collected from the heads of many families. The belief is that it will preserve his health and lock him to life.

Pegasus (see Familiars)

Pentagram See Star

Phallic Charms

From the early history phallic charms have been used, not only to increased virility and sexual prowess, but also to increase other aspects of daily life. The Phallus in history, never had the obscene connotations it has now, it was simply the miracle of procreation.

The earliest phallus ever found was carved from siltstone, measuring 20cm x 3cm and is 28,000 years old and was unearthed in Germany's Hohle Fels Cave. Although it is obviously impossible to tell if this Phallus is a usable object or a mystical charm or both. A Phallus comes in all sizes from tall pillars to small charms, in Peru there is a temple dedicated to the Phallus.

In Roman times the phallus belonged to Priapus a God of fertility and growing plants, both crops and gardens were under his care. Which may be the link in later Roman times to a Greenman phallus.

The Celts carved their Phallus' from antler horn, which would have been sacred to the God.

The Phallus charm is still used to this day in Thailand, it is suspended by a cord inside the clothes near the real penis to divert evil eye and spells on to the fake phallus. Even special phallus charms for boy children are made to ward off jealousy and the evil eye. A real penis is said to have an 'eye' is this the link with the 'evil eye'?

In Thailand all phallic charms were made from carved bone, brass or silver some with added animals, to bring into your life the aspects of the animal. From this we can deduce the meaning of these charms in the ancient world.

Black Panther representation on a Penis- for success when you must work by stealth or strategy.

Crocodile representation on a Penis- courage, strength and increasing mastery over situations.

Lion representation on a Penis- Protection, good fortune and sexual happiness.

Lizard representation on a Penis- sex, marital joy, peaceful home and family fertility. In hot lands small Gecko lizards live on all walls of the houses, eating insects that may harm the members of the family.

Some families have larger lizards as household pets, to protect from poisonous snakes. So lizards and the family are closely interlinked, with this charm, your family is protected by the spirit of the great lizard.

Tiger representation on a Penis- protection, bravery and protection from attack by weapons.

Green Man representation on a Penis- Fertility.

Lady riding, were the only ones to be worn by women, as this helps to protect from unwanted sexual attention and to increase fertility.

Winged Penis A Winged Penis is an all round good luck and protection from evil. I was most surprised to read in the newspaper.

Archaeologists in Southwark had found a very similar charm in a medieval dig and had no idea what it was; they had never seen one before!

Little did they know we were still making them and they are still being used in magic to this day!

See also cowry shells

Penis Bone   Badger, Seals, Racoons, Whales and walruses are some of the God and Goddess's more favored animals, having been given a Penis Bone. Given by a man to his sweetheart and tied with a red ribbon for her to wear round her neck! As a love charm to hold her to him only. I can't think what that was supposed to represent! A happy and fruitful life, I can but assume. In America they are thought to be lucky to wear and are carried for good luck with gambling.

Phoenix The (see Familiars)

Pins

Pins being sharp and made of metal were very expensive until recently and are steeped in magic. Evil could be kept from the house by pushing pins in doorposts.

A bent or crooked pin can be thrown into a well for a wish, reminding me of Celtic swords found in water bent or broken.

It is lucky to pick up a pin, but they must never be given as a gift.

If you loose an item, get a pin and a cushion. Circle the pin three times round the cushion and say "I pin the sprite" once with every circle. Then secure the pin into the cushion and carry on looking, you will find the lost item soon. And if like mine you have a friendly sprite about the house, you may find other things that you have forgotten about or will need in the near future.

Planetary Sigils

Not truly only planetary sigils, as they also include the Sun and Moon. Planets were called "the wandering ones" as they moved amongst the fixed stars. Each planet is dedicated to a Roman/Greek God or Goddess. You can use these signs to bring into your life the energy of that God or Goddess. Use them in candle magic or written talisman.

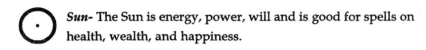

Sun- The Sun is energy, power, will and is good for spells on health, wealth, and happiness.

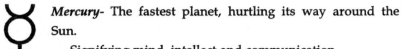

Mercury- The fastest planet, hurtling its way around the Sun.

Signifying mind, intellect and communication.

Mars- The red planet as seen from Earth, offers Primal energy and action, named after the Roman God of War this often shows itself as aggression and lust.

At first glance Mars seems very uncomplicated God but His early beginnings was as a fertility God, almost a Greenman.

He was God of crops and guardian of the fields. Drew on this energy for positivity and courage.

⊕ **Earth-** stability

☽ **Moon-** The Moon shows the traditional feminine energies of emotions, the unconscious mind, psychic energies and self expression. Without the Moon life could not be sustained on our planet, not only does the Moon govern the tides of the seas and rivers but also the tides of magic. She holds the Earth on Her axis, giving us the seasons, so that we do not roast or freeze.

In 1997 a new tiny moon was found to be orbiting the Earth, Cruithne. Only three miles (5k) wide and too small to be seen by the naked eye it has a horseshoe orbit around the Earth that takes 770 years to complete. Of course unknown by the ancients, it may play some part in Astrology but so few know if its existence yet, that it has not been studied.

♀ **Venus-** Venus shows us love of beauty in a far wider sense than just personal, draw love, health and wealth into your life.

484

Jupiter- The largest of the planets of our Solar System brings with it happiness, good fortune, growth and communications.

Saturn- Saturn is one of the most beautiful of our planets with a exquisite skirt of rings stately twirling in a slow orbit deep in the cold of space. Saturn offers us limitations, discipline and unmoving tradition.

Uranus (This planet was not known of by the ancients)- Innovation, inventiveness and non-conformity.

Neptune (This planet was not known of by the ancients)- Neptune the God of Water His sphere of influence are veils and illusions.

Pluto (This planet was not known of by the ancients and is now not thought big enough to be a planet)- Formally Pluto was concerned with introspection and transforming energies.

Sedna- A new planet that has just been found in our Solar System, has been named Sedna, who is an Inuit Goddess of the Ocean. I don't now if it has been given a sign, as yet. But personally I can't see that if Sedna has, the sign will have built up any energy.

Try meditating on what this new planet teaches us. Alone, deep within the Ocean of the Universe, Sedna floats far from the Sun and its warmth. Is She the Crone or the unborn Virgin, how do you see Her.

Whether you choose to use the "new" planets are, as ever, your choice.

You can do a wonderful meditation to the planets while listening to Holst's "Planets Suite" as it takes you on a musical tour of our Solar System.

Rose A symbol of eternity and of the Goddess, in the east it is the Lotus but in the west the rose. The rose slowly opening to reveal the secret Goddess with in. This ring contains an Amethyst carved into the shape of a rose, but nothing improves on the beauty of the Goddess's living flowers.

Rowan Berry Necklace

Thread fresh Rowan berries on to strong cotton with a needle and hang near the hearth, door or wear in circle. Strangely I have found this spell in many parts of the world, in Peru the red berries are worn while casting good spells.

Rings

Rings signify eternity. Legend tells us that the ring was invented when Jupiter chained Prometheus to a rock, for stealing fire from heaven to aid mortal man. However Jupiter soon relented, but decreed that Prometheus must wear a link of his chain and a piece of the rock that he was chained to, for all time.

Buckle Ring Self defence and protection.

Claddagh Ring Worn in the town of Claddagh, Ireland, and passed from mother to daughter on her wedding day.

It has an older meaning than the Christian one given today, of the heart of Christ as King of Heaven. Traditionally it meant the crown depicts loyalty, the hands depict friendship and the heart depicts love.

Elemental Rings Set with a gem stone strengthening the connection with a particular Elemental Quarter and bringing that attribute into your life.

Earth-Protection, Air- Knowledge, Fire- Courage, Water-Happiness.

Gem Rings- Worn to carry the gem and impart its energy to the wear.

Handfasting Rings- Of many types are exchanged in a Witch wedding.

Healing Rings- Very often a snake (as in the Caduceus) or gem set ring.

Hallowed or cramp ring Made from coffin nails, worn to cure cramp and especially powerful if blessed by a king or queen (Hallowed Rings).

Knot Rings in which the two strands of metal is linked into a knot, has direct connection to magic and as the ends of the knot are not in evidence, the eye once more travels round the design and breaking the gaze of fascination, the Evil Eye. A good example of this would be a Knot of Hercules or True-Lovers Ring a knot binds the love with magic, for all time. The custom originated as a healing charm in ancient Egypt, but is best known for its use in ancient Greece and Rome as a protective amulet, most notably as a wedding ring and as a knot on the girdle worn by the bride. This custom is the origin of the phrase 'tying the knot.', which may be the beginnings of the Witches handfasting cord. When making a knot ring, a spell by its very nature is tied into the ring, and so we come back to Smiths being magic users once again. Some talismanic rings were made of both gold and silver joined. But this unfortunately is now illegal in England, due to hallmarking regulations.

Posy Rings- A ring with a motto inside, such as 'I love you'.

Rune Rings- To bring the energies of this magical script into your life.

Seal Ring This particular seal is a pentagram. Seals have been used since Babylonian times and can be used for magical documents or spells.

Use sealing wax (which can be bought in many

colors). Melt with a candle and drop onto your document at the appropriate place.

Wait a moment or two until it forms a skin, then push the seal firmly and an impression of your seal will be left in the wax.

Salus ring Worn in ancient Rome as a charm against ill health, a five pointed star surrounded by a snake. With this ring you asked Salus the daughter of the physician God Asclepius to heal you.

Signet Rings- One of the earliest form of rings developing from the Cylinder seal.

Widow Ring- Believe it or not, a skull and cross bones ring. Widows in the middle ages, took if they chose, a vow not to remarry, to remain married to their dead husbands. If they did this, they kept their house and all moneys from their previous marriage. If they remarried the house and money would belong to their new partner.

These are only a few of the many types of rings; rings would need a book on their own to explain them all.

Scarab

Scarab, sounds so much nicer than Dung Beetle, which is what the scarab is. He rolls the Sun across the sky in the same way as Dung Beetles roll around a ball of dung; so much larger than themselves.

A Sun symbol, an Egyptian talisman of rejuvenation, worn for health, strength and virility.

Sea Shells

Shells are obviously dedicated to the water quarter and sacred to Water Goddesses, bringing happiness and wealth.

In Europe the earliest shells found with Neolithic burials are periwinkles.

Shells are used extensively in Peruvian magic, both as containers and to symbolize water. In the pre-Inca civilization the Mochica's they used a special red shell for its magical quality. Unfortunately we have no idea whether the shell was used for protection or good luck, as no written records remain. In Neolithic burials, both red ochre and shells are present. Possibly as red is used extensively in magic as a substitute for blood, and is therefore life giving, it may have the same meaning as without water of course, life does not exist.

Conch shell is one of the eight emblems of Buddha and brings oratory, learning, protection, good fortune and riches. Used in Tibet to dispense blessed water by the monks. A conch shell can also be used as a ceremonial horn, the spiral within adding to its spiritual meaning, the noise needing to travel the sacred labyrinth before issuing forth.

Cowrie Shell. They have been found in graves as far afield as Europe, Ancient Rome and Egypt, Jordan, China, and used by Scythian Kurgans several hundred of which were found in one tumuli.

They have been used since Upper Palaeolithic (BCE 40,000 to 10,000), in a berial in the Dordogne they are arranged in pairs on the body. In the Neolithic period (BCE 8,500) in England and mainland Europe, cowrie shells were found in graves of important women and children only.

The first question is, how? As the cowry shell is found no nearer than the Red Sea, there must have been trade over a very wide area, for the shells to travel so far so early in history.

This possibly was to bring protection and wealth in the afterlife or to insure a quick rebirth, as well as insuring their status in both realms. In the subsequent Pre-Pottery Neolithic period, skulls were often plastered with a clay face and given cowry shells to look like half closed eyes in Britain. A large eastern cowrie shell was found with a phallus in a woman's grave in Nimes, France.

China BCE 1200 are cowrie shells earliest use as money and later depictions of cowries in bronze made the first coins. Cowries have been used in many other parts of the world, in Africa until the 20th century. Orange cowries at one time sold for large sums on the market. In Fiji and the New Hebrides in the Pacific they are still worn as badges of rank by the chiefs.

In Africa and the religions of Santeria and Hoodoo cowries are used in divination, face up is a positive sign; face down means bad luck is coming. The cowrie was thought of as a mouth giving wisdom of the Goddess. You contact the Goddess, through the cowrie shells, and She advises you how the Gods and Goddesses are affecting your life.

The cowrie shell is used in the modern Middle East as an amulet of protection, in this instance worn by men.

The cowrie is also a female phallic charm, (as with the woman's grave in Nimes, France found with a phallus) The Goddess herself, as with the Sheela- Na- Gig, a bringer of fertility and good luck. In traditional Japan, women hold cowries shells during childbirth to ease the birth. As the 'Giver of Life' the cowrie would protect you from the dangers of life and with its association with water the cowrie has the extra advantage of protecting from the Evil Eye.

You can give cowries as a gift to a woman, with this you offer both wealth, knowledge and protection. As our ancient ancestors did, place cowrie shells in the coffin for the last journey.

Thought of as bringers of wealth (due to its use as money), oratory, fertility and knowledge. To wear a cowry shell you attract food fortune, in all its guises.

The only thing that one should never do with a cowrie shell is to burn it, as this is an insult to the Water Goddesses.

Serpents Tongues
No serpents were harmed; they are Fossilised Sharks teeth and are of course protection.

Skull and Skeleton
Human skulls in Peru are still kept in houses by older people, as protection. But the practice is dying out with the younger and less interested in magic generation. Shaman also use human skulls in

Peru, in some areas to facilitate spell work. By using the ex-owner of the skull as a guide to the other side of the veil that divides life and death, to help bring about a happy conclusion to a spell. In Tibet the top of the skull is used as an offering bowl, they are decorated in many ways, some inlayed with brass others with rows of pressed metal skulls around the rim. As with Death in the Tarot pack, skeletons and skulls are not as dark as they may seem, with a meaning of regeneration and new beginnings.

Spirals

The spiral was probably the first attempt at art ever tried by the ancients and was brought to the peak of perfection by Celtic and Viking art. The spiral may turn with the Sun (diesiel, Sunwise, clockwise) and represents growth. The unfolding  Universe and nature which often forms spirals in its designs as with a shell, galaxy or the seeds on a sunflower. The Spiral can be also be drawn anti-clockwise or Moonwise (widdershins) with its deep mystery of endings and protection. The feminine snake with its coils also represents the spiral, as the spiral may represent the snake.

The Scottish sword dance, starts by dancing widdershins to build power and protection and finishing the dance diesiel bringing victory. The Pagan Spiral Dance that you will participate in hopefully, at open rituals, has the same meaning.

Double Spiral A double spiral is often thought of as the eyes of the God (right) and Goddess (left) therefore duality of dark and light, birth and death.

Triple Spiral has appeared in Celtic art for 3000 years but is far older. Newgrange in Ireland has one of the most famous of the many carvings of Neolithic triple spirals. It was 2500 years old when the Celts first saw it, to explain this remarkable place, they told the story of Oenghus the God of Love who lived with in, while He lived at

Newgrange he never aged. Interestingly, the light at dawn, runs along the floor each day until at the Winter Solstice it floods the inner sanctuary with light, where lies the famous triple spiral. It is for me, the Sun God fertilizing the Earth Goddess, changing the tomb into the womb and giving life in the "other world" to those who's bones were laid to rest there in the side chambers. Possibly this thought was the origin of the later Celtic stories of the God of Love and Fertility, living there.

Star

"Come quickly! I am tasting stars!" Dom Perignon, at the moment of his discovery of champagne. (Although it was discovered in 1612 in England first).

A star is a good luck symbol in all countries from the beginning of time, whether thought of as the light of heaven showing through holes in the sky or thrown across the black velvet of the sky by the hand of the Goddess. Jewel or pendant in the shape of a star brings good fortune in fighting evil.

Four pointed star of the Elemental Quarters

Five pointed Star Five points radiating out from the centre, like a starfish is the Egyptian symbol for stars and in particular Sirius, Isis' star.

Five pointed Star- Pentagram –Druids Foot- Pentagrammon – Star of the Witches Penta meaning five and to Pagans this is the most

important of all symbols representing as it does Spirit, Earth, Air, Fire and Water. In Ancient times until the advent of modern science, everything was thought to be made of these four elements plus spirit, held in balance. The circle around the edge correspond to infinity. The design is made from five lines, this naturally forms a pentagon in the center, if you use a ruler to link the points, of the pentagram, you will form a second pentagon, this time the other way up.

The pentagram appears in the Tarot representing coins and on Pagan altars it represents Earth and the physical world.

From at least far back as 4000BCE in Sumeria, the pentagram has embodied life and health and has links to the apple core of the Earth Mother. By cutting an apple in half around the waist you have natures own pentagram. Apples are therefore the sacred fruit of the Great Mother.

Pentagram is a protection symbol against all evil, it can be written without letting the pen leave the paper, and is said to trap the evil in its labyrinth of interweaving paths, running forever never to escape. In the same way a pentagram if worn, also deflects back magic sent against you and if the altar pentacle is held high will protect you from any unpleasant entity that wanders past. The Pentagram has been adopted by Pagans as a recognition symbol, both as a ring and pendant. With one point up, it is spiritual and sacred to all Pagan Goddesses. The pentagram with its single point down, dates back to Ancient Babylon far earlier than Christianity. This today is male and represents the Horned God, as warrior and guardian but is not worn in this way very often today, due to 'Hollywood' connecting it with Satanism and everything bad.

Interestedly, the planet Venus can be plotted in her synodic periods on a map of the Solar System this forms a pentagram, as seen from Earth.

Each angle of the pentagram is 72 degrees 7+2 = 9 the perfect number. It is said in Eastern philosophy that 3 is the number of the uninitiated and 9 the number of the Knowing.

In the Middle Ages the Pentagram for Christians stood for the five wounds of Christ. Though why a church in Addington, England has an upside down pentagram, I have no idea, unless it represents St Peter crucified upside down? Sir Gawain carried a Pentagram on his

shield to remind him of the knightly virtues. It was worn by Ceremonial Magicians to protect them from evil spirits while working magic. To the Muslim the pentagram stands for the five virtues of Islam.

In Geometry, the Pentagram hides the Golden Mean with in its five lines, Agrippa of Nettesheim's famous pentagram containing a man, points to the Golden Mean of the human body. (See page 00)

Pentacle Although I was taught that a pentacle with a circle around was a pentagram the Oxford Dictionary finds no difference.

What do I think is the difference? If you are going to wear a Pentacle to sleep in, the Pentacle points stick into you.

Rune Pentagram Adding Runic energy to the energy of the pentagram.

Elemental Pentagram Not a traditional design but emphasising the Pentagram's elemental associations.

Six pointed Stars- Seal of Solomon, Star of David, Hexagram, Shatkona (Hindu), Shield of David.

This Symbol preserves its wearer from

dangers when travelling on this, and any other, plane. Seal of Solomon has been used throughout history, as well as by the Jews to which it is now heavily associated.

It consists of two triangles, one of female and water plus one male and fire.

Together, they form all life encompassed 'as above so below'.

Said to seal demons from entering in a similar way as the Pentagram, in the middle ages the two names were interchangeable.

Solomon, a great magician, as well as being a King of Israel understood magic and used it to control demons and
Elemental Quarters. The Seal of Solomon has
adopted his name.

Seal of Fatima or Seal of Miriam This
composite charm is very unusual; it has the
Hand of Fatima in the center, the Seal of
Solomon around, six eyes in each of the spaces and finally a circle of
infinity around.

Seal of Fatima makes a very formidable amulet
of protection.

Uni-Cursal Hexagram was designed by
Crowley, and is written without letting the pen
leave the paper, a classic protection from evil. But
has all the magical qualities of a Seal of Solomon.

*Seven pointed Star, Septagram, Heptagram or
Elven Star* Represents the original seven planets
known to the ancients and since Hellenistic times, the
seven days.

It is also sacred to the Faery Tradition of Magic.
Two different ways of drawing a seven pointed star.

Eight pointed Star or Octagram representing
fullness and regeneration. In Paganism the eight

pointed star represent the eight festivals. In its history the eight pointed
star has represented both Venus and as two four pointed stars set at
angles to each other the Star of Ishtar. An Octagram can be drawn in
five ways, as a continuous line, as with all continuous line designs, it
protects from evil, two interacting squares, as a square and a diamond
interweaving, Ishtar's Star and as a cross with double points.

Nine pointed Stars, Enneagram or Nonagram Representing the
perfect number and all Nine phase Goddesses, Nine Muses and the
modern nine planets (we have just lost Pluto and gained Sedna). In
Christian iconography the nine-pointed star represents the nine gifts
of spirit.

The nine-pointed star can be represented in two ways, as a continuous line platted or as three triangles interlaced.

Sword

Spiritual aggression. The sword is also a fire symbol. A curved symbol is the feminine or lunar principle, a straight sword being male. Justice, authority, courage, strength and liberty, beneficial for all commercial undertakings.

Shield

This can be symbolized by a brooch or pendant, as mentioned earlier, as well as a shield used for its defensive protection on the spiritual plane. Much as Athena's Medusa shield and brooch are.

Shieldknot

This symbol is Viking and represents a shield and therefore protective. Viking and Celtic work are very similar, in there highly decorated complex patterns, the idea of evil thoughts being trapped in it's design running round and round applies as much to Viking as

Celtic. The Shieldknot is sacred to Thor, notice the hidden swastika within the design, this also represents Thor's hammer as the Sun spinning through the air and adds the light of happiness to this amulet.

Spoon

An amulet of protection, take a soup spoon preferably silver but an ordinary soup spoon will do. Bend the handle over, and cut it off, so that the handle has formed a loop for a cord to pass through. Worn round the neck, this will reflect back any negative thoughts sent against you. I remember seeing a Christian cross at a

Stately Home I visited, hanging with many of these amulets. There are many people in Witchcraft today that think this type of spell is unethical but I'm afraid I feel, don't throw it out if you aren't prepared to have it back! It will not return to an innocent party and if no one wishes you ill luck then the Amulet will be inactive.

Swastika

Probably the most misunderstood of the charms. People have asked me why I have included it in a book on Witchcraft, as it will give a wrong idea of what we do. My answer, I don't like suppressed information.

Roman Mosaic floor from Tunisia 200CE

Many years ago, I was walking around the British Museum through the Roman section and there on a Roman silver platter was a black Swastika. This provoked my curiosity, what was a Nazi symbol doing on a Roman plate? When I got home I phoned the museum and except for telling

me it was genuine Roman, they would give me no more information.

The swastika, I eventually found out, is probably the oldest good luck charm in the world. It has been found in carvings the world over and as far back in time as the Neolithic period. Also known as a gammadion because it seems to be made from two gamma letters of the Greek alphabet meaning good fortune, its name is Sanskrit not German, su means good and aste- to be, the English name is Fylfot. It

497

represents the sun crossing the heavens, the arms depicted spiraling in the direction of the sun and the Autumn and Spring Equinox or the male and female, associated with the wheel, the circle of the year and the four Cardinal points of the compass or possibly all four meanings. In Europe the Swastika was associated with Thor's hammer and is good luck charm, was raised as a benediction in Viking Times. Swastikas of straw were attached to cart wheels and the Germanic peoples traditionally rolled these flaming wheels on St John's Eve. They were called 'hail-wheels', the Sun (the swastika) burning away the hail that may damage the harvest. In the Middle ages the Swastika was cast on bells including Church bells to protect them.

It was carved on cave walls in Mayan South America, in Native North America, seen in Rome and Roman North Africa (Tunisia & Algeria) in Greece and even the Celts used it.

The Hindus and Buddhist still use it and the Jains a Buddhist sect, introduced it to China from India in BCE 200, where it is called a thunder-scroll, which fits nicely with its later use by Thor the Thunder God. Still prevalent in India where its reputation is unsullied and can be seen on many Duwali cards. I bought one at my local post office the other year. In Tibet it is used as a Buddhist good luck charm when it rolls 卐 clockwise and a Bon (a religion that predates Buddhism in which every tree or rock has a spirit) good luck charm when it rolls 卍 anticlockwise.

The Anglo-Indian writer Rudyard Kipling used a swastika, as did Robert Baden-Powell's Boy Scout movement, on the cover of their books. But of course that was before the WW11, that changed the

meaning of this symbol in the Western world forever. I have a set of English cigarette cards, that feature well-known talisman and amulets including the swastika but they were printed in the 1920's.before the taint of the Nazis attached itself this symbol. There is a postcard from the same date, boldly featuring a swastika with a

lucky black cat and horseshoes, to be sent to wish the recipient good luck with any project.

Many swastikas from around the world are very different from the traditional design, men, birds and winged rattlesnakes, have been depicted at various times. Some swastikas have circles on the end of the arms, some dots on the spaces between the arms. I have heard people say that the Nazi's reversed the swastika, but in Rome and in Tibet at least, it faced in both directions. The Nazi's used it to draw good luck to them, not because it was bad luck, even they weren't that stupid. Although it may never be accepted as a Pagan lucky charm again, I though it best to put the record straight.

Tattoo

A defensive talisman used by Celtic warriors and many other nationalities in sympathetic magic, a form of self-sacrifice, the blood shed during its production a gift to the Gods.

Women were tattooed in Ancient Egypt, some with a small God Dwarf Bes on the thigh to ease childbirth. A swallow tattooed on the ankle of an 18th Century sailor was thought to make him good at climbing the rigging of old sailing ships. The Crucifixion tattooed on a sailor's back was used to help him if he displeased the Captain, as he hoped that the lashing would not be laid on so hard upon the depiction of Christ. Runes are a good choice if you are contemplating a tattoo, as you will forever bring into your life the energy of the runes.

Choose wisely, remember a tattoo is for life.

Torc

Worn by the Celts as a sign of a warrior, both male and female.

The Gunderstup cauldron shows

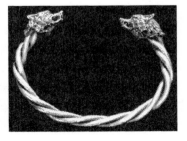

the Cernunnos with the torc in one hand, representing the warrior's valor, holding it high. To collect the torcs in battle may have showed one's power as a warrior.

Touch Wood

A Touchwood is very protective- any small piece of protective wood, oak, ash, yew or rowan worn on a thong or attached to your key ring.

Touch Stone

Is a stone used until recently to test gold

Thor's Hammer

The Viking God of thunder and lightning. Thor was a giant of great strength, a warrior and worshipped by both warriors and peasants alike.

Thor was known for his remarkable ability to down ale and food, Loki (the trickster God) always picked on Thor, making Him look foolish.

The God Thor's hammer was called Mjolnir, lightning was thought to be sparks from his blows and thunder was its sound. His symbol worn by all followers of the thunder God from about the 10th century, bestowing favor and protection, honoring treaties and consecrating marriages.

Smiths were thought to be special favorites of Thor, due to their use of hammers in their work.

Three Hares

This curious charm is known the world over, three hares joined by only three ears. The earliest known example of the Three Hares is found painted on the ceilings of Buddhist cave temples at Mogao, near Dunhuang, China around 600ADE. Following the silk trade routes, woven into the design of the silk, this then traveled across Asia and Europe to English Churches in 1200ADE ending up beside the Greenman. A strange journey for three little hares to make, crossing the Mogul Empire, being placed in Jewish Synagogues, used as a design on Iranian coins, through Europe they traveled. Ending on roof bosses and even Cathedral bells, all over England.

In Buddhist Temples Buddha and many local Gods and Goddesses sit together happily. So I see no reason why the Hare that the Chinese thought lived on the Moon, may in this charm represent the three phases of the Moon which moves anticlockwise through its phases, as does this charm, for ever chasing round and round after each other.

Triangle

In numerology, three stands for creativity and success. Many people still say "everything happens in three's". This harks back to Celtic Britain where three was a sacred number. All forms of the triangle are part of the very special energy of three. As the square is known as a male shape and all even numbers are male, uneven numbers are female, so the triangle is female and therefore today is seen as the Triple Goddess. The square and the triangle together represent a perfect union, of God and Goddess and is one reason the number seven was so greatly revered. Plato thought that all nature was made from triangles and made representations of the Earth, Air, Fire and Water from triangles, that expressed the energy of each.

Earth   Air   Fire   Water

Triangle of the Elements- A sigil for each of the elements from Ceremonial Magic. These triangles can be made with the hands, by placing the tips of the thumbs together and the tips of the first fingers with the second finger brought up behind touching the inner knuckle, at the Elemental Quarters if using Ceremonial Magic.

Abracadabra - Not just a stage magician's word but truly magical and used to diminish, illness, pain, fever or anything that needs dwindling. Abracadabra was used by Gnostics in Rome and very popular throughout the Middle ages.

Samonicus, a celebrated doctor instructed that the charm, which was used for curing aches and fevers, was to be written and folded into a cross shape, worn for nine days around the neck. Before sunrise, cast it behind the patient into a running stream.

Extensively used during the Plague in London of the Black Death of 1665. Abracadabra is of course an upside down triangle with all the power that brings to this charm (see triangle). Make on a waning moon.

Dragon's Eye Stone A gem cut as a triple triangle, sacred to the nine-fold Goddesses and the nine Muses, meaning Love, Power, Wisdom and imparts protection to the wearer no matter which gem it is cut from.

It is also Empedocles' geometric sign for Fire from ancient Greece and in Mediaeval Grimoires, it was used to call female spirits.

Eye of Fire or Dragon Eye represents the element of Fire. As a drawn sigil it is the ancient German a sign for danger.

Triquetra This symbol may have originally been associated with the God Frey and dynamic energy and adopted by the Christians as a depiction of the Holy

Trinity. Now, this very intricate sign represents the Triple Goddess female genitalia interlaced. The Triquetra forms another of the continuous designs thought to keep evil on the trot, interlaced with the magic of the circle.

Triscol A Celtic charm now said to be depicting the Triple Goddess, Maiden, Mother and Crone.

Valknot Sacred to Odin, a symbol made up of three triangles, is not to be taken lightly. A giving of yourself to Him, on His terms, a consenting to be taken when

He sees fit. The Valknot is depicted on the Gotland stone in Sweden, on which an apparent sacrifice is depicted. Do not enter into this contract without due consideration.

Tooth

Around the Mediterranean from an early period, it was thought that as horses loose their first set of teeth like humans, if they were hung one around a child's neck it would help with cutting their first teeth, both magically and practically.

Pliny says that wolf's teeth tied on a child kept away childish terrors and ailments due to teething, also that the largest tooth of a wolf if hung on a horse would give it stamina and speed.

A tooth gives both courage, strength, drawing the energy of the ferocious animal to the carrier and said to be a legendary cure for

toothache. Wolf teeth were joined with silver to make a crescent moon shape, to invoke the Goddess protection. Wolf's teeth were also used as a hunting charm, in the 16th and 18th century rings were set with wolves' teeth. The Irish used wolf's teeth set in silver or fossilised brown bear's teeth set in gold, against fasination and our old friend the Evil Eye. Pliny says that a beaver has incredibly strong teeth and so is a good charm for toothache and for the growing of stronge teeth.

Tusk A boar is a very strong animal with a bad temper, having no wish to die. A hunter that has been brave and succeeded in this task, would take the tusks and wear them proudly. The Etruscan, Greeks and Romans appreciated the power of the tusk as an amulet. A real tusk or a depiction of it, in any material, is a bringer of good fortune. The Roman Tacitus in his book 'Germania' written in 98 CE tells us that the emblem of the tribe Aestii in honour of the 'Mother of the Gods' wore masks of boars, which ensured there safety better than helmets.

In Anglo –Saxon times men wore tusks on there shields or horses. Women and children wore them pierced on as a pendant or with other beads on a necklace. They were considered the epitome of fertility and ferocity and also looked good worn, if you or your man were brave enough to kill a boar, you would want the world to know.

A pair of linked tusks has a connection to Diana The Moon Goddess as they form Her symbol. In Her aspect as protector of animals, a pair of tusks in the shape of the moon were used in earlier times before horse brasses and hung on animals in the fields to protect them. Still today you will find many horse brasses have a moon in the design, continuing the same tradition.

Boar's tusks are still worn in Corfu with cowrie shells and in Spain and Italy a boars tusk is an amulet against the Evil Eye.

Not only boars of course all tusks are protections for horse, human or home. More so for the warrior that braved the ferocity of the animal and killed it, in ancient societies.

When hung from other charms a tusk enhances the magic.

Stags Antlers have in the main the same meaning as boar's tusks. In the Anglo- Saxon period it is a slice from the base of the dropped horn that is used, sometimes left plain, sometimes with many decorations of two concentric circles with a dot in the center or decorated with a phallus. Stags renew their antlers every year and so like snakes where considered a symbol of immortality, worn to promote life and youth. Any part of a deer was thought to drive away snakes but Pliny preferred to burn scraps of horn. The Lithica of Ancient Greece recommends that a man take a stag's antler to bed on his wedding night to ensure a long and happy life together.

Horn of either the bull, stag or ram, signifying the power of the forces of nature and for Witch's the Horned God. In Turkey cow or goat horns are attached to boats as protection and to bring fertility, which in this case would be a large catch of fish (see Capricorn). They also represent the Goddess Hathor as the horns of the Moon. In Scandinavian legend, three horns inter-linked bring good luck

Claw Pliny tells us that Eagles claws were worn for pain in the side, a right claw for pain in the right and a left claw for pain on the left side. Please remember that even in pre-historic times any item could be replaced by a copy in silver or carved in stone it was not thought necessary to wear the original.

Unicorn (see Familiars)
Weapons

Small representations of weapons represent the hero's struggle against the known monsters of life, and were the symbol of valor amongst the Greeks and Romans. During the Anglo- Saxon period women wore small swords, hammers, spears, billhooks on chatelaines hanging from their belts, as a protection amulet, later buckets wine strainers and sickles and symbolic keys were added.

Wheel

This sign is probably older than the Egyptians civilization, both the four and the eight spoked wheel. The wheel is thought to be a sun sign, four spokes for the sun festivals, eight spokes of
the turning wheel of the year and our eight great festivals.

Also seen in Tibet, and is a Buddhist symbol of reincarnation. (see photo on Tibet). It can also represent the eight winds of Ancient

Greece, four cardinal and four cross quarter, that is still engraved on the Tower of the Winds in Athens.

It also protects against evil and protects the house from fire, protecting against ill luck, turning it to good with the turning of the wheel. On the Gundestrup Cauldron, Cernnunos is depicted with a eight spoked wheel. The Celtic four spoked wheel may be the precursor of the Celtic Cross.

Yin Yang

The Yin Yang Charm is very old and was born from Chinese philosophy in which opposite factors rule the Universe.

Yin is, sad, passive, downward flowing and female, dark mystery, the moon and night. Yang is happy, active, the light of the Sun and day upward flaming, but always with a spot of dark in the light and a spot of light in the dark. Both follow each other around, day into night, Summer into Winter, eternally. Nothing is ever static all is in constant change. Carry this charm for balance in your life.

Zodiac Charms

A Zodiac Sun Sign is carried to bring into your life the best attributes of your sign. The ancient symbols that we use originally came from Babylon and the meanings have developed and stayed popular through Greece and Rome to Egypt adapting in the Middle ages to today. Capricorn, half goat half fish, is a Babylonian God Suhur Mas. Scorpio changed during the Middle ages from a Scorpion (as seen in the Temple of Dendra) to a lobster to try to make sense of Scorpio being assigned to water, but then changed back.

Bindrunes and Runescripts

Runes are borrowed from the Heathen branch of the tree of Paganism, those that follow the Norse, Anglo-Saxon, and Vikings ways. Even though not strictly speaking Witchcraft they are still very popular with many traditions of the Craft.

Rune means secret thing or mystery. They are both a language and a mystical system, which has changed and developed over more than 2000 years. Runes could be as old as BCE 200, brought to England in about the 5th century, and used until they were banned in 1639 by the church as being too unchristian. They are perhaps now, more secret than ever. Runes certainly are a mystery; the runes can be read but the meaning behind the words has been lost over the centuries and the deeper knowledge died with the last rune master 500 years ago.

Nothing is as easy to carve or write as runes. With simple strokes to form each letter, you don't have to be an artist to produce runes. Runes have been used over a long period of time and over a very wide area of Europe and beyond, during this time variations have crept in. There are three main forms of Rune script, choose which feels right for you. I use the Elder Futhark, which has 24 characters which makes it easy to translate into Modern English. Elder Futhark is a pre Norse (the earlier version of the Vikings) version of runes that comes from the are that was to become Germany and was used in the 2nd to 8th century. These were very secret indeed known by only a few priests with only 350 inscriptions surviving. There are other rune scripts- Anglo-Saxons Runes can have up to 33 characters and was used in England from 500CE onwards. Younger Futhark are Scandinavia, having only 16 characters originating 800 CE by this period knowledge of writing had improved considerably with 6000

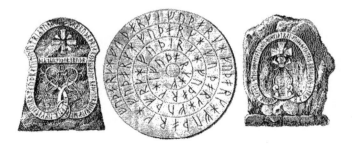

rune (Grave stones) stones still surviving.

But investigate all runescripts, one may be right for you. I feel Runes are invaluable in magic, although any script from any time or place can be used in the Craft; you will find a further selection at the end of this chapter.

How much do we really know about runes?

Not much is the answer.

One of the earliest examples of the prototype written rune language was found in 1811 in Negau in Slovenia. Along with 27 other helmets was a magnificent example of metal work dating back to the 1st century BCE, a long dead warrior had had the word *Harigast* inscribed on the helm. Was this the owners name or an offering to the Gods perhaps Odin? The inscription could have been written no later than BCE 50. The helmet was buried as the Romans invaded (we can only wonder why the owner never returned for the helmets).

That the inscription bore a Germanic name is very unusual and written in the Etruscan runic alphabet, which is situated in modern Tuscany, Italy. This may be the earliest contact of Germanic speakers with an alphabetic writing system, which would later develop into runes.

Etruscan 7th - 5th centuries BCE

The Runes spread to the Germanic tribes in one direction, as well as the Berbers of North Africa in the other. I was very excited on finding a runic type inscription in Tunisia attributed to the local Berber tribes.

Berber Runes

B   G   D   H   H   W   Z   Z   Z   T or D   Y

K   L   M   N   S   S   G   F   Q   R   S   T

The Legend of how the Runes came into being

We must thank Odin (although Odin is His Viking name, He has had many names prior to this) for the magic of the runes.

The stories were discovered in Iceland in collection know called the Poetic Edda, which was first written down in 1000-1300 CE but the stories contained within it are far older. The poem tell of how Odin hung Himself on Yddrasil, the world Ash tree for nine wind swept nights, without food or water. Wounded by His own spear, Odin an offering to Odin. Until in a Shamanic delirium He reached within Himself and found deep in His own unconscious the runes and their meanings.

Runes and their uses

Runes can be used in many ways, Runescripts or (writing), Bindrunes, single runes charms, placing magic onto an item such as jewelry, ritual tools and for divination. Runes were also placed, in the past on weapons and Rune Stones (Grave-Stone). Runes can be used in other ways but that is for you to be given by Odin at a more advanced stage of your work with runes.

Runescripts are the simplest; any phrase that you would like can be translated into runes. Runes can be written from left to right or from right to left or from top to bottom, however words feel right to you. You can place a full stop between words.or a colon:or a flying full stop or just run your words on haveyourwordsrunonuntilyoufin-ishwhatyouaresaying

Many people choose to have their name and the name of the one they love put onto the same ring or pendant, uniting them for all time. Perhaps your God or Goddesses name, worn on a ring or written and placed in a locket. Runes can also be chosen a few at a time as they appeal to you or are the energies that you need at this point in your life. Perhaps you may choose a rune of protection, perhaps with travel or Jera the rune of harvest, to start your year and a day of initiation. You can put the two together, your name first and then what you would like to come to pass. You then write the rune or runes that appeal to you three times, to emphasize and strengthen the power. If translating your magical name into runes, remember that many people can read them as easily as you can read this book. So either place them on an item such as a wand and then cover it, binding with cord or intersperse your magical name with other magical runes or if you do choose not to cover them, be very careful who sees your magical equipment. You can place runes onto any charm to add extra magic to it and to add a little of yourself to an item bought, like a pentagram. All charms should be empowered to bring them alive, runes are no exemption.

People sometimes have runes tattooed on to the skin so that they are always a part of themselves, as warriors would have dug into their skin to incise a rune of Algiz. But for temporary protection and less painfully, you can always draw the runes on to your skin with henna, traditionally woad would also have been used or very untraditionally a ballpoint pen.

Single Rune Charms Choose a rune that seems to be right for the situation that you need to resolve. Cut a slice of fruitwood, incise the rune and drill a hole in the top for a cord or metal ring. Empower the

Rune Charm as described below, on either a Wednesday for Odin (Wodin is another variant of His name, from which Wednesday takes its name) or on the day of the week dedicated to the God or Goddess ruling over that rune.

Bindrune are very similar but you select the runes that, when combined into a single rune pattern, sum up the idea that you wish to express; for example, to draw love to you, to increase health, wealth or for joy.

Runes in a Bindrune can be placed both back to front and upside down as in the Icelandic Bindrune earlier in the chapter. Be careful not to include runes that have meanings which will clash with each other.

Play with the runes until you find a pleasing combination. Inscribe them on paper, metal, vellum, parchment or wood using red ink or traditionally in your own blood. Women have the advantage here as they may use moon blood. Blood is a potent ink for runes; it animates the rune, bringing it to life making it a living enterty. Once more Wednesday is the best day to create your Bindrune.

Both Bindrunes and Runescripts are best if energised and then dedicated to your chosen deity. Norse, Viking, Anglo-Saxon or at a pinch Celtic deities are, of course, best as these are the traditional source of the runes.

How to make your own run Rune set

If you wish to use runes, you must make your own set, Odin tells us through the Poetic Edda.

'Do you know how to cut them, know how to stain them,
Know how to read them, how to understand?
Do you know how to evoke them, know how to send them,
Know how to offer, know how to ask?'

And with this, your journey into understanding the runes begins.

Odin's Questions

'Do you know how to cut them,'

Odin

Runes are straight lines to make them easy to carve into stone, bone, wood or stamped into metal. If using wood, Runes should be cut from a fruit-bearing tree. Knock on the tree and ask it to withdraw its life force from the branch that you have chosen. If any contrary signs are indicated, try again with another branch or a different tree. Leave an offering of mead to the tree and to Odin. A contrary sign may be any strange aggressive noise or feeling, a good sign would be the wind blowing gently or a good feeling. If a Crow or Raven calls, Odin's bird, the choice is yours, how you interpret it at the time.

On a Wednesday, cast a circle and call your quarters elementals that are so very similar to Norse Elves and fairy folk.

Call Odin and possibly your God and Goddess into your circle, as you see fit.

Cut the branch into slices or into staves and sand each rune.

'know how to stain them,'

First draw your runes with pencil, then carve the runes into the wood. Carving towards yourself drawing the runes into yourself. Runes are traditionally stained red and as mentioned above with your own blood or blood mixed with red ink or paint. You could even use a red felt tip pen and then a little blood painted on top with a fine paint brush. If you are not careful with your carving, you will have enough blood for all your runes.

Blow your energy into each rune while singing its name, at least three times each rune. Perhaps at this point do a visualization of each rune while you wait for the blood to dry. Make a note of your findings. Rub beeswax or olive oil into the runes to finish and seal them.

Ask Odin and/or your God and Goddess to bless your new rune set.

Close circle.

Know how to read them, how to understand?

Divination by Runes

Although knowing how to 'read' them may not apply to just reading the letters placed on an item but the deeper meaning of what each rune means magically and of divination with runes. Divination by runes is very controversial. But Tacitus writes of divination in 98BCE with in the Germanic Tribes. Knowing how runes themselves have passed down through the centuries, I can't see any reason to think that this form of prediction would go out of fashion.

Tacitus writes '*To divination and the casting of lots they pay attention above other people. Their method of casting lots is a simple one: they cut a branch from a fruit bearing tree and divide it into small pieces which they mark with certain distinctive signs and scatter at random onto a white cloth. Then, the priest of the community, if the lots are consulted publicly, or father of the family, if it is done privately, after invoking the Gods and with eyes raised to heaven, picks up three pieces, one at a time, and interprets them according to the signs previously marked on them*'

Tacitus gives us no idea as to whether the marks on the wood are runes but I personally see no harm in surmising that they were or that runes could be used in this way.

In Viking mythology the Norns guard the Urda's Well, so holy that none may drink.

The Norns or Weird Sisters, who decided fate

Allot their lives to the sons of men,

And assign to them their fate.

The three are Urda (weird fate- the Past), Verdandi (what is emerging- the Present) and Skuld (debt, necessity- the Future), pick three runes, three was a very magical number to the Norse, one for each of the Norns to see what can be seen.

'*Do you know how to evoke them,*'

To draw out the runes energies and to use them on this realm, write them or carve them into a charm, empower them as we did with each rune. Invoking the God or Goddess of the rune to empower them.

'*know how to send them,*'

This is work better left until you are more experienced.

'*Know how to offer*'

What you choose to offer is up to you. Your time, certainly your energy, perhaps some herbs or a small gift buried in the ground at the foot of an Ash tree. You have already offered your blood in the making of the runes, for you have no right to any other. Odin does tell us not to pledge more than we are willing to give, for it will be taken. With the Norse and Viking an Oath must never be taken if you have any doubt that you can for fill it. A promise to give anything to a God, have no doubt, is an Oath.

'*know how to ask?*'

Not on both knees imploring, nor standing and demanding, to call Odin or the God or Goddess of a particular rune, sing the name of the rune or runes three times, ask for help with the situation.

Understanding the runes is a long journey, I give you below some of my thoughts but sit and think on the runes and the poem, read the other two poems. Although you may find that it is best not to mix meanings of the runes from different poems, as this can get confusing. Try to understand the conclusions that I have come to. Then throw these away and find your own.

What follows is a list of the runes and an idea into their meaning. The runes shown are known as the Elder Futhark. These runes are the simplest to draw and carve, therefore has become the most well known.

The name comes from the first letters used in the first group of runes, this spells out FUTHARK, in the same way as Alpha and Beta are the first two letters in Greek and make the word alphabet.

In runic divination, some experts think that if a rune is drawn out of your pouch upside down, it has the opposite and therefore darker meaning to the rune. Some runes are the same both ways and their meaning does not change. But whether you choose to use the upside down method or just good and bad runes, the choice is yours. With runes there is not enough information to be categorical about anything.

I've also added the Anglo- Saxon Runic Poem as no poem survives for the Elder Futhark runes. This and two other poems on different rune scripts, are all the information that has survived on runes, as all of the Norse traditions were oral. As you read the poems you will notice that to say the least the poems are cryptic, in jokes and a play on words forms a large part of Viking poetry. If in five hundred years an interpretation of someone saying "Wicked man!" may end up as (putting the words into my Thesaurus I get) "Iniquitous gentleman!" or "Depraved bloke!", not what was originally intended. We have only scraps of information to work with, Rune means mystery and they are now an even deeper mystery than they have ever been. Today, we must return to Odin for the true meaning and power of each rune. That I think, is the true meaning of 'Know how to ask'.

Some Rune sets you may encounter have a blank rune; this was added in the 1980s and is not traditional.

I have taken the liberty of taking out the Christian references in the Anglo-Saxon poem and returning them to the old Viking Gods, as befits the Elder Futhark.

Runes

Freyr's Aett

Fehu F
Wealth is a comfort to all men;
yet must every man bestow it freely,

515

if he wish to gain honour in the sight of Odin.

Cattle – the shape of the rune depicts the horns of cattle.

How many head of cattle you owned indicated your wealth and status within the tribe. This Rune draws increased wealth or property and will also protect your valuables and increases sexual energy and vitality. The Head of the household would gave gifts at Yule to his friends and relations, so be generous if you have been fortunate with this rune.

A Rune of God Frey.

Uruz U
The aurochs is proud and has great horns;
it is a very savage beast and fights with its horns;
a great ranger of the moors, it is a creature of mettle.

Auroch- a form of extinct wild Ox, domesticating this beast was not possible, for it had great strength and endurance. It was said to be the size of a small elephant. To kill this animal took great strength, by the killing, the warrior then added the might of the heroic Auroch to his own. The great horns were proudly hung on the walls and mounted with silver as drinking horns and were shown off at banquets to mark manhood and pride in accomplishments.

Boldness, masculine energy and freedom are the attributes of this rune. It is the rune of untamed potential. This rune adds energy for those weak due to illness.

Thurisaz TH
The thorn is exceedingly sharp,
an evil thing for any knight to touch,
uncommonly severe on all who sit among them.

Thorn - This rune has a strong energy with in, a raw energy. This Rune was thought to have the power to draw demons from the underworld. As a thorn, which this rune resembles, on the stem of a beautiful rose, beware the barb and the blood it draws. This rune is like a step in the dark, in a rune reading it donates situations over which you have little or no control. If you fall into thorns by accident it can be very painful, falling into debt or problems of any kind are like being surrounded by thorns it is difficult to find your way out.

Boundary fences were protected by growing thorny bushes around them, if you surround yourself with thorns you stand protected. But a boundary of thorns can keep away friends as well as enemies and then the thorns are truly sharp.

Ansuz A
The mouth is the source of all language,
a pillar of wisdom and a comfort to wise men,
a blessing and a joy to every knight.

Communication- Use this rune for anything connected with education and communication: teaching, learning, negotiations, public speaking, truth, wisdom or writing. Blessing and naming are spells that are spoken using breath to form and place magic with in. The Heathens valued stories and poetry above all other arts; this rune to them would have a very high value.

Inspiration and all forms of art come under the influence of this rune.

Raido R
Riding seems easy to every warrior while he is indoors
and very courageous to him who traverses the
high-roads on the back of a stout horse.

Riding- This rune tells us to stop planning and put our plans into action, literally to get off our bum and get on with the job.

Excellent for protection while travelling, including anything associated with transport- luggage, even cars or flying these days.

517

Although the deeper meaning of this rune is the journey that we make of life, finally into death. Good to place on a loved one on their final journey.

Kenaz K

The torch is known to every living
man by its pale, bright flame;
it always burns where princes sit within.

Torch- A light in the darkness. This rune can be a flame, a gentle fire of the hearth, a fire of transformation or a light of honor. Use this rune in visualization, carrying Kenaz into the darkness. If the way ahead seems unclear or you need to see clearly your thoughts and understand the knowledge that you need to right a situation, this is the rune.

Gebo G

Generosity brings credit and honor,
which support one's dignity;
it furnishes help and subsistence to
all broken men who are devoid of aught else.

Gift- Partnership, a gift from the Gods, a chieftain to his loyal band or a gift from you to the Gods. This rune is a source of great harmony in all partnerships or relationships, both business and love, strengthening them. This rune possibly survives as the kiss on the bottom of a letter, a gift to a loved one.

If you have nothing else to give, give kind words.

Wunjo W

*Bliss he enjoys who knows not suffering, sorrow nor anxiety,
and has prosperity and happiness and a good enough house.*

Bliss- positive progress in all endeavors. Especially good in love or career matters, in fact with any undertaking.

This rune seems to say that money <u>does</u> bring happiness, comfort and pleasure. Personally, I think without money, happiness flies out the window, bringing tension and stress. In Viking times food, home, family and your place within the tribe were all that was needed.

Be happy with whatever you do have, not wasting time envying others.

A rune of prosperity.

Hiemdall's Aett
Hagalaz H

*Hail is the whitest of grain;
it is whirled from the vault of heaven and is tossed
about by gusts of wind and then it melts into water.*

Hail – Nature at Her most destructive, a rune of Winter.

A time of testing, trial, the Gods will be done; a journey into the darkside of oneself. It represents delays and limitations. But as it says in the poem, even hail melts into life giving water. Spring, always follows Winter, even though it can seem interminable, before you see the first green shoots.

Only use this rune in a Bindrune when you are sure you can go no lower and it is time for the waters to melt.

Nauthiz N

*Trouble is oppressive to the heart;
yet often it proves a source of help and
salvation to the children of men,
to everyone who heeds it betimes.*

Need- This rune to me, always looks as if it is crossed out, the opposite of Isa steadfastness. It may also represent a 'need fire' a fire started by rubbing two sticks together. All other fires must be put out for a 'need fire' to work. What do you 'need', not want. Heed the warnings of this rune; look for the reasons and cause of your problems. You learn by over coming problems. To live in bliss, teaches you nothing.

It is a rune of hardship, again not one to use deliberately in a Bindrune.

Isa I

Ice is very cold and immeasurably slippery;
it glistens as clear as glass and most like to gems;
it is a floor wrought by the frost, fair to look upon.

Ice- Immobility, peace, conservation, beauty and solitude. But things that are beautiful may be very dangerous and strong. A glacier is made from flowing water but with natures help becomes solid and invincible. Sometimes we stand too long and become frozen.

This is a very useful rune in a script or Bindrune. Isa will hold a situation at its current position, including the situations that the other runes in the script are helping to promote. Although, to be truthful it is impossible to do a Bindrune without one!

Jera J

Summer is a joy to men, when The Mighty All Father,
suffers the earth to bring forth shining fruits
for rich and poor alike.

Plenty- Fruitfulness. As well as pillaging the Heathens were great farmers, but farming is hard work. Even though Odin places fruit on the trees, it still needs to be planted, gathered and even possibly made into alcohol. Wherever a positive result is needed in return for money, time or trouble this rune will be of great help. The result can be financial, or a promotion but you will reap your harvest. But summer is also enjoyable don't forget to enjoy life as it passes.

Eihwaz E

The yew is a tree with rough bark,
hard and fast in the earth, supported by its roots,
a guardian of flame and a joy upon an estate.

Yew- Yew is both a tree of life and of death, it will grow to a great age, five thousand years, if its roots are strong. But its needles are poisonous and Yew gives off a deadly miasma under the heat of the Sun. Shaman would sometimes sit under a Yew tree on a hot day breathing in the energy to journey to the other world, a dangerous pastime.

The best Bows are made from the flexible but strong Yew. The stave of the bow is especially cut to combine the energies of the sapwood just under the bark, this is flexibly, and the heartwood this is hard and tough. A bow and arrows are good defense and so with this rune. The Yew was planted in graveyards not only for the practical reasons, poisonous to sheep and good for bows. But it was hoped that its seeming immortality would be transferred to the bones and ashes of loved ones.

A Yew tree is an evergreen, providing hope at midwinter when all around is bleak and appears dead, a promise of Spring to come.

Yew will bend but not break and so with this rune, which is a rune of strength, defense, wisdom, protection and banishing.

Perthro P

Perthro is a source of recreation and
amusement to the great, where warriors
sit blithely together in the banqueting-hall.

Possibly a gaming cup on it's side throwing the dice of life – not much is known of this rune and its energies but it seems a rune of strategy and chance. By whether you win or lose, trust to powers greater than yourself. Is it a step in the dark? An initiation is a step in the dark. With this rune you give yourself over to Fate.

Algiz Z

The Elk-sedge is mostly to be found in a marsh;
it grows in the water and makes a ghastly wound,
covering with blood every warrior who touches it.

Protection- As you can see from the Icelandic Bindrune Charm earlier in this chapter, this is an excellent Rune for protection. Elk-Sedge has leaves that are blade shaped, in the 'Doctrine of Signatures' this makes it protective and may account for the reference to blood in the poem. In fact in herbal lore Sedge, Calamus or Sweet Flag to give some of its other names, is protective the world over and although sweet smelling is very poisonous. It gives off a great deal of heat when in flower. The rune also resembles the horns of an elk and Frey fights with a single Elk antler at Ragnarok, the end or change of the world, in replacement for his sword. This Rune also shows itself in the CND badge as a symbol of protection.

This symbol is far older than the Elder Futhark and can be found in the Etruscan scripts, during this time it has built up a strong magical energy. This is a rune of great power and is the rune I personally reach for when feeling the need for protection.

The arms of this Rune reach up to your Gods and Goddesses for protection, as a child reaches for its mother.

This rune protects from both evil thoughts and deeds.

Sowulo S

The sun is ever a joy in the hopes of seafarers
when they journey away over the fishes' bath,
until the courser of the deep bears them to land.

Sun- This Rune I always feel, has great power strong and true as the

Sun and Baldur its guardian. It promotes health, physical strength, clear thinking and self-confidence. The Rune is shaped like a flash of inspiration. If you cross two of these runes, you have a swastika mentioned earlier in this chapter, it was the Vikings sigil of good luck and of course a Sun symbol.

This Rune also, of course, protects with travel over water.

Tyr's Aett

Teiwaz T

Tyr is a guiding star; well does it keep faith with princes;
it is ever on its course over the mists of night and never fails.

Justice- Warrior God Tyr. Tyr is also the Northern Star, guiding travelers across uncharted waters. This is a Rune of the warrior, both on the Earthly plane and on the Astral. Tyr gave His sword hand to protect the Viking Gods, by placing His hand in the wolf Fenrir's mouth while they bound him. He was the God that presided over the halls of justice, sometimes this was dealt with by law and sometimes by single combat, both protagonists knowing that Tyr would give strength to the just. A rune of struggle and of overcoming adversity, fighting for justice but always with honor.

Tyr's sword of justice hangs over your head in the using of this rune. Nothing will happen to you if your cause is just, but never call upon Tyr if you are not an honorable person.

Berkana B

The poplar bears no fruit; yet without seed it
brings forth suckers, for it is generated from its leaves.
Splendid are its branches and gloriously adorned
its lofty crown which reaches to the skies.

There are two species of Poplar tree Black and White, to which does our enigmatic poet allude?

The Black Poplar is the tallest growing to 30 meters and is therefore one of the tallest trees with a ' *lofty crown'*. In Winter its silhouette, with its slight lean and lower branches that sweep to the floor and the turning upwards, stands against the skyline proudly and distinctively. Black Poplars are either male or female needing both in close proximity to bring forth seed, male catkins appear in March and are red long and thick, with female catkins lime green and fluffy appearing in June.

The White Poplar tree most distinctive feature are the under side of the leaves which are covered in a white curly down that shimmer in the Sun light and when the wind blows the leaves rustle and speak to those with ears to hear, it was called the Whispering Tree. The White Poplar too has long and thick catkins.

As with the poem both forms of Poplar tree's seeds are not easily propagated, it sends out suckers to form new trees. In this the tree is very successful and is a bane to modern gardeners. Poplars grow best near water, and will send out its roots over long distances to reach its needs. The wood for both types of Poplar was used for shields, oars and paddles being very light weight. But a shield in battle must not only protect you from blows but from magic and this wood is known to do that. It also protects from fire, as it is slow burning not one to be used on the hearth.

So what do we learn from the Poplar tree, as to the nature of this rune?

The Poplar tree in Ancient Greece was a tree of death but the runes do not come from Greece. But out of death new life is formed and the poem does speak of birth and propagation. The later rune poem refers to Birch rather than Poplar and Birch is another tree meaning birth and growth. Birch trees are sacred to Frigga and Freya who are Viking Goddesses and Eostra an Anglo-Saxon Goddess, all are Goddesses of fertility. For me, both Poplar trees within the context of this poem have the same meaning- B for birth. Fertility meant as many children, animals and wealth as possible, with all this came honor and possibly a loft crown?

Growth

Ehwaz E

The horse is a joy to princes in the presence of warriors.
A steed in the pride of its hoofs, when rich men on
horseback bandy words about it; and it is ever a
source of comfort to the restless.

Movement- Due to its speed and beauty, a horse has always been a sacred animal and a symbol of power and the Sun. A horse, is a status symbol and lifts you above the crowd and this rune moves you on to new and better house, new job or new love. It is a good rune to use when Astral journeying, draw it upon yourself or carry the rune. Of course it is also good for all modes of travel, whether by land, sea or even air. Odin rode across the skies in an eight legged horse, Sleipnir

Mannaz M

The joyous man is dear to his kinsmen;
yet every man is doomed to fail his fellow,
since Odin by his decree will commit the
vile carrion to the earth.

The Self- You, how you react with your family, your friends or mankind. This rune brings change within. Mannaz is the primal waters of life, duty, responsibility and death. No one is perfect, we all make mistakes and it is having the courage to admit and put right our blunder that the honor is found. But it is very true that if you are happy, you are better liked than a sullen person. Happiness breeds happiness and misery breeds misery, but even a happy person and a joy to all must bring sadness with their death. This rune is very helpful in bringing new attitudes into your life and giving up old habits.

Live, laugh and help where you can for tomorrow we all must die.

Laguz L

The ocean seems interminable to men,
if they venture on the rolling bark
and the waves of the sea terrify them
and the courser of the deep heed not its bridle.

Flow- Water brought wealth with trade and fishing, but it brought loss as well, adventure and death; water was always respected. Water and emotion is inevitably linked, as with West in our circle, the water bringing with it love, fertility, sensitivity and widening your psychic ability. Emotion can sweep you away like a tide, if you allow it. Deep mysteries of the moon and the Well of the three Norns, are interlinked with this rune.

Here the water is frightening and deep, the waves are high and life is out of control. Bring it to a safe harbor with this rune.

Inguz NG

Ing was first seen by men among
the East-Danes, till, followed by his wagon,
he departed eastwards over the waves.
So the Heardingas (a tribe of tough guys) named the hero.

Fertility- Ing (earlier probably the God Frey) is the Anglo-Saxon God of Fertility to whom many English Kings claimed descent. This rune symbolizes Ing's seed, the seed of new beginnings; it could be an idea, a project or a child. The rune Inguz bears a great similarity to the twisted strands of DNA but also to a seed that is planted in the Earth sending out both roots and shoots. This rune is a force for good, a happy hearth and home.

Dagaz D

Day, the glorious light of the Sun,
is sent by the Lord Odin;
it is beloved of men, a source of hope and

happiness to rich and poor, and of service to all.

Daybreak- dawn coming up after a long dark night. In the Viking homeland night lasts for six months and so to see the Sun once more after so long was indeed a hope and a change for the good. A Viking day went from Sundown to Sundown, through the safe day to the mystery of night. This rune looks almost to be one side for night and one side for day or one side for life, another death. Life was hard until very recently; death was a constant companion, of friends, children and animals on which all depended. War was fought with abandon, those who died a hero's death would go to the Halls of Odin and Freya to fight all day, drink and make love all night, until the day of Ragnorock when they would fight shoulder to shoulder with their Gods.

An excellent rune to change a situation, from dark to light.

Othila O
An estate is very dear to every man,
if he can enjoy there in his house
whatever is right and proper in constant prosperity.

Inherited Land- Nobility, tradition, values and family.

The shape of this rune seems to indicate a sacred enclosure. You are owned by the land, you do not own the land; you are only its guardian.

If life is happy at home, nothing else is important.

A Ceremony of Dedication of your Amulet or Talisman

Talismans and amulets work best if dedicated to your God and Goddess.

Do this on the phase of the moon that matches the type of charm you wish to dedicate.

Have ready: - Your talisman or amulet

- Some salt, incense, a red candle, water

- A charcoal block

Cast circle with your finger or Athame
Draw up cone of power
Draw pentagram in the North, with your finger or Athame
Call Elemental Quarters.
Purify Elements
Chant
Anoint
Call down the Moon

The first part of the dedication is for a commercially bought Talisman, Amulet or Charm, not one made by yourself or any Witch who you trust. Turn to the

North

Sprinkle a little salt on your charm as you say

"Element of Earth, cleanse this charm, let nothing impure remain there in."

West

Sprinkle a little water on your charm as you say

"Element of Water, cleanse this charm, let nothing impure remain there in."

South

Wave the charm through the Red candle as you say

"Element of Fire, cleanse this charm, let nothing impure remain there in."

East

Wave the charm through the incense as you say

"Element of Air, cleanse this charm, let nothing impure remain there in."

Start here if this is a non-commercial charm.

Hold the charm high to your Goddess

"I call to you Maiden, Mother and wise one Crone,
Place within this ... ... (name of charm) ... ... Your power,

Enliven and waken this charm of... (name the powers that the charm has)....

Bring these powers into my life.

Lady of Enchantment and Mystery, my thanks."

Dab with anointing oil if it will not harm your charm.

North

Sprinkle a little salt on your charm as you say:-

"Element of Earth, imbue this charm with your protection."

East

Wave the charm through the incense as you say

"Element of Air, imbue this charm with understanding."

South

Wave the charm through the Red candle as you say

"Element of Fire, imbue this charm with your energy."

West

Sprinkle a little water on your charm as you say

"Element of Water, imbue this charm with the emotion of happiness."

Place the charm to your breast and close your eyes, bonding with it.

"Thou art mine! I am thine! We are one!"

Place the charm on your Athame or any consecrated ritual tool, if you have any.

Add anything you wish to say.

"SO MOTE IT BE!!! NINE TIMES ETERNAL!!!"

If this is a Full Moon finish any other spell work that you wish to do.

Bless cakes and wine.

Place on your charm, before closing circle.

Close circle in the normal way.

Place remaining cakes and wine on the Earth.

529

With this your ceremony is done.

May you wear your talisman or amulet in health
And may luck and love always be with you.

Blessed be.

Other Scripts you can use in magic

When making scripts for spells, a mystic language helps concentration and adds power to the work. Any script will is fine, you don't have to use runes, use whichever script appeals to you most. Here are some to start you off.

Cuneiform script is one of the earliest known forms of writing, created by the Sumerians. It was written in wet clay with the corner of a cube or triangular stick, from left to right. They baked clay tablets that they wished to keep and recycled their shopping lists.

Cuniform Script

Discovered in the ruins of a Syrian temple in Ras Shamara, this alphabet dates from 1,400 BC

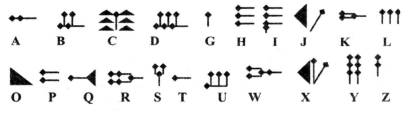

Numbers

Hieroglyphics (Ancient Egyptian). There are over 2000 picture symbols representing either a letter or a word Egyptian Hieroglyphics. The Egyptian began to formulate their elaborate picture writing BCE 3000. A picture of a woman may represent just that the word 'woman' but what is she doing, is she raising her arms in salutation to the God, then she is preying or is she on her knees, then she is in mourning. Egyptian Hieroglyphics are written either way or up or down or left to right or right to left, you read Hieroglyphics from the direction the heads face. Egyptian Hieroglyphic is written in a continuos stream no space between the words and have no punctuation.

The Witches' Alphabet or Theban Script

Also known as the Alphabet of Honorius, the Witches' Alphabet, *etc.* It is referred to the Latin alphabet and written left to right (the last character, referred to the Greek Omega, is not generally used as a

The Witches' Alphabet or Theban Script

letter, rather as a period or separator). This script was popularised by Agrippa's *De Occulta Philosophia* (it appears in lib. III cap. XXIX, "De characteribus et sigillis sprituum"), although it may have appeared in earlier works such as the *Polygraphia* of Trithemius. The alphabet is traditionally ascribed to one 'Honorius the Theban', probably the author of the *Liber Juratus* (the Sworn Book of Honorios), a medieval work on Ceremonial magic.

Passing the River described by Heinrich Cornelius Agrippa in his Third Book of Occult Philosophy 1513. It is derived from the Hebrew Alphabet. The name may refer to crossing of the Euphrates by the Jews on their return from Babylon to rebuild the Temple (some old witchcraft tools may be inscribed with this script).

Passing the River

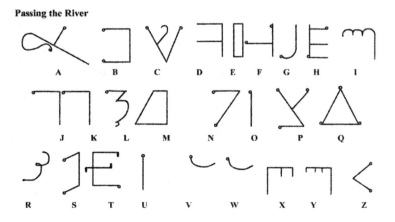

Celestial or Angelic Script (Ceremonial Magic)

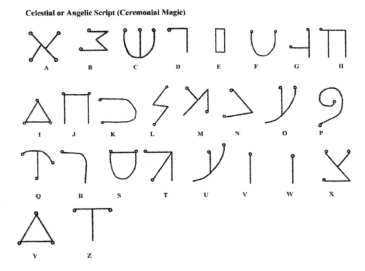

Celestial or Angelic Script (Ceremonial Magic)

Although I don't work personally with Angels in Witchcraft, many do.

The Characters of Celestial Writing, the writing called Malachim and the writing called Passing of the River all appeared in *De Occulta Philosophia* lib. III cap. XXX, 'Alius characterizandi modus a cabalistis traditus', and are referred to the Hebrew alphabet. They do not include distinct final forms for any letters, although Malachim has a variant form of Samekh that may correspond to the otherwise unknown 'Samekh final' alluded to in some works on Magic. Malachim is also called 'Angelic' or 'Regal' (from Heb., MLKIM, 'Kings') by Agrippa.

The Alphabet of Daggers or Athames

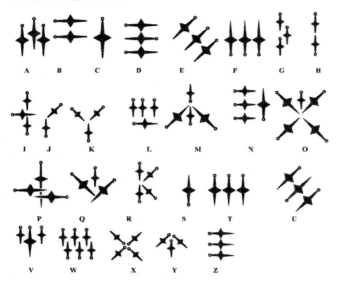

The Alphabet of Daggers

This is a magical alphabet, which appears in Aleister Crowley's *The Vision and the Voice*. It corresponds to the letters of the English alphabet

Exercise- Write your name in Runes and look at the meaning of each letter. If you have "bad" runes this only tells us to look at what we can change about ourselves.

CHAPTER 11

Esbats and Spells

An Esbat (possibly from Old French s'esbattre – 'to frolic') is a Fullmoon ritual, for us a time to cast magic.

An Esbat opens and closes as a Sabbat ritual does, but the content changes to spell work, rather than a celebration of the season.

Now you are well practiced by having worked your Sabbats, it is now time to progress on to Esbats and spell casting, but only if you feel prepared.

Never rush in magic; never progress until you are ready.

Everyone can learn to cast spells, but some do have a natural aptitude for it. Some people are natural musicians, so it is hardly strange that some will have a greater ease at spell casting than others. But whether your forte is spell casting, tarot or writing rituals, you will have a talent, which is valuable. If the Goddess hasn't called you, you would not be reading this book.

Magic was born when humans first developed from apes. One of their first acts was to draw on the walls of our caves the animals that we wished to kill in the hunt. You see our ancestors shooting arrows or attacking with spears, in these paintings they always win their animal and there are always plenty of animals to kill. This type of spell is called sympathetic magic; you project what you wish to see happen. This brought the early humans much needed food for the tribe and honored the animals to be killed, wishing them rebirth, as life and death are ever repeating circles.

With us, the coven will gather at the fullmoon to perform all the spells that have been asked of individual members over the last month. Over tea and biscuits or a glass of wine before circle or during the teaching nights, we discuss how each spell is devised. Whether it will be a Spell Bag, a Verbal Incantation or an amulet. All members evaluate each problem and the best way decided on. If it is a teaching coven, as many types of spell as possible will be covered, to allow all a chance to experience and participate in every form of spell work. There is nothing frightening in a Witchcraft circle.

Oh goodie Spell work! But do we have to bother with all this casting circle?

Well actually, yes.

A circle holds in the power that you are creating, as it holds in the heat of the candles that you lit for the Sabbats. It cuts the area that you are working in, out of time and space, taking it to another dimension were magic happens.

Do we have to do Sabbats as well as the Esbats?

If you want to be a Witch, you must work with the Goddess and God and celebrate the seasons with them. Doesn't your Mum and Dad want you over for Christmas? Well it's like that with the God and Goddess, if they are going to help you with your magic they want to see that you are serious about what you are doing. Although within most Sabbats there is a spell hidden, only for you, to advance you on your journey, sometimes it's a spell for Love, Work or to take away you problems, as with Samhain. Possibly we learn more at Sabbats about magic than we do at Esbats. So don't be so quick to dismiss Sabbats as not being of interest.

Esbats

Esbats are the time to see how the knowledge of the herbs, oils, gems and charms, come together. How they combine crafting into spells, to heal and protect the community.

Three spells at most should be cast, but sometimes, the need outweighs practicability. But always be sure to keep it to an uneven number of spells, the numbers of magic. Between each spell chant and circle to change the psychic energy, from one spell to the next. Any chant will do for this, something about changing would be a nice idea, try your hand at writing a chant. Repeat the chant as many times as you feel you need but at least three, rhyming

Change and turn, change and turn,
From this magic may I learn,
Power of dark, power of light,
Make my magic flow tonight!

or not as you choose. Remember a bad rhyme is not a bad spell.

Be very sure that you want the spell to work, for all spells DO work, but think carefully, sometimes you may not want the spell when you have it.

Spells, what are they?

Spells change the web of life, how each strand reacts and interweaves with every other. Magic is the same the world over, we may wave our hands that way, and the Shaman in Peru may wave his hands this way but the energy that both tap into is always the same, no matter through which God or Goddess it is channeled.

Spells cause change to occur, by the output of your energy, changing the world around you. Magic is using nature, and is a natural act. Tapping into a science that at the moment we have no name for, for which we only know the answers not the questions. It works, but we cannot explain how. Magic changes the probability of an outcome of a subject; will you get the job? Will you find love? Will the health problem go? Yes, it will. But, can I grow my hair by a foot in a month? Can I loose three stone in weight by next Wednesday? No. Only if your are living in a magical TV program and believe it or not that is not real life. Films are fun, I am the first in the queue to see them, but they aren't real, enjoy and forget; they are not a learning experience. Unfortunately young girls are phone me each week asking for these spells to be done. Magic can and does work wonders, when a woman holds her child and you know that your magic helped, it is a wonderful feeling but even magic will not work if she has no man in her life. It would be wonderful to be able to light the fire down the forest with a click of my finger but it does not happen, and no other witch that can do it either! Just in case you are about to ask. I'll just add I have been privileged to see some wonderful sight of natural magic down the forest. My dream is that perhaps one day; I may find the way to tap into that magic.

The press like to brand us as White Witches, because it makes them feel more comfortable. In reality there is no color to magic, no good or bad, like electricity it will run an incubator or an electric chair. Magic will, on the instigator's behalf, do the deed asked. Note, on the instigators behalf, part of you is in all magic that you do. All magic is on your record when, at the end of all time you answer to Her upstairs, as I affectionately call my Goddess. Will you have done your best at all times? If you keep that in mind, you will choose wisely how to handle any situation.

Surely, spells are just all psychological?

Spells not only have a magical aspect to them but also a psychological one. By psychological, a modern day term, I mean using the hidden part of the brain, the part that can heal if it chooses, the part that under hypnosis can allow if it chooses, operations with out anaesthetic. This dark side of the brain that access to is denied by ordinary means, that magic can influence and use, in the hope of healing the spirit.

'Getting the brain to cure itself' isn't that easy. Chemical companies run vast expensive tests with their new drugs and sugar pills to be sure that their new drugs work. If placebos worked every time, then these tests would be useless. Getting access to this healing area of the brain is not as easy as people dismissively believe. Yes, there is a psychological element to spells. Do not be so quick however, to dismiss the entire spell as 'just psychological'. There is far more to a spell than that. How, for instance would 'just psychological', affect a promotion or love?

"Ah, that's coincidence" I hear.

But when it happens time and time again, how long can you shout coincidence. The Coven have cast spells for jobs, return of stolen property and healing for those that could never have known that the spell was working its magic around them. So how can coincidence or 'just psychological' affect an object? When you have cast spells for so many years and seen so many come to pass, you to will be left with only one conclusion.

Shaman on Lake Titicaca doing a spell for good health

So, you want to do a spell?

What do you want to do this spell for? Let's take a love spell. Is it for a partner in life or just in general? Let us assume a new partner. Is there a time limit to your work, if the spell did not work right away would this mean it had not worked at all? Have you an eye on the man or woman down the street? Do you want he/she to fall head over heels in love, blinded by the spell? Loving someone they would never have looked at? If after you have done this spell for this super -person, you decide they were not what you wanted after all, how then do you make them fall out of love with you?

You can't play with other people's emotions so readily.

Have I the right to do that? A Pagan is a believer in the old Gods and does no magic and therefore takes no responsibility but a Witch takes the responsibility into her or his own hands, and at the end of the day must answer to the Crone Goddess herself for their use of the powers.

So, how do we tackle this problem? Many books will tell you that you don't interfere with other people's lives. Is this right? Remember that in magic, what you do both takes and gives to you, the Witch, the user of the magic.

The way to tackle a spell like this would be to do a general love spell around you, which will remove their shyness, and remove obstacles (but not their wife or husband!). As a side effect they will be more loveable in all ways, getting on better with their Mum, The Boss and that special person down the road.

Remember that your spiritual advancement depends on how you handle spells. Use your judgement, the same judgement that you would apply to any situation in any aspect of life. Think the problem through, see where it takes you and only then act.

Can heal with magic?

Even great illnesses like Cancer can be cured and certainly helped by magic. However, never encourage the patient to rely on you to cure the illness. Always insist that they carry on with medical help. Teach them visualization. How to visualize tiny white knights or perhaps nanobots, a type of futuristic minute robot that can fix problems from inside the body, whichever the patient would understand and relate to most. See them cutting away the problem or healing the area, whichever is needed. In some hospitals now they are teaching self-hypnosis to burns patients, visualizing cool grass and seeing their skin without harm. This has done wonders, it cools the skin so that the burns do not damage the skin as deeply as they may have done, it also helps with shock, as in many cases this is what the patient dies from. Perhaps as well as the visualization, a spell bag that the patient can hang on to and rub when they feel afraid.

As a generalization, men's ability very often lies with healing but they have difficulty with visualization; women can develop their innate intuition and become talented psychics.

Yes, you can do spells for yourself.

I have heard some people say that to do spells for yourself is black magic. This is a hang over from Christian times, when you were not allowed to pray for yourself, as this was thought to be selfish. But in my opinion you must practice on yourself, before letting loose on others.

Yes, you can do money spells.

I have often done spells to attract money, running a business in any day and age is a headache. But with a money spell you will only acquire enough money to cope with your problem, never enough to bank. Don't waste your magic and energy on doing the lottery, there are too many witches pulling in too many directions. I know!

Be precise with your spell.

Magic will take the shortest route possible for a spell to reach its goal. Don't do a money spell without a way for it to come to you, preferably - the spell works best through how you earn your living. If you don't, the easiest way may be to bump off your favorite aunt, leaving you all her money. Don't take that chance. One spell I would not do is a slimming spell, "I want to be slimmer" – you get Diabetes, "I want to loss weight" you lose a leg and yes, you do weigh less but do you want to! I pondered this for sometime, as I am chubbier than I would like to be. I decided to do a Body Balancing spell. Nothing I thought could go wrong. My doctor decided to test me for a Thyroid problem, guess what; yes, perfectly balanced Thyroid, low choles-terol and high energy levels! But still no slimmer.

Is there a payment demanded by Fate?

Some people feel that if you ask for a spell, that you must expect to lose something. I have not found this to be the case; with all the spells my Coven does, we would not have a bowl to "wee wee" in. Sabbats are how you pay, by giving energy to the Goddesses and Gods; you can't take without giving. During the last two millenniums when only the Christian's God was recognized, he was all powerful. Now his millennia has drawn to a close, the time of the old Gods and Goddesses began to emerge from the darkness of neglect, as more and more people began to remember Them, their light grows stronger.

Time Limit
Place a time with in which you wish the spell to come about or add a little ginger to make sure the spell doesn't take too long.

For some spells the answer is no.

Charging money for a spell.
By all Witchcraft traditions, you are not allowed to charge for spells, over and above a fair price for spell components. Nor are you allowed to charge for training your coven, although this takes up a lot of time, it is done for love. You will however be expected, if you are lucky enough to join a coven, to bring wine, food and candles and not let all the expenses fall on the HP and HPs or you may be asked for a small donation to cover this.

Energy needed for a spell is like the energy of casting a circle.
When you gather together the components of spells, the words, at the right time of the month (see below), cast circle, call quarters, all set. But what do you do? It's all right to say the words, wave your arms about, but there must be more to it? There is, you must draw out of yourself the same energy that you used to cast circle and throw it at the spell. Think of the energy that you are creating as a whirlpool if you like. Allowing the power to build, circling round you, until the air almost begins to crackle with the energy you have produced and as it reaches it peak (and no one but you will know when) throw the power you have created at the problem. This is where, in a coven

situation, a group mind comes into play. All must feel the energy and know the point to throw the spell. If it is a verbal spell the spell is sent off with a shout or into the components that you have gathered if it is a spell bag or any similar type of spell. As a child didn't your mother always tell you never to point, in so doing you are directing energy at the individual, and therefore casting magic. Every spell that you do must have the same amount of energy thrown at it; this can be very tiring. This is why only three spells must be done on any one evening. We do break this rule all too often but not until you are more practiced.

Group Mind

This is the energy of the circle. The aim of a Coven is to build a group mind. It allows, when in circle and spell work is to be done, everyone to operate as a single unit. As well as ritual, this is achieved with parties, outings, in short being good friends. When coveners understand each other without the need for words, complete concentration on the spell is achieved. The sum of the whole is greater and stronger than the individuals within. When all have reached initiation, this is a very powerful entity, enabling concentration on deep magics.

Visualization

We have practiced visualization, as a way to enter the Astral plain, now we use the same technique to visualize the out come of the spell. In your minds eye, see your patient walking or your friend happily skipping through a field with their new love. Exaggerate the visualization, no hesitant steps but winning a marathon. A visualization of a sickly sweet over the top love film scenario for our sad and lonely friend; will bring about the desired outcome.

Which spell to use.

A Spell should be chosen for the type of people to receive them. Many will benefit from a tangible spell like a spellbag, as they can gain comfort from its presence and know that you have set the spell in motion. Sometimes a verbal spell is all that is needed, as they may not wish to be in possession of anything that might be found by an unsympathetic spouse. You must choose which spell will fit the situation best.

Some People get Addicted

Some people get addicted to spells; I usually limit the number that I do for each person. If it's an on going illness, that is different matter but if they ask for a love spell, then a new job, then a new home, the person is asking you to take control of their life, you can't do that. They must live life themselves and make their own decisions. You need to weigh up the person and decide, is this spell necessary or not. I limit to one spell every 6 months or only three spells and no more.

Spells don't have to be formal

They can be fun, if you are doing a spell to bring happiness into someone's life you can stand around slowly saying boring words. You need to put a bit of go into it, sing, and dance or make up a silly poem and like my **very** bad rhyme!

"Earth, Air, Fire and Water,

Make this spell do what it ought ta!"

The more the coven laughs with this type of spell the better the universe knows what is wanted.

Stubborn spells

If it is a very stubborn problem you may choose to do a three-part spell, repeating every month on the fullmoon the same spell, done in the same way.

You're shouting to the Universe that something needs to be done.

You're shouting to the Universe that something needs to be done.

You're shouting to the Universe that something needs to be done.

Energy of the Spell

Your right (or your leading hand if you are a lefty) hand is your projecting magic hand, your left is your drawing in magic hand. So to cast a spell you would use your right hand to throw energy down through your fingers and any tool you may be using, into the world. Use your left hand to draw into yourself (remember not to take pain-see healing), for example to take energy from the Earth or a crystal.

Something of the person for whom the spell is to be done can be included in the spell, to strengthen it; this can be a lock of hair, or a possession that is carried every day but nothing expensive. Though I have not found it necessary to always use this.

Then its just a matter of reaching into the heart of the Universe grabbing some energy tying it into a knot and throwing the knot at the problem. This sounds complicated, but it isn't. Just focus your energy down through any tool you are using, this can be your finger, wand or Athame according to the type of spell, while concentrating on the person and problem. The Universe and your Goddess will do the rest.

The Timing of Spells

Spellwork should, wherever possible, be performed on the fullmoon. If you must work a week after or before, it is better to adapt your spells to suit. Make a healing spell that you intended to do on the fullmoon, to an increase of health spell, if you find yourself unable to work on the fullmoon and only able to work before on a waxing (increasing) moon. Your spell of healing should be changed to one of diminishing pain or ill health, if you are forced through circumstance to work on a waning moon (decreasing moon). The tides of magic are like the tides of the sea, which the moon also influences. You must catch the right tide or your spell won't travel anywhere.

There are complicated tables of when to do spells on what month, day and time but this comes again from Ceremonial Magic not from Witchcraft, I have always kept only to the Waxing, Full and Waning moon, with 95% of my spells coming to fruition. So I see no point in waiting till a month of Venus or getting up at 3am to do a spell when 11pm tonight will do just as well. As long as I angle the spell to be cast, to the right phase of the moon, the spell will work

Phases if the Moon

*A **Waxing moon**-* Spells to grow in strength- health, animals and plants- work with the Maiden. Plant all vegetables that grow above the ground.

Fine seeds then sow,
Whilst moon doth grow.

Also if you should have any pruning or your hobby is sheep shearing now is the time to do it, whilst the moon increases, an increase in yield will then be expected.

This is when the moon is growing in size to a fullmoon, a time when the points or horns point to the left as seen from the Earth.

 *A **Fullmoon**-* all magic – Strictly the time of the Mother but a time when all aspects of the Triple Goddess come together, as waxing- full- waning moons are at their closest and all forms of magic can be performed. A time when she smiles down upon the earth with her full round face, if it is a clear night the edges of the moon should be crisp for it to be full on that night. If soft on the left, it is either a fullmoon tomorrow or on the right, it was yesterday.

*A **Waning moon*** – A time to let go of pain, attachments, etc. work with the Crone. Plant all root vegetables, that grow within the womb of the Goddess.

This is when the moon is diminishing in the sky, a time when the points or horns point to the right as seen from the Earth.

The Crone because she is wisdom-
She that sweeps all to her,
She that weaves the web of life,
She that knows all there is to know,
All the strands converge and twist meeting and parting, at any

one time.

She that wields the shears that ends the strands.

It is therefore to Her you turn for help with divination.

Darkmoon a time when the Goddess is at rest, She draws a cloak over Her face and does not appear in the sky, while She changes from Crone to Virgin. We believe, She is in a chrysalis stage, not that She is unknowing but that she is not to be disturbed. This she tells us by her invisibility to us.

 You can see from this that the Moon moves anti-clockwise or Widdershins, through her cycle. If Deisiel is Sunwise, then Widdershines is Moonwise.

We call this time the Dark Moon but in diaries you will see it marked as a New Moon.

Diaries will mark one minute after midnight as the next day. So if you are looking to cast circle at the fullmoon, check the actual time that the moon is full or you will be casting you circle up to a whole day late. Sometimes the fullmoon falls in the middle of the day but still do it in the evening. It's best if it falls before 12 noon do the spell on the day before, after 12 noon the date mentioned in the diary. Spells that need to be cast in daylight can be aimed at the God, the best here are protection, strength, victory and happiness, all Sun attributes.

So Mote it be!

You will see this at the end of many spells. The words, send the spell on its way with a push. "Make it come to pass" would be a good alternative but not so dynamic.

Types of Spells

Blessing- To give the love of the God and Goddess to who or whatever you bless.

Consecrating- To dedicate a tool to the service of the God and Goddess (or a person as in an initiation).

Empowering- To place energy within an item.

Healing- To heal person, place or thing.

Love- To draw love, partner, mother or general.

Protection- To protect, yourself or others. Remember others may not have the same scruples as you, so set protection around your home and yourself.

Banning - To make someone feel uncomfortable in a presence or area.

Binding- To stop someone from performing a deed.

Cursing

One final note; it is said that spells rebound on you three times, this makes cursing a bit of a no, no. The Wiccan words some up the situation nicely,

"If it harm none, do what thy will." **If it harm none.**

I have been offered a thousand pounds to do a curse, but I would never entertain it. Much to the person's surprise, asking how much it would cost then! As he was prepared to go so high, perhaps I should have done it; he might have had them bumped off instead!

If you follow this route, you will find yourself playing with very dark forces; like attracts like. Both my mother and my grandmother, on my fathers side were well known for their curses. Many years ago when I was untutored in the ways of Witchcraft, my mother was staying with me and asleep in the sitting room. I heard a whining noise and went down to investigate. I saw my mother lying in bed, rocking from side to side, very distressed. What to do, should I wake her? I thought of sleepwalkers, you are not meant to wake them. I put my hand out to touch her foot and I noticed a dark presence in the corner of the room, with glowing eyes, very tall flowing up and on to the ceiling with arms over-hanging the bed. I kept my eye on the presence while waking my mother, thinking it in my imagination. On waking she told me that she had been calling me for hours to wake her. She said the Devil was in the corner and had been pushing on her chest, stopping her screaming, pointing to where I had seen the apparition. Strangely, the following evening at the same time the front door blew open and then the back, I thought I was dreaming after last night's escapade and turned over and went back to sleep. Leaving my mother to get up and relock both doors. I wonder what would of happened if my mother had been at home alone that night? I managed to stop my mother from cursing and the entity never appeared again.

I have never needed to curse, all problems can be tackled without cursing, at worst you may consider doing a binding, this will stop a person from causing hurt to an innocent party. As in an ex-lover causing a nuisance at the work place or the parent's home. Always keep in mind that you may only hear one side of the story, the other half of the problem may tell a different tale entirely! You may not be in full possession of all the facts of a problem, especially if you have been told the dilemma by only one side of an argument. In this case do a spell for the best outcome for all concerned. People can very easily be manipulated and drawn into taking sides in divorces and broken friendships, stay above all interference by doing a spell for peace and tranquillity to wash away the bitterness. The Coven did a spell at one time which I still feel was justified, but later the same woman came back asking for retribution on someone that had upset her. This I didn't feel was warranted and made me concerned over the truth that we had been told of the first spell. Luckily we had only done a blessing that all would be settled and no more harm done. So whether she had told all the truth or only as she saw it, was irrelevant. But it did draw the problem to my notice, that with out knowing both parties- beware!

We have only needed to do a binding spell a few times in more than twenty years; more often it can be tackled by a protection spell. Although there was one time we were sorely tempted do a binding, after much discussion with physical violence being suggested, by the men of the coven. We gave the person three warnings that took the shape of three blessings. If these had not been heeded we would have gone ahead with the binding; a time, in my opinion, that to do nothing would have caused more harm than to act. Can you stand by and let others be mentally and physically hurt by your inaction? Or do you chance the consequences? At the end of my time I am confident that my Goddess, if I had not used a binding when needed, would have given me minus marks for inaction, if I had left the situation unrectified. But these are problems for a more experienced Witch, with many years of work and practice behind them.

I feel that I can stand before Anubis or the Black dog of The Morrigan when I die and have my heart weighted against Ma'at's feather, and be assured of the outcome – will you? If you keep this scenario in mind you won't go far wrong. According to the Egyptians the penalty if your heart failed the test, was to have it be eaten by monsters- don't say you weren't warned!

Use magic to enhance your and others life, bringing love, health, joy, and protection and to take control of who you are.

Old names of the Moons

Wolf Moon	January –	Time of hunger
Storm Moon	February –	Rough weather
Chaste Moon	March- in this month	Vernal (Virgin) Equinox falls
Seed Moon	April-	Time to plant
Hare Moon	May-	Beltane and fun abounds
Dyad Moon	June-	Latin for pair, two bright stars, easily seen in the constellation of Gemini
Mead Moon	July-	Honey at its best, time to make mead
Wort Moon	August-	Time to gather herbs for the winter
Barley Moon	September-	Time to harvest and make beer. Beer was used instead of water to drink in Medieval times as alcohol sterilizes.

Hunters Moon or Blood Moon	October-	Samhain, time to choose which animals would have been slaughtered and salted down for the winter. Diet supplemented with hunting.
Snow Moon	November-	First of the snow, winters started earlier
Oak Moon	December-	Oak trees should only be felled at this time of year for the best timber.
Goddess Moon		13th moon There is no thirteenth moon name, I don't know why, I can only assume that this list does not go back in history far enough. So I invented my own, sorry, all moons are the Goddesses but she is left off the list.

A Blue Moon is when two full Moons occur in one calendar month. Be sure of the times of the full moon for this. As the full moon may fall just before or just after midnight, not agreeing with your calendar and changing which night the full moon truly is on.

Divination by the Moon (Moonmancy)

Moon divination was one of the first forms of Astrology in Babylon in 2300BC.

When the Moon has two equal horns- luck.
When the Moon has right horn longer- a present.
When the Moon's horns are dim- a flood will come.
Halo around the Moon- good luck.
Dark halo around the Moon- clouds gather rain in a month.

Bright Moon- crops will prosper.

When the Moon appears low on the horizon- bad luck

When a river surrounds the Moon – great rains

Sun and Moon in the sky together- good luck, stand in silence.

First day after the Fullmoon- thunder and rain, good for the crops.

No Moon or Sun (darkmoon) – increase in wisdom.

When Venus shines (the bright 'star', low on the horizon)- the hearts desire

And from English folklore when the Moon has two horns pointing up, comes this little ditty

There she's sat

With Her arms in Her lap

Waiting for the rain to come

Rainbow Magic

Colors for spells

Spells are linked with the colors of the rainbow that The Goddess placed in the sky, in Babylonian myth (the forerunner of Noah's story), promising never to allow the God to get his hands on Her magic again! So we link ours spells to Hers by color coding our magic.

Pink-	love, romance and friendship.
Red-	sexual love, energy, strength, health, aggression
Purple-	luck, joy, health and wealth
Blue-	healing and wisdom
Gold or orange-	energy, wisdom, creative pursuits, happiness and luck.
Green-	fertility, success, money
Brown-	Earth blessing and harvest

White of course, is all colors combined and black is the absence of any color.

White or silver-	spirituality, remembrance and peace.
Black-	protection and divination. In old folklore tradition children should never wear black without good cause, as black falls under the domination of Saturn, who is old age. I don't think the Dark Goddess minds.

Of cause many colors can be combined for spells, pink and red for love for example.

For a good harvest, brown (soil), gold (sun) and green (fertility of the crop) will help.

Mixing colors, oils, gems and magic
Here are some examples of how the herbs, gems and oils can be mixed and used in a spell bag or candle magic.

White –Pure Spirit-	Gem ~ Diamond, Quartz Crystal, Amber, Ametrine Herb or oil ~ Amber, Benzoin
Silver- Goddess-	Gem ~ Amethyst, Moonstone Herb or oil ~ Lavender, Myrrh, Fennel.

Herbs for incense, either for the Moon or the Goddess are often grouped together in books on Ceremonial Magic. In witchcraft, I find it better to separate them out into Maiden, Mother and Crone, as it makes no sense to have an incense with camphor for the virgin and with sandalwood for the sexy Mother/Seductress, both under Moon.

Virgin-	Gem ~ Moonstone, Pearl or Mother of Pearl Herb or oil ~ Camphor, Hyssop, Lemon, Juniper.
Mother/ Seductress-	Gem ~ Garnet or Ruby

Herb ~ Rose, Sandalwood, Neroli, Jasmine,
Chamomile, Musk, Ylang Ylang.

Crone-   Gem ~ Onyx, Diopside or Smokey Quartz

Herb or oil ~ Patchouli, Mugwort,
Wormwood, Nutmeg, Mandrake, Hyacinth,
Galbanam, Violet.

Gold- God-   Gem ~ Citrene, Sunstone
Herb ~ Orange, Oakmoss, Cardamom,
Ginger, Frankincense, Cederwood,
Cinnamon.

Pink- Love-   Gem ~ Rose Quartz
Herb ~ Rose, Patchouli, Musk, Sandalwood,
Ginger.

(for love you can work with Venus and then you will need to use
green, Her color)

Red- Energy,   Gem ~ Ruby, Garnet, Carnelian, Haematite
Sexuality, Courage- Herb or oil ~ Frankincense, Cinnamon,
Cardamon, Chilli, Dragons Blood,
Sanderswood, Galangal,

Purple- Success- Gem ~ (An exception that proves the rule)
Lodestone
Herb or oil ~ Bay, Grains of Paradise, Tonka
Bean, Rose, Cinnamon

Blue- Healing-   Gem ~ Blue Topaz, Sapphire, Lapis,
Turquoise
Herb or oil ~ White Willow, Chamomile,
Lavender, St. Johns Wort

Yellow- Communication-	Gem ~ Clear Quartz, Yellow Beryl Herb ~ Frankincense.

Green- Wealth-

Gem ~ Aventurine, Emerald
Herb or oil ~ Oakmoss, Patchouli, Bay,
Tonka Bean, Frankincense, Orange, Basil.

Black- Protection-

Gem ~ Onyx, Diopside
Herb or oil ~ Mandrake, Myrrh,
Frankincense, Angelica, Oak, Yew, Ash,

Elm,

Beech, Ebony, Star Anise, Spelani.

Divination-

Gem ~ Crystal, Beryl
Herb or oil ~ Wormwood, Mugwort,
Sandalwood, Nutmeg, Myrrh.

Some Types of Spells

Each type of spell can be done in many ways, Candle magic, Spell bags, Cords, Incantations, Amulets, Talisman, Knot Magic, Sex magic, water magic, earth magic, the list is endless.

Once a spell has been cast, no word must be spoke of it. Until after it has come to pass.

A Birthday cake

A Birthday cake with candles is a spell, one to which it has become customary to blow on candles. But if you tell what you have wished, like a real spell, it will never come true.

Cards

A Birthday card is a spell, wishing the person a years worth of happiness.

A Get Well card is a one that we have used often. With Healing oil or Lavender oil, mark out a pentagram on to the card, marking it at just the points with your finger. As the recipient opens the card the spell and pretty smell is delivered!

Chanting

Chanting to raise energy, say a little rhyme as many times as you need to.

This is an example of a chant you might choose, when a problem is playing on your mind.

For this spell, have a bowl of water or better still a running stream, place your hands, into it and chant as many times as necessary.

Into the water, let it flow
See it gone, let it go.

A chant for raising energy for a spell.

Out of darkness,
Out of light,
Goddess send your power tonight!

or

Waxing, waxing, growing, growing
The Goddess's power is flowing, flowing.

Chants are needed on Sabbats as well as Esbats, this chant works well for Samhain.

Samhain night, Samhain night.
Ancestors, drew to my light,
Remember me, celebrate with me,
Now that the Craft is free.

There are many good CD's on the market, with well known Pagan chants that will cover most spells that you may need to do.

Cloutie Tree

A tree with rags hanging, this should be situated near a holy well or pond. I started a Cloutie Tree in a near by wood by the pond, which is fed by an underground stream from the holy pond in a local Iron Age fort, in which a church has been built. By the pond is a fallen tree that will not let go of life and from the few roots left within the earth, it has re-grown. Tie rags or ribbons on to the tree in a color to compliment the spell or if it is for healing rub the rag onto the affected part before tying it to the tree. Cloutie is an old word for clothing; I can remember my Grandmother saying "never cast a clout until May be out!"

Drumming Spells

Drumming Spells this is a brilliant way to raise energy for a spell but best used outdoors. When the energy has reached its peak stop with a crash, perhaps shouting the name of the person, whom the spell is for.

Ecstatic Dance Spells

Ecstatic Dance Spells, using dance to generate the energy for a spell. Dance round and round the circle until you are dizzy, all the time keeping in mind the reason for the spell and its recipient. Very good with added drumming if you have anyone that can do this for you. At the peak, let the spell go, and drop to the ground.

Knot Magic

Knots bind in good and are a hindrance to all evil, in itself it is a spell for longevity and averts the Evil Eye. Knot magic or cord magic, is a very old form of magic. The ancient Egyptians may have been one of the first to use knot magic, they felt that it was a unification of the Earth and the Gods.

Knot Magic will tie lovers hands, as in a handfasting but also it will hold the dying to this plane of existence. In the past, people would remove any knots from around a dying person, to allow them to pass over. A woman giving birth must have no knots not only on her but also near her; the midwife would be sure not to wear anything that was knotted. This would make her job far harder, holding the baby in the womb. There are legends of witches selling three knots in a rope or a lock of their hair to sailors, undo one for a breeze, two for a good wind but three would cause a gale.

A good example of a knot spell is found in the Handfasting ceremony, a witch wedding. Never untie the knot or the magic tied into the handfasting will be set free. The only time the cords must be untied is when the couple have decided to go their own ways. We use a red cord to bind their hands in honor of the Mother Goddess, as they slip their hands free the knot is formed. The couple tie a new knot on the anniversary every year. In China a similar idea is used but with a red and a green ribbon being tied together at the wedding, the green is held by the women and the red by the man.

Another good example of knot magic is *"The Spell of Nine"*

A 3ft length of cord appropriate in color to the spell.

Tie a knot in the center, one at either end, and then one between the center and the end each side, then one in each gap, this equals nine.

As with all magic as you tie the knots zap in your power.

As you do this, chant the rhyme.

X	X	X	X	X	X	X	X	X
2	6	4	7	1	8	5	9	3

"By the knot of one, I call the God of the golden Sun,
By the knot of two, I call the Goddess of a Midnight hue,
By the knot of three, I call the Oak, Ash and Rowan tree,
By the knot of four, I call the rushing wind as is the lore,
By the knot of five, I call strength and light to be my guide,

By the knot of six, I call on power from beyond the river Styx,
By the knot of seven, I hear the wings of the night black Raven,
By the knot of eight, this spell I <u>can</u> create,
By the knot of nine, -(spell for...) — and magic (or healing) are
irrevocably intertwined!!
So mote it be!!"

In 1880 in the magazine 'The Antiquary' it mentions a still older article written in 1635, a man from the Orkney Isles who had a spell cast by nine knots into a blue thread and given to his sister. Unfortunately the spell is not elaborated on, it would be very interesting to have some more information but at least we know that "The Spell of Nine" was at work in 1635.

Love Spell

This love spell, to be done on the handfasting night with hair from both partners.

"Three times a true love's knot I tie secure,
Firm be the knot, firm may our love endure".

Keep in a very safe place, do not untie.

In Mexico, a statue of a draped skeleton, Saintisima Muerte- most Holy Death is supposedly the Virgin Mary dead. But in truth she seems to be the Aztec Goddess of Death thinly disguised. There is a groove around the base of the statue to accept a cord. The Cord is knotted within ritual with seven knots, dipped into a husband's sperm and tied onto the statue, asking the Goddess of death to keep a close eye on him in case he wanders. This type of magic is considered controlling and therefore not done by English Witches. But does show yet another form of knot magic and that it is prevalent all over the world.

The Chinese in particular love knot magic, they

tie good luck into a red cord with a special fancy knot. Sometimes hanging charms from the cord to enhance the magic. This is hung in every home in China.

In China the main street in Beijing has light decorations that hang at the side of the road, just like Yule lights in High Streets in England. The street in Beijing is very long and the decorations run for miles, right though the year not only at Yule. The decoration is the same red knot, to bring everyone and the city good luck.

Red Thread Red thread was another way of averting the Evil Eye and fascination, in many countries. It was tied to the wrist or neck (not a good idea) of a young child until it rotted off, the child was thought then to be old enough to wear other forms of protection.

"Rowan tree and red thread, will put witches to their speed" goes an old Scottish rhyme. Equal armed crossed twigs of Rowan were tied with red thread and placed over stables, this must be done without the touch of iron. They were also placed on the animals left in the fields; people sewed the crosses into the lining of coats, as protection against fairies on particularly on May and Mid Summers Eve. Riders, who had no choice but to be out and about on that day, wore sprigs of Rowan in their hats for protection. Red was though the best color against enchantment, such a bright color, catches the Evil Eye and therefore detracts it away from the victim. With both red thread and the tree that would later bear red berries, a very strong charm is made. Rowan Day is the 3rd May, a day to cut the Rowan to place over the door and to carry in our pockets. In the 1618 Margaret Barclay was brought to trial for witchcraft in Ayrshire, Scotland, the evidence- a Rowan twig tied with red thread.

Use red thread to tie madder and plantain to your head for a headache or to tie buttercup around the neck of a mentaly distressed patient when at the moon is waning in April and October only mind.

Red Cord with a blue bead, probably these should have originally been turquoise but later replaced by blue faience beads. Again this breaks the eye of fascination.

Blue Cord another spell mentioned in 'The Antiquary' magazine again quoting from the older article written in 1635 *"On the banks of the Ale and Teviot (Scottish Borders) women have a custom of wearing around their necks blue woolen thread or cords till they wean their children, doing this for the purpose of averting ephemeral fevers. These are handed down from mother to daughter, and esteemed in proportion to their antiquity. Probably these threads had originally received some blessing or charm and this we should suppose to have been the properly colored thread to receive such a blessing..."*

Blue in our tradition is used for healing and cooling temperatures, this works very well with this spell.

Witches Ladder or Witches Garland is a length of cord or wool with feathers braided in, the feather is placed across the cord.

In a secret room in a house in Wellington, Somerset the first recorded Witches Ladder was found in 1887. Charles Godfrey Leland also found evidence of the same spell; the Italian Witches called the spell a Witches Garland. There the feathers were knotted into the cord rather than braided, but the main difference between the English version and the Straga's is that an image of a cock cut from cotton was placed with the finished cord. As the cock bird is a euphemism in Italy for a phallus and during the Roman Empire the bird was sacred to Apollo the Sun God, adding to the empowerment of the spell and a happy conclusion.

For this spell you will need a new length of cord or wool, it will need to be five foot when finished, tie a loop at one end and braid together with nine feathers inserted as you braid equally distanced (other items can also be added). Both the cord and the feathers should be in an appropriate color. This spell is very good with crow feathers for protection or if your spell is for healing use blue cord and either natural colored feathers or dyed blue. Chant and empower this as you braid, adding a last extra effort when you tie the knot to finish. Hide it in the house near the hearth or door, if for protection it will always be on guard.

Hands on healing

Hands on healing this is done by many religions around the world, Witchcraft among them. NEVER take pain away, this is the easiest way to relieve any problem, but you take it into YOU.

Lay your hands on or just above, however you feel more confident, the person to be healed. Pour through your hands blue healing light, you can imagine a sun within the body of the person radiating healing heat and energy around their body. This can be done from a distance (Absent Healing) if the need arises. I did absent healing on my Grandmother in America when I found she was ill, she recovered and lived to 95. After any hands on or even absent healing, clap and throw away from you any remaining energy from the healing, being careful not to throw it at anyone either. This breaks the tie that has been created between you both and in particular breaks contact with the pain or illness that you were curing.

Hypnosis

English Law of the 13th century against *'Enchantment as those who send people to sleep.'* Although it is clamed to have been "discovered" in the 1773, hypnotism has been around for hundreds, if not thousands of years. Hypnosis played a big part in the Cunning person's arsenal of weapons against illness and injuries. As it does in today's Witchcraft. Hypnosis works, it can block pain so that operations can be carried out. It is a great help in dropping unwanted habits and in visualization.

There is a true story of hypnotism, when it was rediscovered. A beautiful Famous but blind concert pianist came to a hypnotist to help her, the doctors had told her that there was no physical reason for her not to be able to see. She was hypnotized and low and behold once more she could see, for the first time since she was five, when she fell from a tree. She was ecstatic, but when she sat down to play, she was completely confused and unable to play a note. All her concerts dates were cancelled, her family that depended on her were starving. She returned to the hypnotherapist and asked him to reverse the presidia, so that she might play again.

Today, this story seems horrific, but it was of it's time. It does however, show how strong hypnotherapy is. But it will only work with the full co-operation of the subject.

Nothing can be done against the will of the person being hypnotized, no matter what fiction tells us.

Herb Picture spell

Scatter appropriate dried and pounded leaves onto a clean white sheet of paper into a pattern, "draw" what you would like to happen in your spell. This is probably easiest in symbols, anything that has a meaning for you, chant and empower these with in your circle. Sweep them into a bag and carry it with you, or sprinkle around a person to be healed, all the magic of the symbol is now with in every grain, as in Homeopathy.

Hair Spell

If you and your intended wish to stay together for repeated lifetimes. After thirty years together, place three hairs of yours with three hairs of your beloved together deep into a crack in an young Oak tree. As the tree grows it will seal your hair together for hundreds of years.

Half a six pence-Love Spell

Traditionally you would cut in half a six pence, two lovers who must be parted, each taking half. These two halves of the coin would strive to be reunited and so bring the lovers safely back together again. But for the coins help, once reunited, you must forever after keep the two halves of the coin in the same box or bag.

Money Spell

Another spell using money, but this time to attract it.

Take the smallest note, unfortunately this now needs to be a £5 note. Place a nutmeg on the note and roll it towards you. Secure it by binding it with green thread or wool and keep it rolled up in a spell box. There is a similar spell in Hoodoo using a piece of High John the Conqueror Root, another example of the crossover of magic or is it a Universal Constant of magic?

Moving-in Gift

If a friend has moved house, this is a lovely spell to bless the new house. On first crossing the threshold sprinkle salt across the door say

> *"May evil never pass your door"*
> Offer a loaf of bread,
> *"May you never hunger"*
> Offer a bottle of wine,
> *"May laughter and happiness always have a place here in"*
> after that go in and open the wine.

Pregnancy Spell

This Spell will not work without a man in your life, Witches aren't that good at spells!

 You will need- a walnut shell that has neatly broken in two. Mugwort to line your shell and a representation of a baby, this can be plastic, something carved or a silver charm. Place your baby with in its womb in circle, chanting a little rhyme. Then keep it with you at all times. This spell has worked for many ladies wanting children.

Poppets, Fif Faffs or Tobies (names from different parts of the country)

These are dolls made from cotton, for the person concerned. You normally hear of this in cursing magic, but it can be used in healing. But I find one big draw back with this type of spell. Once made you are honor bound to take care of that poppet, I know that it is said that you can deconscrate it, but I am not happy with this. So in case of fire or flood and you have to run around rescuing your poppets first before Granny, use another method to cast a spell. So strongly do I feel about this I won't tell you how to make them.

Rose Spell the rose is of course the flower of the Goddess. If you would like a spell to come to pass, cast it on a rose bud that is standing in a pretty vase on your altar. As the rose opens the spell comes to pass. If you wish to give a thank you for a spell that has worked very well, place an open red rose on your altar at the next Sabbat or full moon.

Spell bags

This type of spell has many names in many areas of England and in many countries around the world. It is known as Mojo bags in Hoodoo as in the song "I've got my Mojo Working." Hoodoo is the magic from the Deep South of America.

There are many crossovers between Hoodoo and European spell craft. European magic and folklore, as well as Native American knowledge of local plant lore, would have influenced the Afro-Caribbean people, as much as they were influenced by the Christian religion. In some ways, parts of Hoodoo might have a clearer memory of our spell history, than we have.

In Mexico to this day, a similar idea is still used, dried small humming birds (today a life would never be taken in Witchcraft) are placed in red bags and a wish is cast upon them. Is this the remains of the Aztec religion or European influence? In Peru they use small glass jars, in this they place herbs, seeds and small sacred objects, this is filled with Pisco, Peru's famous spirit and again a charm is placed within the jar. Across the world the universal knowledge of magic, is the same.

Take a bag, the color of the spell that you wish to cast or black as this is the absence of all colors and therefore adds no adverse influences. Place within it a crystal or semi-precious gem, herbs, perhaps a charm (pentagram etc.) a piece of horn or feather. Then bless and empower this, in all the quarters starting with North. This is where keeping the elemental representations separate, on the altar, is used to its best advantage. Add salt from the North and ask for Earth's protection, add incense from the East and ask for Air's knowledge, add the fire from a taper and ask for South's energy, add a few drops of water and ask for West's emotion (mostly happiness). Adding appropriate oil for Spirit, either love, protection or anointing according to the spell being cast and you have a spell bag of great power!

TREAT IT WITH GREAT RESPECT. If it is for yourself add appropriate oil to it each full moon.

If it should break at anytime, its work is done, bury the remains in the garden.

Spell Boxes

A place to put all spells that are awaiting an outcome. Do not mix protection with love or healing spells. It is best if you can have a separate box for each type of spell.

Verbal Incantations any spell said in rhyme. Make up your own, they will be stronger that way, but here are some to get you thinking.

This chant can be used for any personal work with the Goddess you choose to do.

"I call to the Great Goddess three,
For all that you would show to me.
I come as I did in times of old
To stand before you strong and bold."

I'm sure that you can do better than my feeble efforts.
One that is not said in rhyme but equally powerful.
A general blessing.

"May Sunshine and luck bless your endeavors,
May the Moon shine its magic on you,
May Earth protect you and give the beauty of a flower,
May Air give you understanding and the song of a bird,

May Fire give you passion and cozy warmth in winter,
May Water bring you happiness and cleanse your spirit,
As you walk through this life, may your steps tread lightly.
So mote it be!"

Another to use to background a spell (needs at least two, one to chant and one to lead with the words)

Earth, Air, Fire, Water (repeat as many times as you need to)
With a rhyme of your own making.

Witch Bottle

Witch Bottles are a protection spell, sending back to the sender any evil thought or spell. This is an old tradition and is found under the doorsteps or in fireplaces of many old houses. These used to be made in a Bellarmine bottles, that was a strange bottle that had a face, said to have looked like Cardinal Bellarmine. But bottles with faces have been in existence since Roman Times, although I have as yet, found no proof that they were used as spell bottles.

Find a nice bottle, with a cork or the type of beer bottle that has a wire clip fastening, soak off the label. If you are travelling to Tunisia they make excellent copies of the Roman bottles, for just a few pounds. Add a good pinch of pins, broken glass and other sharp objects. Then add your urine, next empower it within your circle taking the bottle to the Elemental Quarters, asking them to add their power. Adding salt from Earth, incense from Air, Fire from the fire quarter (you must use your imagination on this quarter) and finally a little Water from the west. Ask the God and Goddess, to energize the spell for you, as we have discussed. I usually use wax to drip the face of the horned God, onto the bottle, if it is plain, to give it a traditional finish.

This forms a guardian for you and your house. Even when you are not at home to guard the house, the Witch bottle will do its work and will protect on the magical level your home, happiness and business. The essence of you stands guard at all times with pointy things in hand, to ward off evil thoughts from all that is yours.

A variation on a Written Spell (See Charms)

Copper Love Spell- Sheet Copper (copper is sacred to Venus/Aphrodite) can be bought from craft shops in thin sheets, for inscribing pictures; this can be cut up into small pieces with an old pair of scissors, inscribed with your burin and used for love magic. Adding sigils that you think are appropriate; hearts, Gebo rune- X you will probably know this rune as a kiss or any symbols that takes your fancy. Roll it up and keep safe in a spellbox.

Candle Magic

Candles come in many shapes and sizes, color and smells, where to start?

You need a plain small candle, if you choose you could make them yourself the shape can be appropriate to the spell, such as a heart for love for example. Choose one of the colors above that you feel would suit the spell that you are working on.

Now carve any appropriate words into the candle, with your Boline or Burin. You may choose to use the name of the person that you are working for, or their star sign. Your magical name if you have one yet, if the spell is for you. Add the intent whether it be love, health or a symbol for the intent, a heart, a pentagram for a protection spell or just to enhance the magic. The flame upon the candle represents your willpower, the remains of candle magic show in the birthday cake where you blowout the candles and make a wish.

So we have our candles, what next?

The oils that we have made, now come into use.

Choose an oil that suits the spell, for this fictitious love spell that we started with at the beginning of this chapter, we will need Love oil, or a mixture you create yourself. You could use Rose oil, ouch, expensive. Use either an essential oil or a mixed magic blend to "dress the candle", until then, the candle is just a candle but to then dress it with oils you begin to make the magic.

Love oil

I use Ylang-Ylang (for its aphrodisiac effect and calming)

Patchouli (for love)

Ginger (to speed things along and for its spice and warmth)

Three drops of Rose oil

Almond oil base

It is essential to use a virgin candle - a candle unburned, but it need not be full size. You don't want it to last three days, so choose a small candle or trim a dinner candle to an appropriate size, three inches is ideal. Choose a small candle for safety and because you can keep your concentration on it, by just keeping an eye on it until it burns out completely.

Anoint the candle from the middle up and the middle down. You are the center and you anoint up to the Gods and then down to the physical plane. As it burns through the first half, the message is heard by your Goddess, as it burns through the second half, it comes to fruition on the Earth Plane. While anointing the candle, work into it your spell, visualizing the spell working, if for love feel loved; see yourself reaching out to a new person in your life, holding them close. Light your candle and say the words of your spell, then leave the candle to burn out completely. Like the birthday candles, do not tell anyone about the spell until after it has came true.

A Rainbow of Candle Magic Spells

These are simple spells; feel free to mix and match, change the Courage spell to a Love Spell by changing the red candle to a bright pink and the oil and incense to Love. Change the words from "Courage I ask" to "Love I ask" changing courage to love, every time it is mentioned.

Feel free to elaborate these spells in any way you choose, chant or dance. The wording is only an example to get you going, feel free as you get more confident to add any words that come from the heart.

A Love Spell

This is a spell to draw all forms of love to you.

This spell should be carried out on a waxing or a Fullmoon.

Have ready:

. A deep pink candle and candleholder

. Love oil.

. Love incense.

. A charcoal block.

. Pink cord or ribbon

. Silver heart pendant.

Cast Circle and call quarters in the normal manner.

Anoint the pink candle from the center up and from the center down with love oil.

Light your pink candle and call to your Goddess and God to be with you.

Visualize love coming from all quarters.

Turn to the north and say:

"I call to the North to draw love to me.

I call to the East to draw love to me.

I call to the South to draw love to me.

I call to the West to draw love to me."

Take the heart pendant and wave your talisman through the incense.

Anoint the heart with love oil.

Take the pink cord (or ribbon) and tie a knot in the center and continue as numbered, saying with each knot:

X	X	X	X	X	X	X	X	X
2	6	4	7	1	8	5	9	3

Use the Knot of Nine magic spell at the beginning of this chapter.

"Draw to me my true love, that we may spend our time in this realm in happiness."

Make a circle of the cord around the candle and place the heart within this circle.

Meditate on having a person to love you, see yourself running through fields together, kissing, laughing, and making love. See only happiness surrounding you.

Now you can add anything else that you would like to say.

Close Circle

Allow the candle to burn out completely.

Knead the cooled candle wax with the cord together and hide in a secret place or place in your spell box. Wear the pendant as a talisman.

With this your spell is done.

Finally, get out where your new love can find you. Join clubs and go dancing for they will never find you if you stay at home. No matter how good your spell, they may wander aimlessly looking for you, if you stay at home.

A Courage Spell

This spell should be carried out on a waxing or a Fullmoon.

Have ready:

- Red candle and candle holder
- Crucible of Courage oil.
- Crucible of Courage incense.
- A charcoal block.

Cast Circle and call quarters in the normal manner.

Meditate for a while on what you are about to do.

Anoint the red candle in the center of the circle from its center up and from its center down with Crucible of Courage oil, and then light it.

Call the Great Goddess and God to be with you

Once more draw the Earth energy up through your body slowly to your head. This time instead of allowing forming the cone of power, hold it at its peak. Let the energy vibrate throughout your entire body.

Say

"Courage I ask
Courage I call
Courage I ask
Courage I call
Courage I ask
Courage I call
Great God and Goddess,
I ask your strength,
Let your power imbue my body.
Give me courage to face this time
Power and strength,
Courage and fortitude
I feel within me.
I know that you walk with me
And that I never need worry knowing that you guard me.
So mote it be!"

Hold your hands above your head and let the power flow around you.

Start to breath more slowly. Allow the power to ebb away, keeping the courage within.

Now add anything else that you would like to say.

Say goodbye to the quarters and cut circle in the normal manner.

Allow the candle to burn out completely.

With this your ceremony is done.

A Business Success Spell

This spell should be carried out on a waxing or a full moon.

Have ready:

- A purple candle .

572

- Five green candles.
- Six candle holders.
- Money oil.
- Jupiter oil.
- Jupiter incense.
- A charcoal block.

Cast Circle and call quarters in the normal manner.

Anoint the purple candle from the center up and from the center down with Jupiter oil and the green candles with money oil in the same way.

Set the purple candle in the center and the five green candles equally around it. The green candles form a pentagram, the Pentagram, is the symbol of Earth and therefore money.

Light your purple candle and then the green candles. Call to the Goddess and God to be with you.

Pick up your purified salt.

"In the circle, the flame of purple encircled with flames of green.
I bless the pentagram with Earth."

Sprinkle salt clockwise around the circle of candles.

"I bless the pentagram with Air."

Sprinkle incense on the charcoal and smudge (fan) it in the direction of the candles.

"I bless the pentagram with Fire,"

Wave your hand clockwise, high over the flame.

"I bless the pentagram with Water."

Sprinkle water clockwise around the circle of candles.

Move the green candles a little nearer to the purple candle.

Circle above the candles with your hand as if stirring, while you chant:

"Earth, Air, Fire, Water.

Earth, Air, Fire, Water,
Earth, Air, Fire, Water."
(As many times as you feel necessary).

Say:
"Draw to me success.

Circle above the candles with your hand as if stirring, while you chant:
Earth. Air. Fire, Water.
Earth, Air, Fire, Water.
Earth, Air, Fire, Water."

Move the green candles tight together around the purple candle. Now add anything else that you would like to say.

"Now my spell it is begun
Success in work, I ask of thee,
All is ready, all is done
And as ever, so mote it be!"

Close Circle in the normal way
Allow the candle to burn out completely.
With this your ceremony is done.

A Healing Spell
This spell should be carried out on a full moon.

Although this spell is not meant to replace medical treatment, it will boost, compliment, and promote health.

Have ready:

. A blue candle or a Zodiac color candle and candle holder,
. A Boline, Burin or tooth pick.
. Healing oil.

. Healing incense.
. A charcoal block.
. A small bag.
. A quartz crystal
. Healing herbs (see list)

If the person to be healed is not yourself and not present at the ceremony, choose the appropriate Zodiac color candle to represent them.

Before the ceremony, wash the crystal, rotating it in the water three times anti-clockwise, and three times clockwise.

Cast Circle and call quarters in the normal manner.

Write the name of the person to be healed with the Boline or burin onto the candle. Add any other symbols that you think appropriate, a pentagram for protection, an Ankh for life or the triple moon, or all three!

Anoint the candle from the center up and from the center down with healing oil.

Light your candle and call to the Goddess and God to be with you.

Visualize the one to be healed in perfect health, see them running, pain free, enjoying their life.

Place the herbs in the bag and say:

"Great Goddess and God, heal me (or persons name).
Remove the pain (or any other problem)
Give me strength."

Anoint the crystal with healing oil and place it in the bag.

Stand and hold your arms above your head, facing north. Say:

"Grant me the power to see the strength of the life-force.
The life-force shall permeate and infuse me and bring long lasting
well being."

See the life force flowing down from the stars, flowing over you or the person for whom you are doing the spell, through you, bathing you in a glowing blue aura.

Now add anything else that you would like to say.

Close Circle in the normal way

Allow the candle to burn out completely.

Put a little of the candlewax into your charm bag. Wear the charm bag or place under your pillow. Whenever you have need, draw on the life-force, for you are now connected to it.

With this your ceremony is done.

Repeat every three months, if it is a problem that has to be kept at bay.

A Happiness Spell

This spell should be carried out on a full moon at noon, at that time you then have both God and Goddess's energies.

Have ready:

. A gold candle and candleholder

. Sun oil.

. Sun incense.

. A charcoal block.

Cast Circle and call quarters in the normal manner.

Anoint the candle from the center up and from the center down with Sun oil. While you are doing this chant: *Happiness I call to thee* repeat as often as you need.

Light your candle and call to The God and Goddess to be with you.

Great God of the fiery golden Sun, burn away gray depression from my life.

Face North. Stand and hold your arms up to the sky.

"I call happiness from the Four Corners of the Universe.

I call happiness from the North.	Turn.
I call happiness from the East.	Turn
I call happiness from the South.	Turn.
I call happiness from the West ."	Turn

Feel the Suns energies spiral clockwise around you. As the eye of the hurricane, you are at peace, but around you *joy* comes filling your entire home, into every nook and every cranny.

Slowly allow the winds to die down, as they do, absorb them into yourself. Feel the happiness permeating your very being. Be uplifted; let joy into your life. Close your eyes and drop your arms to your sides with palms up. Feel the Suns heat on your body. Tip your head back and feel the Sun on your face warming you all through. Allow the Sun to melt any sadness still left in your heart. Smile at the Sun. (Smiling releases a chemical in your brain that actually makes you feel happier.)

"So mote it be!"

Close Circle in the normal way.

Allow the candle to burn out completely.

With this your ceremony is done.

And SMILE !!

For the next day you need to be positive, in everything you do. Smile at people, even if necessary pretend to be happy as the spell gets to work. It will not work, if after doing the spell you stop it from working, by negative thoughts. Depression is a very strong feeling; the spell may have to be repeated for three fullmoons.

A Money Spell

This spell should be carried out on a Waxing moon,

Do not be afraid of a money spell. It is not wicked to ask for what you need. Magic will never make you rich, it will never bring you a Mercedes or a Porsche. You can never save with magic money but it will pay the electricity bill or the mortgage.

Have ready:

. A green candle and candleholder
. money oil.
. money incense.
. A charcoal block.
. A coin.
. Green ink.
. Parchment.

Cast Circle and call quarters in the normal manner.

Anoint the candle from the center up and from the center down with Money oil.

Rub the coin with money oil and place coin under the candle.

Light your candle and call to the Goddess and God to be with you.

Visualize money coming from all quarters to you. See the bills paid, see the clerk stamping the receipt PAID IN FULL!

Draw with green ink, a money (£ or $ what ever is right for you) sign on the parchment and say:

"Great Goddess and God I call upon your might
With love I call to you this night
To pay my bills I do aspire
To have my life in balance I do so desire."
Burn the money sign in the candle.
Add any other words here.
"So mote it be!"
Close circle in the normal way.
Allow the candle to burn out completely.
Keep the coin as a lucky piece and rub whenever you have need.
With this your ceremony is done.

An Earth Blessing Spell

This spell should be carried out on a full moon,

Our green and pleasant land, today is less green and a lot less pleasant. We can never harm the Earth, whatever we do, She will be forever the same. She may change the color of Her dress, She may wear desert gold instead of green and be My Lady of the Scorpions. If we do not do away with nuclear weapons, She may wear a dress of atomic glowing purple. But the Earth will not change, so perhaps this is a blessing for our preservation, not for Hers.

This rite is best done in the open air. To get the feel of the Earth, remove your shoes and socks, feel the Earth with your bare feet.

Have ready:

- A Brown candle and candleholder
- Earth oil,
- Earth incense.
- A charcoal block.

Cast Circle and call quarters in the normal manner.

Anoint the brown candle from the center up and from the center down with Earth oil.

Light your brown candle and call the Goddess and God to be with you.

"I bless the Earth that we may live.

I bless the Earth, my strength to give."

Walk around anti-clockwise within your circle

Stop and hold your hands to the sky.

Throw incense onto the fire (if you have one, or use the charcoal block)

"I call to the North to help me cleanse the land of peoples careless deeds."

Throw incense onto the fire

"I call to the East to help me cleanse the air of factories foul vapors."

Throw incense onto the fire

"I call to the South to help me cleanse the fires that they may

burn clean.

Throw incense onto the fire.

I call to the West to help me cleanse the sea of pollution."

Draw from the four quarters, strength, into yourself and send it out through your hands to clean and clear the Earth.

Now change direction and walk clockwise around your circle. Stop and say:

"Mother Earth.
I see the beauty of your hills.
I see the beauty of your valleys.
I see the beauty of your deserts.
I see the beauty of your oceans.
What Mother Nature makes beautiful,
Humans try to destroy.
I ask that You open their eyes to Your beauty
And that our steps may tread lightly, upon the Earth.
Now add anything else that you would like to say,
So mote it be!"

Close circle in the normal manner.

Allow the candle to burn out completely.

With this your ceremony is done.

Requiem for the Departed

White light has all colors with in it and so is the color of spirituality.

At this point in your life the energy is lacking to sit and write spells so I hope that this will come in handy.

Sometimes a funeral does not seem enough when a loved one dies. Now days it may well be a non- denominational ritual, that does not fulfil your needs, as a Pagan or Witch. This is a spell that you can do to help them pass on, and perhaps it is as much for yourself as for the departed, to help you say goodbye.

Have ready:

- A white candle and candle holder
- Frankincense.
- Frankincense or Amber oil.
- A charcoal block.
- A red rose
- Rosemary.
- Red wine.

Cast Circle and call quarters in the normal manner.

Anoint the white candle from the center up and from the center down with the oil, whilst doing this remember the person, happy and laughing.

Light your white candle and call to the Goddess and God to be with you and say:

"I light this candle for ... ... (name)... ...

Great Goddess and Great God, gather them into your gentle arms.

Take from us all sadness at their passing, leaving only happy memories.

Comfort all who love them.

I ask that all friends and loved ones that have passed before, be ready to receive them.

May time spent in the Golden land make them ready for rebirth once again."

Sit in front of the candle and close your eyes. Relax your muscles and breathe deeply. Imagine the person beside you, take their hand, kiss their cheek and gently squeeze their hand. Smile at them without sadness, for they go on to a green and pleasant land. Time passes at a different rate than here. It will not seem long to them, before you join them again, although it may seem many years to you.

Mentally stand and see a door in front of you, knock and wait for the door to open. When it opens, see through the door, a golden land, green grass, blue skies and a warm sun. A lady dressed in silver stands in this golden land, She beckons to your loved one. Give them one last kiss upon the cheek and proffer your hand towards the door as if to invite them to step through. They pass through the door, turn to look once more at you, Smile, give them the confidence to go on. The door closes.

Feel happy, for you have done the hardest deed, allowing them to go on with your blessing.

Drink some wine; hold it high above your head and toast to all friends departed.

Add anything else that you would like to say.

Close circle in the normal way.

Allow the candle to burn out completely.

Press the rose and rosemary in a special book.

Tip some wine onto the Earth in remembrance.

With this your ceremony is done.

Novena of Protection
This spell should be started on a fullmoon.

This spell uses black candles. Hopefully by now you will not tear this page from the book, despite Hollywood's fantasies, a black candle is just a candle and nothing to be frightened of. Candles must be anointed with oil to be enlivened, if you anoint with good oil, you get good candles for good magic. There is only evil in a black candle if you choose to put it there.

Black is sacred to the Crone Goddess of Wisdom, Protection and Divination.

A Novena is a spell that takes nine days to complete and is much older than Christianity. Nine is sacred to the moon and is only used in spells of great importance. It's rather like knocking at a door, you sometimes have to knock a few times to be heard.

Have ready:

- A black candle and candleholder

- Protection oil.
- Protection incense.
- A charcoal block.
- Nine pins.

Cast Circle and call quarters in the normal manner.

Place nine pins in equal spaces down the candle; anoint the first portion with oil.

Light your candle and call to the Goddess and God to be with you.

"Great Goddess and God I call on your help

Flow your protection over me

Protect me with you love

Build a wall of protection around my home,

My loved ones, and myself

Let a wall of mirrors be erected,

Reflecting back to the sender any thoughts sent against me."

Visualize a blue Eye of Horus above the wall of protection around your home or place of business. See it strong and impregnable. The Eye of Horus is your guardian.

Now add anything else that you would like to say.

"So mote it be!"

"My thanks to you great Goddess and God for coming to my circle, my thoughts are ever with you."

Close Circle in the normal way.

Pinch or snuff out the candle, do not blow on a candle, never use one element

against another.

Repeat for nine days at the same time every evening.

With this your ceremony is done.

Exercises:- Look at the moon and watch the Waxing-Full-Waning moon, get to know the Virgin-Mother-Crone Goddess phases and feel their energies. When you are ready start to do a Fullmoon Ritual.

CHAPTER 12

Familiars or Spirit Animals

Familiars or as the Shamans call them Spirit or totem animals, can be very remarkable teachers. Bringing into our lives the powers that we lack or that we will need as we move further along our chosen path but they do have a deeper use, teaching many lessons in life. You may not always keep the same familiars as you change and develop. As you learn lessons you may pass on your familiars to others or add to them as your experience deepens. They not only teach on the Astral plane but also at times show themselves, by the use of your third eye, on the physical plane. Familiars are also friends helping you in times of stress.

One day, I was driving back from Birmingham, where the museum was holding an exhibition of my jewelry. It was late at night, and I was tired after a long day. The car started to have breather problems, it would sputter and then started to get slower and slower until finally stopping. After a few moments it started again fine but then half an hour later it repeated again. This it did frequently every half-hour, then every quarter of an hour and then every ten minutes! I asked my two spirit wolves attach themselves to the end of my bonnet like Huskies and pull my car home, they were happy to help and from that moment on, I did not brake down or even slowed again the rest of the trip.

But of course, there are other more interesting ways to work with familiars. To visualize yourself running with wolves, smelling what they smell, with their power, to see humans and the glow of their campfires, smell them as wolves do and feel the fear. To feel the fur rippling up and down your bones as you stretch your legs in long strides and cover miles in a short time. With this you begin to under-stand who and what your familiar is. Some familiars will speak, and teach you of things you must know, others like my wolves, never say a word but take me to a place or to see an object that I need to know about, in visualization. All animal familiars on this or any other plane, will help you understand the mysteries deeper.

Trace memories of our forebears still remain with us in our own culture today, although even these are now changing, we may eat rabbit but never hare, we may eat pigeon but never raven, we may eat cow but never horse. There is still a deep-seated respect for these animals that once adorned our pennants and guarded us as supernatural beings.

The list below is not only the meaning of familiars but also how to use representations of animals as amulets to draw into your life the energies of that animal.

This is the traditional meaning of the animal that has chosen you. But remember this can be changed by your perception of the animal, this applies to the all symbols in dreams too. For example a cat, can mean home and family to some but if you are afraid of cats, it symbolizes something very different. So examine how you perceive the familiar that moves with you. For this may be its first lesson.

Visualization to find your familiar

Relax; allow the cares of the day to fade away.

Slowly tighten the muscles of your feet, and then your legs. Tighten the muscles of your chest, shoulders and then your face.

Allow it all to relax, float on a sea of nothing.

Breathe out the dark air of the day; breathe in the white light of the universe. Do this for a little while.

Visualize yourself at the top of a flight of stairs, descend slowly and as you descend allow your breathing to slow.

Descend again, breathing in and out more slowly.

Descend again, feel the banister under your hand.

Descend again, feel the tread of the stair under your feet.

Descend again, at the bottom there is a door, knock on the door and you will find that it opens, allowing you to enter.

Beyond the door you once more see your temple, that is now

familiar to you. Cross the grass and enter, your ritual tools are arranged upon your altar as you left them. Place incense on the burner in your temple. Take your wand and hold it out in the direction of North and say

"Great Goddess and God of my chosen path,
Send to me my magical helper,
Whether by Earth,
Turn to East,
Or by Air
Turn to South,
Or by Fire
Turn to West,
Or by Water,
For I would see,
That which you wish for me."

Sit quietly facing the door until your familiar comes to you.

When you see the animal, go gently, as you would with a real creature; encourage it soothingly to come to you. Perhaps you may have some food in your pocket, if so, lay it on the floor in front of you. Put your hand out to stroke him, if it will allow you.

Is it a he or a she and does it matter?

Try speaking to it, does it speak your language?

Or does it communicate in thought or not at all?

Try to feel its energy, will it take you on a journey?

Can you shapeshift into that animal?

Can you travel with it, feeling as it does, seeing as it sees?

If so shapeshift and follow it run, swim or fly ....

For a time be that creature and talk to it, understand what it has been sent to teach you.

This will be enough for your first visit, so thank your familiar for coming to your call. Stand and return to the door. Slowly ascend the stairs and as you do, you return to normal breathing, until by the time you reach the top step you will feel happy and fully awake.

Write everything down, particularly if you have been lucky enough to follow your familiar, recount every impression of smell, taste and feeling.

Repeat this exercise as soon as possible to fix your experience.

Below is a list of animals that often offer themselves as familiars but of course yours could be any animal that has taken a liking to you.

Sometimes, it can be a surprise as to which creature you have been given. Do not be disappointed however if it was not what you were hoping for. It may only be the first of many familiars during your magical life.

Try to acquire a representation of your animal, if a deer perhaps a dropped horn, a photo or statue to place on your altar or carry a silver talisman of them, to cement a link between you.

Your familiars and what they may mean.

Bat

A bat brings with it long life and good fortune. Bats fly at fullmoon and twilight, which is of course a very magical time when the Sun God and the Moon Goddess inhabit the sky at the same time, wisdom, secret knowledge and initiation are their gifts. Five Bats

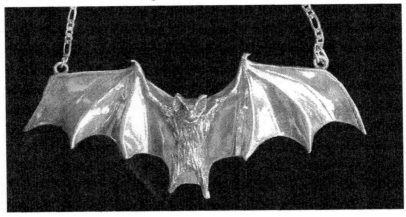

linked together is an interesting Talisman from China with a meaning of 'that which all people desire' -luck, wealth, longevity, health and peace.

Bear

Brings good luck and teaching, to know oneself.

Bee

A bee is a symbol of many Goddesses of the Ancient world, including Demeter, Aphrodite and Artemis. The honey was used for a wonderful alcoholic drink, Mead. That has been brewed for 10,000 years possibly the oldest alcoholic drink in the word. But that is not all there is to honey, for it is a superb preservative, due to this it represents immortality, birth and rebirth of the soul. The bee is a familiar of wealth through hard work, inspiration, creativity and artistic work.

Boar

Both the Celts and Vikings felt this to be a very important familiar sacred to the element of Fire extremely protective, teaching leadership, virility and fertility. Eaten at Celtic feasts, a warrior must put his life in danger to procure one for the banquet. One of the most feared animals of its time, a boar will hold it's ground, never giving up until death. A special spear was used to kill a boar, it had a bar a foot from the point of the spearhead. A boar will not stop charging even when the hunter has wounded the boar, without the bar, it will force its way up the spear in an attempt to kill the hunter. Their power was transferred symbolically to war helms as a personal or tribal emblem. Due to boar farms being re-established in Britain, many have escaped and in some places boar have re-established colonies. Use the boar for positive thinking and success.

Bull

The symbology of the Bull is used for success with love, fertility and to secure lasting friendship. The bull and its horn have been used as a fertility symbol since the Stone Age. An Earthquake in Ancient Crete was thought to be the stamping of the Monitor in his Labyrinth. Symbolizing good health and long life, the bull was the symbol of Thor, Osiris, Apis, Baal and Jupiter.

Cow Cow seems to be a representation of the Great Earth Mother like no other animal. The Norse primordial cow of creation, Audumia, her name means creation of the Earth. From her udder flow the four primordial rivers that nourish the oldest Norse race of Gods. In Egypt She was Hathor, Goddess of Love and Abundance. The Cow is still sacred in India, where She is known as the fountain of milk and curds.

Butterfly

The spirit soaring upward towards the light of immortal life, thought to have been a soul ascending to paradise. A butterfly also signifies a metamorphosis of body or/and of outlook. The butterfly has a totally different DNA from the caterpillar, so change will come to you whether you like it or not, if you are given this familiar. On the Scottish border red butterflies were thought to be shape-shifted witches, so there is a strong connection with this beautiful and delicate creature.

Crocodile

Worshipped in Ancient Egypt, Sebek, called The Crocodile God of Reason, because he could see clearly even when his eyes seemed to be veiled by nectatious membrane. On the banks of the Nile, a temple was built to Sebek, where the crocodiles could bathe and laze in the hot sun. The Sunstone Carnelian was Sebek's sacred stone.

Cat

It was said that witches transformed into cats, unfortunately the spell is lost but the witches association with cats is still well known. The lucky black cat is renowned and a depiction appears on many horseshoes at weddings, passing on harmony, happiness, fruitfulness and luck. The Goddess Bast in Egypt, is depicted with a cat's head on a human body, surrounded by kittens or in Her full cat form. Her image adorns the systrams (rattle) of Hathor the Goddess of health and happiness. When a cat died in Ancient Egypt the women of the household would shave off their eyebrows in mourning.

Cats were also sacred to the Viking Goddess Freya, who rode in a chariot pulled by cats.

Witches were thought to always have cats as familiars and so Christians became uncomfortable around cats and so the saying "beware if a black cat crosses your path" came into general use. It is said the Cat Goddesses will send you blessings if you adopt a stray cat.

Condor

In Peru, since Inca times, the condor is thought of as a sacred bird of the Skies. The condor has an impressive wing span of nine and a half feet and are birds of prey. The have a long life 50 –80 years and mate for life. Condors teach of Spirit, strength and beauty. Summed up in the tune that you hear wherever you go in Peru, El Condor Pasa, which is almost a National Anthem.

Dog

The emblem of faithfulness and healing, perhaps the animal most associated with humans. Bred by humans from the wolf centuries ago and having many of its qualities. Guarding the gate to the "Other World" of fairies and death. Cerberus is the three-headed dog that guards the entrance to the underworld in Greco- Roman legends. A black dog is connected with The Morrigan and the white coated red eared hounds of Annwen, that appear in Celtic fable are also part of the stories that surround this animal.

Dragon

In legend the fabled, dragons are both winged and wingless. They are known by many names, worms and giant snakes as well as dragons.

It has always intrigued me that Dragons are a creature depicted in art the world over. From Ancient Babylon, Egypt, Greece, China, Japan and even in South America dragons are mentioned. The dragons of China are a different species from European dragons. In Europe dragons are more reptilian with horns, pointy tails and breathing fire. In China however, dragons are a mixture of other animals. They are described as having the head of a camel, cow ears, the horns of a deer, paws of a tiger and many other creatures' aspects are adopted into the body of the dragon. Each of the animals used in the structure of the dragon adds to its eventual power, each bringing their special energies into the creatures eventual form. But it is very surprising that two so different descriptions should produce two such similar animals. It is as if a dragon had shown itself to artists from different cultures and different artistic styles, for only a short glimpse and they both tried hard to portray what they had seen.

Dragons are not only found all over the world, but throughout history as well. In 1940 a prehistoric cave painting of a dragon a full three metres long was found in cave in France at La Baume, by Siegfried Giedion, some scientists have dated the cave painting as early as 20,000 years ago; this is possibly the earliest drawing of a dragon.

Next the story shifts to Mesopotamia, which is situated between the Tigris and Euphrates rivers, now Iraq. Here we meet the great Dragon Goddess Tiamet, who created the Universe in Chaldean legend. She was killed by Marduk who tore Her in half, making the home of the Gods from one half and the Earth from the other half of Her. Many peoples say that when earthquakes happen it is the dragon moving. Perhaps Tiamet is not dead, just shifting to get a bit more comfy. After all, if you cut a worm in two, you get two worms.

Tiamet was remembered in the Chaldean constellation of Draco. Draco, meaning dragon of course, wraps itself around the North Star. Back then, Thuban (Alpha Draconis or First Dragon) within the Draco constellation, was the star to follow when traveling North, but time and even stars move on.

In Egypt, Apophis a many headed dragon with a long snake like body, is the enemy of Ra the Sun God. In Egypt where the cobras are deadly poisonous, I suppose the Egyptians can be forgiven for not taking dragons to their heart.

In Thailand and surrounding countries, to this day, they worship water dragons called Nagas. Sticky rice, the stable diet of the people, as well as jos sticks and flowers are left as offerings. Nagas are long and sleek like an eel with the head and tail of a Chinese dragon, but can be phenomenally long, although the number of heads that the Nagas have differs, varying from one, three or five. During the rainy season, the rivers overflow and the Nagas escape into the rice paddies, long beautiful boats are used to encourage the Nagas to follow and return to the river. Depictions of Nagas cast in concrete, some spangled to catch the sunlight, line the stairways of many Buddhist temples. On the fullmoon in October, there is a strange phenomenon that happens on the in the Mekong River. Balls of a ruby color rise from the water; legend has it, that the Nagas are responsible. Scientists of course differ in their opinion, but they can give no explanation of the phenomena. Nagas like dragons bestow luck, longevity, wealth and protection.

In China, the earliest illustration of dragons was in the Yin Dynasty 3000 years ago. China is famous for their dragons, which were believed to be messengers of the Gods and gave advice. The Emperor was the only one allowed converse with the Imperial Dragons, on pain of death. The dragon had five claws and it is said that the further a dragon strays from China the more claws he will loose, with Japanese and Korean dragons having only three or four claws. The Chinese dragons have 81 scales 9X9. In Spring and Summer the dragon rides the skies and in Winter and Autumn they hibernates in the water, they can be as small as a silkworm or fill the sky, as they choose. Thunder is a dragon roaring.

There are nine dragons in China folklore or possibly nine stages in a dragon's life-

Celestial Dragon supports the homes of the Gods.

Earth Dragon guards the Earth and its body is the mountains.

Spiritual Dragon when they fly through the air and disturb the clouds it brings wind, rain and therefore a good harvest.

Treasure Dragon guards gems and precious metals.

Coiling Dragon lives on the Ocean floor.

Yellow Dragon of scholarly knowledge. "*His intelligence and virtue are unfathomable; moreover he ensures the peaceful air, and sports in the pools*".

The Horned Dragon grows his horns when he is 500 years old and acquires wings at 1000 years.

Winged Dragon of air, this dragon is the only Chinese Dragon with wings.

And most importantly *The Imperial Dragon* that became the symbol of the Emperor Kao Tsu in the Han Dynasty 206BCE and remained so throughout Imperial Chinese history.

As dragons of all elements exist and it is perfectly feasible to call dragons to each of the elements quarters, if you are a great friend of this wondrous creature.

Dragons were then, and still are in China, considered bringers of longevity, prosperity and luck, bestowing protection on all those whom they like. Chinese people keep representations of dragons on many items to encourage dragons to bestow good luck on themselves or homes. On New Years day in China and now wherever Chinese people have roamed to around the world, dragon dancing takes to the streets. Under the dragons' jaw they carry the Peal of Wisdom. Accompanying the dragon are drums, cymbals, gongs and flags, to scare away the demons that bring bad luck.

The color of the dragon is important, as with our own red dragon bringing energy to our festivals. The longer the dragon, the more luck it will bring with it, ours is twenty-five feet! But this is not exceptional in China where seventy-five feet is quite normal. In China, people train to Dragon Dance with as much dedication as a martial art and collect money by performing the acrobatics that the

Chinese are so famous for. The dragons will climb walls to retrieve a note from a first floor window.

Greek stories abound with dragons some good, some bad. Doesn't it remind you of humans? The name Dragon comes from the Greek word Drakon, before this dragons had no group name. But the Greeks and Romans added knowledge and nobility to the attributes of the dragon.

Unfortunately by the time we get to the Christian era, the Egyptian view that dragons are bad had prevailed. In Revelations chapter 13 we read of a war in Heaven. Satan is depicted as a seven headed red dragon, cast from heaven with a third of the Angels. The red dragon of Revelations waits for the Virgin Mary to give birth, to eat her child, on wings (like Isis?) Mary flies to the wilderness. But in Matthew 2:16-18 we are told that Mary flees to the wilderness to escape Herod and slaughtered of all the children (although there is no historical evidence for this) under two in the hope of killing Jesus. Herod represented the greatest evil threat of the conquered nations of the time- The Roman Empire. Seven headed dragon and the seven hills of Rome, a coincidence? In battle the Roman Armies would lock shields and form a 'Testudo Formation' likened to a turtle or to my mind a modern tank but without the wheels and engine. With the army's red capes flying, there tall dragon horns blearing they marched into countries, demanding taxes and imposing their laws. Rome may well have been written about by the early Christians as the red dragon of Revelations.

By the Middle Ages however the Virgin Mary place had been taken by fine young virgins princesses, now needed to satisfy the dragons appetite, the dragon had become synonymous with evil. St George and his many friends went on a killing spree across Europe and North Africa, slaughtering the evil Pagan dragons.

One bad dragon ruins it for all the rest!

Dragons do resemble the dinosaurs that once roamed the Earth or soared in Her skies. But dinosaurs had long gone by the time the first human stepped foot on to green grass. So why this preoccupation across the world with our noble friends? Perhaps it is a DNA memory, or those with vision above the norm can see through the veil to the land beyond? What I do know is that as Paganism returns to the world so do dragons. Almost without fail every Pagan home I have ever entered displays a dragon, so perhaps they **are** synonymous with Paganism.

Although the dragon is in essence male, human females have in the last fifty years been shown in art in command of this powerful creature. This amalgamation forms Yin Yang energy, as the Goddess grows stronger, re-affirming her place in today's society. She reins in and controls the Earth energies of dragons and is once more in command.

European Dragon (wingless) An Earth elemental very protective, it also stands for strength and speed. It is the guardian of underground treasure and temples. Wingless dragons usually signify Earth magic.

European Dragon (winged) A Fire elemental and male, spitting fire at your enemies and those of the Earth, in some legends the pointed tail is full of venom.

All dragons are luck bringers, along with power and prosperity.

Dragons can be familiars, if you are lucky enough to be given one, they are excellent teachers. As with the Chinese Emperors being given divine knowledge and guided on their path, so if you are granted a dragon cherish his counseling, as all dragons are closely entwined with magic.

Dolphin

Safety while travelling especially over water, as a charm but as a familiar, it teaches us about the water element. A mammal of the sea, the dolphin has the highest brain capacity except man. Sacred to sea deities of many cultures, dolphins are depicted on some Roman coins carrying Apollo a Sun God, on their back. It is not just in modern times that dolphins have had an affinity and swam with humans. Although I am personally unhappy with Water Parks that catch and keep dolphins teaching them to perform tricks. I love the latest idea of an open area that allows dolphins to swim in when they feel like it, to play with humans. Due to dolphins navigating by echo location, they live in a world of sound, everything that we would see with our eyes facing forwards, they "see" by sound and can move around in complete darkness easily. Dolphins are able "see" if a woman is pregnant, as they can feel the sound picture of the child within her body, moving very gently around her.

Eagle

The eagle symbolizes strength, freedom, courage, high ideals and teaches of the knowledge of the Air element. In ancient Greece it symbolized Zeus, in Rome the symbol of the legions. Their cries foretell great events. A solitary bird on a high place foretold an enemy advance. When they fly low disease or war will follow. When the Eagle circles, soaring high in the sky the omens were seen as good. In stormy weather, the wind was said to be eagles flapping their wings. Even a depiction of a feather would transfer bravery.

Frog

A frog is a charm against illness and may be worn to hasten recovery and to win friendship. In part this is due to the cleansing and purifying water element in which they live but it is also due to their strange DNA, changing so completely from a water creature into a land creature.

Frogs lay an enormous amount of eggs and so were thought of as charms of abundance and fertility, hatching into swarms of tadpoles but then they change their body completely becoming land creatures and in great change they were thought to bring health out of sickness. They can lie for long periods buried without light or air and rise unharmed. Frogs were sacred to the Egyptian midwife Goddess Heket (strange fact- in the western world frogs in the 1940 and 50 were used to test the if a woman was pregnant by injecting the frog with her urine). Frog charms were placed on mummies to help find rebirth. Frog talisman was also given as gifts in Egypt at the New Year, they appeared every year at that time, from the mud of the Nile after the flood and are a symbol of Osiris (the new crop) after his murder and resurrection.

Not surprisingly Frogs also figure widely in rain charms. The fertility of the frog and it being born of the foam on water made it sacred to Venus in ancient Rome. A frog teaches us to attract love and mix with those of like-minded attitude, sharing our knowledge and in turn receiving new knowledge.

Fly

Sacred fly of Egypt. Given as an honor, like a medal is today, by the Egyptian Pharaoh for perseverance in the face of the enemy. Understandable if you have ever tried to shoo a fly away from your dinner.

Fish

Fish have been used, from its inception of Christianity as a secret sign and recognition symbol. Earlier a fish symbolized Venus/Aphrodite, who rose from the sea and as such is a charm for lovers but Venus also brings with Her health and wealth. It protects from the drying effects of the Evil Eye by bringing a representation of water to the problem. The fish is also the symbol of the first incarnation of Vishnu, when He saved Manu from the flood to become the father of a new race. A fish also brings an understanding of the emotions of Water and its ebb and flow.

Falcon see Eagle.

Fox

A fox is a talisman for business success. It teaches us cunning, to walk alone by night, is courageous and clever. There are many stories of witches turning themselves into foxes. It is lucky to see a single fox but to see more than one is considered is unlucky. Be a little wary of this one, as it can also teach us cruelty, a fox is one of the few creatures along with man, that will kill for pleasure as well as food. The fox was worshipped as a totem in ancient Lydia.

Goat

The goat is one of the symbols of the horned God and it teaches us of leadership and fertility. Rings worn with this symbol are meant to control the energy of the animal, placing it under your power and attuning you to the power of the Horned God.

Ram Egypt's ram God Amon, 'the virile male, the holy phallus which stirreth up the passions of love, Ram of Rams!' The ram is a virility charm, surprise, surprise!

Griffin

The Griffin had the head and wings of an eagle and body of a lion. Originating in Ancient Persia the Griffin was symbolic of the seasons he is the legendary guardian of treasure and the Sun to which the lion along with nobility and strength is always associated; added is the

eagle's strong power of flight. Teaching of the God in His Solar aspect.

Romans, Greeks and Lydians used depictions of Griffins to guard tombs. Very popular in Medieval heraldry and legend, the Griffin was adopted by the Christians as a symbol of Christ's ascension, possible due to the Griffins link with the Sun God.

The Griffin as a familiar teaches nobility and the knowledge of the Sun God.

Hare

An animal sacred to Moon Goddesses the world over, having a connection with Spring, fertility and divination. The Chinese thought hares lived on the Moon. When the moon is waxing, from about the eighth day to the full, it requires no very vivid imagination to see on the westward side of the lunar disk a large dark patch very noticeably resembling a hare. The Egyptians have a hieroglyph for hare and this may be its first recognition as a sacred animal. Hares accompanied the German Goddess Harek, the Roman Goddess Hecate and in Saxon times the Goddess Oestara or Eostre, who was said to rule over the spring and the dawn. Hares have a gestation period of about 28 days, the same as the Moon's month and a women's menstrual cycle. Hares have a strong connection to Paganism and so have acquired an undeserved reputation for bad luck from Christians. It is lucky for a Pagan to have a hare cross your path.

It was an animal that witches were said to turn into by using this rhyme.

I shall go as a hare,
With sorrow and sych and meikle care;
And I shall go in the Goddesses name
Ay while I come home again.

On returning they must say.

Hare, hare, God send me care.
I am in a hare's likeness just now,
But I shall be in a woman's likeness even now.

Witch hares were often hunted but never caught and could only be shot with a silver bullet.

Hares are the true animals of Spring and not the Christian rabbits (see more on Spring Equinox).

Horse

A horse is one of the most magical of creatures, its very discarded footwear brings luck into the home. It was also sacred in Norse myth to the God Frey.

Stallion A stallion is a sun symbol often portrayed in Celtic times with a wheel of the year and so he is fertility, harvest and even the Corn Spirit. The 'Obby 'Orse, that dances in the streets in the Summer, is a means to bring this energy to the people. To dance with the 'Obby 'Orse, is to become pregnant within the year. In the Bronze Age, a horse was worth as much as a Rolls Royce is today. It was used for travel and farming, it gave prestige, sexual vigor, fertility and prowess in war, which are the Sun God's attributes, to its owner. The Celts and Vikings traveled to war on horseback but dismounted to fight not wishing to use such valuable animals. Oden's horse Sleipnir was eight legged and able to travel between the worlds of life and death. Cut into the very chalk hills of England stamped on coins and probably sewn as flags or pennants, the horse was the emblem of many Celtic tribes. In Rome horse skulls were often attached to the underside of roofs as a protection of the home.

Mare Many Goddesses are linked to mares, perhaps the best known is Epona who was worshipped across Britain, Gaul and into Rome itself. More statues have been found of Epona than any other Celtic deity. Her power was not confined to mares but springs and rivers, which are the entry into "the other world" both of the fay (fairies) and death. She is not all death but also carries in some depictions a cornucopia bringing good luck and life. Found near Thermal Springs Epona's statues depict Her naked lying on the back of a horse rather like a water nymph. Water with it's association to emotion and happiness, would make Epona a beneficial statue to have in the home, you can see why She was so popular a Goddess.

So precious were horses of either sex that roses were used to decorate stables on festival days. A stallion in Celtic times represents the God and the Sun and a mare with its connection to water and divination embodies the Goddess and the Moon. Together they form a strong familiar, these mighty animals so wild and yet so gentle, teaching many things. Only those given a horse, or if you are truly lucky a pair, will find the answers to what the horse has come to teach you.

Lion

A Sun symbol, the possessor of strength and the masculine principle of virility, might, majesty, law and justice, health and protection. The Lion is group energy teaching leadership, working together for full protection and for the good of all within the pride.

Lioness The woman as mother, huntress and leader, as lionesses have a dominant female within it's Pride. As huntress the lioness feeds her young and her mate. Learn from her to walk silently and she teaches that only when necessary should you to use your strength.

Lizard

Teaching the power of all seeing wisdom and good fortune. A green lizard was thought to be connected to emerald and so help weak eyesight and so rings with a lizard on were said to aid eyesight. If a pregnant woman sees a lizard cross her path, it will bring good luck to her and her child.

Mouse

The mouse is a symbol of Apollo and a soul symbol in Europe. Said to be seen around a birth or death, bringing or taking the soul. A mouse also gives us an eye for detail if this is missing from your character.

Owl

Worn as a talisman, the Owl is a familiar of wisdom. All over Europe the owl is a bird of divination. In Ancient Babylon, Owl amulets protected women during childbirth. In France an Owl seen on the way to cut the harvest, would means that all will go well. They also believed that when a pregnant woman hears an Owl hoot that her child will be a girl. If a woman is pregnant and she alone hears an owl hoot outside her house at night then her child will be blessed.

The Incas venerated the Owl for its beautiful eyes and thought them to be a Female Shamans bird. When I visited a sacred site in Peru in broad daylight, two owls sat watching me, the guide commented that she had never seen owls there before.

An owl is the bird of the Crone Goddess; it swoops silently on its thick downy wings by night, to its prey. Silence is one of the aspects that the Crone teaches us.

Pegasus

The beautiful winged horse Pegasus, sprang from the blood of his dying mother, Medusa, as Perseus sliced off her head. Pegasus father was the Sea God Poseidon, he had been conceived much earlier. The Goddess Minerva caught and tamed Pegasus, giving him as a gift to the muses, for whom he produced a stream with a kick of his hoof. But an idyllic life was not Pegasus fate, life had yet more in store for him. Minerva was called to Her temple by Bellerophon asking a boon, he wished to use Pegasus to fight the fire breathing Chimaera whose front half was both lion and goat, with the hind quarters dragon. While Bellerophon slept in Her temple, Minerva gave him a golden bridle and whispered into his ear where he could find Pegasus. The handsome winged white horse came quietly to the owner of the golden bridle. Together they defeated the Chimaera and had many more adventures. Bellerophon married a beautiful princess but that still was not enough and he became obsessed with his own brilliance. Bellerophon mounted Pegasus, determined to ride into the sky to the very home of the Gods! The old saying pride comes before a fall and so fell Bellerophon. Zeus the Father of the Greek Gods, sent a gadfly to sting Pegasus and Bellerophon was thrown from his back, his fall left him lame and blind. He wandered the world as a beggar for the rest of his days. But our story is of Pegasus, not Bellerophon, what happened to him? Pegasus was allowed to continue his flight to Mount Olympus, there he delivered thunderbolts for Zeus. You can see him as he crosses the sky as the constellation of Pegasus, always to look down on the stupidity of human frailty.

Pegasus symbolizes the strengthening of natural forces and spirituality, changing the evil of the Medusa to the nobility of the Pegasus.

Phoenix The

The story was first told 7000 years ago in Ancient Egypt of the beautiful Bennu bird as he was then called, which means 'rise in brilliance'. The Bennu, who was larger than an eagle, was associated with Atum and Ra, Egyptian Sun Gods and described as 'the one that came into being by himself'. But at this time, the only hint of the fire legend that was to come, was his association with the Sun Gods of Ancient Egypt. Herodotus, a Greek historian who visited Egypt in the fifth century BCE, adopted the story of the Bennu bird and renamed it The (The - attesting that there is only one) Phoenix and Diodorus completes the legend as we know it today.

The Egyptian Sun God Ra (later Apollo) would stop His chariot every morning to hear the wonderful sound of The Phoenix singing, as he washed in the spring, droplets of water falling from his luminous scarlet and gold feathers. The Phoenix lives a long life some say 500 years, others 1461 years. When he becomes very old and tired he gathers together a nest of aromatic woods, sitting in the middle he is consumed by flames. His old body is burnt but from the ashes he arises again young and full of vigor. The Phoenix then places his ashes within an egg made of Myrrh and flies to the "City of the Sun" Heliopolis. There he places the egg on the altar to Ra, as a expression of gratitude for his eternal youth.

The Phoenix story has traveled the world and can be found in Egypt, Greece, and Arabia, in the Hindu and Chinese culture and even the early Christians. In China The Phoenix is considered female and is called Si ling, a bird that belongs exclusively to the Empress. The Phoenix represents her throughout China's history, as the Dragon represents the Emperor. The five cosmic tones of Chinese music, which the phoenix sings correspond to the five organs in the

603

human body and helps to regulate the circulation of the Life Force, represent loyalty, honesty, decorum and justice. In any representation drawn or carved, she brings good luck, and is power sent from the heavens and of course is female energy. The Phoenix was used extensively on jewelry, to show high moral values but was strictly reserved for those of importance. She also represents South which fits very well with Witchcraft in which South is Fire. But in truth The Phoenix represents all of the elements in some way; it is of course born of fire, bathes in water, flies in air and lastly makes an egg from Myrrh, which it must gather from trees.

How did this legend originate? Ravens have a strange habit of "Anting" which is to sit on an ant's nest and allow the ants to crawl into its feathers and eat the mites that live there. Then to get rid of the ants the Raven will sit over a heat source and the ants will leave to find a more comfortable home. Some times the heat source can be a dying fire, on taking off the air from the wings fans the fire and you have what looks remarkably like The Phoenix, resurrected from the flames, with the light from the fire reflecting on its glossy black feathers.

Robin Edgar has put forward an interesting thought that The Phoenix represents the total eclipse of the sun. Egyptian priests could predict when this would occur. During this phenomenon, sometimes there is a bird like effect. Wings and a tail appear to spread out on either side of the Sun. In art from around the world, there are depictions of this both in the Old World and the new. The total eclipse would be seen at different times over a large area, accounting for the story's adoption all over the world.

But I like the story the way it is, without trying to work out where it came from, for me it diminishes it some how.

The Phoenix represents both change and immortality, day and night, the changing wheel of the year Summer into Winter, even the greatest change of all death and rebirth. The solar symbol of transformation, renewed youthfulness and opportunity.

If you are lucky, you may be granted The Phoenix as a familiar but it is a precious gift of the Gods and not one to be demanded. The Phoenix is given only to those that stand apart, a person of rare quality.

The story of the phoenix started at the birth of the world. The Phoenix was there at the beginning and will be there at the end.

Pig

Blessing. A pig is believed to see and smell the wind. All around the world the Pig is a bringer of good luck, but that may be because of its ability to fill the table. In Ireland they describe the Pig 'as the gentleman that pays the rent'.

Rat

Worn as an amulet against plague and rats, it also has ties with the Gods of the Underworld and depicted on the statue of Cernunnos as a soul taker. Sea folklore says the sailors know that a ship will sink if the rats left, they have an ability to smell doom. There is a Buddhist temple in India, dedicated to the rat, where it is a great honor to have them eat from your plate. The rat also pulls the chariot of Ganesh; the elephant headed God of Prosperity. The rat's name is Chua and represents wisdom, judgement and knowledge. Do not reject this familiar if it has decided to work with you.

Rabbit

Are strange creatures, place them on their backs and stroke them gently on their tummy and you can hypnotize them, wonderful if you need to administer cream or cut the toenails of a pet. Hypnotism works on many animals that are hunted by stronger creatures. Over coming timidity and stress represents itself as this familiar, although there is also gentleness to be learnt from it but be aware that the Goddess may have given you a warning of danger nearby. Rabbits also represent luck and fertility.

Raven and Crow

The Crow and Raven are very similar to look at and are of the same family, Corvidae. The Raven, however is larger up to 26 inches and can have a four-foot wingspan, having a slightly different tail and shaggier plumage. Both are the color of the midnight and the Dark Moon, a deep and mysterious black. To Pagans black is knowledge and magical power but to Christians the color is frightening and so to them Ravens and Crows were considered birds of ill omen. Previously the Ravens was regarded as a special bird of many Celtic and Anglo-Saxon Gods and Goddesses. Associated with The Morrigan, Bran the Blessed, Lugh and Odin as messengers and are associated with oracles, shape-shifting and are teachers of magic. The Morrigan sends the Ravens on to the battlefields as choosers of the slain picking at the corpses, looking for the spirit of the dead heroes. In the Ogham script it speaks of the great Raven.

Snamchain feda, most buoyant of wood,
that is ebad, aspen, with him, for fair swimming is wood;
that is a name for the great raven.

Like all Corvids the Raven is noisy, aggressive and a meat eater. Getting the blame from farmers for eating corn, when they were eating the caterpillars and worms. Strangely the Raven has been observed to work in close harmony with wolves. Alerting wolves to prey, waiting until the pack has finished, then going in for her share of a nice dinner, even playing chase together after.

In one Native American culture, the Raven married the Great Mother Goddess. In another tribe, the Shamans project their spell on to a Raven familiar, asking him to kindly drop his spell where it is needed.

A delightful story of how the crow acquired his wonderful color comes from Greek myth. Apollo loved Coronis a mortal girl but she deceived him (or fell in love while pregnant) with Ischys, an Arcadian. When the crow, then a white bird told Apollo this, he shot Coronis with his bow, the crow turned black in grief. The child Coronis was to bear was saved by Apollo and sent to Charon the

Centaur to be brought up, this child grow up to be Asclepius the Greek God of Healing. Coronis was set in the heavens as the star constellation Corvus the crow, in grief at his actions by Apollo.

A Raven was the first bird to be sent from the ark by Noah to fly forever, never to find land and the Dove was only the second bird to be sent. The reason the Raven was sent from the ark first has always intrigued me, until I found out that the Vikings carried them on board ship. When they were out of sight of land a Raven was released, spiralled around until sensing land and then flying off in that direction, with the Vikings paddling furiously behind.

Vix and Leslie The Ravens Dancers at The Halloween Festival

Ravens fed Elijh in the desert and Paul the Hermit, so not so bad for a bird of ill omen.

The first stage initiate to the very secret Roman Mithraic Mysteries took the title of Raven, which was linked to the lunar sphere.

Legend has it that if the Ravens ever leave The Tower of London, the monarchy and the Tower will fall. Bran was a giant from Celtic times and Ravens followed him where ever he went. His head is supposedly buried under Tower Hill on which stands The Tower of London. I can only assume that if the Ravens leave it will mean that the head of Bran has left and there will be no hill for the Tower of London to stand on. But the story is taken very seriously and always there are six (and one spare) Ravens kept in the Tower with their wings clipped, so that this prophesy will never come about. During WW11 the Tower was bombed, Churchill sent bird catchers quickly to Wales for more Ravens, just to be sure.

Ravens and Crows are the most intelligent of all bird species, using tools, learning how to profit from human behavior and able to learn to speak, most important for a messenger! Ravens have learnt to use humans, in Scotland they are the only birds to fly toward a gunshot. Why? Because after shooting a deer, the hunter will gut the animal, making it easier to carry. Leaving a nice lunch for the Raven.

Sadly, the group name of Ravens are "An Unkindness or Conspiracy of Ravens" and of Crows it is " A Murder of Crows". I much prefer Humming birds that have a "Charm", I'm sure it's a Christian "misunderstanding" again. Perhaps Pagans could all start a new colloquial saying "A Mystery of Ravens"?

In Ireland the saying goes "The Raven told it" so it must be true.

Corvidaemancy (mancy just means divination) or Divination by Crow and Raven

1 Bird- To meet a single crow or raven was thought to be unlucky,

To hear one crowing on the left side in the morning was a very bad sign.

If a crow or raven called from the right, it foretold the weather.

Good weather if its cries came in even (Sun God) numbers and bad in odd numbers.

If they tumble about in the air, bad weather is on its way

If a single bird flies three times round the roof and then perches on it, it is a death omen for someone within the house.

If one were to croak three times near a dwelling, it would also be a sign of imminent death.

2 Birds- Two seen at once, a wedding will follow shortly or if they fly over a house a birth will be announced.

3 Birds- To see three crows in a row is very lucky.

4 Birds- Four fly over a house sorrow is coming.

More Birds- If all the crows suddenly leave a wood, a famine is imminent.

The Raven Drummers, have appeared in the Jack-in-the-Green Festival in Hastings for many years with The Morrigan our Giant. As the Parade stops The Raven Drummers beat the drums and call "Morrigan". Ravens have now been spotted on Hastings cliffs after an absence of hundreds of years. As Paganism and Witchcraft return it seems Ravens are now returning to their traditional haunts.

Salmon

The search for knowledge.

Snake

Snakes have the power to imbue the wearer with long life and good health and creativity. Snakes are not liked by all, many have told me they think the skin to be slimy, in fact the skin of a snake is as smooth as silk. As a familiar they are very powerful, teaching Earth wisdom. One of the oldest symbols of feminine power and with a high sexual energy. In the Middle East, the female serpent was the embodiment of wisdom. I wonder if that is the reason the snake is chosen as the baddie in the Garden of Eden? Neither the Jews nor the Christians had much truck with Goddesses, wise or otherwise.

Many Goddesses are depicted carrying a snake, Artemis, Hecate and Persephone; they are teachers of healing and of the mysteries of immortality.

In Egypt, the snake was Vazit, *"the giver of food for eternal life"*.

In Roman times snake rings and bangles were worn to engender health, probably in the hope of acquiring the favors of Asclepius the Roman God of Healing, that He carried on his staff (see Caduceus). Snakes are the guardians of immortality, also of subterranean riches of the spirit that are symbolized by hidden treasure, as is the Dragon. In the old testament, one of the many trials the Jews faced in their thirty years of wandering in the wilderness, looking for the promised land was the plague of serpents. Moses is depicted in the Bible curing people by just showing them a staff with a brass snake curled round it. In this example like cured like, as in the Doctrine of Signatures.

In Peru the Inca marked Earth energy with a snake. This can be seen in a burial area near Lake Titicaca on a standing stone marking the entrance to a burial site. There a snake is carved onto the rock's surface. If you take a compass and run it up and down the side of the stone, by the carving of the snake the magnetic North pointer will turn to the carving, is so great that the compass needle spins. Above and below the carving the needle points North as usual. As with Earth energy, the shedding of the snake's skins represents the regenerative powers linked to fertility, as seeds planted in the earth grow into flower in the Spring.

Snake- Cobra Uraeus, the Egyptian Goddess as Creatrix. The symbol of the cobra was worn on the third eye for insight. This represented wisdom; protection and a healing spirit. Although perhaps not a traditional familiar of this country, with our new ability to travel, this familiar seems to appear more and more.

Horned Headed Snakes depicted held by Cernunnos on the Gundestrup Cauldron, in one hand and a Torc in the other. Probably the snakes meaning is plenty, prosperity, longevity and fertility, a mixing of symbols from the ram a very male symbol and snake which can be interpreted as a phallic symbol, taking the energy of both. This strange reptile actually exists in North Africa (and a version of the horned rattlesnake in America). Did the legend of the snake that lived in far away North Africa come to the ears of the makers of the Gundestrup Cauldron or was it of the artist's imagination? There are many very strange creatures depicted on the cauldron, possibly elephants and a lion or tiger, prompting some to suggest that an itinerant Silversmith made the cauldron. He may of had knowledge of far away places and strange animals or did the legends of the animals traveled with Cernunnos or should we call him Pashupati, the Indian Stag Horned God of 6000 years ago? How long has Cernunnos and the horned snake kept company before being recorded by the makers of the cauldron? We may never know.

Scorpion

Natives of Central and South America say mother scorpion receives the souls of the dead. Both Selket, the Egyptian Goddess and Isharn Tamtim, the Babylonian Goddess, were seen in the sky as the scorpion of the Zodiac. Selket's priests and priestesses were magicians and medics dealing with poisonous bites. The scorpion teaches us of the Crone Goddesses.

Stag or Hart

Hart is the old name for a male deer over five years old and teaches leadership and gives knowledge. The symbol of masculinity and virility, it signifies Herne and Cernunnos.

A friend and I were in the Forest of Dean, some many years back, when we saw a Red Deer about five foot six inches, run into our path. It stood and held the path for his mate to cross and then one final look at us and he followed. The strange thing being he only had one horn. If stags drop their horns they stay near, pawing the ground, trying to put them back on. So why this deer was in such a hurry, running with only one horn, remains a mystery. Why only one horn? About a year previous my friend had found a horn that I bought and asked if he could have it, as it was his familiar, to carry in circle. I had bought the horn, when I was about twelve, from an antique stall and never done anything with it. I had no idea why I bought it but had never thrown it away, always carrying it from home to home, ever since. On returning from holiday, I phoned the Forest of Dean's inquiry office, to find out what type of deer it was that we had seen. We were very naive in those days but you only learn by asking questions. To find, that they don't have Red Deer in the Forest of Dean. Not always are your familiars seen in visualizations, sometimes they are real.

The size of the deer and shape of the horns will tell you which deer has come to your call for a familiar. From the large Red to the tiny Mont Jac deer all have their own personalities. Usually though a familiar will be the Red Deer of Celtic legend, which is the only deer native to Ireland but England, Scotland and Wales also have the Roe Deer that are far smaller. The Red Deer have had a continuous presence since the end of the last Ice Age (10,000 BCE) crossing the land bridge from France. The Red has a rich red colored coat, darkening down to a greyish brown in winter. The Lead or Master deer will have the largest rack of antlers in the herd, which are at peak condition in the early autumn for the rut, when they are used for bouts of sparring between rivals. A fully-grown Red stag can stand 41"-54'" high at the shoulder and can weigh an impressive 190kg (420Ibs).

He will fight all comers for supremacy of his territory. As mating time draws near, the stag becomes very territorial, his neck double in size as male hormones are pumped into the system, and he will fight all the males in his herd for the right to mate. Then to further the mystery, the shedding of the horns like the leaves of the forest and their re-growth, completes the cycle

In the poem of Amergin he refers to a stag of seven tines (see chapter on Gods), tines are the points on his horns, this stag is a mature male. Each amount of tines has its name, Imperial stag however one with more than fourteen tines, is considered the Lord of the Forest. So count your familiars tines to help you understand what he has come to teach you.

As Lord of the Forest the stag is a totem of the Horned God with his majestic antlers, strength and fleet of foot, teaching leadership, mystical signs and leading you through illusion into a place of safety. In Celtic mythology, both the Red Stag and Hind, the female equivalent, are magical creatures able to move between the worlds. With this Familiar listen to the whispers on the wind, you will become more attuned to both nature and the secrets of Cernunnos.

The Sun throughout history is closely connected to the Stag, Cernunnos antlers also represent the rays of the Sun, His blessings falling on all that feel His warmth.

To the Mayans of Mexico the deer were sometimes depicted carrying the Sun. To the Pawnee Native Americans, the deer will guide you to the light of the Sun. To the Chinese the deer symbolizes immortality and nobility and is featuring in many carvings.

One deer in a friend's Deer Park decided to try for Alpha deer against his father, they had fought before but the son had always backed down. This time he caught his father against a barbed wire fence, he charged him again and again until not one inch of his hide was without punctures. This type of behavior is how deer's get their reputation in fighting.

Doe or Hind Female deer, gentle motherly wisdom and inquisitive, fleet of foot also teaching leadership. In most deer, only the male has antlers; in reindeer the female has antlers too, but smaller than in the male. So look to the shape of the horns before jumping to the conclusion that your familiar is a stag.

In the Celtic tradition, the hunting of a hind was symbolic for the pursuit of wisdom. One of the tasks of Hercules was to capture the hind of Mount Ceryneia. She had golden antlers and hooves of bronze and it took Hercules a full year to capture her alive. This he accomplished by shooting an arrow in to her front leg, between bone and tendon, so that no blood was spilled.

At the same deer-park that my friend helps to run, we were lucky to be shown around, a chance to see the Red Deer up close. We stopped the car, and sat there in silence, the lead female deer came over to the car and almost put her head into the car window. She was a very nosy lady, you felt she would go back and tell all the other ladies what she had seen and I would not be in the least surprised if the lead stag was hen pecked.

Spider
The creative power of the spider in weaving the web of life. The

center of the web is the center of the Universe, all strands of Her web are lives interweaving with one another, teaching us to know how we interact and change the lives of those around us, for good or ill.

Spider's webs were said to heal cuts if bound tightly round. In times past women were the weavers of cloth and weavers of magic, able to look to the past and to the future in divination. Spiders were carried for success in trade, hence the name of money spider.

Starfish

Nature's own pentagram, as are five pointed flowers. A starfish, as with the pentagram, teaches us how to protect ourselves and invisible stands with us, protecting at all times.

Seahorse

In Italy, the seahorse is worn as a protection from the evil eye and learning to handle the energies of the water quarter.

Seahorse charms depicting seahorses both real (real seahorses were actually ground up and added to medicine) and imaginary, half horse and half fish, were considered to have great healing powers, for respiratory disorders, impotence, general lethargy and pain. Seahorses also due to their 'wetness' protected from the Evil Eye.

Toad

Toads were often cited as familiars to witches. The Bufo Marinus or Cane Toads, when excited, excretes a hallucinogenic through parotid glands on its skin, which were said to be licked by witches at Sabbats or used in potions. But this specific type of toad is indigenous to America not Europe so most unlikely. The Bufo toad appears in the Art of the Olmecs, Incus, Aztecs, and Mayans as far back as 2000 BC. The Mayans used a drink called Chicha in their rituals, this consisted of sugar fermented with a live toad and toad poisons. European witches may not have used this familiar but other Pagan societies did for its hallucinogenic properties.

There are various forms of Bufo toad, which live in many other areas of the world. These are said to secret poisons rather than hallucinogenic from their glands, and have evolved this gland to deter or kill any animal trying to eat them. The Chinese for thousands of years have used the Bufo toad extractions in a medicinal preparation called Ch'an Su for heart problems, although it is a variant poison. It is also used in such diverse countries as Tibet, Nepal, India, Germany, and Africa, for centuries for the same purpose. The Greek Gods and Goddess Dionysus, Zeus and Diana, and Hera are all associated with Bufo toads. In Hoodoo it is rumored that toad venom is part of the recipe for the infamous "Zombie Potion".

Bufotenine the active ingredient in toad venom is also found in several species of Amanita mushrooms, the ones so loved of fairy stories, red with white spots. The English word "toad stool" dates back to 1398, linking toads and mushrooms together. So we are back at the beginning again, if toads are so connected with a hallucinogenic mushroom are they in someway hallucinogenic? Or were they in the past used as in many countries as medicine, possibly by witches to heal or for magic?

Toads are strange creatures; the tongue is to quick for the human eye as it strikes out for an insect. They can stay hidden under the earth for many months. I remember digging one up as a child and it making me jump as it bounded from its lair.

Within its head so the legend goes can be found a gem called a Toadstone. Carried by Horse Whispers to control and train horses and by witches for healing. Though in truth no toads need be killed for a toadstone, as they are fossilized teeth.

Depictions of toads are used in charms of sexuality, fertility, and rain.

Unicorn

Early in the Unicorns career it was described as either a goat or a horse with a single horn, and could be found in many strange colors. Slowly it settled into the shape of a horse with cloven feet of the goat, with his beard and with a lion's tail and totally white the color of purity. Although even over the past hundred years that image has continued to change, due to Hollywood films. The unicorn is depicted as a beautiful white horse with a silver horn, loosing all traces of its goat ancestry and lion tail, but perhaps that is right as a goat is traditionally thought of as anything but pure.

The first account of the Unicorn comes from Ancient Babylon, where the Sun was considered to be a Lion and the Moon considered to be a Unicorn and chasing each other across the sky. Found in Ancient Egypt and now in the British Museum is a papyrus of a game that looks suspiciously like chess between a Unicorn and a Lion. Could our Egyptian papyrus just be another 'game' of the Sun and Moon copied from Babylonian myth?

Later, in 434BC Ctesias wrote *"There are in India certain wild asses which are as large as horses, and larger. Their bodies are white, their heads are dark red, and their eyes dark blue. They have a horn on the forehead which is about eighteen inches in length. The dust filed from this horn is administered in a potion as a protection against deadly drugs."*

In the Indus Valley were we find our first sighting of the Stag Horned God, there are also depictions of the Unicorn engraved on seals, in resent finds, that date from 4000 years ago. Had the legend of the Unicorn survived in India until Ctesias wrote about them 1500 years later?

Alexander the Great was given a Unicorn as a gift! Some suggest that this could be Bucephalus his horse, wearing a horned helm but of course we know this to be propaganda, from the disbeliveers. (Smile).

A strange book was written in Christian Alexandria, The Physiologus, citing every creature that god ever made, including the Unicorn. *"He is a small animal, like a kid, but surprisingly fierce for his size, with one very sharp horn on his head, and no hunter is able to catch him by force. Yet there is a trick by which he is taken. Men lead a virgin to the place where he most resorts and leave her there alone. As soon as he sees this virgin he runs and lays his head in her lap. She fondles him and he falls asleep. The hunters then approach and capture him and lead him to the palace of the king."*

The Church compared the Unicorn to Christ due to its strength and meekness.

There is a set of six magnificent tapestries to be found in Paris at the 'The National Museum of the Middle Ages'. 'The Unicorn Tapestries' are woven from fine wool, silk and gold thread, in about 1495-1505 the time when knights were bold and damsels needed to be saved. They depict a Unicorn and Lady Claude Le Viste, widow of Geoffrey of Balzac with a "Mille Fleurs" background and represent the five senses and desire. By the Middle Ages the Unicorn's horn had grown to three foot in length, he had left all his goat properties behind with the exception of the beard and grown into a full size horse, becoming pure white. The horn that is depicted in the tapestries is much longer that we visualize now and is in fact a horn from a Narwhal. These strange whales grow a single twisted tooth to great lengths sometimes up to 8ft.

Although not truly a tusk but a strange twisted tooth, normally only one tooth will grow long. The Narwhal is avidly sort after for their magical qualities, for many hundreds of years. To own a whole horn was an incredible price and even a small part was sold for £24 per ounce, an inconceivable sum of money so long ago. Mary Queen of Scots, King James's mother only owned a small piece with which she ate her food; it has a reputation of nullify poison.

King James of Scotland, who became King of England on the death of the Virgin Queen Elizabeth and brought with him his Coat of Arms which, had two Unicorns supporters. This he changed for one English lion and one Scottish Unicorn and can be still seen on England's Coat of Arms to this day. But whether anyone was fooled by this attempt at reconciliation, we shall never know but what we now think of as a children's rhyme, was a political statement and sung in the taverns of the day.

The Lion and the Unicorn were fighting for the Crown:
The Lion chased the Unicorn all around the town.
Some gave them white bread and some gave them brown,
And some gave them plum cake and drummed them out of town!

Now days the Unicorn has returned to its beginnings as a female power symbol of the Virgin Goddess phase of the Moon, both virile and pure. A noble animal very sacred to the Goddess, teaching a gentle acceptance and inner strength, a lunar symbol that wards off evil influences and guards against harm, it has an invincible force contained with in its magical horn. If you have this magical familiar, the Virgin Goddess may grant you a wish on its magical horn.

Wolf

The Goddess as the great She-wolf, defender of her cubs and as provider, a popular totem animal of both Witches and Warriors.

The wolf in many cultures is a teacher, a guide through the dark corridors of your mind. Helping you to understand the magic on its many levels. The Goddess in her mother phase, a mother that teaches her children to become teachers themselves and pass on Her wisdom. Rome was in legend founded when a she wolf nurtured twin boys, who went on to establish an Empire. The wolf, according to the Mongolian nomads is as intelligent as a human and often out wits them in the hunt. The wolf is sacred to both Apollo and Odin. In Sweden, old women that lived in the forest were credited with the ability to control wolves and were known as Wolf-crones. I can well imagine this to be true, many people feed foxes on London, I can see where an old lady could easily make friends with a wolf, feeding it.

Surprising only the Alpha (or lead) pair, mate. The wolf pack is a true family and will protect its pregnant female, both the dogs and bitches baby-sitting the cubs for Mum to feed herself and stretch her legs.

The wolf, since ancient times, has always been linked with the fullmoon and is a charm of good fortune, valor and protection. To have a pair of wolves on a pendant or ring will attract love to you, as wolves bond for life.

Since records began in Canada, no report of a wolf having hurt any human has ever been recorded. Yet, in Europe during the Christian Middle Ages, they were hunted to extinction, seeming to underline their Pagan symbolism. Wolf heads were nailed on town gates as protection; squares of wolf fur were placed on horses to protect them, and outlaws were also known as Wolf Heads.

But like Pagans, wolves are now returning to the quiet and secret places.

Visit your familiar often, bonding with them, in time they will teach you many mysteries of the Goddess and God.

CHAPTER 13

Self Dedication

Self-Initiation or dedication as some are now calling it, is a very important step. If you have followed this book, you will now possibly feel ready for Initiation. This is a huge commitment and not one to be undertaken lightly. Do not be swayed by dark capes billowing in the wind and large impressive jewelry, that is not Witchcraft, the Goddess or God speaking through you, that is Witchcraft. Many today do not appreciate the gravity of initiation, taking it far too lightly. You can not undo initiation; an initiation is for life. You may decide that you do not believe in the old Gods, but they may still believe in you. You give your word, your honor, and swear to the principles of the Craft. You are expected to understand and to adhere to these principles.

There is no hurry for initiation, the minimum length of time is a year and a day, but you can take as long as you choose. It gives you time to consider what you are about to do and to have experienced the Year Wheel through the eyes of a novice witch. Even within a coven I have had one initiate who took five years, five months, take as long as you need, no one must rush you. When you are comfortable in circle, know all your words, understand the energies, only then are you ready.

As you come up for initiation it is time to review your life so far, did you make the changes that we talked of in the first chapter? I have talked through many problems with coveners over the years. What remains to hold you back, is it your childhood, a teacher at school, your career, your health? Witchcraft teaches us not to be afraid of the dark, neither the dark within nor the dark without.

You have now passed on and become an adult; it is time for you to take responsibility for yourself. It stops here.

Re-evaluate who you are and where you are going. Initiation

means death, the death of the old you and the birth of the new. Most covens during initiation re-enact a death of the initiate. You hold the power of the universe in your hands. It is time to take charge of your life, a time to find who you truly are.

What is the difference between Self -initiation and dedication?

Dedication is when you give yourself to the Goddess and initiation is when you are accepted into a coven and a tradition and self–initiation is when you initiate into witchcraft, by yourself, without anyone giving you permission. But what is the common factor in all these? The Goddess and God, if they don't accept you, the initiation no matter by whom it is given is invalid. Who initiated the first witch- The Goddess and God, so they are the only ones you have to please. I self-initiated first before finding and being initiated into the path that I now follow, so perhaps more than most I see it from both sides of the argument, neither suffered because of the other. You may find a coven at a later date, you may not wish to. There are many paths that lead to the center. Call it what you will, initiation or dedication, a word is unimportant. The decision is important, the ritual between you and the Gods is important. In our initiation we call down the God into the High Priest to initiate the women and the Goddess down into the High Priestess to initiate the men. The only exception to that is of a mother to daughter, father to son. So in fact it is still the Goddess and God that initiates and not the coven; at least not for us.

Magical meaning of names.

Now is the time to pick a new name for your new life.

Names hold magic with in, both the Jewish god Jehovah and the Egyptian God Ra have secret names by which the world was made and can be destroyed. Your magical name is a secret name between you and the Gods, the name by which you are known to them and this is a channel by which they can feed you energy to help with your spell work. If someone finds out your magical name they can use this knowledge to work magic against you, by feeding you dark magic through this same channel. The more names of yours they know, the closer to your core they get. So never tell anyone your true magical name, some people however have a second magical name that they use for their public name, as with writers. This is fine to reveal to people, as only as much magic as your given name at birth will stick to it.

It's a little presumptuous to choose the name of a God or Goddess, but anything else that feels right will do. You may wish to test your name with numerology, how this is done is in many books, to see how it will reverberate with your new life or you may not care, it just feels right. You may add to your name at a later date, as you grow. You never lose a name merely add to the list. Your names are a kind of history of who you have been and where you have come to, on your witchcraft journey.

Initiation into Elemental quarter

Although this is not relevant to lone witches but just to complete the picture of what happens in our coven. At this time we ask the initiate to choose a quarter, to be its Elemental Guardian, if they choose to. Though not all choose to specialize in an element. They will call that quarter to the circle, make the candles for use in that quarter throughout the year. Teach new initiates all about the element and teaching them how to set circle.

How do I start on self initiation?

You have now made your decision. You wish to self-initiate and pledge your allegiance to the old Gods or even to a particular Goddess and/or God.

Firstly consult your calendar, you will need to find a Waning Moon between Imbolc and the Autumn Equinox. The time before or later and you will be in the dormant time of the Earth, when nothing grows, as this is a fertility religion, your initiation needs to be in the growing season. The Waning Moon is for a ritual of self-assessment, in which you examine who you are and where you are going. On the following Waxing Moon, which is the Virgin, that as a witch you are about to become, as this is the best time for your initiation. This moon is also about growth and so with Her help you will grow stronger into your full prime. We give our initiates to the Virgin Goddess, as like the children under her care, they take their first faltering steps as a witch.

Think about what you are about to do, which pledges do you wish to make to the Goddess and God? An oath is a very serious business that applies to any oath that you take, in Celtic times to break an oath would surely spell your death.

Never, make an oath you can't keep. Oaths were very often sworn on the sword, as with our Coven, by this you imply that you offer your neck to the sword edge. Not that any coven will use the sword if you don't keep your word but it is not to us that you swear but to Her upstairs.

So what will you swear to? In our Coven, we swear to uphold the virtues of witchcraft, never to use our power unwisely and to help our brothers and sisters of the craft. If you do not feel confident enough to write your own words and are going to use mine, read them through first to be sure that you agree with them.

Waning Moon Ritual

Three days prior to the Dark of the Moon just before your initiation, which is a time of reflection, take a candle, large mirror, pen and paper, into a darkened room and open circle (cast, call quarters etc), if you have followed this book you understand how to do this. Light your candle, meditate with closed eyes, open your eyes and look into the mirror. Look past your face and into your spirit, there is none here but you. Write down all the thoughts that hold you back, what or who held problems, for you, that are left unresolved. What would you like to see in the future, what are your goals? In all aspects of your life not only in your witchy future, write everything down. It is now time for you to move on.

Examine your list; who can you forgive for hurting you?

Who do you need to just forget and refuse to allow the pain to hold you back any longer?

Who can you say, "You were wrong" to?

Who do you need to say "forgive me" to?

Bitterness eats at your spirit, now is the time to let it go.

Visualize these people in the mirror; say the words that set you free.

On the positive side, where are you going?

Who are you going with?

How do you get there?

Positive energy feeds you spirit. Make a note of all of your thoughts.

Call your Goddess into you.

After, make a note of what She has said to you and work on all your conclusions.

Keep your paper in your magical diary; you will need it later.

For initiation you will need
Preferably, write the words for your ritual rather than relying on mine, allow them to come from your heart.

You will also need to arrange the day off from work or do the initiation at the weekend.

A cauldron or bowl

Three strands of red cord and your usual equipment.

A silver pentagram and chain.

On the Day of the Virgin Goddess
Set up your working space, if possible. So that on your return you do not need to do this.

Go to the local woods or any special place that means a lot to you. Take food and drink or eat out in a pleasant restaurant not a fast food chain, you need to be fortified for your journey.

Eat at about 12 noon so that you will have an empty stomach for your initiation but don't starve yourself either, we don't want you passing out!

Walk in the woods and feel nature all around you. You are already one with nature but your initiation will give you a deeper bond. See if the wood gives you something, it might be a feather, a pretty stone or a leaf. When you are ready return home.

If you are given a gift, place it on your altar for your initiation and after keep it safe.

Take a bath and add consecrated salt from your last ritual, lavender oil, rose petals and star anise to your usual bubblebath.

Initiation Ritual

Take into circle your paper with the positive and negative attributes on.

Sweep the circle with the besom, visualizing sweeping all evil from the area

Lay out white boundary cord

Place your silver pentagram on your altar

Light the spirit candle.

Place incense on the charcoal blocks.

Meditate to clear the mind and prepare for this most important ritual.

Open circle in the usual manner.

Use your own words here or

"Lord and Lady of Magic

From deepest woodland glade

And over sacred and enchanted hills,

At the still of night when spirits walk.

Ride the tides of magic to my circle

Spinners of Birth, Fate and Death.

Vast and shadowed, from deepest realms unseen

By the dark cauldron of your inspiration.

You power I invoke to aid me!"

Call the Goddess or God into you and listen to the words you speak

Burn the paper with positive and negative qualities

"This old me I burn, that from the ashes like the phoenix I will rise,

A new and vital person will stand before your eyes."

Place burning paper into your cauldron or bowl

Stand with arms raised and visualize the old you being destroyed and the new you growing from the ashes.

Take a moment to be sure that you are truly ready for this change. When ready continue.

Hold your Athame high with both hands and with feet apart

"I wish that you accept me as a Child of the Goddess.

I will do my best to serve you in every task that you set,

I will honor all my brothers and sisters of the craft,

I will never use my powers in anger, but only in love.

I will help all that ask,

And serve the God and Goddess (or any special God and/or Goddess name you have chosen) all the days of my life.

To this I give my oath"

Kiss Athame and replace it in its sheath.

Initiation Visualization

Relax as usual

Go down the stairs

Through the door.............

You find yourself in the pitch black, with your eyes open or closed it makes no difference, you can see nothing before you. You know that you are in a short tunnel or chamber. It has a blunt end behind you; there are only a couple of feet above your head and about ten feet in front of you. You can not stand or move too much. You are not afraid. You have been sent here to 'see visions'. You try with eyes open and with eyes closed but you see nothing, only the dark. By now you are getting very cold, the cold seeps into your body; you try to warm up by rubbing your cold and frozen limbs. A time passes; by now hunger has taken a grip on your body, biting hunger is consuming your body from the inside. Gnawing hunger on the inside, intense cold on the outside. You curl into a ball on the floor to try to keep warm. Time passes; you drift into sleep and dream, dreams. All at once, you find that the tunnel is larger, you stand, something is chasing you down the tunnel, and you are running for your life! Some form of monster is chasing you down the tunnel, something dark and frightening. Your mind finds all manner of legends tucked in the recesses Monitors, Dragons, things without name. The stones of the floor hurt your bare feet, you leave a trickle of blood on the stones that the beast can follow, the dark and fearful monster is close behind you now. You can feel its hot breath on your back and the smell of its rank breath envelops you. You run and run, you see a light ahead and run into a cavern.

All around the walls of the cavern it is lit by masses of small candles. In the center is an old woman dressed in dark coarse cloth, stirring a cauldron over a small fire, you walk towards her, forgetting the monster that was so close behind.

"What is your name?" she asks in a voice as old as the universe. You reply she shakes her head,

"What do you do?" you answer.

"Why come you here?" you answer. She shakes her head and points to where you came in. You turn towards the passage.

You find yourself back in the dark but the hunger has passed and you now do not feel so cold. You think of what the old woman said…….. you think…… you dream………

You are running in the tunnel again. The monster, once more is nipping at your heels. Once more, you come to the old lady. Once more she asks you the three questions.

"What is your name?"

"What do you do?"

"Why come you here?"

With the shaking of her head you find yourself back in the dark again. Once more you think of what the old woman said to you. You know now you are dying, you have passed hunger and thirst you have been here too long, you just wish to sleep forever. Once more you dream of dreaming……..

You are running through the tunnel again chased by the same monster as before. This time he is very close, you are just too tired. You feel a claw or fingernails rake your back, the warmth of your own blood runs down and drips on your legs as you run. You know with the next swipe you will be down, and he will feed on your entrails. You see the light of the cavern just in time; your hand reaches out to touch the cavern mouth as if claiming sanctuary. With you last breath you push yourself through the door, the old crone is still there and she asks you.

"What is your name?"

This time you answer "I have no name"

"What do you do?"

"The unborn do nothing."

"Why come you hear?"

"I come for wisdom." you answer.

She takes the spoon that she stirs the brew within the cauldron and offers you some. She picks up from the floor bones and leaves and herbs, ties them into a bundle, dips them into the cauldron and shakes them three times around your body, then kisses you on both cheeks. You know that you are accepted and dismissed in one and turn to leave.

You find yourself back once more in the dark but now you hear singing, the stones being removed and light filtering in. You know that you have passed your initiation test.

Return up the stairs to the candles on the altar.

Take a well-deserved sip of wine.

Plait the red cord and place it round your waist.

Take your pentagram from the altar; hold it by its chain between your two hands.

Take the pentagram to North first, hold it high towards North

"I announce to the Powers of Earth that I am (witch name) Witch and Priest/ess"

Then to East

"I announce to the Powers of Air that I am (witch name) Witch and Priest/ess"

Then to South

"I announce to the Powers of Fire that I am (witch name) Witch and Priest/ess"

Then to West

"I announce to the Powers of Water that I am (witch name) Witch and Priest/ess"

Place pentagram on your neck.

"Be it sealed"

Bless wine and drink all the contents.

Do or say anything else that you feel you wish to.

Close Circle

Eat and **Congratulations!!!**

After Self- Initiation

After your self-initiation as a witch, this will give different feelings to different people, in some it can be a flash of light and actually seeing the Goddess within your room. For others it is a warm feeling and yet others it develops slowly over the coming months, no one can say in advance how you will react.

So what happens next?

Now is the time to hone your new Craft, practice, practice, and practice. Listen to what the Goddess and God teach you.

You have given yourself to the Virgin for Her to strengthen; there are 12 -13 fullmoons every year, in this you work with the Mother Goddess and eight Sabbats in which you work with both the God and all the Goddesses. One ritual each year after Samhain on the waning moon before the Sun turns at Yule, honor the Crone, with a very somber and serious circle as for a grand Grandmother. At least one at High Summer in the open air, exclusively to the God; a warrior circle.

In our coven it is a little more complicated. It is a balance for us; we give our initiates to the Virgin, on the waxing moon and we work all our magic on the Fullmoon. We do some Sun rituals at high Summer, around a lovely old oak tree. Post initiation only, we continue the work started at initiation by working just before the Darkmoon with the Crone. At this time, we do regression (but not with anyone suffering depression) divination, Astral projection and power work. We also look within to the dark side of our being. Here we strive to uncover our full potential, to find a deeper under-standing of who we are, and a sum of the new depths that we find, being greater than the whole. Karl Jung called this work "Owning your own Shadow", but Jung placed a name on an idea that has been used for centuries to investigate who you are and to be stronger from the knowledge. You should work towards a unification of both the dark and the light within each of us. For a witch, this can only be found by holding the hand of your chosen Goddess and God and walking their path. They teach you to strengthen your inner spirit. When you know who you are, the power begins to flow. The stronger as a person you are, the stronger the power flows. The Goddess and God teach you, where to find and how to unlock the power that is latent in us all. I can but point you in the direction of your guide; no one but they can unlock the gate.

The Darkmoon as we call this time, even though technically it isn't. I like to think of as our time, we do very little spell work for others, the only exception to this would be protection workings of close friends.

But don't let go of the thought that circle should be fun, fun and laughter are very much a part of the Craft, despite my concentration on improving yourself. For some people improving your inner-self means finding out how to laugh and have fun.

Laughter is infectious, infect everyone!

The only problem then is, if you enjoy life it passes faster.

Silent Circles

When we have an experienced coven we usually do a silent ritual, by this I mean that not a word is spoken from the time robes are put on until the Spirit candle is put out, at the end of the ritual. In every case you can hear every word that is thought, by every member. In some ways you can see the energies clearer in a silent circle. You might like to try this as an exercise.

Start a Group

Books are not the easiest way to learn, if you can find a teacher, so much the better. I know in some parts of the country, it is still very difficult to find a group to work with. If you get a chance to join a coven, of whatever tradition, it will be far easier to practice, as long as you feel comfortable with them and they with you.

It can be very exhausting having to coming home from work tired and then having to start circle. It is much more fun to work in a group. You can of course get a few friends together and work fullmoons and Sabbats by yourselves, as long as you tell them that you are self-initiated this is no problem. This is not a coven, more usually this is called a Clan, Tribe or any other name meaning group.

Choose people that enjoy each other's company, forming a group is difficult enough with everyone on the same wave length, without understanding each other it is almost impossible. With people that you are not comfortable with, you can't open your spirit and blend to the same extent, as when you feel relaxed, the circle should be a place of complete trust. A coven becomes a family unit, who you call in times of problems. Whether it is a death in your family and you call them for emotional support or you break down on the motorway and need a tow!

Organize outings together, go to sacred sites; go along to festivals together.

Perhaps moving round the HP and HPs roles among all attending?

You may choose not to ask so much commitment as a coven

would, only turning up when they choose or you may decide that all Sabbats and Fullmoons must be fully attended. The choice is yours or a joint decision of you all.

In a coven situation, when a couple are ready to go off on their own and start a new group, we have a leaving ceremony to wish them well. Here the HPs passes on the words and sigils to the new HPs, HPs to HPs only, allowing them to open their own coven and so another coven is born.

If there are no Moots or meetings in your area, organize something. Put adverts in New Age shops where like minded people are going to cluster or health shops, possible Newsagents windows to meet in a local pub. All the Moots round the country had small beginnings. My local moot meets in a pub restaurant, those who choose have dinner first or people come along just for the after dinner speakers. A few pound is charged for the speaker's expenses and a good evening is had by all.

Trolls

But unfortunately you will run into some of the same problems covens do –Politics. No matter how carefully you choose your members, you will find them. To borrow a name from Eran the kind author of this concept, whom I understand, is writing a book that will be very interesting reading when it comes out, that type of person known as a troll. Unfortunately from Christian Churches to synagogues and bike clubs, it matters not. Trolls get bored and wish to smash something that someone else has created. It happens to every coven I know unfortunately, but don't let it put you off of forming a group. Destruction is their one joy in their sad little lives. Unfortunately Witchcraft is no exception to the general rule.

If people are having difficulties with one another, ask them to discus their problems and not to return to coven until this is done or if it is that bad, ask them to choose whom is staying and who is leaving. You can not go into ritual unhappy with the coveners that you stand in circle with.

In Conclusion

There is still a great deal to re-learn, so much of our magical heritage has been lost. But, countries are at last exchanging ideas on this momentous subject and we are uncovering new or old ideas all the time. While I was in Egypt, in the Great Pyramid of Cheop, in the Kings Chamber, three ladies linked hands and hit a certain note. The whole pyramid began to vibrate! It was a very strange experience. I am so pleased that I got up at 4am, flew on the Goddesses wings (well it couldn't have been me running up the hill to beat the coaches for a ticket, as only a few people are allowed in everyday). Just for that moment to be there, to understand more about the ability of sound and a little more of the abilities people who built the pyramids and how much has still to be remembered. I love to travel to countries and learn of magic from every tradition.

I have found that Witchcraft has been a great fulfilment in my life and I have met some wonderful people over the many years. I'm sure that you will find Paganism, in all its different guises to bring something very special, as a gift into your life.

Thank you for walking with me through these pages. I have enjoyed the experience and will feel lost now without you, dear reader. I hope you found with in its pages what you were looking for, or at least something to add to your knowledge.

Finishing as I started, the most important piece of information I can give you –

Witchcraft teaches us not to be afraid of the dark, neither the Dark within nor the Dark without.

Don't do anything that does not feel right to you and enjoy everything you do.

The Goddess, God and Elemental Quarters contain all that you need for a happy life-

May the God and Goddess guide your steps
May Earth protect you,
May Air blow wisdom in your direction,

May Fire warm you and give you courage,
May Water send you only happiness.
May you live long and prosper.
Merry Meet, Merry part and Merry meet again!

Blessed Be
Jeanette

Caduceus Pagan Festivals

Jeanette organizes two of the largest Pagan Festivals in the world every year.
There are the best speakers and entertainers on the Pagan scene!
A warm welcome to all traditions and to new comers to Paganism especially.

The International *Halloween Bash!!*
The weekend before Halloween see website for exact date
Closing with a candle lit parade 'Night of the Ancestors'

And

The International BeltaneBash!!
The Last Weekend in May -Sunday and Bank Holiday Monday
!! The Oldest PAGAN PRIDE PARADE in the World !!
Lining up at 10.30am on the Sunday outside Conway Hall, the parade goes around the British Museum with giants, drums, voices, costumes and laughter!! Everyone welcome, lets make every year bigger than the last and then on to.............
at Conway Hall, Red Lion Sq., Holborn, London WC1R 4RL
http://www.paganfestivals.com
Gigantic Pagan Craft market! Tarot!
FREE entertainment, FREE lectures, FREE workshops,
FREE parking!!
Please book early to avoid disappointment!!
Opening ritual and then onto
an explosion of Pagan Folk and Rock Music, Drumming and Dancing
Wild Bedlam Morris!!
All the best in Pagan creative entertainment, the only festival like it.
Talks and Workshops by leading speakers in the Pagan field all going on in different parts of the building all at the same time, you can't see everything, there's just too much.
Ending on Sunday with a Grand Samhain Witchcraft Ritual by
The Raven and The Rose.

B O O K S

O is a symbol of the world, of oneness and unity. In different cultures it also means the "eye," symbolizing knowledge and insight. We aim to publish books that are accessible, constructive and that challenge accepted opinion, both that of academia and the "moral majority."

Our books are available in all good English language bookstores worldwide. If you don't see the book on the shelves ask the bookstore to order it for you, quoting the ISBN number and title. Alternatively you can order online (all major online retail sites carry our titles) or contact the distributor in the relevant country, listed on the copyright page.

See our website **www.o-books.net** for a full list of over 500 titles, growing by 100 a year.

And tune in to myspiritradio.com for our book review radio show, hosted by June-Elleni Laine, where you can listen to the authors discussing their books.